the
BADEN
EMIGRATION BOOK
(including emigration from Alsace)

compiled by
Cornelia Schrader-Muggenthaler

International Standard Book Number
1-55856-107-2

In preparing this script, I wish to express my appreciation to Carmen Schrader-Muggenthaler, Martin Bergmann, Otto Greis, Daniel Fuchs and Tobias Hauzeneder, for their eager assistance.

Appreciation is also extended to Dr. Rehm and the General Lands Archive in Karlsruhe for granting permission to use their records (see sources).

Special thanks, too, to Mrs. Doris Weisner who allowed me to include her collection of emigrants (see sources) and Mr. Norbert Stich, who compiled the computer program for this endeavor.

Finally...
I want to thank my husband, Wolfgang, for his support, patience, and understanding.

CONTENTS

FOREWORD

This is the first volume of "The Baden Emigration Book." It includes emigrants leaving the Baden area to go to America during the 18th and 19th centuries. In addition to the Baden emigrants listed, there are several hundred Alsacian emigrations to America.

Many records of the villages in Baden have already been microfilmed by the Church of Jesus Christ of Latter Day Saints. This volume includes a list of those villages. These microfilmed records can, of course, be viewed at any of the LDS Church Family History Center libraries throughout the world.

It is the compiler's sincere hope that this book will be of great hep for anyone tracing their roots.

Please carefully read the introduction and source explanation pages. They should prove to help you to understand the lists and avoid any misinterpretations.

INTRODUCTION

The emigrants enumerated in this book came primarily from Baden and Alsace.

During the 18th and 19th centuries many people were unable to read and write and, therefore, were unable to fill out their own passports or emigration applications. The officers wrote down the information as they heard it. Names and places were thus often spelled phonetically. Due to this fact, there may be some misspellings.

Every effort was taken to make the book as complete and accurate as possible. If you cannot find the village you are looking for, look for the closest spelling.

Many men migrated with their families. In some cases it is noted as to who migrated with who and the total number of family members involved. There are also single men and women listed. It is not shown if they migrated alone or with a family. Occasionally you will find "the same person" listed twice. This was done when names were repeated in the lists and differences were found in the birth or emigration date. It cannot be determined from these records as to which one is correct.

When an emigration date shows up as 01/01/1848, this does not mean they emigrated 1st January 1848. It is a default in the program. The year only is correct. Emigration dates are very vague. In many cases the people migrated before or after the date.

ABBREVIATIONS

f = father
m = mother
s = son
d = daughter
mn = maiden name

w ch = with children
w parents or w paren. = with parents
w family = with family

w p = with parents
w f = with family

If someone migrated with their family or children, then his/ her name is at the end of the listing of this surname.

Umlaut Ö = oe , Ü = ue, Ä =ae

These letters are at the end of each letter. The computer cannot sort Umlauts.

EXPLANATION OF THE SOURCE

EMIGRATION FROM BADEN

Source F1 to F9

With the permission of the General Lands Archive in Karlsruhe, the collection of emigrants to America and other countries in the 18th, 19th, and 20th centuries were sorted out. Only the 18th and 19th century emigrations to America were extracted for this particular book.

This collection was not in alphabetical order and, therefore, was very difficult to use in its original format. By alphabetizing and organizing the emigrant names, the genealogist now has full and easy access to this most valuable material. Plans to continue with a second volume are underway.

This material has been microfilmed by the Church of Jesus Christ of Latter Day Saints.

For your reference -
Film Numbers:

Source F1/F5 = Film Number 934610
Source F2 = Film Number 1125248
Source F3 = Film Number 1125250
Source F4 = Film Number 1125251
Source F6 = Film Number 1125254
Source F7 = Film Number 1125249
Source F8 = Film Number 1125252
Source F9 = Film Number 1125253

EXPLANATION OF THE SOURCE

EMIGRATION FROM ALSACE

Source F2 is from the same microfilm as the Baden emigrations. This film included emigrants from Alsace.

Source F2 = Film Number 1125248

Source But = This source includes emigrants from a collection of Mrs. Doris Weisner, Riesweiler Hohl 1, 6540 Simmern.

HISTORY OF BADEN

Baden is located along the Rhine River and today belongs to the federal state, Baden-Wurttemberg. Stuttgart is its capitol.

Baden was defeated by the Palatinates in 1462. It lost all its territories located east of Pforzheim to Wurttemberg (1300-1603). It was divided into two margrave counties: Baden-Durlach (capitol Durlach) and Baden-Baden (capitol Baden).

After several religious disputes, Baden remained Catholic (1571). In 1689 the two residential capitols were destroyed by the French. In 1715 Karlsruhe was proclaimed as the residential capitol.

During 1730 to 1737 many natural disasters destroyed the country. This caused many inhabitants of Baden during the following years to migrate to America and other countries.

With the "Reichsdeputationtreaty" in 1803, many territories reverted to Baden.

As a result of the Liberal Constitution of 1818 Baden was declared a constitutional monarchy.

After the resignation of Friedrich II in 1918, the free state of Baden (with a Reichspresident as a political leader) was formed.

After the Second World War Baden was an American occupied zone (1945-1951).

HISTORY OF BADEN

In 1952 the "Sudweststaat Baden" was combined with Wurttemberg to form the federal state, Baden-Wurttemberg.

Today Baden is one of the most beautiful areas in Germany. Its beautiful landscape (Black Forest) and its lovely historical towns attract tourists from all over the world.

HISTORY OF ALSACE

The area of Alsace has historically been a very troubled one. This beautiful region was always in the interest of the surrounding countries.

The first settlements in Alsace were Celtic. In 58 B.C. it was conquered by Caesar and then belonged to the Provincia Germania Superior.

During the Migration-of-Nations period, it became Alemanic. With the victory of Chlodwig against the Alemannes, the Franconians conquered and christianized the Alsace area in 496.

With the Empire Division in the contract of Mersen in 870 it became part of the East Franconian Empire. Through this contract Ludwig II received, after the death of Lothar II, the east half of Lothringen.

Since 925 Alsace belonged to the Dukedom of Swabia. After the reign of the House of Staufer, it was separated into the countries, Lower and Upper Alsace. The Free Cities beside Strassburg and Muelhausen built the Ten-City-Alliance in 1354 (=Zehnstadte Bund).

With the "Westfalian Peace" the properties of the House Habsburg were given to France.

Louis the 14th extended his power and control to the Free Cities (Reichsstadte) also. Strassburg was occupied, but its connections to Germany still existed.

HISTORY OF ALSACE

During the French Revolution the Alsace became part of France.

Many young men migrated in the 1840's because they did not want to become soldiers. About 125,000 Alsacians and Lorraines migrated at this time to America as well as to Algeria.

When Bismarck and his troops beat Emperor Napoleon II in 1871 the Alsace was taken over by Germany. It became the German Reichsland Alsace Lorraine, including Bas-Rhin (Lower Alsace) and Haut Rhin (Upper Alsace). The western part of Haut Rhin fought against the annexation by Germany. This part was born in 1871 and named the Territory of Belfort.

In this time period many inhabitants migrated because they did not want to be German. They migrated to America and Algeria and were replaced with German citizens.

In 1918 it became French again, and still remains to this day, except for a short break in the years of the Germany Occupation (1940 to 1944).

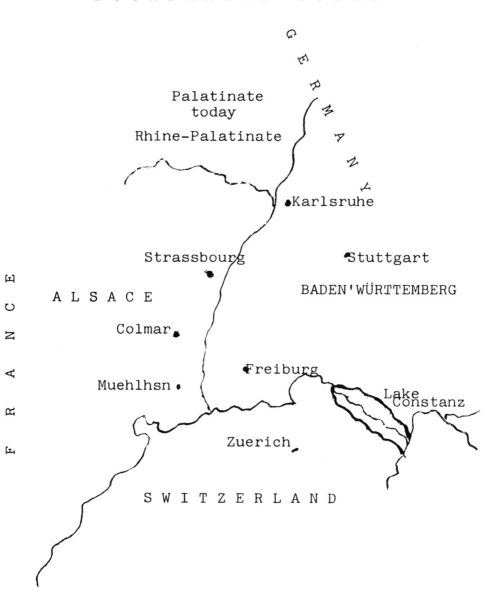

BOUNDARIES TODAY

GERMANY

Palatinate
today
Rhine-Palatinate

•Karlsruhe

Strassbourg

Stuttgart

BADEN'WÜRTTEMBERG

ALSACE

Colmar•

Muehlhsn •

•Freiburg

Lake
Constanz

FRANCE

Zuerich

SWITZERLAND

EMIGRATION

FROM

BADEN

Lastname	Firstname	Birth Year	Birthplace	Emigration	De	Prof	Source
ABELE	ALBERT	1850	RÜPPUR	01/01/1871	A		F8
ABELHÖR	FRIEDRICH		LANGENSTEINBACH	01/01/1853	A		F8
ABEND	ANTON	1849	SPESSART	10/15/1866	A		F4
ABEND	LUITGARD	1827	BURBACH	01/01/1856	A		F4
ABEND	VIKTORIA	1796	BURBACH	/ /	A		F4
ABERLE	JAKOB		WÖSSINGEN	01/01/1854	A		F4
ABRESCH	LUISE		KARLSRUHE	01/01/1851	A		F3
ACKERER	ERNST	1847	KARLSRUHE	01/01/1880	A		F3
ACKERMANN	CARL	1840	DURLACH KARLSRUHE	01/01/1867			F7
ADE	WILHELM	1831	DURLACH KARLSRUHE	/ /	A		F7
ADELMANN	GEORG		OFTERSHEIM	01/01/1784			F1
ADELMANN W 8 PERSON	ADAM		OFTERSHEIM	06/02/1784			F1
ADLER	JOSEF	1863	KARLSRUHE	01/01/1883	A		F3
ADLER	VERONIKA	1860	ÖNSBACH	01/01/1883	A		F5
ALBENER	SIGMUND		MÖRSCH	07/28/1832	A		F4
ALBERT	NIKOLAUS		ALTFELD	01/01/1754	A		F5
ALBERT W F	LORENZ		MICHELRIET	03/13/1854	A		F5
ALBRECHT	ALBERT	1841	DURLACH	01/01/1869	A		F7
ALBRECHT	FRANZ GERH.		DURLACH KARLSRUHE	01/01/1835			F7
ALBRECHT	JOHANN MATHäUS		DURLACH KARLSRUHE	01/01/1862			F7
ALLGEIER	SIMON		MÖSBACH BÜHL	01/01/1839			F1
ALT	MARTIN		DURLACH KARLSRUHE	01/01/1846			F7
ALTENBACH	WILHELM		ETTLINGEN	01/01/1886	A		F4
ALTFELIX	HEINRICH CHRIST		DURLACH KARLSRUHE	01/01/1845	A		F7
ALTFELIX	KARL GEORG	1860	DURLACH KARLSRUHE	01/01/1886	A		F7
ALTFELIX	RUDOLF	1831	DURLACH KARLSRUHE	/ /			F7
AMANN	FRANZ		WÖSSINGEN	01/01/1854	A		F4
AMANN MN BEILLON WID	MARIE W CH	1843	BRETTEN	01/01/1885	A		F8
AMANN W M	HEINRICH JOHANN	1878	BRETTEN	01/01/1885	A		F8
AMANN W M	JULIUS FRANZ	1871	BRETTEN	01/01/1885	A		F8
AMBS	GEORG		KARLSRUHE	/ /	A		F3
AMMAN	LEOPOLD	1829	DURLACH KARLSRUHE	/ /			F7
AMOLSCH W FAMILY	CHRISTIAN	1818	BLANKENLOCH	01/01/1866	A		F4
AMOLSCH W P	CHRISTIAN	1855	BLANKENLOCH	01/01/1866	A		F4
AMOLSCH W P	LISELOTTE		BLANKENLOCH	01/01/1866	A		F4
AMOLSCH W P	LUDWIG	1850	BLANKENLOCH	01/01/1866	A		F4
AMOLSCH W P	LUISE	1851	BLANKENLOCH	01/01/1866	A		F4
ANDER	PAUL	1873	KARLSRUHE	01/01/1894	A		F3
ANDERER	JOSEF	1874	ETZENROT	01/01/1881	A		F4
ANDERSON MN HOFFMANN	LUISE		KARLSRUHE	/ /	A		F3
ANDREAS	KARL	1876	KARLSRUHE	01/01/1893	A		F3
ANKERER	ERNST KARL		KARLSRUHE	01/01/1868	A		F3
ANSPACH	JOHANN		BRETTEN	01/01/1868	A		F4
ANTENRIETH	JAKOB		BRETTEN	01/01/1850	A		F4
ANTSCHLER	JOHANN MICHAEL		KARLSRUHE	01/01/1861	A		F6
APPENWEILER	GUSTAV	1853	KARLSRUHE	01/01/1871	A		F3
ARBOURT W F	CHRISTOPH		KREUZWERTHEIM	06/22/1791	A		F5
ARGAST	WILHELM FRIEDRI	1877	KARLSRUHE	01/01/1895	A		F3
ARHEIT	CONRAD		GRÖTZINGEN	01/01/1830	A		F5
ARHEIT	WILHELM		GRÖTZINGEN	01/01/1864	A		F5

Lastname	Firstname	Birth Year	Birthplace	Emigration	De	Prof	Source
ARMBRUSTER	HERR		SöLLINGEN	/ /			F7
ARMBRUSTER	PHILIPP JAKOB		SöLLINGEN	01/01/1861	A		F7
ARMBRUSTER	REGINA		PFORZHEIM	01/01/1852	A		F6
ARMBRUSTER	REGINA		RUFT	01/01/1854	A		F6
ARMBRUSTER W F	JAKOB JUNIOR		SöLLINGEN	01/01/1865	A		F7
ARMBRUSTER W F	JOHANN GEORG	1823	SöLLINGEN	01/01/1854	A		F7
ARMBRUSTER W S	JAKOB		SöLLINGEN	01/01/1865	A		F7
ARRHEIT	ANDREAS		GRöTZINGEN	01/01/1785	A		F3
ARRHEIT	ANDREAS		GRöTZINGEN	01/01/1795	A		F5
ARTMANN	JOSEF		BURBACH	01/01/1790	A		F4
ARTMANN W FAMILY	JOHANNES	1799	BURBACH	08/06/1850	A		F4
ARTMANN W P	AMALIA	1839	BURBACH	08/06/1850	A		F4
ARTMANN W P	ANTON	1837	BURBACH	08/06/1850	A		F4
ARTMANN W P	HELENA	1845	BURBACH	01/01/1860	A		F4
ARTMANN W P	JOHANN	1831	BURBACH	01/01/1856	A		F4
ARZNER	LUDWIG	1857	KARLSRUHE	01/01/1883	A		F3
ASAL	ERNST WILHELM	1860	KARLSRUHE	01/01/1880	A		F3
ASKANI	JOHANN		HOCKENHEIM	01/01/1859	A		F6
AST	JOHANN GEORG		KARLSRUHE	01/01/1876	A		F3
ATZMANN	ADOLF	1872	BULACH	01/01/1890	A		F6
AUER	JOHANN		THENGEN	01/01/1859	A		F6
AUGENSTEIN	HERMANN	1875	MALSCH	01/01/1892	A		F2
AUTENRIETH	ENGELHARD		BRETTEN	01/01/1805	A		F4
AUTENRIETH	KONRAD	1802	BRETTEN	01/01/1872	A		F4
AUTHENRIETH	WILHELM		BRETTEN	01/01/1881	A		F4

Lastname	Firstname	Birth Year	Birthplace	Emigration	De	Prof	Source
BAAM	CHRISTINE	1851	RÜPPUR	01/01/1870	A		F8
BAAM	FRIDERIKE	1853	RÜPPUR	01/01/1870	A		F8
BABBERGER	WILHELM	1856	KARLSRUHE	01/01/1883	A		F3
BABER	HANSJÖRG		BLANKENLOCH	01/01/1737	A		F4
BACH	JULIANE	1814	LANGENSTEINBACH	/ /	A		F3
BACH	KARL	1817	LANGENSTEINBACH	/ /	A		F3
BACH	KONRAD	1854	RINKLINGEN	01/01/1870	A		F6
BACH	MAGDALENA	1823	LANGENSTEINBACH	/ /	A		F3
BACH	MICHAEL	1847	LANGENSTEINBACH	/ /	A		F3
BACHMANN	ELISABETH		HASLACH	01/01/1859	A		F6
BADENBROD	ARTHUR	1866	ETTLINGEN	01/01/1882	A		F4
BADER	WILLIAM		KARLSRUHE	/ /	A		F3
BADER MN BRAYER	LUISE CäCILIE	1837	GRABEN	01/01/1867	A		F3
BADER W FAMILY	GEORG SIMON	1837	GRABEN	01/01/1867	A		F3
BADER W PARENTS	CHRISTIAN	1866	GRABEN	01/01/1867	A		F3
BAGER	LYDIA	1861	STAFFORT	01/01/1880	A		F6
BAGER	WILHELMINA	1862	STAFFORT	01/01/1880	A		F6
BAGMEIER	HEINRICH	1862	MÜHLBERG	01/01/1865	A		F6
BALBACH	EDUARD		KARLSRUHE	01/01/1828	A		F3
BALDENECKER	FRIEDRICH	1843	KARLSRUHE	01/01/1868	A		F3
BALDES	JAKOB		MÖRSCH	01/01/1862			F7
BALL	HUBERT	1827	MÖRSCH	12/18/1852	A		F7
BALL	JOSEF		MÖRSCH	01/01/1842	A		F7
BALL MN FITTERER	SCHOLASTIKA		MÖRSCH	01/01/1832	A		F7
BALL W F	ADAM		MÖRSCH	01/01/1832	A		F7
BALLES	JOHANN MICHAEL		SCHLOSSAU	01/01/1859	A		F6
BALSER	KATHARINA	1825	MALSCH	02/14/1862	A		F2
BALZER	KATHARINA	1825	MALSCH	01/01/1850	A		F1
BANDEL	KATHARINA		ETTLINGEN	01/01/1861	A		F4
BANNAD MN HEINRICH	MAGDALENA	1873	MALSCH	01/01/1890	A		F1
BANNER	FRIEDRICH WILHE	1870	STAFFORT	01/01/1887	A		F6
BARK	MARIA WILHELMIN	1846	LANGENSTEINBACH	/ /	A		F3
BARNSTEDT	KARL WILHELM	1861	KARLSRUHE	01/01/1880	A		F3
BARTBERGER	AUGUST		KARLSRUHE	01/01/1849	A		F3
BARTH	CHRISTINE		BLANKENLOCH	01/01/1845	A		F4
BARTH	ELIONORE	1850	MALSCH	10/05/1880	A		F2
BARTH	GOTTLIEB		BRETTEN	01/01/1832	A		F4
BARTH	JAKOB		MÜNZESHEIM	01/01/1853	A		F5
BARTH	JOHANN	1864	MALSCH	10/05/1880	A		F2
BARTH	KAROLINE	1845	MALSCH	01/01/1880	A		F2
BARTH	PETER	1856	MALSCH	10/05/1881	A		FE
BARTH	PHILIPP JAKOB		SÖLLINGEN	01/01/1860	A		F7
BARTH	VALENTIN	1855	MALSCH	10/05/1880	A		F2
BARTH	WILHELM	1846	MALSCH	10/05/1880	A		F2
BARTH	WINZENS	1859	MALSCH	10/05/1880	A		F2
BARTH MN OCHS	APPOLONIA	1820	MALSCH	10/05/1881	A		F2
BARTH W FAMILY	MARZIAN	1820	MALSCH	10/05/1881	A		F2
BARTH W W	CHRISTOF		SÖLLINGEN	01/01/1857	A		F7
BARTHBERGER	KARL FRIEDRICH		KARLSRUHE	02/14/1850	A		F3
BARTHOLOMä	KARL FRIEDRICH	1869	GRÖTZINGEN	01/01/1884	A		F3

Lastname	Firstname	Birth Year	Birthplace	Emigration	De	Prof	Source
BARTHORN MN WERNER	PHILIPPINE	1842	GRABEN	01/01/1868	A		F3
BARTHORN W FAMILY	CHRISTOPH	1840	GRABEN	01/01/1868	A		F3
BASEMANN	MAX	1866	KARLSRUHE	01/01/1884	A		F3
BASLER	MARGARETHA		SPöCK	01/01/1782	A		F4
BASS	LUISE		SöLLINGEN	/ /	A		F7
BASTIAN	ALEXANDER	1839	DURLACH KARLSRUHE	/ /			F7
BASTIAN W FAMILY	OSWALD	1857	KARLSRUHE	01/01/1882	A		F3
BASTIAN W PARENTS	WILBERT	1879	KARLSRUHE	01/01/1882	A		F3
BATSCHAUER	FRANK	1894	KARLSRUHE	/ /	A		F3
BAUCHERT	CHRISTIAN	1825	LANGENSTEINBACH	/ /	A		F3
BAUCHERT	KATHARINA	1829	LANGENSTEINBACH	/ /	A		F3
BAUCHERT	MATHäUS	1837	LANGENSTEINBACH	03/15/1864	A		F3
BAUCHERT	ROSINA	1834	LANGENSTEINBACH	01/01/1861	A		F3
BAUER			DOCKENROTH?BOCKENROD	04/26/1773	A		F5
BAUER	ANDREAS		FORBACH	01/01/1857	A		F6
BAUER	CHRISTIAN	1844	MALSCH	06/20/1868	A		F2
BAUER	DOROTHEA		MÜNZESHEIM	01/01/1853	A		F5
BAUER	FRANZ	1848	MALSCH	06/20/1868	A		F2
BAUER	FRIEDRICH		BLANKENLOCH	01/01/1891	A		F5
BAUER	FRIEDRICH ADOLF	1856	KARLSRUHE	01/01/1887	A		F3
BAUER	GABRIEL	1839	BURBACH	01/01/1864	A		F4
BAUER	JOHANN		BRETTEN	01/01/1850	A		F4
BAUER	JOSEF		BRETTEN	01/01/1855	A		F4
BAUER	KARL	1872	KARLSRUHE	01/01/1882	A		F3
BAUER	KARL HEINRICH	1838	LANGENSTEINBACH	/ /	A		F3
BAUER	MARIA		FORBACH	01/01/1857	A		F6
BAUER	MATHIAS	1834	BURBACH	01/01/1854	A		F4
BAUER	MICHAEL		SPöCK	01/01/1737	A		F4
BAUER	THOMA		SPöCK	01/01/1737	A		F4
BAUER	VIKTORIAN	1854	MALSCH	06/20/1868	A		F2
BAUER	WILHELM LUDWIG	1861	BLANKENLOCH	01/01/1879	A		F8
BAUER W FAMILY	JOHANN		WöSSINGEN	01/01/1834	A		F4
BAUER W FAMILY	THOMAS	1812	HöRDEN MURGTAL	06/20/1868	A		F2
BAUMANN	BARBARA		LANBERBISCHOFSHEIM	/ /	A		F6
BAUMANN	FRANZISKA		ALTSCHWEIER	01/01/1857	A		F6
BAUMANN	THEODOR		KARLSRUHE	/ /	A		F3
BAUMANN MN WOHLSCHEL	MARGARETHA	1848	LANGENSTEINBACH	02/14/1882	A		F3
BAUMANN W FAMILY	CHRISTIAN	1844	LANGENSTEINBACH	02/14/1882	A		F3
BAUMANN W PARENTS	CHRISTIAN	1869	LANGENSTEINBACH	02/14/1882	A		F3
BAUMANN W PARENTS	CHRISTINE	1874	LANGENSTEINBACH	02/14/1882	A		F3
BAUMANN W PARENTS	LUISE	1876	LANGENSTEINBACH	02/14/1882	A		F3
BAUMANN W PARENTS	MAGDALENA	1872	LANGENSTEINBACH	01/01/1882	A		F3
BAUMANN W PARENTS	PHILIPP FRIEDRI	1880	LANGENSTEINBACH	01/01/1882	A		F3
BAUMANN W PARENTS	PHILIPPINE	1878	LANGENSTEINBACH	02/14/1882	A		F3
BAUMEISTER MN KäSSLR	ELISABETH	1811	SPESSART	03/27/1847	A		F4
BAUMEISTER W FAMILY	ANTON CHRISTOPH	1808	SPESSART	03/27/1847	A		F4
BAUMEISTER W P	AUGUST	1835	ETTLINGEN	04/21/1835	A		F4
BAUMEISTER W P	GEORG	1840	ETTLINGEN	03/27/1846	A		F4
BAUMEISTER W P	JOHANNA	1840	ETTLINGEN	03/27/1847	A		F4
BAUMERT	KARL	1876	KARLSRUHE	01/01/1893	A		F3

Lastname	Firstname	Birth Year	Birthplace	Emigration	De	Prof	Source
BAUMERT	WILHELM	1876	KARLSRUHE	01/01/1891	A		F3
BAUMGARTNER	PETER		SPÖCK	01/01/1737	A		F4
BAUMGäRTNER	JAKOB		NEIDINGEN	01/01/1866	A		F6
BAUS	CHRISTIAN		WÖSSINGEN	01/01/1849	A		F6
BAUSCH MN MÜLLER	SUSANNE	1848	SCHÖLLBRONN	01/01/1881	A		F7
BAUSCH W F	FRIEDRICH	1840	SCHÖLLBRONN	01/01/1881	A		F7
BAUSCH W P	CHRISTIAN	1880	SCHÖLLBRONN	01/01/1881	A		F7
BAUSCH W P	JAKOB	1871	SCHÖLLBRONN	01/01/1881	A		F7
BAUSCH W P	KARL	1879	SCHÖLLBRONN	01/01/1881	A		F7
BAUSCH W P	KATHARINA	1878	SCHÖLLBRONN	01/01/1881	A		F7
BAUSCH W P	MAGDALENA	1875	SCHÖLLBRONN	01/01/1881	A		F7
BAUSER	WILHELMINE	1840	ETTLINGEN	12/02/1861	A		F4
BAUTZ	KARL	1847	KARLSRUHE	01/01/1871	A		F3
BAYER	FRIEDRICH	1851	KARLSRUHE	01/01/1870	A		F3
BAYERLE	RUDOLF WIEDEMAD	1875	DURLACH	01/01/1891	A		F6
BECHLER	ADELHEID	1837	MALSCH	01/01/1850	A		F2
BECHLER	ANNA	1798	MALSCH	01/01/1839	A		F2
BECHLER	BONIFAZ	1818	MALSCH	/ /	A		F2
BECHLER	CYRIAS	1844	MALSCH	07/25/1846	A		F2
BECHLER	DOROTHEA	1809	MALSCH	09/22/1864	A		F2
BECHLER	FLORIAN	1823	MALSCH	01/01/1851	A		F2
BECHLER	FRANZISKA	1831	MALSCH	01/01/1855	A		F2
BECHLER	GERTRUD	1841	MALSCH	04/09/1841	A		F2
BECHLER	GUSTAV		MALSCH	01/01/1850	A		F2
BECHLER	HILDEGARD		MALSCH	01/01/1850	A		
BECHLER	HILDEGARD	1854	MALSCH	10/13/1857	A		F2
BECHLER	JOHANN	1838	MALSCH	07/05/1855	A		F2
BECHLER	JOHANNES	1838	MALSCH	04/09/1841	A		F2
BECHLER	JOSEF		MALSCH	01/01/1839	A		F2
BECHLER	JOSEF		MALSCH	01/01/1846	A		F2
BECHLER	JOSEF CORNELIUS	1842	AMERIKA	/ /	A		F2
BECHLER	KATHARINA	1857	MALSCH	10/13/1857	A		F2
BECHLER	KONRAD	1820	MALSCH	/ /	A		F2
BECHLER	LEO	1841	MALSCH	01/01/1855	A		F2
BECHLER	LUDWIG	1849	MALSCH	10/13/1857	A		F2
BECHLER	MAGARETHE	1836	MALSCH	01/01/1839	A		F2
BECHLER	MARIA ANNA	1806	MALSCH	01/01/1839	A		F2
BECHLER	MARTIN	1804	MALSCH	01/01/1839	A		F2
BECHLER	MARTIN MICHAEL	1835	MALSCH	01/01/1839	A		F2
BECHLER	MATHIAS		MALSCH	01/01/1823	A		F2
BECHLER	MATHIAS	1812	MALSCH	01/01/1851	A		F2
BECHLER	MEINRAD	1847	MALSCH	10/13/1857	A		F2
BECHLER	PELAGIUS	1830	MALSCH	01/01/1839	A		F2
BECHLER	ROBERT	1852	MALSCH	10/13/1857	A		F2
BECHLER	SEBASTIAN	1805	MALSCH	04/30/1832	A		F2
BECHLER	STEFANI		MALSCH	04/30/1832	A		F2
BECHLER	THERES ALBINA	1846	MALSCH	07/25/1846	A		F2
BECHLER	VALENTIN	1823	MALSCH	10/03/1857	A		
BECHLER	VERONIKA		MALSCH	01/01/1850	A		F2
BECHLER	VERONIKA	1810	MALSCH	01/01/1839	A		F2

Lastname	Firstname	Birth Year	Birthplace	Emigration	De	Prof	Source
BECHLER MN BEIGER	THEODORE			07/25/1846	A		F2
BECHLER MN EISENER	LEOSADIA		MALSCH	10/03/1857	A		F2
BECHLER MN HERTMED	ELISABETH		MALSCH	04/30/1832	A		F2
BECHLER MN MEISHAUPT	GERTRUD	1806	MALSCH	04/09/1841	A		F2
BECHLER W FAMILY	ANTON	1806	MALSCH	04/09/1841	A		F2
BECHLER W FAMILY	JOSEF	1812	MALSCH	07/25/1846	A		F2
BECHLER W M	APPOLONIA	1839	MALSCH	01/01/1839	A		F2
BECHLER W P	ANTON	1841	MALSCH	07/25/1846	A		F2
BECHLER W P	THERESE	1846	MALSCH	07/25/1846	A		F2
BECHLER.MN.NIPLER.VB	ALOISE		MALSCH	/ /	A		F2
BECHT	PETRUS	1830	BURBACH	/ /	A		F4
BECHTOLD	BARBARA	1858	KNIELINGEN	01/01/1882	A		F6
BECHTOLD	GOTTLIEB FRIEDH	1864	KNIELINGEN	01/01/1882	A		F6
BECHTOLD	JAKOB	1855	KNIELINGEN	01/01/1882	A		F6
BECK	ANDREAS	1845	DURLACH KARLSRUHE	/ /			F7
BECK	ANTON	1820	DAXLANDEN	01/01/1873	A		F6
BECK	CHRISTOPH HEINH		SöLLINGEN	01/01/1855	A		F7
BECK	JAKOB		BRETTEN	01/01/1845	A		F4
BECK	JOHANNES		KREDENBACH	05/17/1754	A		F5
BECK	LEONARD		HASSELBERG	04/30/1840	A		F1
BECK	LEOPOLD		HASSELBERG	04/30/1840	A		F5
BECK W F	CHRISTOPH		SöLLINGEN	01/01/1857	A		F7
BECKER	ALBERT		KARLSRUHE	01/01/1852	A		F3
BECKER	ANNA MARIA	1818	DIETENHAUSEN	01/01/1853	A		F3
BECKER	ANTON	1834	DURLACH KARLSRUHE	/ /			F7
BECKER	AUGUST		GRABEN	01/01/1888	A		F5
BECKER	AUGUST	1852	GRABEN	01/01/1876	A		F3
BECKER	AUGUST	1888	GRABEN	/ /	A		F3
BECKER	AUGUST BERNHARD		GRABEN	01/01/1876	A		F3
BECKER	AUGUST FERDINAN		GRABEN	01/01/1876	A		F5
BECKER	CHRISTOPH	1830	LANGENSTEINBACH	01/01/1869	A		F3
BECKER	CHRISTOPH	1839	LANGENSTEINBACH	/ /	A		F3
BECKER	FRIEDRICH	1850	LANGENSTEINBACH	10/15/1869	A		F3
BECKER	GOTTLIEB	1801	LANGENSTEINBACH	01/01/1852	A		F3
BECKER	GUSTAV ADOLF	1863	KARLSRUHE	01/01/1884	A		F3
BECKER	HEINRICH	1876	KARLSRUHE	01/01/1893	A		F3
BECKER	JAKOB		GRöTZINGEN	01/01/1817	A		F5
BECKER	JAKOB	1840	LANGENSTEINBACH	05/25/1866	A		F3
BECKER	JAKOB	1843	LANGENSTEINBACH	05/23/1866	A		F3
BECKER	JOHANN	1813	LANGENSTEINBACH	01/01/1853	A		F3
BECKER	KARL		GRABEN	01/01/1879	A		F3
BECKER	KARL FRIEDRICH		GRABEN	01/01/1882	A		F3
BECKER	KARL LUDWIG	1858	GRABEN	01/01/1876	A		F3
BECKER	MAGDALENA	1834	LANGENSTEINBACH	02/03/1854	A		F3
BECKER	MARTIN		GRABEN	01/01/1830	A		F3
BECKER	MICHAEL	1836	LANGENSTEINBACH	01/01/1869	A		F3
BECKER	MICHAEL	1837	LANGENSTEINBACH	01/01/1854	A		F3
BECKER	PHILIPP	1810	LANGENSTEINBACH	01/01/1854	A		F3
BECKER	PHILIPP JAKOB		GRABEN	01/01/1830	A		F3
BECKER	SIMON		GRABEN	01/01/1850	A		F3

Lastname	Firstname	Birth Year	Birthplace	Emigration	De	Prof	Source
BECKER	SIMON		GRABEN	01/01/1867	A		F3
BECKER	WILHELM		GRABEN	01/01/1873	A		F3
BECKER	WILHELM		GRABEN	01/01/1873	A		F5
BECKER	WILHELM		GRABEN	01/01/1876	A		F3
BECKER	WILHELM		GRABEN	01/01/1877	A		F3
BECKER MN RAUSCH	REGINA	1810	LANGENSTEINBACH	01/01/1848	A		F3
BECKER MN SCHMIDT	KATHARINA	1857	LANGENSTEINBACH	03/09/1883	A		F3
BECKER MN ÜBERHÖR	MAGDALENA	1804	LANGENSTEINBACH	01/01/1852	A		F3
BECKER W F	CHRISTOPH		GRABEN	01/01/1835	A		F5
BECKER W F	SIMON		GRABEN	01/01/1867	A		F5
BECKER W FAMILY	CHRISTIAN	1793	LANGENSTEINBACH	01/01/1848	A		F3
BECKER W FAMILY	CHRISTIAN	1807	LANGENSTEINBACH	01/01/1848	A		F3
BECKER W FAMILY	CHRISTOPH		GRABEN	01/01/1835	A		F3
BECKER W FAMILY	JAKOB	1841	LANGENSTEINBACH	03/09/1883	A		F3
BECKER W PARENTS	CHRISTINE	1844	LANGENSTEINBACH	01/01/1848	A		F3
BECKER W PARENTS	CHRISTINE	1883	LANGENSTEINBACH	01/01/1883	A		F3
BECKER W PARENTS	CHRISTOPH	1831	LANGENSTEINBACH	01/01/1852	A		F3
BECKER W PARENTS	EMILIE	1878	LANGENSTEINBACH	03/09/1883	A		F3
BECKER W PARENTS	FRIEDRICH	1835	LANGENSTEINBACH	01/01/1848	A		F3
BECKER W PARENTS	GOTTLIEB	1824	LANGENSTEINBACH	01/01/1852	A		F3
BECKER W PARENTS	JAKOB	1846	LANGENSTEINBACH	01/01/1848	A		F3
BECKER W PARENTS	JAKOB	1871	LANGENSTEINBACH	03/09/1883	A		F3
BECKER W PARENTS	JOHANN	1876	LANGENSTEINBACH	03/09/1883	A		F3
BECKER W PARENTS	KARL	1836	LANGENSTEINBACH	01/01/1852	A		F3
BECKER W PARENTS	KAROLINE	1877	LANGENSTEINBACH	03/09/1883	A		F3
BECKER W PARENTS	MAGDALENA	1836	LANGENSTEINBACH	01/01/1848	A		F3
BECKER W PARENTS	SUSANNE	1873	LANGENSTEINBACH	03/09/1883	A		F3
BECKER W PARENTS	WILHELM	1833	LANGENSTEINBACH	01/01/1852	A		F3
BECKER W WIFE	PHILIPP JAKOB		GRABEN	01/01/1830	A		F5
BECKER-KURZ	FRIEDERIKE		GRABEN	01/01/1882	A		F3
BED	MATHäUS	1817	SANDHAUFEN	01/01/1817	A		F2
BEDE WID MN VOGEL FA	THERESE	1787	ETTLINGEN	01/01/1847	A		F4
BEDER				/ /			
BEDER	ANNA MARIA	1836	VÖLKERSBACH	01/01/1853	A		F4
BEDER	AUGUST	1852	KARLSRUHE	01/01/1876	A		F3
BEDER	FRANZ JOSEF	1869	STUPFERICH	01/01/1892	A		F6
BEDER	JAKOB		GRÖTZINGEN	/ /	A		F3
BEDER	KARL	1878	KARLSRUHE	01/01/1893	A		F3
BEDER	KARL LUDWIG	1858	KARLSRUHE	01/01/1876	A		F3
BEDER W MOTHER	CHRISTINE	1821	ETTLINGEN	01/01/1847	A		F4
BEFFLER	KARL	1876	KARLSRUHE	01/01/1894	A		F3
BEH	CHRISTOPH LUDWG		SÖLLINGEN	01/01/1852	A		F7
BEHIER? W F	JOHANN		BRUCHSAL	01/01/1866	A		F6
BEHLER	JOHANN		DORFWEIER	01/01/1859	A		F6
BEHRINGER W F	PETER		HASSELBERG	05/16/1754	A		F5
BEIDECK	KARL LUDWIG	1851	HOCHSTETTEN	01/01/1882	A		F8
BEIGER	CHRISTIAN		BERGHAUSEN	01/01/1864	A		F4
BEILE	JOHANN		BADEN?	01/01/1866	A		F6
BEILMANN	LEOPOLD		GRABEN	01/01/1861	A		F6
BENDER	ANTON		ETTLINGEN	/ /	A		

Lastname	Firstname	Birth Year	Birthplace	Emigration	De	Prof	Source
BENDER	FRIEDRICH WILHE	1870	BÜHL	01/01/1890	A		F5
BENDER	MARIE		SÖLLINGEN	/ /	A		F7
BENKERT	JOHANN		BRETTEN	01/01/1847	A		F4
BENKERT	JULIANA ELISABH		BRETTEN	01/01/1865	A		F4
BENKERT	LEONHARD		BRETTEN	01/01/1842	A		F4
BENZ	CHRISTOPH		GRÖTZINGEN	01/01/1810	A		F3
BENZ	CLEMENS		VÖLKERSBACH	01/01/1826	A		F4
BENZ	KARL		VÖLKERSBACH	01/01/1861	A		F4
BENZ	KAROLINE		GRÖTZINGEN	01/01/1858	A		F5
BENZ	KATHARINA		GRÖTZINGEN	/ /	A		F3
BENZ	MAGDALENA		GRÖTZINGEN	01/01/1855	A		F5
BENZ	MARTIN		GRÖTZINGEN	01/01/1852	A		F5
BENZ W FAMILY	PETER	1812	GRÖTZINGEN	01/01/1851	A		F3
BENZ W FATHER	CHRISTINE	1850	GRÖTZINGEN	01/01/1851	A		F3
BENZ W FATHER	KARL FRIEDRICH	1847	GRÖTZINGEN	01/01/1851	A		F3
BERBERICH	ADOLF	1877	ETTLINGEN	01/01/1894	A		F4
BERCHTOLD	LEONHARD		BAUERBACH	01/01/1862	A		F6
BERGER	ANNA		ETTLINGEN	/ /	A		F1
BERGER	ANNA	1881	ETTLINGEN	/ /	A		F3
BERGER	ANTON ANDREAS	1855	ETTLINGEN	01/01/1872	A		F4
BERGER	ANTON ANDREAS	1856	ETTLINGEN	01/01/1872	A		F4
BERGER	EDUARD WILHELM	1838	ETTLINGEN	01/01/1867	A		F4
BERGER	JOHANN		WEHR	01/01/1862	A		F8
BERGER	JOSEF		ALTDORF	01/01/1833	A		F6
BERGER	WILHELM		DURLACH	01/01/1866	A		F8
BERGER	WILHELM	1847	DURLACH KARLSRUHE	/ /			F7
BERGER W FAMILY	LUDWIG	1803	ETTLINGEN	01/01/1845	A		F4
BERGER MN BARAL	SUSANNE	1810	ETTLINGEN	01/01/1845	A		F4
BERGER MN JOURDAN	SUSANNE	1807	ETTLINGEN	01/01/1845	A		F4
BERGER W FAMILY	STEFAN	1806	ETTLINGEN	01/01/1845	A		F4
BERGER W PARENTS	CHRISTIAN	1829	ETTLINGEN	01/01/1845	A		F4
BERGER W PARENTS	LUDWIG WILHELM	1844	ETTLINGEN	01/01/1845	A		F4
BERGER W PARENTS	LUISE	1838	ETTLINGEN	01/01/1845	A		F4
BERGER W PARENTS	SUSANNE	1833	ETTLINGEN	01/01/1845	A		F4
BERGER W PARENTS	SUSANNE	1834	ETTLINGEN	01/01/1845	A		F4
BERISCH	WILHELM		BRETTEN	01/01/1853	A		F4
BERNER	HERMANN	1883	MALSCH	01/01/1899	A		F2
BERNHARD	ERNST		ETTLINGEN	01/01/1858	A		F4
BERNHARD	PHILIPP	1875	KARLSRUHE	01/01/1894	A		F3
BERNHARD	THEODOR		BÜHLERTHAL	01/01/1854	A		F6
BERNHARD MN BAUREITL	KATHARINA		ETTLINGEN	01/01/1858	A		F4
BERNHARD W FAMILY	FRANZ	1799	ETTLINGEN	01/01/1858	A		F4
BERNHARD W PARENTS	ERNST	1831	ETTLINGEN	01/01/1858	A		F4
BERNHARD W PARENTS	KAROLINE	1842	ETTLINGEN	01/01/1858	A		F4
BERNHARD W PARENTS	KATHARINA	1835	ETTLINGEN	01/01/1858	A		F4
BERTHäUFER	NORBERT AUGUST		GRABEN	01/01/1781	A		F3
BERTRAND	ALFRED			/ /			
BERTSCH	FRIEDRICH	1849	KARLSRUHE	01/01/1872	A		F3
BERTSCH	KARL FRIEDRICH		GRABEN	01/01/1872	A		F3
BERWANGER	LEOPOLD		KLEINEICHOLZHEIM	01/01/1866	A		F6

Lastname	Firstname	Birth Year	Birthplace	Emigration	De	Prof	Source
BEST	SEBASTIAN		BLANKENLOCH	01/01/1737	A		F4
BETHäUSER	ROBERT AUGUST E		GRABEN	01/01/1781	A		F3
BETZ	ADAM	1870	WEINHEIM	01/01/1891	A		F5
BEURER	THOMA		SPöCK	01/01/1737	A		F4
BEUTEL MN		1853	KARLSRUHE	01/01/1882	A		F3
BEUTEL W FAMILY	JOHANN	1853	KARLSRUHE	01/01/1882	A		F3
BEUTEL W PARENTS	FRIEDRICH	1878	KARLSRUHE	01/01/1882	A		F3
BEUTEL W PARENTS	HEINRICH	1870	KARLSRUHE	01/01/1882	A		F3
BEUTEL W PARENTS	KARL	1875	KARLSRUHE	01/01/1882	A		F3
BIBERGER	JOHANN GEORG		BRÖTZINGEN	01/01/1796	A		F7
BICHLER	SIMON	1862	BRETTEN	01/01/1879	A		F4
BICKEL	AUGUST		GRABEN	01/01/1880	A		F3
BICKEL	CHRISTOPH		WEINGARTEN	01/01/1857	A		F8
BICKEL	FERDINAND		GRABEN	01/01/1880	A		F3
BICKEL	HEINRICH	1859	GRABEN	01/01/1888	A		F3
BICKEL	HEINRICH FRIEDR	1838	RINKLINGEN	01/01/1864	A		F4
BICKEL	JAKOB		GRABEN	01/01/1781	A		F3
BICKEL	KARL LUDWIG		GRABEN	01/01/1868	A		F3
BICKEL	KONRAD AUGUST	1816	RINKLINGEN	/ /	A		F4
BICKEL	LORENZ	1847	RINKLINGEN	01/01/1896	A		F4
BICKEL	LUDWIG		GRABEN	01/01/1880	A		F3
BICKEL	LUDWIG		GRABEN	01/01/1880	A		F5
BICKEL	NINA		GRABEN	/ /	A		F5
BICKEL	SIMON		GRABEN	01/01/1835	A		F3
BICKEL	WILHELM AUGUST	1854	WEINGARTEN B. OFNBRG	01/01/1870	A		F4
BICKEL MN SEGER	KATHARINA ELISB	1822	GRABEN	01/01/1871	A		F3
BICKEL MN VOGEL	KATHARINA	1862	GRABEN	01/01/1888	A		F6
BICKEL W F	AUGUST RUDOLF	1852	GRABEN	01/01/1871	A		F6
BICKEL W F	CHRISTOPH	1821	GRABEN	01/01/1871	A		F6
BICKEL W F	FERDINAND	1856	GRABEN	01/01/1871	A		F6
BICKEL W F	HEINRICH	1849	GRABEN	01/01/1888	A		F6
BICKEL W F	JAKOB FRIEDRICH		GRABEN	01/01/1824	A		F5
BICKEL W F	JOHANN ADAM		GRABEN	01/01/1819	A		F5
BICKEL W F	PHILIPP		GRABEN	01/01/1819	A		F5
BICKEL W F	SIMON		GRABEN	01/01/1835	A		F5
BICKEL W FAMILY	CHRISTOPH	1821	GRABEN	01/01/1871	A		F3
BICKEL W FAMILY	HEINRICH		GRABEN	01/01/1888	A		F3
BICKEL W P	CHRISTOPH FRIED	1855	GRABEN	01/01/1871	A		F6
BICKEL W P	HEINRICH	1888	GRABEN	01/01/1888	A		F6
BICKEL W P	KATHARINA ELIS	1850	GRABEN	01/01/1871	A		F6
BICKEL W P	MARIA	1887	GRABEN	01/01/1888	A		F6
BICKEL W P	STEFANIE	1856	GRABEN	01/01/1871	A		F6
BICKEL W PARENTS	AUGUST RUDOLF	1852	GRABEN	01/01/1871	A		F3
BICKEL W PARENTS	CHRISTOPH FRIED	1855	GRABEN	01/01/1871	A		F3
BICKEL W PARENTS	FERDINAND	1856	GRABEN	01/01/1871	A		F3
BICKEL W PARENTS	HEINRICH	1888	GRABEN	01/01/1888	A		F3
BICKEL W PARENTS	KATHARINA ELIS	1850	GRABEN	01/01/1871	A		F3
BICKEL W PARENTS	MARIA ELIS	1887	GRABEN	01/01/1888	A		F3
BICKEL W PARENTS	STEFANIE	1856	GRABEN	01/01/1871	A		F3
BIDEL	CHRISTOPH FRIED	1831	KARLSRUHE	01/01/1871	A		F3

Lastname	Firstname	Birth Year	Birthplace	Emigration	De	Prof	Source
BIDEL	HEINRICH	1859	GRABEN	01/01/1888	A		F3
BIDEL	JAKOB		GARBEN	/ /	A		F3
BIEL	HERRMANN	1870	WEINGARTEN	01/01/1889	A		F6
BIEL	HERRMANN	1873	WEINGARTEN	01/01/1889	A		F6
BIEL	WILHELM	1871	WEINGARTEN	01/01/1888	A		F6
BIEMER	KARL	1865	KARLSRUHE	01/01/1882	A		F3
BIER	FRANZ	1863	KARLSRUHE	01/01/1881	A		F3
BIERENBREIER	AURELIA		WINDEN	01/01/1808			F1
BIERIG	LUDWIG	1867	KARLSRUHE	01/01/1885	A		F3
BIESCHOFF MN	ANNA	1874	KARLSRUHE	/ /	A		F3
BILDERBACH	KARL	1866	KARLSRUHE	01/01/1883	A		F3
BILGER	IGNAZ		ÖHNINGEN	01/01/1859	A		F6
BINENAGEL	KARL		GROSSENHOLZHEIM	01/01/1859	A		F8
BIPPER	AMALIE	1871	SPöCK	01/01/1880	A		F9
BIPPER	LUDWIG	1865	SPöCK	01/01/1880	A		F9
BIPPER MN ZIMMERMANN	CAROLINE	1839	SPöCK	01/01/1880	A		F9
BIPPER W F	JAKOB	1836	SPöCK	01/01/1880	A		F9
BIPPER W P	FERDINAND	1864	SPöCK	01/01/1880	A		F9
BIPPER W P	JULIUS	1868	SPöCK	01/01/1880	A		F9
BIPPER W P	SOPHIE	1873	SPöCK	01/01/1880	A		F9
BIPPES	JAKOB			/ /			
BIPPES MN	CHRISTINE	1828	SPöCK	01/01/1867	A		F4
BIPPES MN ZIMMERMANN	CAROLINA		SPöCK	01/01/1890	A		F4
BIPPES W FAMILY	JAKOB	1836	SPöCK	01/01/1890	A		F4
BIPPES W FAMILY	KARL MARTIN	1825	SPöCK	01/01/1867	A		F4
BIPPES W P	AMELIE	1883	SPöCK	01/01/1890	A		F4
BIPPES W P	LUDWIG	1876	SPöCK	01/01/1890	A		F4
BIPPES W P	MARIA	1863	SPöCK	01/01/1867	A		F4
BIPPES W P	WILHELMA	1849	SPöCK	01/01/1867	A		F4
BIRKENMAIER	KARL	1852	KARLSRUHE	01/01/1868	A		F3
BITSCHE	KONRAD LEOPOLD	1861	BRETTEN	01/01/1880	A		F4
BITSCHE	KONRAD LEOPOLD	1861	BRETTEN	01/01/1880	A		F8
BITTIGHOFER	ELISABETH		SÖLLINGEN	01/01/1865	A		F7
BITTMANN	KARL	1876	MALSCH	08/23/1892	A		F2
BLANKENHEIM	BARBARA	1850	BRETTEN	01/01/1867	A		F4
BLANKENHEIM	BARBARA	1850	BRETTEN	01/01/1867	A		F8
BLANKENHEIM	FRIEDRICH	1847	BRETTEN	01/01/1867	A		F4
BLANKENHEIM	JOHANN	1847	BRETTEN	01/01/1867	A		F4
BLANKENHEIM	JOHANN	1849	BRETTEN	01/01/1869	A		F4
BLANKENHEIM	KATHARINA		BRETTEN	01/01/1862	A		F4
BLANKENHEIM	WILHELM	1865	BRETTEN	01/01/1882	A		F4
BLANKENHEIM	WILHELM JAKOB	1865	BRETTEN	01/01/1882	A		F4
BLAU	AUGUST		GRABEN	01/01/1879	A		F3
BLAU	FRIEDRICH		GRABEN	01/01/1879	A		F3
BLAU	HEINRICH		GRABEN	01/01/1879	A		F3
BLAU	JAKOBINE	1837	GRABEN	01/01/1857	A		F3
BLAU	JOHANN JAKOB	1861	GRABEN	01/01/1877	A		F3
BLAU	KARL		GRABEN	01/01/1869	A		F3
BLAU	KARL SIMON		GRABEN	01/01/1888	A		F3
BLAU	KAROLINA	1860	GRABEN	01/01/1888	A		F3

Lastname	Firstname	Birth Year	Birthplace	Emigration	De	Prof	Source
BLAU	LUDWIG		GRABEN	01/01/1880	A		F3
BLAU	MAGDALENE		GRABEN	01/01/1870	A		F3
BLAU	MARTIN		GRABEN	01/01/1879	A		F3
BLAU	PHILIPP		GRABEN	01/01/1882	A		F3
BLAU	PHILIPP		GRABEN	01/01/1882	A		F5
BLAU	PHILIPPINE		GRABEN	01/01/1878	A		F3
BLAU	PHILIPPINE		GRABEN	01/01/1878	A		F5
BLAU	WILHELM KONRAD	1854	GRABEN	01/01/1884	A		F3
BLAU W FAMILY	KARL SIMON	1856	GRABEN	01/01/1888	A		F3
BLAU W PARENTS	EMMA KAROLINA	1884	GRABEN	01/01/1888	A		F3
BLAU W PARENTS	KARL LUDWIG	1881	GRABEN	01/01/1888	A		F3
BLAU-KLINGER	KAROLINE		GRABEN	01/01/1891	A		F3
BLAZ	LEONARD	1818	RINKLINGEN	01/01/1848	A		F4
BLAZ	MARTIN	1823	RINKLINGEN	/ /	A		F4
BLEICH	FRIEDRICH	1838	BRETTEN	01/01/1867	A		F8
BLEICH	FRIEDRICH	1847	BRETTEN	01/01/1867	A		F4
BLEIDERN	CARL	1834	DURLACH KARLSRUHE	/ /			F7
BLEIER	FRIEDRICH		GRABEN	/ /	A		F5
BLEIER	HEINRICH		GRABEN	01/01/1873	A		F3
BLEIER	HEINRICH		GRABEN	01/01/1880	A		F3
BLINN	LUDWIG	1864	KARLSRUHE	01/01/1882	A		F3
BLISCH	WILHELM		BRETTEN	01/01/1853	A		F4
BLOCKMANN	ALBERT	1859	KARLSRUHE	01/01/1892	A		F3
BLOS	FRIEDRICH	1854	BRETTEN	01/01/1870	A		F8
BLOS	FRIEDRICH	1854	BRETTEN	01/01/1880	A		F4
BLUM	LUDWIG	1863	KARLSRUHE	01/01/1883	A		F3
BLUST WW	GEORG		MÖSBACH BÜHL	/ /			F1
BOBARTH	FRIEDRICH			/ /			
BOD	MICHAEL JOSEF		KARLSRUHE	01/01/1857	A		F3
BODEMER	BALTASAR	1820	BURBACH	01/01/1851	A		F4
BODEMER	CÄZILIE	1826	BURBACH	01/01/1856	A		F4
BODEMER	FRANZ XAVER	1830	BURBACH	01/01/1863	A		F4
BODEMER	JOSEF	1818	BURBACH	01/01/1851	A		F4
BODEMER	LEOPOLD	1823	BURBACH	01/01/1851	A		F4
BOETH	WILHELM	1869	KARLSRUHE	01/01/1870	A		F3
BOHLICH W FAMILY	REINHARD	1852	KARLSRUHE	01/01/1883	A		F3
BOHLICH W PARENTS	ROSA	1865	KARLSRUHE	01/01/1883	A		F3
BOHLICH W PARENTS	RUDOLF	1871	KARLSRUHE	01/01/1883	A		F3
BOHLICH W PARENTS	THERESE	1870	KARLSRUHE	01/01/1883	A		F3
BOHN MN GLASER	GERTRUD	1778	PFAFFENROTH	01/01/1830	A		F4
BOHN W FAMILY	JOSEF	1776	SPESSART	01/01/1830	A		F4
BOHNER	DAVID	1869	KARLSRUHE	01/01/1883	A		F3
BOLLER	GEORG KASPAR		HASSELBERG	/ /	A		F5
BOLLWEBER	HEINRICH	1876	KARLSRUHE	01/01/1893	A		F3
BOMLICHER WW 1CH	ANTON		BALM/ WALDSH.	01/01/1737			F1
BORGER W F	HANS MICHEL		VOCKENROTH	05/18/1852	A		F5
BORST	EMIL	1864	KARLSRUHE	01/01/1881	A		F3
BORST	FRIDA	1863	KARLSRUHE	01/01/1882	A		F3
BORST	KARL	1862	KARLSRUHE	01/01/1882	A		F3
BORST	MARIA	1862	KARLSRUHE	01/01/1882	A		F3

Lastname	Firstname	Birth Year	Birthplace	Emigration	De	Prof	Source
BORST	STEFAN	1859	KARLSRUHE	01/01/1882	A		F3
BOSSERT WW CH	LUDWIG		WÖSSINGEN	01/01/1846	A		F1
BOTT	CHRISTOPH		GRABEN	01/01/1774	A		F3
BRANCH	CHRISTINE		WÖSSINGEN	01/01/1853	A		
BRANCH	MICHAEL		WÖSSINGEN	01/01/1791	A		F1
BRANCH	PHILIPP		WÖSSINGEN	01/01/1844	A		F1
BRANCH MN KUNZMANN	CHRISTINA BARBR		WÖSSINGEN	01/01/1864	A		F1
BRANCH W 5 PERSONS	JOSEF		WÖSSINGEN	09/24/1782		FARM	F1
BRANCH W FAMILY	JAKOB FRIEDRICH		WÖSSINGEN	01/01/1832	A		F1
BRANCH WW 5CH	PETER		WÖSSINGEN	01/01/1848	A		F1
BRANCH WW CH	PETER		WÖSSINGEN	01/01/1864	A		F1
BRAND	CHRISTOPH		NÖTTINGEN	06/05/1802			F1
BRANDNER	JOHANN JAKOB	1830	RINKLINGEN	01/01/1858	A		F4
BRANDNER	JOHANNES	1761	LANGENSTEINBACH	01/01/1792	A		F6
BRANNETH	WILHELM	1872	KARLSRUHE	01/01/1891	A		F3
BRAUCH	CHRISTINA		WÖSSINGEN	01/01/1853	A		F1
BRAUCH	FRIEDRICH		GRABEN	01/01/1883	A		F3
BRAUCH	FRIEDRICH WILHE	1870	GRABEN	01/01/1886	A		F3
BRAUCH	LUDWIG		GRABEN	01/01/1878	A		F3
BRAUCH	MICHAEL		WÖSSINGEN	01/01/1741	A		F1
BRAUCH	PETER		WÖSSINGEN	01/01/1864	A		F1
BRAUCH	PHILIPP		WÖSSINGEN	01/01/1844	A		F1
BRAUCH W F	JAKOB FRIEDRICH		WÖSSINGEN	01/01/1852	A		F1
BRAUCH W F	PETER		WÖSSINGEN	01/01/1848	A		F1
BRAUN	CHRISTIAN		OFTERSHEIM	01/01/1784			F1
BRAUN	EVA		GRABEN	01/01/1855	A		F3
BRAUN	FRIEDRICH		GRABEN	01/01/1832	A		F3
BRAUN	FRIEDRICH		GRABEN	01/01/1833	A		F3
BRAUN	FRIEDRICH		GRABEN	01/01/1852	A		F5
BRAUN	HERMANN		KÜLSHEIM	01/01/1859	A		F6
BRAUN	HERMANN	1874	BÜHLERTAL	01/01/1896	A		F5
BRAUN	JAKOB		GRABEN	01/01/1819	A		F5
BRAUN	LUISE	1865	LINKENHEIM	01/01/1881	A		F8
BRAUN	PHILLIP		WÖSSINGEN	01/01/1844	A		F4
BRAUN	SIMON JAKOB		GRABEN	01/01/1862	A		F5
BRAUN	VALENTIN		DAXSLANDEN	04/02/1803	A		F1
BRAUN	WILHELM		GRABEN	01/01/1855	A		F3
BRAUN MN FRIES	HERTA		ETTLINGEN	01/01/1895	A		F4
BRAUN W WIFE	AUGUST HERMANN	1870	OPPENAU OFFENBURG	01/01/1895	A		F4
BRAUN W WIFE	FRIEDRICH		GRABEN	01/01/1853	A		F5
BRECHNITZ	JOHANN ANDREAS		BRETTEN	01/01/1858	A		F4
BRECHT	CHRISTIAN		SPÖCK	01/01/1750	A		F4
BRECHT	CHRISTINE		SPÖCK	01/01/1750	A		F4
BREHM	KATHARINA	1817	SPESSART	/ /	A		F4
BREINING	MAX	1864	KARLSRUHE	01/01/1882	A		F3
BREMEIER	WILHELM GEORG	1875	KARLSRUHE	01/01/1891	A		F3
BRENDLE	LEOPOLD JOHANN	1862	RINKLINGEN	01/01/1880	A		F4
BRENNER	HEINRICH	1808	SPÖCK	01/01/1881	A		F8
BRENS MN AIDT	AGATHE			01/01/1847	A		F4
BRENS W FAMILY	BENJAMIN	1817	GISINGEN PFORZHEIM	01/01/1847	A		F4

Lastname	Firstname	Birth Year	Birthplace	Emigration	De	Prof	Source
BRENS W PARENTS	FRANZ KARL	1841	ETTLINGEN	01/01/1847	A		F4
BRONNER	EUGEN	1875	KARLSRUHE	01/01/1891	A		F3
BRUDERLE	MARIA ANNA		BERGHAUPTEN	/ /			
BRUDERLE W CHILD	MARIA ANNA		BERGHAUSEN	01/01/1866	A		F6
BRUECKEL	KURT		KARLSRUHE	/ /	A		F3
BRUEDEL	KURT		KARLSRUHE	/ /	A		F3
BRUNKEN	A.		SöLLINGEN	/ /	A		F7
BRUNNER	CIRIAK	1834	SCHÖLLBRONN	/ /	A		F1
BRUNNER	ERNST ALBERT	1874	KARLSRUHE	01/01/1892	A		F3
BRUNNER	JOSEF		SCHÖLLBRONN	01/01/1853	A		F7
BRUNNER	KATHARINA	1832	SCHÖLLBRONN	01/01/1867	A		F7
BRUNNER	LUDINA	1864	SCHÖLLBRONN	01/01/1867	A		F7
BRUNNER W F	JOHANNA	1835	SCHÖLLBRONN	01/01/1867	A		F7
BRUNNER W P	CÄZILIE	1856	SCHÖLLBRONN	01/01/1867	A		F7
BRUNNER W P	PIUS	1864	SCHÖLLBRONN	01/01/1867	A		F7
BRUNNER W P	ROBERT	1866	SCHÖLLBRONN	01/01/1867	A		F7
BRÜCKNER	ADOLF	1859	KARLSRUHE	01/01/1883	A		F3
BRÜNNER	WILHELM	1866	KARLSRUHE	01/01/1883	A		F3
BRÄUNIG	LEONHARD	1853	BRETTEN	01/01/1875	A		F8
BRÄUNING	ERNST	1843	BRETTEN	01/01/1882	A		F4
BRÄUNING	LEONHARD	1853	BRETTEN	01/01/1875	A		F4
BRÄUNING MN MOSETTE	LUISE	1852	BRETTEN	01/01/1882	A		F8
BRÄUNING W F	ERNST	1852	BRETTEN	01/01/1882	A		F8
BRÄUNING W P	ERNST	1879	BRETTEN	01/01/1882	A		F8
BRÄUTIGAM	JOSEF		MÖRSCH	01/01/1858	A		F7
BRÄUTIGAM	MAGDALENA		MÖRSCH	01/01/1880	A		F7
BUCHLEITER MN MÜLLER	KATHARINA		SPIELBERG	02/03/1854	A		F3
BUCHLEITER W FAMILY	GOTTLIEB	1817	LANGENSTEINBACH	03/02/1854	A		F3
BUCHLEITER W PARENTS	KATHARINA	1849	LANGENSTEINBACH	02/03/1854	A		F3
BUCHLEITER W PARENTS	MAGARETHA	1844	LANGENSTEINBACH	03/02/1854	A		F3
BUCHLEITER W PARENTS	PHILIPP	1846	LANGENSTEINBACH	02/03/1854	A		F3
BUCHLINGER	KATH. PHILIPPIE	1851	MALSCH	/ /			F2
BUCHLINGER MN FAUTH	WALBURGA	1812	MALSCH	01/01/1855	A		F2
BUCHMAIER	ANTON	1810	MALSCH	01/01/1847	A		F2
BUCHMAIER	CYRIAL	1876	MALSCH	08/30/1892	A		F2
BUCHMAIER	ISIDOR	1853	MALSCH	11/09/1866	A		F2
BUCHMAIER	JOSEF OSWALD	1831	MALSCH	01/01/1860	A		F2
BUCHMAIER	KARL	1839	MALSCH	01/01/1860	A		F2
BUCHMAIER	MICHAEL	1836	MALSCH	/ /	A		F2
BUCHMAIER MN W.V.WEN	LUISE			01/01/1877	A		F2
BUCHMAIER W FAMILY	THEODOR	1852	MALSCH	01/01/1877	A		F2
BUCHMÜLLER	JOHANN ADALBERT		DURMERSHEIM	01/01/1850	A		F7
BUCKLINGER	ANTON	1866	KARLSRUHE	01/01/1882	A		F3
BUDER	KLARA	1832	BURBACH	01/01/1853	A		F4
BUGER WW 4CH	JOSEF		BALM WALDSH.	01/01/1737			F1
BUHLINGER	AMALIA	1842	MALSCH	01/01/1855	A		F2
BUHLINGER	BABARA	1800	MALSCH	01/01/1832	A		F2
BUHLINGER	FRANZ			/ /			F2
BUHLINGER	FRANZ	1873	MALSCH	01/01/1891	A		F2
BUHLINGER	HERMANN		MALSCH	01/01/1889	A		F2

Lastname	Firstname	Birth Year	Birthplace	Emigration	De	Prof	Source
BUHLINGER	IGNAZ	1800	MALSCH	01/01/1848	A		F2
BUHLINGER	IGNAZ	1809	MALSCH	01/01/1848	A		F2
BUHLINGER	JOSEF		MALSCH	01/01/1877	A		F9
BUHLINGER	MARIA ANNA	1809	MALSCH	01/01/1832	A		F2
BUHLINGER	MARTIN	1800	MALSCH	01/01/1832	A		F2
BUHLINGER	MECHTILD	1802	MALSCH	01/01/1832	A		F2
BUHLINGER	MICHAEL	1788	MALSCH	01/01/1832	A		F2
BUHLINGER	MICHAEL	1827	MALSCH	01/01/1837	A		F2
BUHLINGER	THOMAS	1848	MALSCH	01/01/1889	A		F2
BUHLINGER MN IHLY	GERTRUD		MALSCH	01/01/1832	A		F2
BUHLINGER MN KOCH	ADELHEID		MALSCH	01/01/1889	A		F2
BUHLINGER W FAMILY	BALTASAR	1812	MALSCH	01/01/1855	A		F2
BULINGER	BERTHOLD	1861	MALSCH	01/01/1880	A		F2
BULINGER	FRANZ	1873	MALSCH	01/01/1891	A		F2
BULINGER	FRANZISKA	1835	MALSCH	01/01/1855	A		F2
BULINGER	IGNAZ	1877	MALSCH	/ /	A		F2
BULINGER	JOHANNES	1891	MALSCH	01/01/1892	A		F2
BULINGER	RUDOLF	1848	MALSCH	01/01/1855	A		F2
BULINGER MN BOOS	MARGOTH	1731	MALSCH	01/01/1770	A		F2
BULINGER W FAMILY	FRANZ ANTON	1742	MALSCH	01/01/1770	A		F2
BULLINGER	BERNHARD	1823	MALSCH	01/01/1848	A		F2
BULLINGER	BERNHARD	1835	MALSCH	01/01/1848	A		F2
BULLINGER	FLORA THERESE	1844	MALSCH	01/01/1848	A		F2
BULLINGER	FRANZ ANTON	1847	MALSCH	/ /			F2
BULLINGER	FRANZ KARL	1838	MALSCH	01/01/1848	A		F2
BULLINGER	KARL	1857	MALSCH	01/01/1880	A		F2
BULLINGER	MARIA ANNA	1838	MALSCH	01/01/1848	A		F2
BULLINGER	SUSANNE	1836	MALSCH	01/01/1848	A		F2
BULLINGER	THEODOR URBAN	1847	MALSCH	01/01/1848	A		F2
BULLINGER	WILHELM ALEXANR	1841	MALSCH	01/01/1848	A		F2
BULLINGER MN DOLL	BARBARA	1811	MALSCH	01/01/1848	A		F2
BULLINGER MN KRäMER	THERESE	1821	MALSCH	01/01/1848	A		F2
BULLINGER MN LANG	KATHARINA		MALSCH	01/01/1873	A		F2
BULLINGER W FAMILY	ANTON	1846	MALSCH	01/01/1873	A		F2
BULLINGER W FAMILY	IGNAZ	1809	MALSCH	01/01/1848	A		F2
BULLINGER W FAMILY	THOMAS	1816	MALSCH	01/01/1848	A		F2
BURG	FRIEDRICH	1813	DAXLANDEN	01/01/1832	A		F6
BURGFAHLER MN KANAL	EMMA	1838	SPÖCK	01/01/1880	A		F8
BURGFAHLER W F	GOTTLIEB	1836	SPÖCK	01/01/1880	A		F8
BURGFAHLER W P	ERNST	1865	SPÖCK	01/01/1880	A		F8
BURGFAHLER W P	ERNSTINE	1870	SPÖCK	01/01/1880	A		F8
BURGFAHLER W P	FRIEDRICH WILHM	1863	SPÖCK	01/01/1880	A		F7
BURGFAHLER W P	NINA	1877	SPÖCK	01/01/1880	A		F8
BURGHARD	KARLFRIEDRICH	1835	SÖLLINGEN	01/01/1856	A		F7
BURGSTAHLE W PARENT	LINA	1867	KARLSRUHE	01/01/1883	A		F3
BURGSTAHLER	GOTTLIEB		SPöCK	01/01/1880	A		F4
BURGSTAHLER	KONRAD		SPöCK	01/01/1835	A		F4
BURGSTAHLER	LEONHARD		SPöCK	01/01/1879	A		F4
BURGSTAHLER MN DüRRE	ANNA	1843	KARLSRUHE	01/01/1883	A		F3
BURGSTAHLER MN KACH	KAROLINE	1836	SPöCK	01/01/1881	A		F4

Lastname	Firstname	Birth Year	Birthplace	Emigration	De	Prof	Source
BURGSTAHLER MN KUNZ	KATHARINA	1841	KARLSRUHE	01/01/1879	A		F3
BURGSTAHLER W FAMILY	LEONHARD	1836	KARLSRUHE	01/01/1879	A		F3
BURGSTAHLER W FAMILY	LUDWIG	1836	SPöCK	01/01/1881	A		F4
BURGSTAHLER W FAMILY	WILHELM	1837	KARLSRUHE	01/01/1883	A		F3
BURGSTAHLER W PARENS	ALBERT	1880	SPöCK	01/01/1881	A		F4
BURGSTAHLER W PARENS	GOTTLIEB	1867	SPöCK	01/01/1881	A		F4
BURGSTAHLER W PARENS	HEINRICH	1876	SPöCK	01/01/1881	A		F4
BURGSTAHLER W PARENS	MAX	1865	SPöCK	01/01/1881	A		F4 BUS
BURGSTAHLER W PARENT	BERTA	1873	KARLSRUHE	01/01/1883	A		F3
BURGSTAHLER W PARENT	BERTA	1878	KARLSRUHE	01/01/1879	A		F3
BURGSTAHLER W PARENT	CHRISTIAN	1875	KARLSRUHE	01/01/1879	A		F3
BURGSTAHLER W PARENT	JOHANN JAKOB	1872	KARLSRUHE	01/01/1879	A		F3
BURGSTAHLER W PARENT	KARL	1873	SPöCK	01/01/1881	A		F4
BURGSTAHLER W PARENT	KATHARINA	1869	KARLSRUHE	01/01/1879	A		F3
BURGSTAHLER W PARENT	LEOPOLD	1869	SPöCK	01/01/1881	A		F4
BURGSTAHLER W PARENT	LUIS	1876	KARLSRUHE	01/01/1879	A		F3
BURGSTAHLER W PARENT	WILHELM	1866	KARLSRUHE	01/01/1883	A		F3
BURGSTAHTER W FAMILY			SPöCK	01/01/1867	A		F4
BURKARD	DIETER		MöRSCH	01/01/1847	A		F2
BURKARD	KASIMIR		MöRSCH	01/01/1847	A		F7
BURKARD W P	KLEMENTINE	1852	MöRSCH	08/10/1853	A		F7
BURKARDT	ANTON	1875	MöRSCH	10/09/1880	A		F7
BURKARDT	FLORIAN	1873	MöRSCH	10/09/1880	A		F7
BURKARDT MN LAIER	LUISE		MöRSCH	08/10/1853	A		F7
BURKARDT W F	KONRAD	1850	MöRSCH	10/09/1880	A		F7
BURKARDT W F	LUDWIG		MöRSCH	08/10/1853	A		F7
BURKARDT W P	BARBARA	1849	MöRSCH	08/10/1853	A		F7
BURKARDT W P	GREGOR	1848	MöRSCH	08/10/1853	A		F7
BURKARDT W P	WILHELMINE	1870	MöRSCH	10/09/1880	A		F7
BURKART	LUDWINA		MöRSCH	04/05/1852	A		F7
BURKHARD	AUGUST		SöLLINGEN	01/01/1864	A		F7
BURKHARD	BENEDIKT		MöRSCH	01/01/1831	A		F7
BURKHARD	BENEDIKT		MöRSCH	01/01/1859	A		F7
BURKHARD	JOSEF		SöLLINGEN	01/01/1855	A		F7
BURKHARD	KARL		SöLLINGEN	01/01/1855	A		F7
BURKHARD	THEODOR		KARLSRUHE	01/01/1852	A		F3
BURKHARD	VALENTIN		WALLDPSF/WIESLOCH	01/01/1866	A		F6
BURKHARD W CH	WIDOW OF JOHANN		SöLLINGEN	01/01/1855	A		F7
BURKHARD W M	ELISABETH		SöLLINGEN	01/01/1855	A		F7
BURKHARD W M	KARL		SöLLINGEN	01/01/1855	A		F7
BURKHARDT	CHRISTOPH		SöLLINGEN	01/01/1860	A		F7
BURKHARDT	DOROTHEA BARBAR		SöLLINGEN	01/01/1855	A		F7
BURKHARDT MN KELLER	REGINA		MöRSCH	10/09/1880	A		F7
BURKHARTH	LUDWIG		MöRSCH	01/01/1852	A		F7
BURS	JOHANN WILHELM		GRöTZINGEN	01/01/1864	A		F5
BURSGTAHLER W PARENS	FRIEDRIECH	1866	SPöCK	01/01/1881	A		
BURST	JOHANN WILHELM		GRöTZINGEN	/ /	A		F3
BUSJäGER	KARL	1857	DURLACH KARLSRUHE	/ /	A		F7
BUTZJäGER	KARL		KARLSRUHE	09/01/1856	A		F3
BüCHLE	GEORG DANIEL		KARLSRUHE	01/01/1851	A		F3

Lastname	Firstname	Birth Year	Birthplace	Emigration	De	Prof	Source
BüCHLER	LOUIS	1848	KARLSRUHE	01/01/1868	A		F3
BüHLER	ANNA MARIA	1832	GRöTZINGEN	01/01/1853	A		F3
BüHLER	AUGUST		GRöTZINGEN	01/01/1865	A		F3
BüHLER	CHRISTOPH		GRöTZINGEN	01/01/1838	A		F5
BüHLER	MAX	1852	KARLSRUHE	01/01/1870	A		F3
BüHLER	PHILIPP		GRöTZINGEN	01/01/1887	A		F3
BüHLER MN KUMM	KATHARINA		GRöTZINGEN	01/01/1838	A		F5
BüHLER W WIFE	CHRISTOPH		GRöTZINGEN	/ /	A		F3
BüHLER WW	MARTIN		WöSSINGEN	01/01/1803			F1
BäCKER	ALBERT GEORG		GERCHSHEIM	01/01/1859	A		F6
BäR	CHISTOPH		MALSCH	01/01/1969	A		F2
BäR	CHRISTIAN		DURLACH	/ /	A		F3
BäR	CHRISTIAN	1877	DURLACH	01/01/1894	A		F3
BäR	HEINRICH	1774	DURLACH	01/01/1894	A		F5
BäR	HEINRICH	1872	DURLACH	01/01/1890	A		F3
BäR	JOSEPH		BADEN	01/01/1869	A		F2
BäR	JOSEPH	1851	MALSCH	04/27/1869	A		F2
BäR	JULIUS	1864	KARLSRUHE	01/01/1879	A		F3
BäR	KARL	1879	DURLACH	01/01/1894	A		F3
BäR	KARL	1879	DURLACH	01/01/1894	A		F5
BäR	KAROLINE	1873	MALSCH	09/02/1880	A		F2
BäR	KONRAD	1869	MALSCH	09/02/1880	A		F2
BäR	MARIA ANNA	1840	MALSCH	01/01/1869	A		F2
BäR	VERONIKA	1868	MALSCH	09/02/1880	A		F2
BäR MN BUHLINGER	KATHARINA	1842	MALSCH	09/02/1880	A		F2
BäR W F	SIMON		STEBBACH	01/01/1866	A		F6
BäR W FAMILY	CHRISTOPH	1838	MALSCH	09/02/1880	A		F2
BäR W P	AMALIE	1875	MALSCH	09/02/1880	A		F2
BäUERLER	EMIL	1879	KARLSRUHE	01/01/1895	A		F3
BöCKLE	ANDREAS		RINKLINGEN	01/01/1880	A		F4
BöCKLE	GEORG HEINRICH	1849	RINKLINGEN	01/01/1898	A		F4
BöCKLE	JOHANN KONRAD	1807	RINKLINGEN	04/25/1834	A		F4
BöCKLE	KARL	1872	RINKLINGEN	04/23/1893	A		F4
BöCKLE	KARL AUGUST	1872	RINKLINGEN	04/22/1893	A		F4
BöCKLE	KAROLINE	1856	RINKLINGEN	01/01/1876	A		F4
BöCKLE	KAROLINE	1856	RINKLINGEN	01/01/1878	A		F4
BöCKLE	MAGDALENA		RINKLINGEN	01/01/1863	A		F4
BöCKLE	MAGDALENA	1813	RINKLINGEN	04/23/1834	A		F4
BöCKLE W FAMILY	CHRISTIAN	1798	RINKLINGEN	01/01/1850	A		F4
BöCKLE W FAMILY	CHRISTOPH		RINKLINGEN	01/01/1817	A		F4
BöCKLE MN RÄTZ	ELISABETH		RINKLINGEN	01/01/1817	A		F4
BöCKLE MN WüRZ	ANNA MARIA	1794	RINKLINGEN	01/01/1850	A		F4
BöCKLE W P	BERNHARD	1812	RINKLINGEN	01/01/1817	A		F4
BöCKLE W P	ELISABETH	1807	RINKLINGEN	01/01/1817	A		F4
BöCKLE W P	IMANUEL	1831	RINKLINGEN	01/01/1850	A		F4
BöCKLE W P	LEONHAR	1810	RINKLINGEN	01/01/1817	A		F4
BöCKMANN	DANIEL		EISINGEN	01/01/1825	A		F9
BöGLI	KARL BERTOLD	1856	KARLSRUHE	01/01/1875	A		F3
BöHLER	JOSEF		DEISENDORF	01/01/1855	A		F6
BöHRINGER	KARL		DURLACH KARLSRUHE	01/01/1836			F7

Lastname	Firstname	Birth Year	Birthplace	Emigration	De	Prof	Source
BöRST	JOHANNES	1868	KARLSRUHE	01/01/1882	A		F3
BöTTLE	KONRAD	1861	RINKLINGEN	01/01/1880	A		F4
BÖCKLE	JAKOB		RINKLINGEN	01/01/1866	A		F8
BÖGER	JAKOB		LANGENSTEINBACH	01/01/1825	A		F6
BÜCHLE	GEORG DANIEL		KARLSRUHE	01/01/1851	A		F5
BÜHLER	ANNA MARIA		STEIN	01/01/1795	A		F6

Lastname	Firstname	Birth Year	Birthplace	Emigration	De	Prof	Source
CANCRIN	LUDWIG	1847	KARLSRUHE	01/01/1869	A		F3
CARRIER	EMIL	1859	KARLSRUHE	01/01/1885	A		F3
CHRIST	FRIEDRICH		KARLSRUHE	/ /	A		F3
CINCO	KARL HEINRICH		KARLSRUHE	01/01/1878	A		F3
CONRAD	FRIEDRICH	1848	KARLSRUHE	01/01/1868	A		F3
CONRAD	PHILIPP JAKOB		SÖLLINGEN	01/01/1862	A		F7
CORADE-MORITZ	ELISABETH	1892	KARLSRUHE	/ /	A		F3
COTIAUX	FRANZ	1875	KARLSRUHE	01/01/1891	A		F3

Lastname	Firstname	Birth Year	Birthplace	Emigration	De	Prof	Source
D				/ /			
DAHM	HEINRICH		WÖSSINGEN	01/01/1828	A		F1
DAHMEN W CH	OTTO	1827	KARLSRUHE	01/01/1875	A		F3
DAHMEN W FATHER	ANNA MARIA	1862	KARLSRUHE	01/01/1875	A		F3
DAHMEN W FATHER	JAKOB BABTIST	1855	KARLSRUHE	01/01/1875	A		F3
DAHMEN W FATHER	KARL OTTO	1857	KARLSRUHE	01/01/1875	A		F3
DAHMEN W FATHER	MARIA	1866	KARLSRUHE	01/01/1875	A		F3
DAHMEN W FATHER	MARIA AMALIE	1868	KARLSRUHE	01/01/1875	A		F3
DAHMEN W FATHER	MARIA PID WANDA	1870	KARLSRUHE	01/01/1875	A		F3
DAHMEN W FATHER	OTTO WERNER	1860	KARLSRUHE	01/01/1875	A		F3
DAHN	FRIEDRICH		WÖSSINGEN	01/01/1805	A		F1
DAHN	HEINRICH		WÖSSINGEN	01/01/1845	A		F1
DAHN WW 4CH	JAKOB		WÖSSINGEN	07/19/1782			F1
DALER	ANDRE	1828	DURLACH KARLSRUHE	/ /			F7
DAMBACHER	LUDWIG	1819	LANGENSTEINBACH	02/16/1856	A		F3
DAMBARTH MN SCHAUSBE	MAGDALENA	1802	GRÖTZINGEN	01/01/1843	A		F3
DAMBARTH W FAMILY	CHRISTIAN	1795	GRÖTZINGEN	01/01/1843	A		F3
DAMBARTH W PARENTS	AUGUST	1842	GRÖTZINGEN	01/01/1843	A		F3
DAMM	HEINRICH		HASSELBERG	05/16/1754	A		F5
DAMMBACHER	ANNA MARIA	1823	LANGENSTEINBACH	/ /	A		F3
DAMMBACHER	CHRISTIAN	1844	LANGENSTEINBACH	/ /	A		F3
DAMMBACHER	CHRISTOPH FRIEH	1813	LANGENSTEINBACH	05/24/1843	A		F3
DAMMBACHER	GOTTLIEB	1827	LANGENSTEINBACH	02/16/1856	A		F3
DAMMBACHER	JAOHANN	1825	LANGENSTEINBACH	09/27/1863	A		F3
DAMMBACHER	JOHANNES	1825	LANGENSTEINBACH	/ /	A		F3
DAMMBACHER	KATHERINA	1820	LANGENSTEINBACH	/ /	A		F3
DAMMBACHER	MICHAEL JAKOB	1840	LANGENSTEINBACH	/ /	A		F3
DANCH	JOHANN JAKOB		BRETTEN	01/01/1852	A		F4
DANNEMAIER	AUGUST	1866	DAXLANDEN	01/01/1884	A		F6
DAPF	JOHANN GEORG		GRÖTZINGEN	/ /	A		F3
DAPF W WIFE	JOHANN GEORG		GRÖTZINGEN	01/01/1848	A		F5
DAUBENBERGER	JOHANN		GRÖTZINGEN	/ /	A		F3
DAUBENBERGER	JOHANN		GRÖTZINGEN	01/01/1862	A		F5
DAUBENBERGER W CHILD	MAGDALENA	1823	GRÖTZINGEN	01/01/1851	A		F3
DAUBENBERGER W MOTHE	ELISABETH	1848	GRÖTZINGEN	01/01/1851	A		F3
DAUBENBERGER W MOTHE	KARL FRIEDRICH	1846	GRÖTZINGEN	01/01/1851	A		F3
DAUM	APPOLONIA	1832	VÖLKERSBACH	01/01/1852	A		F4
DAUM	KATHARINA	1833	VÖLKERSBACH	07/14/1854	A		F4
DAUM W FAMILY	MARIA EVA	1837	VÖLKERSBACH	06/14/1866	A		F4
DAUM W P	ANTON GREGOR GU	1865	VÖLKERSBACH	01/01/1866	A		F4
DAVID	SIMON	1855	MALSCH	01/01/1871	A		F2
DEBATTIS	ADOLF PHILIPP		KARLSRUHE	01/01/1852	A		F3
DECK	DAVID	1857	MÖRSCH	02/15/1881	A		F7
DECK	LUDWIG	1864	MÖRSCH	03/03/1882	A		F7
DECK	MARIA EVA		MÖRSCH	01/01/1865	A		F7
DECK MN BAIER	MARIA	1859	MÖRSCH	03/14/1889	A		F7
DECK MN BAIER	MARIA EVA	1849	MÖRSCH	03/14/1889	A		F3
DECK MN BECHTOLD	REGINE	1841	MÖRSCH	10/09/1880	A		F7
DECK MN KOCH	JOSEFA		MÖRSCH	02/21/1831	A		F7
DECK W F	DOMINIK	1841	MÖRSCH	10/09/1880	A		F7

- 32 -

Lastname	Firstname	Birth Year	Birthplace	Emigration	De	Prof	Source
DECK W F	JOHANN	1852	MÖRSCH	03/14/1889	A		F7
DECK W F	VINZENS		MÖRSCH	02/21/1831	A		F7
DECK W FAMILY	JOHANN	1852	MÖRSCH	03/14/1889	A		F3
DECK W P	ALOIS	1877	MÖRSCH	10/09/1880	A		F7
DECK W P	ANTON		MÖRSCH	02/21/1831	A		F7
DECK W P	BERNHARD	1881	MÖRSCH	03/14/1889	A		F7
DECK W P	ELISABETH		MÖRSCH	02/21/1831	A		F7
DECK W P	FRANZ		MÖRSCH	02/21/1831	A		F7
DECK W P	JUSTINA	1881	MÖRSCH	03/14/1889	A		F7
DECK W P	KLARA	1889	MÖRSCH	03/14/1889	A		F7
DECK W P	SIMON		MÖRSCH	02/21/1831	A		F7
DECK W P	SOPHIE	1873	MÖRSCH	03/14/1889	A		F7
DECK W P	SOPHIE	1873	MÖRSCH	10/09/1880	A		F7
DECK W P	THERESE	1868	MÖRSCH	10/09/1880	A		F7
DECK W P	VIKTOR		MÖRSCH	02/21/1831	A		F7
DECK W P	WILHELM	1869	MÖRSCH	10/09/1880	A		F7
DECK W PARENTS	BERNARD	1881	MÖRSCH	03/14/1889	A		F3
DECK W PARENTS	JUSTINA	1881	MÖRSCH	03/14/1889	A		F3
DECK W PARENTS	KLARA	1888	MÖRSCH	03/14/1889	A		F3
DECK W PARENTS	LUDWIG	1879	MÖRSCH	03/14/1889	A		F3
DECK W PARENTS	SOPHIE	1873	MÖRSCH	03/14/1889	A		F3
DECK WP	LUDWIG	1879	MÖRSCH	03/14/1889	A		F7
DECKER MN WIPFLER	MARTHA	1803	SCHÖLLBRONN	01/01/1851	A		F7
DECKER W F	LEOPOLD		SCHÖLLBRONN	01/01/1851	A		F7
DECKER W P	JOHANN	1827	SCHÖLLBRONN	01/01/1851	A		F7
DECKER W P	KATHARINA	1836	SCHÖLLBRONN	01/01/1851	A		F7
DECKER W P	MARIA ANNA	1833	SCHÖLLBRONN	01/01/1851	A		F7
DECKER W P	MATHILDE	1831	SCHÖLLBRONN	01/01/1851	A		F7
DECKER W P	THERESIA	1841	SCHÖLLBRONN	01/01/1851	A		F7
DECKER W P	WILHELMINE	1839	SCHÖLLBRONN	01/01/1851	A		F7
DEFER	LUDWIG	1880	KARLSRUHE	01/01/1895	A		F3
DEGLER	KARL FRIDRICH	1878	MALSCH	08/20/1894	A		F2
DEHLINGER	AUGUST		GRABEN	01/01/1873	A		F3
DEHLINGER	LUDWIG		GRABEN	01/01/1863	A		F3
DEHN	JAKOB		KARLSRUHE	01/01/1839	A		F3
DEHN	PHILIP HEINRICH		WÖSSINGEN	01/01/1857	A		F1
DEHN	WILHELM		KARLSRUHE	01/01/1836	A		F3
DEILEY	FRIEDRICH		DURLACH	01/01/1861	A		F5
DEIMLING	FRANZ CHRISTIAN		WÖSSINGEN	/ /	A		F4
DEIMLING	UWE		KARLSRUHE	01/01/1849	A		F3
DEITERLE	TOBIAS		FORBACH	01/01/1864	A		F6
DEITH	HEINRICH	1853	GRÖTZINGEN	01/01/1868	A		F3
DEMMLER	FRIEDRICH		KARLSRUHE	01/01/1852	A		F3
DEMMLER	JOHANN PHILIPP		KARLSRUHE	01/01/1863	A		F3
DENDLER	KARL FRIEDRICH	1853	BRETTEN	01/01/1871	A		F4
DENGEL	BARBARA		EPSENBACH	01/01/1859	A		F6
DENGEL	MARIA KATHARINA		EPSENBACH	01/01/1859	A		F6
DENGLER	MICHAEL		BRETTEN	01/01/1810	A		F4
DENNIG	PHILIPP		WILFERDINGEN	01/01/1795	A		F6
DENNINGER	CHRISTINE	1827	LANGENSTEINBACH	/ /	A		F3

- 33 -

Lastname	Firstname	Birth Year	Birthplace	Emigration	De	Prof	Source
DENNINGER	GOTTLIEB	1824	LANGENSTEINBACH	/ /	A		F3
DENNINGER	JAKOB	1822	LANGENSTEINBACH	/ /	A		F3
DENNINGER	JOHANN DANIEL	1801	LANGENSTEINBACH	01/01/1836	A		F3
DENNINGER	KARL		MANNHEIM	01/01/1860	A		F6
DENNINGER	MATHäUS	1804	LANGENSTEINBACH	01/01/1829	A		F3
DENNINGER	PHILIPP	1808	LANGENSTEINBACH	01/01/1830	A		F3
DENNINGER MN ICKELE	MAGDALENA	1801	LANGENSTEINBACH	01/01/1829	A		F3
DENNINGER MN ITSCHNR	SUSANNA	1804	LANGENSTEINBACH	03/12/1832	A		F3
DENNINGER W FAMILY	JOHANN GEORG	1801	LANGENSTEINBACH	03/12/1832	A		F3
DENNINGER W FAMILY	JOHANN KRAFT	1797	LANGENSTEINBACH	01/01/1829	A		F3
DENNINGER W P	ANDREAS	1828	LANGENSTEINBACH	01/01/1832	A		F3
DENNINGER W PARENTS	ANNA MARIA	1829	LANGENSTEINBACH	03/12/1832	A		F3
DENNINGER W PARENTS	JAKOBINA	1830	LANGENSTEINBACH	03/12/1832	A		F3
DENNINGER W PARENTS	JULIANE	1826	LANGENSTEINBACH	01/01/1829	A		F3
DENNINGER W PARENTS	MARGARETHA	1824	LANGENSTEINBACH	01/01/1829	A		F3
DENZIL	WILHELM		GRABEN	01/01/1846	A		F3
DESER	AUGUST	1876	KARLSRUHE	01/01/1893	A		F3
DETTER	JOSEF		SCHLATT	01/01/1859	A		F6
DEUBEL	ANTON	1884	MALSCH	03/23/1899	A		F2
DEUBEL	AUGUST	1856	MALSCH	01/01/1880	A		F2
DEUBEL	EDUARD	1817	MALSCH	06/14/1865	A		F4
DEUBEL	FRANZ ANTON	1869	MALSCH	01/01/1891	A		F2
DEUBEL	JOHANNES	1823	MALSCH	06/15/1866	A		F2
DEUBEL W FAMILY	WENDELIN	1822	MALSCH	01/01/1866	A		F2
DEUBEL MN GRIEFINGER	KATHARINA	1824	MALSCH	01/01/1866	A		F4
DEURIDER	MICHAEL		WÖSSINGEN	01/01/1832	A		F4
DEUTSCHER W FAMILY	MICHAEL		WÖSSINGEN	01/01/1832	A		F1
DEWALB	KARL	1866	BRETTEN	01/01/1883	A		F4
DEWATH	WILHELM	1854	KARLSRUHE	01/01/1872	A		F3
DID	FRIEDRICH		WEIL	01/01/1848	A		F2
DIEFENBRONNER	WILHELM	1860	KARLSRUHE	01/01/1877	A		F3
DIEHM	ANDREAS		ALTFELD	05/09/1837	A		F5
DIEHM	CHRISTOPH		BESTENHEID	04/09/1834	A		F5
DIEHM	PAUL		REMLINGEN	01/11/1838	A		F5
DIEHM	WALTER	1892	KARLSRUHE	/ /	A		F3
DIEPPOLTER	KARL		KARLSRUHE	01/01/1856	A		F3
DIESTELHORST	FR.	1862	KARLSRUHE	01/01/1881	A		F3
DIESTELHORST	THEODOR	1864	KARLSRUHE	01/01/1883	A		F3
DIETER W S	JAKOB		SÖLLINGEN	01/01/1865	A		F7
DIETERLE	LUDWIG		FORBACH	01/01/1869	A		F6
DIETERLIN	JULIUS		PFORZHEIM	01/01/1859	A		F8
DIETRICH	GUSTAV	1865	KARLSRUHE	01/01/1884	A		F3
DIETSCH	KARL	1871	KARLSRUHE	01/01/1886	A		F3
DIETZ	JAKOB	1874	SPIELBERG	10/19/1888	A		F4
DIETZ	WILHELMINE		KARLSRUHE	01/01/1853	A		F3
DIFTES	ROSA		ETTLINGEN	/ /	A		F3
DILL	IGNAZ	1783	ETTLINGEN	01/01/1804	A		F4
DILL	JOHANN MICHAEL		HASSELBERG	01/01/1754	A		F5
DILLINGER	ADOLF HEKTOR GE	1882	KARLSRUHE	01/01/1899	A		F3
DILLMANN W DAUGHTER	CHRISTOPH	1802	ETTLINGEN	03/18/1865	A		F3

Lastname	Firstname	Birth Year	Birthplace	Emigration	De	Prof	Source
DILLMANN W FAMILY	ALOIS	1839	ETTLINGEN	/ /	A		
DILLMANN W FATHER	THERESE	1828	ETTLINGEN	03/18/1865	A		F3
DINGER	HEINRICH	1876	KARLSRUHE	01/01/1892	A		F3
DINKEL	GEORG FRIEDRICH		KREUZWERTHEIM	01/30/1840	A		F5
DINKEL	MICHAEL		KREUZWERTHEIM	/ /	A		F5
DINKEL W F	NIKOLAUS		KREUZWERTHEIM	03/22/1785	A		F5
DISCHNER W F	MICHAEL		GRÖTZINGEN	01/01/1737	A		F5
DISCHNER W FAMILY	MICHAEL		GRÖTZINGEN	01/01/1737	A		F3
DISTELHORST	AUGUST	1862	KARLSRUHE	01/01/1878	A		F3
DISTLER	KARL	1857	ETTLINGEN	01/01/1882	A		F3
DITTES	KONRAD		BRETTEN	01/01/1834	A		F4
DITTMAR	LUISE		GRABEN	/ /	A		F5
DOERING	ADOLF		KARLSRUHE	01/01/1836	A		F3
DOLAND	KONRAD	1879	KARLSRUHE	01/01/1896	A		F3
DOLL	ANTON	1839	MALSCH	01/01/1846	A		F2
DOLL	AUGUST	1831	GRÖTZINGEN	01/01/1851	A		F3
DOLL	CHRISTIAN		GRÖTZINGEN	01/01/1848	A		F5
DOLL	ELEONORE		BRETTEN	01/01/1855	A		F4
DOLL	FRANZ	1817	MALSCH	01/01/1882	A		F2
DOLL	HEINRICH	1847	KNIELINGEN	01/01/1871	A		F6
DOLL	JOHANN	1836	MALSCH	01/01/1846	A		F2
DOLL	KARL		GRÖTZINGEN	01/01/1846	A		F3
DOLL	KATHARINA	1823	GRÖTZINGEN	01/01/1846	A		F3
DOLL	LUDWIG		KARLSRUHE	01/01/1886	A		F3
DOLL	MARTIN		GRÖTZINGEN	01/01/1811	A		F3
DOLL	MARTIN		GRÖTZINGEN	01/01/1820	A		F5
DOLL	SOPHIE KATHARIA		BRETTEN	01/01/1855	A		F4
DOLL	STEPHAN	1845	MALSCH	01/01/1846	A		F2
DOLL	THADäUS	1843	MALSCH	01/01/1846	A		F2
DOLL MN GRäFINGER	FRANZISKA	1851	MALSCH	11/01/1882	A		F2
DOLL MN WETZEL	FRANZISKA	1813	MALSCH	01/01/1846	A		F2
DOLL W CHILDREN	CHRISTIAN	1788	GRÖTZINGEN	01/01/1848	A		F3
DOLL W FAMILY	MICHAEL	1808	MALSCH	01/01/1846	A		F2
DOLL W FAMILY	MICHAEL	1850	MALSCH	11/01/1882	A		F2
DOLL W FATHER	HEINRICH	1829	GRÖTZINGEN	01/01/1848	A		F3
DOLL W FATHER	JULIUS	1826	GRÖTZINGEN	01/01/1848	A		F3
DOLLMER	AUGUST	1866	GRÖTZINGEN	01/01/1883	A		F3
DONFRED MN SCHMID	ELISE		KARLERUHE	/ /	A		F3
DONTSCHER	MICHAEL		WÖSSINGEN	01/01/1832	A		F4
DOPF	CHRISTOPH		GRÖTZINGEN	01/01/1865	A		F5
DOPF W FAMILY	CHRISTOPH		GRÖTZINGEN	/ /	A		F3
DORMÄCHTER	MICHAEL		BRETTEN	01/01/1862	A		F4
DORNER	KARL	1862	KARLSRUHE	01/01/1884	A		F3
DORR	RUDOLF		KARLSRUHE	01/01/1876	A		F3
DORRWARTH	JAKOBINE	1847	BRETTEN	01/01/1866	A		F4
DORRWARTH W FAMILY	ULRICH		BRETTEN	01/01/1854	A		F4
DORSCH	ADAM			/ /			
DORSCH W F	ADAM		VOCKENROTH	01/05/1786	A		F5
DORTISCH	AUGUST		GRÖTZINGEN	01/01/1865	A		F3
DORTISCH	PHILIPP JAKOB		GRÖTZINGEN	01/01/1854	A		F5

Lastname	Firstname	Birth Year	Birthplace	Emigration	De	Prof	Source
DORTISCH	PHILIPP JAKOB	1833	GRöTZINGEN	01/01/1854	A		F3
DOSCH	CHRISTOPH		öDENGESäSS	01/01/1752	A		F5
DOSCH W F	JOHANN CHRISTOH	1752	öDENGESäSS	05/08/1752	A		F5
DOTTRISCH	FRIEDRICH	1788	GRöTZINGEN	01/01/1846	A		F3
DOTTRISCH	JOHANN	1866	GRöTZINGEN	01/01/1883	A		F3
DRACK	MAGNUS	1847	KARLSRUHE	01/01/1869	A		F3
DRUM	TREZENS	1835	MALSCH	04/27/1846	A		F2
DUEBEL	EDUARD	1817	MALSCH	06/14/1865	A		F2
DUFFNER	FRIEDRICH		KARLSRUHE	01/01/1865	A		F6
DUMBERT	MICHAEL KARL		KARLSRUHE	/ /	A		F3
DUMBERTH	CHRISTIAN		GRöTZINGEN	01/01/1830	A		F5
DUMBERTH MN SCHAUFFE	MAGDALENA		GRöTZINGEN	/ /	A		F3
DUMBERTH W WIFE	CHRISTIAN		GRöTZINGEN	/ /	A		F3
DUMBOLD	CHRISTOPH ELIAS		DURLACH	01/01/1848	A		F6
DUMMELDINGER	KARL		KARLSRUHE	01/01/1843	A		F3
DUNZ	FRANZ JOSEF		MöRSCH	05/05/1832	A		F7
DUPPLER	ANTON	1867	KARLSRUHE	01/01/1884	A		F3
DURBAN	KARL		KARLSRUHE	01/01/1860	A		F3
DURM	FRIEDRICH	1838	MALSCH	04/27/1846	A		F2
DURM	ISAIS	1842	MALSCH	04/27/1846	A		F2
DURM	JOSEF	1831	MALSCH	04/27/1846	A		F2
DURM	KAROLINE	1833	MALSCH	04/27/1846	A		F2
DURM	ROMAN	1829	MALSCH	04/27/1846	A		F2
DURM	THOMAS	1840	MALSCH	04/27/1846	A		F2
DURM MN KUHN	MARIANNE		MALSCH	04/27/1846	A		F2
DURM W FAMILY	THOMAS	1802	MALSCH	04/27/1846	A		F2
DüRR	EMIL RICHARD	1881	KARLSRUHE	01/01/1896	A		F3
DüRR	ERNST GOTTLIEB		GRöTZINGEN	01/01/1809	A		F3
DüRR	GEORG FRIEDRICH		GRöTZINGEN	01/01/1809	A		F3
DüRR	JOHANN JAKOB		GRöTZINGEN	01/01/1809	A		F3
DüRR	KARL	1848	HOCHSTETTEN	01/01/1872	A		F8
DöGTLE	ZACHARIAS		GRöTZINGEN	01/01/1880	A		F3
DöGTLE W PARENTS	AUGUST	1868	GRöTZINGEN	01/01/1880	A		F3
DöGTLE W PARENTS	KARL	1861	GRöTZINGEN	01/01/1880	A		F3
DöGTLE W PARENTS	KATHARINA	1866	GRöTZINGEN	01/01/1880	A		F3
DöGTLE W PARENTS	MAGDALENA	1863	GRöTZINGEN	01/01/1880	A		F3
DöRFLER	ADOLF		SöLLINGEN	/ /	A		F7
DöRFLER	AUGUST		SöLLINGEN	01/01/1855	A		F7
DöRFLER	DAVID	1882	SöLLINGEN	/ /	A		F7
DöRFLER	JAKOB	1781	SöLLINGEN	01/01/1845	A		F7
DöRFLER	JAKOB	1854	SöLLINGEN	01/01/1869	A		F7
DöRFLER MN WEISS	ELISABETH	1793	SöLLINGEN	01/01/1845	A		F7
DöRFLER W P	CAROLUS	1834	SöLLINGEN	01/01/1845	A		F7
DöRFLER W P	KATHARINA	1807	SöLLINGEN	01/01/1845	A		F7
DöRFLER W P	SAMUEL	1824	SöLLINGEN	01/01/1845	A		F7
DöRFLER W W	JAKOB		SöLLINGEN	01/01/1855	A		F7
DöRFLINGER	ANNA MARIA		KARLSRUHE	01/01/1868	A		F3
DöRFLINGER	GEORG JAKOB		BLANKENLOCH	01/01/1859	A		F4
DöRFLINGER	JAKOB		KARLSRUHE	01/01/1868	A		F3
DöRFLINGER W FAMILY	GOTTFRIED		BLANKENLOCH	01/01/1835	A		F4

Lastname	Firstname	Birth Year	Birthplace	Emigration	De	Prof	Source
DÖRFLINGER WIDOW OF	JAKOB FRIEDRICH		KARLSRUHE	01/01/1868	A		F3
DÖRRFUSS	ADOLF KARL WILH	1875	ETTLINGEN	09/28/1889	A		F3
DÖTHER	JOHANN MICHAEL		MERCHINGEN	01/01/1859	A		F6
DÖRFLINGER MN	KATHARINA	1836	BLANKENLOCH	01/01/1868	A		F4
DÖRFLINGER W FAMILY	JAKOB	1833	BLANKENLOCH	01/01/1868	A		F4
DÖRFLINGER W P	CHRISTIAN	1859	BLANKENLOCH	01/01/1868	A		F4
DÖRFLINGER W P	GOTTFRIED	1866	BLANKENLOCH	01/01/1868	A		F4
DÖRFLINGER W P	JOHANN	1861	BLANKENLOCH	01/01/1868	A		F4
DÖRFLINGER W P	KARL	1867	BLANKENLOCH	01/01/1868	A		F4
DÖRFLINGER W P	PHILIPPINE	1858	BLANKENLOCH	01/01/1868	A		F4
DÖRNER	LUDWIG	1840	GRABEN	01/01/1868	A		F8
DÖTHER	JOHANN MICHAEL		MERCHINGEN	01/01/1859	A		F6
DÜRR MN FETZNER	KATHARINA		LINKENHEIM	01/01/1870	A		F7
DÜRR MN KESSELSCHMIT	CHRISTINE	1827	LINKENHEIM	01/01/1870	A		F8
DÜRR W F	FERDINAND	1840	LINKENHEIM	01/01/1870	A		F7
DÜRR W F	FRIEDRICH	1821	LINKENHEIM	01/01/1882	A		F8
DÜRR W F	KAROLINE	1854	LINKENHEIM	01/01/1870	A		F8
DÜRR W F	LEOPOLD	1824	LINKENHEIM	01/01/1870	A		F8
DÜRR W P	ALBERT	1870	LINKENHEIM	01/01/1882	A		F8
DÜRR W P	AUGUST	1851	LINKENHEIM	01/01/1870	A		F8
DÜRR W P	KAROLINE LUISE	1867	LINKENHEIM	01/01/1870	A		F8
DÜRR W P	LEOPOLD	1864	LINKENHEIM	01/01/1870	A		F8
DÜRR W P	LUDWIG	1862	LINKENHEIM	01/01/1870	A		F8
DÜRR W P	LUISE	1866	LINKENHEIM	01/01/1882	A		F8
DÜRR W P	RUDOLF	1867	LINKENHEIM	01/01/1870	A		F8
DÜRR W P	WILHELM	1869	LINKENHEIM	01/01/1870	A		F8
DÜRRER	PETER JULIUS	1843	BRETTEN	01/01/1862	A		F4

Lastname	Firstname	Birth Year	Birthplace	Emigration	De	Prof	Source
EBBEDE	KARL	1856	KARLSRUHE	01/01/1882	A		F3
EBEL	ALBERT		GRABEN	01/01/1880	A		F3
EBEL	HEINRICH		GRABEN	01/01/1868	A		F3
EBEL	LUDWIG		GRABEN	01/01/1868	A		F3
EBEL	LUDWIG		GRABEN	01/01/1868	A		F5
EBEL	LUDWIG		GRABEN	01/01/1873	A		F3
EBEL	WILHELM		GRABEN	01/01/1880	A		F3
EBERBACH	WILHELM	1852	BRETTEN	01/01/1866	A		F4
EBERHARD	CHRISTIAN		BLANKENLOCH	01/01/1835	A		F4
EBERHARD	KARL	1871	ETTLINGEN	05/11/1895	A		F4
EBERHARD	KARL	1878	KARLSRUHE	01/01/1895	A		F3
EBERHART	JAKOB		BLANKENLOCH	01/01/1848	A		F4
EBERLE	GEORG IVAN		BRETTEN	01/01/1847	A		F4
EBERLIN	ALBERT JOHANN	1865	KARLSRUHE	01/01/1892	A		F3
EBERSBRONN SCHOCK	HIERONIMUS		FORBACH	01/01/1871	A		76
EBERSBRONN V.	STEPHAN AUGUST		FORBACH	01/01/1869	A		F6
EBERT	HEINRICH	1868	KARLSRUHE	01/01/1888	A		F3
EBI	JOHANN		OBERETTINGEN	01/01/1851	A		F1
EDERT	LUDWIG	1872	KARLSRUHE	01/01/1888	A		F3
EDHARD	THEODOR	1850	KARLSRUHE	01/01/1882	A		F3
EFFERT	AMALIE	1822	MALSCH	01/01/1854	A		F2
EFFNER	FRIEDRICH FRANZ		KARLSRUHE	01/01/1857	A		F3
EGENLAUF W FAMILY	MICHAEL	1851	ETTLINGEN	01/01/1881	A		F4
EGENLAUF W HUSBAND	MAGDALENA	1851	ETTLINGEN	01/01/1881	A		F4
EGENLAUF W PARENTS	LUISE	1879	ETTLINGEN	01/01/1881	A		F4
EGENLAUF W PARENTS	WILHELM	1878	ETTLINGEN	01/01/1881	A		F4
EGGENSBERGER	WILHELM	1867	KARLSRUHE	01/01/1884	A		F3
EGNER	JOSEF	1845	KARLSRUHE	01/01/1879	A		F3
EHENU	PHILIPPE		KARLSRUHE	/ /	A		F3
EHNES	JAKOB	1803	BURBACH	01/01/1829	A		F4
EHNES MN HUD	MATHILDE	1809	BURBACH	01/01/1854	A		F4
EHNES W FAMILY	ERNST	1809	BURBACH	01/01/1854	A		F4
EHNES W P	ANNA MARIA	1845	BURBACH	01/01/1854	A		F4
EHNES W P	HEINRICH	1835	BURBACH	01/01/1854	A		F4
EHNES W P	LUISE	1849	BURBACH	01/01/1854	A		F4
EHNES W P	MARGARETHA	1835	BURBACH	01/01/1854	A		F4
EHNES W P	MARIA MAGDALENA	1836	BURBACH	01/01/1854	A		F4
EHNES W P	PAULINE	1832	BURBACH	01/01/1854	A		F4
EHRET	ADOLF		RASTATT	01/01/1859	A		F6
EHRETT	FRANZISKA		RASTATT	01/01/1859	A		F6
EHRLER	CARL FRIEDRICH	1825	GRÖTZINGEN	01/01/1853	A		F3
EHRLICH W W 7 CH	HEINRICH		WÖSSINGEN	01/01/1782	A		F1
EICH	JOSEF		MÖRSCH	01/01/1831	A		F7
EICHHORN	IGNAZ		VÖLKERSBACH	01/01/1830	A		F4
EICHINGER MN	KATHARINA	1788	VÖLKERSBACH	08/24/1808	A		F4
EICHINGER W FAMILY	MATHIAS	1787	VÖLKERSBACH	08/24/1808	A		F4
EICHINGER W P	JOHANNA		VÖLKERSBACH	08/24/1808	A		F4
EIDERLIN	JOSEF		RHINA	01/01/1708	A		F1
EIERMANN	JOHANN ADAM		TAUBERBISCHOFSHEIM	01/01/1859	A		F7
EIFNEN	GUSTAV	1833	MALSCCH	01/01/1850	A		F2

Lastname	Firstname	Birth Year	Birthplace	Emigration	De	Prof	Source
EILER	KARL FRIEDRICH		GRöTZINGEN	01/01/1853	A		F5
EISEINGEN	FRIEDERIKE		MERCHINGEN	01/01/1866	A		F6
EISELE	AUGUST	1846	BURBACH	01/01/1854	A		F4
EISELE	BARBARA	1843	BURBACH	01/01/1854	A		F4
EISELE	HETMANN	1840	BURBACH	01/01/1854	A		F4
EISELE	JOHANN FRIEDRIH	1820	BRETTEN	01/01/1869	A		F4
EISELE	JOSEF MAXIMILLN	1838	BURBACH	01/01/1854	A		F4
EISELE	MAURUS	1816	BURBACH	01/01/1856	A		F4
EISELE	OSWALD		ETTLINGEN	01/01/1853	A		F4
EISELE	OSWALD	1837	ETTLINGEN	09/27/1880	A		F4
EISELE	PAULINE		ETTLINGEN	12/15/1852	A		F4
EISELE	PHILIPPINE	1831	BURBACH	01/01/1854	A		F4
EISELE MN HäUFER	CRESZENTIA	1823	ETTLINGE	01/17/1848	A		F4
EISELE MN KLEIN	FRANZISKA		ETTLINGEN	01/01/1866	A		F4
EISELE W FAMILY	GREGOR	1818	ETTLINGEN	01/01/1866	A		F4
EISELE W PARENTS	CHRISTIAN	1865	ETTLINGEN	01/01/1866	A		F4
EISELE W PARENTS	EUGEN	1854	ETTLINGEN	01/01/1866	A		F4
EISELE W PARENTS	JOSEFINE	1845	ETTLINGEN	01/01/1866	A		F4
EISELE W PARENTS	LEOPOLD	1847	ETTLINGEN	01/01/1866	A		F4
EISELE W PARENTS	LUISE	1863	ETTLINGEN	01/01/1866	A		F4
EISELE W PARENTS	OTTO	1850	ETTLINGEN	01/01/1866	A		F4
EISELE W PARENTS	RUDOLF	1849	ETTLINGEN	01/01/1866	A		F4
EISELE W WIFE	JOSEF	1823	ETTLINGEN	/ /	A		F4
EISENFOLB	FLORIAN	1812	ETTLINGEN	01/01/1851	A		F4
EISENHUT	JOSEF		OBRIGHEIM	01/01/1854	A		F6
EISENLOHR	CHISTIAN ERNST	1851	KARLSRUHE	01/01/1870	A		F3
EISENLOHR	OTTO AUGUST	1859	KARLSRUHE	01/01/1876	A		F3
EISENMANN	CASPAR		PRINZBACH	01/01/1859	A		F6
EISNER	BALBINA	1836	MALSCH	11/21/1853	A		F2
EISNER	GUSTAV	1833	MALSCH	03/21/1852	A		F2
EISNER	HILDEGARD	1835	MALSCH	01/01/1850	A		F2
EISNER	VERONIKA	1832	MALSCH	01/01/1850	A		F2
EITEL	MARGARETHA		STEINMAUERN	01/01/1754	A		F1
ELLER	JOHANN		BUGGINGEN	01/01/1853	A		F6
EMMERT	JAKOB		RAPPENAU	01/01/1859	A		F6
ENDRES	JOHANN		GLASHOFEN	05/19/1752	A		F6
ENDRES	THOMAS			/ /			
ENDRES W F	THOMAS		MICHELRIET	05/16/1754	A		F5
ENGEL	KARL		WEINGARTEN	01/01/1839	A		F8
ENGEL	WILHELM	1853	ETTLINGEN	01/01/1869	A		F4
ENGEL MN REICH	BARBARA	1821	ETTLINGEN	01/01/1873	A		F4
ENGEL W FAMILY	ZACHARIAS		WöSSINGEN	01/01/1854	A		F1
EPP	JULIUS	1869	KARLSRUHE	01/01/1883	A		F3
EPP	ROBERT FRIEDRIC	1878	KARLSRUHE	01/01/1894	A		F3
EPPENBACH	AUGUST		GRöTZINGEN	01/01/1865	A		F3
EPPENBACH	KATHARINA		GRöTZINGEN	01/01/1863	A		F3
EPPENBACH MN WAGNER	KAROLINE		GRöTZINGEN	/ /	A		F3
EPPENBACH MN WAGNER	KAROLINE		GRöTZINGEN	01/01/1857	A		F5
EPPENBACH W WIFE	CHRISTIAN		GRöTZINGEN	/ /	A		F3
EPPENBACH W WIFE	CHRISTIAN		GRöTZINGEN	01/01/1857	A		F5

Lastname	Firstname	Birth Year	Birthplace	Emigration	De	Prof	Source
ERBERSBRONN SCHOCK	KARL		FORBACH	01/01/1871	A		F6
ERHARD	ALOIS	1789	ETTLINGEN	04/29/1834	A		F4
ERHARD	AUGUST	1859	LINKENHEIM	01/01/1882	A		F8
ERHARD	CARL	1802	ETTLINGEN	04/29/1834	A		F4
ERHARD W FAMILY	JOSEF	1811	ETTLINGEN	08/03/1872	A		F4
ERHARD W FATHER	BERTA	1852	ETTLINGEN	08/03/1872	A		F4
ERHARD W FATHER	KAROLINE	1846	ETTLINGEN	08/03/1872	A		F4
ERHARD W FATHER	RUDOLF	1851	ETTLINGEN	08/03/1872	A		F4
ERHARD W FATHER	WILHELM	1857	ETTLINGEN	08/03/1872	A		F4
ERHARD-BLAU	MAGDALENA		GRABEN	01/01/1873	A		F3
ERHARDT	WILHELM	1861	KARLSRUHE	01/01/1880	A		F3
ERICH W F	ANDREAS		ALTFELD	05/10/1752	A		F5
ERICH W F	JOHANN ADAM		BESTENHEID	01/01/1762	A		F5
ERLEBEN	THEODOR		KARLSRUHE	01/01/1855	A		F3
ERMEL	CHRISTIAN	1882	KNIELINGEN	01/01/1882	A		F6
ERMEL MN	JULIANE	1836	KNIELINGEN	01/01/1885	A		F8
ERMEL W F	GOTTLIEB	1833	KNIELINGEN	01/01/1885	A		F8
ERMEL W P	CHRISTIAN	1872	KNIELINGEN	01/01/1885	A		F8
ERMEL W P	FRIEDRICH	1870	KNIELINGEN	01/01/1885	A		F8
ERNST	CHRISTIAN	1850	SPöCK	01/01/1867	A		F4
ERNST	JAKOB	1813	SPöCK	01/01/1867	A		F4
ERNST	JAKOB	1843	SPöCK	01/01/1867	A		F8
ERNST	KARL		SPöCK	01/01/1866	A		F4
ERNST	KONRAD		SPöCK	01/01/1737	A		F4
ERNST	LUDWIG		SPöCK	01/01/1866	A		F4
ERNST	WENDELIN		SPöCK	01/01/1737	A		F4
ERNST	WENDELIN		SPöCK	01/01/1737	A		F6
ERNST MN STOBER	WILHELMINE		SPöCK	01/01/1867	A		F4
ERNST W BROTHER	KARL		SPöCK	01/01/1866	A		F4
ERNST W BROTHER	LUDWIG		SPöCK	01/01/1866	A		F4
ERNST W FAMILY	CHRISTIAN FRID.		SPöCK	01/01/1868	A		F4
ERNST W FAMILY	CHRISTOPH FRID.		SPöCK	01/01/1768	A		F4
ERNST WID.	JAKOB	1811	SPöCK	01/01/1867	A		F4
ERNY	WILHELM	1867	KARLSRUHE	01/01/1885	A		F3
ESSNER	JAKOB		KARLSRUHE	01/01/1831	A		F3
ETSCHMANN	LUDWIG GUSTAV		DURLACH	01/01/1868	A		F6
ETTLINGER	ABRAHAM	1827	KARLSRUHE	01/01/1871	A		F3
ETTLINGER	ANSELM ALFRED	1852	KARLSRUHE	01/01/1871	A		F3
ETTLINGER	HERMANN	1852	KARLSRUHE	01/01/1871	A		F3
ETTLINGER	JAKOB		GRABEN	01/01/1877	A		F3
ETTLINGER	LUDWIG	1856	GRABEN	01/01/1872	A		F3
EUGEN	KASPAR		ETTLINGEN	/ /	A		F4
EVERT	CHRISTIAN	1851	SPöCK	01/01/1867	A		F8
EWERT	CHRISTIAN	1851	SPöCK	01/01/1867	A		F4

Lastname	Firstname	Birth Year	Birthplace	Emigration	De	Prof	Source
FAHRER	KARL	1860	KARLSRUHE	01/01/1880	A		F3
FAHRER	ZACHARIUS JAKOB		KARLSRUHE	01/01/1864	A		F3
FAHRER W FAMILY	JAKOB FRIEDRICH		WÖSSINGEN	01/01/1852	A		F1
FAHRER W FAMILY	ZACHARIAS		WÖSSINGEN	01/01/1832	A	WEAV	F1
FAHRT	JOHANN FRIEDRIH		KARLSRUHE	01/01/1840	A		F3
FALLER	CHRISTINE		BERGHÖSCHINGEN	01/01/1866	A		F6
FALLER	ETTILIE		BERGHÖSCHINGEN	01/01/1866	A		F6
FALLER	THERESE		KARLSRUHE	/ /	A		F3
FALLER	WENDELIN		NEUSATZ	01/01/1880	A		F5
FARRENTOPF MN SCHNER	FRANZISKA		SPESSART	10/23/1880	A		F4
FARRENTOPF W FAMILY	KARL		SPESSART	10/23/1880	A		F4
FARRENTOPF W P	BERTA	1857	SPESSART	10/18/1880	A		F4
FARRENTOPF W P	KARL	1860	SPESSART	10/18/1880	A		F4
FARRENTOPF W P	ROMAN	1865	SPESSART	10/18/1880	A		F4
FARRENTOPF W P	RUDOLF	1846	SPESSART	10/23/1880	A		F4
FARRENTOPF W P	THEODOR	1854	SPESSART	05/06/1871	A		F4
FASS	ANTON	1829	MALSCH	01/01/1851	A		F2
FASS MN HERTWED	KAROLINE	1830	MALSCH	03/27/1860	A		F2
FASS W FAMILY	JOHANN		MALSCH	03/27/1860	A		F2
FATH	LEOPOLD	1873	KARLSRUHE	01/01/1891	A		F3
FAUL	JOSEF	1763	BURBACH	01/01/1791	A		F4
FAUTH W M	FRIEDRICH	1874	MALSCH	01/01/1880	A		F2
FAUTH W M	JOSEF THEODOR	1870	MALSCH	01/01/1880	A		F2
FAUTH W M	KAROLINE	1876	MALSCH	01/01/1880	A		F2
FAUTH W M	MATHäUS	1872	MALSCH	01/01/1880	A		F2
FAUTH WIDOW OF ANTON	HELENA MN BäR	1847	MALSCH	01/01/1880	A		F2
FECHT	GOTTLIEB BERHAD		KARLSRUHE	01/01/1852	A		F3
FEDERLECHNER	KARL FRIEDRICH	1855	GÄRSCHNENREUTH	01/01/1883	A		F6
FEDERLESCHNER	KARL FRIEDRICH	1855	WENTSCHENNEUREUT?	01/01/1883	A		F6
FELD	KARL FRIEDRICH	1858	MÜHLBERG	01/01/1878	A		F6
FELLMOSER	OTILIE		FORBACH	01/01/1860	A		F6
FERDINANT MN KINSEY	ELISABETH	1857	KARLSRUHE	01/01/1877	A		F3
FERDINANT W FAMILY	HEINRICH	1855	KARLSRUHE	01/01/1877	A		F3
FERTIG	ANDREAS		ALTFELD	01/01/1749	A		F5
FERTIG	ANDREAS		ALTFELD	01/01/1754	A		F5
FERTIG W F	HANS		ALTFELD	05/12/1752	A		F5
FESENBECK	MARIA ELISABETH	1798	RINKLINGEN	06/21/1832	A		F4
FESER	KARL FRIEDRICH	1857	DURLACH KARLSRUHE	/ /			F7
FETZER MN VEES	LUISE	1866	RÜPPUR	01/01/1867	A		F8
FETZER W F	LUDWIG	1839	RÜPPUR	01/01/1867	A		F8
FETZNER	KARL WILHELM		SPÖCK	01/01/1892	A		F8
FETZNER	KAROLINE		SPÖCK	01/01/1866	A		F4
FETZNER	LUISE		SPÖCK	01/01/1866	A		F4
FETZNER	TOBIAS		SPÖCK	01/01/1865	A		F4
FETZNER MN	LUISE	1848	LINKENHEIM	01/01/1883	A		F8
FETZNER MN RöSLER	CHRISTINA	1849	SPÖCK	01/01/1892	A		F4
FETZNER MN RÖSSLER	CHRISTINA	1849	SPÖCK	01/01/1892	A		F8
FETZNER W F	MATHÄUS	1843	LINKENHEIM	01/01/1883	A		F8
FETZNER W FAMILY	KARL WILHELM	1843	SPÖCK	01/01/1892	A		F4
FETZNER W P	CHRISTINE	1882	SPÖCK	01/01/1892	A		F4

Lastname	Firstname	Birth Year	Birthplace	Emigration	De	Prof	Source
FETZNER W P	ELISE CHRISTINE	1877	LINKENHEIM	01/01/1883	A		F8
FETZNER W P	EMMA	1881	SPöCK	/ /			
FETZNER W P	ERNST	1876	SPöCK	01/01/1892	A		F4
FETZNER W P	FRIEDRICH WILHE	1870	LINKENHEIM	01/01/1883	A		F8
FETZNER W P	KARL	1871	SPöCK	01/01/1892	A		F4
FETZNER W P	KARL LEOPOLD	1872	LINKENHEIM	01/01/1883	A		F8
FETZNER W P	LEOPOLD	1874	SPöCK	01/01/1892	A		F4
FETZNER W P	LUDWIG	1874	LINKENHEIM	01/01/1883	A		F8
FETZNER W P	LUISE	1875	SPöCK	01/01/1892	A		F4
FETZNER W P	LUISE WILHELMIE	1868	LINKENHEIM	01/01/1883	A		F8
FETZNER W P	LYDIA	1881	LINKENHEIM	01/01/1883	A		F8
FETZNER W P	MARIE	1885	SPöCK	01/01/1892	A		F4
FETZNER W P	PAULINE CAROLIE	1879	LINKENHEIM	01/01/1883	A		F8
FETZNER W P	WILHELM FRIEDRH	1890	SPöCK	01/01/1892	A		F4
FEUERSTEIN	ALBERT		MALSCH	05/24/1861	A		F2
FICHTENBERGER	JOHANN GEORG		BRÖNINGEN	01/01/1796	A		F8
FINDLING	ALOIS		MALSCH	11/14/1859			
FINDLING	JAKOB	1833	ETTLINGEN	01/01/1850	A		F4
FINDLING	KARL	1846	ETTLINGEN	/ /	A		F4
FINDLING MN FRIES	KATHARINA		ETTLINGEN	05/03/1832	A		F4
FINDLING MN FRIES	LUISE		ETTLINGEN	03/28/1882	A		F4
FINDLING MN RIMMELSB	ANNA MARIA		ETTLINGEN	03/21/1853	A		F4
FINDLING W FAMILY	ALOIS	1798	ETTLINGEN	03/21/1853	A		F4
FINDLING W FAMILY	JAKOB	1846	ETTLINGEN	03/28/1882	A		F4
FINDLING W PARENTS	EMIL	1880	ETTLINGEN	03/28/1882	A		F4
FINDLING W PARENTS	JOSEF	1834	ETTLINGEN	03/21/1853	A		F4
FINDLING W PARENTS	KATHARINA	1840	ETTLINGEN	03/21/1853	A		F4
FINDLING W PARENTS	LEOPOLD	1845	ETTLINGEN	03/21/1853	A		F4
FINDLING W PARENTS	MAGDALENA	1874	ETTLINGEN	03/28/1882	A		F4
FINDLING W PARENTS	MARIANNA	1838	ETTLINGEN	03/21/1853	A		F4
FINDLING W PARENTS	RUDOLF	1878	ETTLINGEN	03/28/1882	A		F4
FINDLING W WIFE	JAKOB		ETTLINGEN	05/03/1832	A		F4
FINFBEIN	MATHIAS	1815	BURBACH	/ /	A		F4
FINK	ERNST AUGUST	1844	BRETTEN	01/01/1873	A		F4
FINK	MECHTILD		SINZHEIM	01/01/1847	A		F6
FIRNER	KARL JAKOB	1868	KARLSRUHE	01/01/1882	A		F3
FISCHER	ANNA MARIA		MUNDINGEN	01/01/1804			F1
FISCHER	JOHANN	1847	MÜHLBURG	01/01/1871	A		F8
FISCHER	MARIA ANNA		RASTATT	01/01/1859	A		F6
FISCHER	WILHELMINE	1864	KNIELINGEN	01/01/1881	A		F6
FISDER	KARL WILHELM	1862	KARLSRUHE	01/01/1882	A		F3
FITTERER	JAKOB	1815	MÖRSCH	01/01/1832	A		F7
FITTERER	JOHANN URBAN		MÖRSCH	01/01/1851	A		F7
FITTERER	KAROLINE	1886	MÖRSCH	01/01/1891	A		F7
FITTERER	OTTO	1888	MÖRSCH	01/01/1891	A		F7
FITTERER MN PIMMELSP	MAGDALENA	1837	MÖRSCH	06/21/1866	A		F7
FITTERER W F	ANDREAS		MÖRSCH	01/01/1891	A		F7
FITTERER W F	FRIEDRICH		MÖRSCH	06/21/1866	A		F7
FITTERER W P	DAVID	1863	MÖRSCH	06/21/1866	A		F7
FITTERER W P	HERMANN	1865	MÖRSCH	06/21/1866	A		F7

Lastname	Firstname	Birth Year	Birthplace	Emigration	De	Prof	Source
FITTERER W P	JOHANNA	1861	MÖRSCH	06/21/1866	A		F7
FLECKENSTEIN	JOHANNES		MALSCH	01/01/1845	A		F2
FLEISCHMANN	FRIEDRICH		DURLACH	/ /	A		F5
FLEISCHMANN	FRIEDRICH		KARLSRUHE	/ /	A		F3
FLEISCHMANN	FRIEDRICH	1895	KARLSRUHE	/ /	A		F3
FLEISCHMANN	JOHANN CHRISTOP	1842	DURLACH KARLSRUHE	/ /	A		F7
FLETSCHINGER MN VOGE	KATHARINA	1815	ETTLINGEN	01/01/1846	A		F4
FLETSCHINGER W F	ANTON		ETTLINGEN	01/01/1846	A		F4
FLETSCHINGER W PAREN	ELISABETH	1836	ETTLINGEN	01/01/1846	A		F4
FLETSCHINGER W PAREN	JOSEF	1838	ETTLINGEN	01/01/1846	A		F4
FLETSCHINGER W PAREN	LUISE	1841	ETTLINGEN	01/01/1846	A		F4
FLETSCHINGER W PAREN	PHILIPP	1833	ETTLINGEN	01/01/1846	A		F4
FLIDERT	JOH. KID		BOCKENRATH	01/05/1786	A		F2
FLOHR	JAKOB		DURLACH KARLSRUHE	01/01/1836	A		F7
FLOHR	MICHAEL		GRABEN	01/01/1771	A		F3
FLOHR	PHILIPP		GRABEN	01/01/1861	A		F3
FLOHR	PHILIPP		GRABEN	01/01/1861	A		F5
FORSCHNER	AUGUST JAKOB	1838	DURLACH KARLSRUHE	/ /	A		F7
FORSCHNER	CHRIST.JAKOB	1839	DURLACH KARLSRUHE	/ /	A		F7
FORST	HUGO		KARLSRUHE	01/01/1878	A		F3
FORSTER	KARL		WALLDORF	01/01/1866	A		F6
FRANK	ERNST		KÜRNBACH	01/01/1851	A		F1
FRANK	FRIEDRICH	1873	RÜPPUR	01/01/1888	A		F8
FRANK	GROEG AUGUST		BREITEN	01/01/1862	A		F6WERR
FRANZ	BERNHARD	1798	ETTLINGEN	01/01/1858	A		F4
FRANZ	EMIL		RASTATT	01/01/1866	A		F6
FRANZ	KARL	1877	OBERHAUSEN	01/01/1908	A		F1
FRANZ	KARL FRIEDRICH		KARLSRUHE	01/01/1771	A		F3
FRANZ MN BAUREITHEL	KATHARINA		ETTLINGEN	01/01/1858	A		F4
FRANZ MN RUPP	MARIA KATHARINA	1818	LANGENSTEINBACH	02/03/1854	A		F3
FRANZ W FAMILY	ANDREAS	1820	LANGENSTEINBACH	02/03/1854	A		F3
FRANZ W PARENTS	ANDREAS	1845	LANGENSTEINBACH	02/03/1854	A		F3
FRANZ W PARENTS	CHRISTINE	1850	LANGENSTEINBACH	02/03/1854	A		F3
FRANZ W PARENTS	KATHARINA	1842	LANGENSTEINBACH	02/03/1854	A		F3
FRANZMANN	KARL	1847	DURLACH KARLSRUHE	/ /	A		F7
FREI	BERNHARD		EBNET	01/01/1866	A		F6
FREI	WILHELM	1826	DURLACH KARLSRUHE	/ /	A		F7
FREI	WILHELM	1876	KARLSRUHE	01/01/1892	A		F3
FREIBURGER	JAKOB LUDWIG		BRETTEN	01/01/1853	A		F4
FREIDINGER	ADAM		SPÖCK	01/01/1820	A		F4
FREUDENBERGER	PETER		ALTFELD	01/01/1833	A		F5
FREUDENTHAL	REBEKKA		TAIRNBACH	01/01/1866	A		F6
FREY	ALBERT		KARLSRUHE	01/01/1841	A		F3
FREY	CARL	1855	MÜHLBERG	01/01/1871	A		F6
FREY	KARL	1849	MÜHLBERG	01/01/1871	A		F6
FREY	OTTO	1853	MÜHLBERG	01/01/1871	A		F6
FREYTAG	ERHARD		KARLSRUHE	/ /	A		
FREYTAG	ERHARD		KARLSRUHE	01/01/1794	A		F3
FREYTAG	JOHANN FRIEDRIH		KARLSRUHE	01/01/1771	A		F6
FREYTAG	JOHANN FRIEDRIH		KARLSRUHE	01/01/1794	A		F3

Lastname	Firstname	Birth Year	Birthplace	Emigration	De	Prof	Source
FRIBOLE MN LUMPP	EVA	1810	SöLLINGEN	01/01/1868	A		F7
FRIBOLE W P	ELISABETH	1846	SöLLINGEN	01/01/1868	A		F7
FRIBOLE W P	JAKOB	1842	SöLLINGEN	01/01/1868	A		F7
FRIBOLE W P	JOHANN	1848	SöLLINGEN	01/01/1868	A		F7
FRIBOLE W P	KARL	1856	SöLLINGEN	01/01/1868	A		F7
FRICK	JONAS		GRöTZINGEN	01/01/1852	A		F5
FRIDOLIN	ELISABETH BABET	1834	SöLLINGEN	01/01/1853	A		F7
FRIDOLIN	HEINRICH		WöSSINGEN	01/01/1803	A		F1
FRIEBEL	FRIEDRICH		WöSSINGEN	01/01/1817			F1
FRIEBOLE	HEINRICH		SöLLINGEN	01/01/1868	A		F7
FRIEBOLE W F	HEINRICH		WöSSINGEN	01/01/1802	A	BREW	F1
FRIEBOLE WW	CHRISTIAN		WöSSINGEN	01/01/1828	A		F1
FRIEBOLE WW	JOHANNES		WöSSINGEN	01/01/1828	A		F1
FRIED	JONAS		GRöTZINGEN	/ /	A		F3
FRIEDEBURG V.	WILHELM		KARLSRUHE	01/01/1860	A		F3
FRIEDEBURG V.	WILHELM		KARLSRUHE	01/01/1860	A		F3
FRIEDEMANN	JOHANNES		KARLSRUHE	06/17/1850	A		F3
FRIES	MATHEUS		ETTLINGEN	05/12/1832	A		F4
FRIESE	ADAM		MALSCH	01/01/1852	A		F2
FRIETSCHY	FRANZ	1872	BÜHL	01/01/1887	A		F5
FRIS	HURTSING		MALSCH	01/01/1832	A		F2
FRITZ	ALBERT		DURLACH	01/01/1893	A		F5
FRITZ	ALBERT		DURLACH	01/01/1893	A		F6
FRITZ	FERDINAND		FORBACH	01/01/1861	A		F6
FRITZ	J.WILLIAM	1893	KARLSRUHE	/ /	A		F3
FRITZ	KLETUS		FORBACH	01/01/1854	A		F6
FRITZ	LUDWIG		FORBACH	01/01/1854	A		F6
FRITZ	WALBURGA		FORBACH	01/01/1854	A		F6
FRITZ	XAVER		FORBACH	01/01/1860	A		F6
FRITZ MN WALZ	JULIANE	1842	BERGHAUSEN	01/01/1885	A		F4
FRITZ W F	STEPHAN		FORBACH	01/01/1854	A		F6
FRITZ W FAMILY	ALBERT		DURLACH	/ /	A		F3
FRITZ W FAMILY	CHRISTOPH	1838	BERGHAUSEN	01/01/1885	A		F4
FRITZ W FAMILY	NICKOLAUS		FORBACH	01/01/1870	A		F6
FRITZ W P	ANNA CHRISTINE			/ /			
FRITZ W P	ANNA CHRISTINE	1881	BERGHAUSEN	01/01/1885	A		F4
FRITZ W P	JAKOBINE	1864	BERGHAUSEN	01/01/1885	A		F4
FRITZ W P	KARL	1875	BERGHAUSEN	01/01/1885	A		F4
FRITZ W P	LUISE BARBARA	1862	BERGHAUSEN	01/01/1885	A		F4
FRITZ W P	MARIA	1869	BERGHAUSEN	01/01/1885	A		F4
FRITZ W P	WILHELM CHRISTO	1871	BERGHAUSEN	01/01/1885	A		F4
FROHMÜLLER	JULIUS FERDINAN	1860	DURLACH KARLSRUHE	/ /	A		F7
FROMMEL	FRANZ		SöLLINGEN	01/01/1848	A		F7
FROMMEL	MR.		SöLLINGEN	/ /	A		F7
FROSCH	HERMANN		DAXLANDEN	01/01/1883	A		F6
FUCHS	HERMANN	1866	KARLSRUHE	01/01/1882	A		F3
FUCHS	ISIDOR	1865	KARLSRUHE	01/01/1880	A		F3
FUCHS	MOSES	1865	KARLSRUHE	01/01/1880	A		F3
FUCHS	PETER		KARLSRUHE	01/01/1789	A		F3
FUCHS W DAUGTHER	CHRISTINE		THENINGEN	01/01/1859	A		F6

Lastname	Firstname	Birth Year	Birthplace	Emigration	De	Prof	Source
FUNK	GEORG		UNTERGIMPERN	01/01/1866	A		F6
FÜHRNISS MN MÜLLER	STEFANIE	1848	HOCHSTETTEN	01/01/1878	A		F8
FÜHRNISS W F	FRIEDRICH WILHM	1851	HOCHSTETTEN	01/01/1878	A		F8
FÜLLER	JULIUS	1875	KARLSRUHE	01/01/1893	A		F3
FÜNFLE	ALBERT	1854	KARLSRUHE	01/01/1873	A		F3
FÜNFLE	FRIEDRICH	1852	KARLSRUHE	01/01/1879	A		F3
FÜNFLE	KARL	1856	KARLSRUHE	01/01/1873	A		F3
FÜRNISS	KARL FRIEDRICH	1851	HOCHSTETTEN	01/01/1880	A		F8
FÜRNISS	KARL LUDWIG	1868	LIEDOLSHEIM	01/01/1885	A		F9
FÜRNISS	WILHELM FRIEDRH	1876	LIEDOLSHEIM	01/01/1891	A		F9
FÜRNISS MN LANG	LYDIA		LIEDOLSHEIM	01/01/1882	A		F9
FÜRNISS MN MEINZER	JOHANNA	1844	HOCHSTETTEN	01/01/1880	A		F8
FÜRNISS W F	ADOLF		LIEDOLSHEIM	01/01/1882	A		F9
FÜRNISS W F	KARL FRIEDRICH	1839	HOCHSTETTEN	01/01/1880	A		F8
FÜRNISS W P	ADOLF	1873	LIEDOLSHEIM	01/01/1882	A		F9
FÜRNISS W P	ELLIE	1874	LIEDOLSHEIM	01/01/1882	A		F9
FÜRNISS W P	ERMA	1873	HOCHSTETTEN	01/01/1880	A		F8
FÜRNISS W P	FRIEDA	1868	HOCHSTETTEN	01/01/1880	A		F8
FÜRNISS W P	KARL	1871	HOCHSTETTEN	01/01/1880	A		F8
FÜRNISS W P	KARL	1876	LIEDOLSHEIM	01/01/1882	A		F9
FÜRNISS W P	LEOPOLD	1879	HOCHSTETTEN	01/01/1880	A		F8
FÜRNISS W P	LUISE	1863	HOCHSTETTEN	01/01/1880	A		F8
FÜRNISS W P	ROSA	1877	HOCHSTETTEN	01/01/1880	A		F8
FÜRNISS W P	THEODOR	1874	HOCHSTETTEN	01/01/1880	A		F8
FÜRNISS W P	WILHELM	1875	HOCHSTETTEN	01/01/1880	A		F8
FÜSSLER	JAKOB		GRÖTZINGEN	/ /	A		F3
FÜSSLERE	JAKOB		GRÖTZINGEN	01/01/1817	A		F5
FäSER	KARL	1874	KARLSRUHE	01/01/1890	A		F3
FäSSER	FERDINAND	1832	RINKLINGEN	01/31/1834	A		F4
FäSSER	KATHARINA	1828	RINKLINGEN	01/01/1854	A		F4
FäSSER	MARTIN		RINKLINGEN	01/01/1854	A		F4
FäSSER	VALENTIN	1875	MALSCH	01/01/1890	A		F2
FäSSER MN MAYER	JAKOBINE	1801	RINKLINGEN	/ /	A		F4
FäSSER W CH	FERDINAND	1838	RINKLINGEN	01/01/1863	A		F4
FäSSER W F	JONAS	1834	RINKLINGEN	01/31/1834	A		F4
FäSSLER	JOSEF		OCHENHEIM	01/01/1859	A		F6
FäSSLER	WILHELM		ISCHENHEIM	01/01/1859	A		F6
FÖCHLER	WILHELM	1855	ETTLINGEN	01/01/1887	A		F4
FÖRCH MN SCHOTTMÜLLE	ANNA BEATE		SPESSART	11/03/1853	A		F4
FÖRCH W FAMILY	JOHANN MICHAEL		SPESSART	11/03/1853	A		F4
FÖRCH W P	ADELHEID	1839	SPESSART	11/03/1853	A		F4
FÖRCH W P	EMIL THEODOR	1850	SPESSART	11/03/1853	A		F4
FÖRCH W P	GUSTAV	1842	SPESSART	11/03/1853	A		F4
FÖRCH W P	JULIUS ROBERT	1852	SPESSART	11/03/1853	A		F4
FÖRCH W P	RUDOLF	1844	SPESSART	11/03/1853	A		F4
FÖRDERER	ALOIS	1876	KARLSRUHE	01/01/1891	A		F3
FÖRDERER	EMIL	1874	KARLSRUHE	01/01/1891	A		F3
FÖRINGER	AUGUST	1821	KARLSRUHE	01/01/1841	A		F3
FÖRDERER	IGNAZ		SCHÖLLBRONN	01/01/1839	A		F7
FÜTTERER	AUGUSTIN		MÖRSCH	04/11/1847	A		F7

Lastname	Firstname	Birth Year	Birthplace	Emigration	De	Prof	Source
FÜTTERER	JULIAN		MÖRSCH	01/01/1832	A		F7
FÜTTERER W F	PHILIPP		MÖRSCH	01/01/1831	A		F7

Lastname	Firstname	Birth Year	Birthplace	Emigration De	Prof	Source
GAAR	EMIL LEONHARD	1863	KARLSRUHE	01/01/1882 A		F3
GAAR	KARL	1857	KARLSRUHE	01/01/1882 A		F3
GAAR	RICHARD	1862	KARLSRUHE	01/01/1882 A		F3
GAERTNER	EUGEN		KARLSRUHE	/ / A		F3
GAGLE	LEOPOLD	1842	RÜPPUR	01/01/1866 A		F8
GAISLE	IGNAZ			/ /		
GAMER	AUGUST		GRABEN	/ / A		F5
GAMER	DANIEL		GRABEN	01/01/1861 A		F3
GAMER	GUSTAV		GRABEN	01/01/1861 A		F3
GAMER	JAKOB		GRABEN	01/01/1799 A		F3
GAMER	JAKOB		GRABEN	01/01/1861 A		F3
GAMER	KARL		GRABEN	01/01/1888 A		F3
GAMER	KARL		GRABEN	01/01/1888 A		F5
GAMER	KARL LUDWIG		GRABEN	01/01/1861 A		F3
GAMER	WILHELM		GRABEN	01/01/1889 A		F5
GAMER MN WENZ	BERTA	1860	GRABEN	01/01/1889 A		F3
GAMER W FAMILY	JOAHNN MARTIN		SPöCK	01/01/1835 A		F4
GAMER W FAMILY	WILHELM		GRABEN	01/01/1889 A		F3
GAMER W PARENTS	HERMANN	1889	GRABEN	01/01/1889 A		F3
GAMER W PARENTS	WILHELM	1887	GRABEN	01/01/1889 A		F3
GANG	FERDINAND	1855	KARLSRUHE	01/01/1873 A		F3
GANNINGER	JOHANN		LANGENBRÜDEN	01/01/1859 A		F6
GANTER	KARL	1862	KARLSRUHE	01/01/1885 A		F3
GANTZ	WILH KARL LUDWG	1856	KARLSRUHE	01/01/1876 A		F3
GARTNER	ALEXANDER	1849	KARLSRUHE	01/01/1867 A		F3
GASSMEIER	MR.		SöLLINGEN	/ / A		F7
GATTMANN	KARL	1875	KARLSRUHE	01/01/1893 A		F3
GAUS	HEINRICH		WöSSINGEN	01/01/1832 A		F1
GAUS	JAKOB		KARLSRUHE	08/15/1850 A		F3
GAUS WW CH	CHRISTOPH		WöSSINGEN	01/01/1848 A		F1
GAUSS	ADAM		WöSSINGEN	01/01/1828 A		F1
GAUSS	FRIEDRICH		WöSSINGEN	/ / A		F1
GAUSS	MARGARETHA		WöSSINGEN	01/01/1862 A		F1
GAUSS	SALOMEA		WöSSINGEN	01/01/1865 A		F1
GAUSS W FAMILY	JAKOB FRIEDRICH		WöSSINGEN	01/01/1832 A		F1
GAUST	MARGAERETHA		WöSSINGEN	01/01/1854 A		F1
GAUTH	FRIEDRICH	1874	MALSCH	09/02/1880 A		F2
GAUTH	JOSEF THEODOR	1870	MALSCH	09/02/1880 A		F2
GAUTH	KAROLINE	1876	MALSCH	09/02/1880 A		F2
GAUTH	MATHäUS	1872	MALSCH	09/02/1880 A		F2
GAUTH MN BäR	HELENA		MALSCH	09/02/1880 A		F2
GAUTH W FAMILY	ANTON	1847	MALSCH	09/02/1880 A		F2
GEBERT	KATHARINA JOHAA		VOLKSHAUSEN	01/01/1859 A		F6
GEDAUER	HERMANN	1869	KARLSRUHE	01/01/1886 A		F3
GEDLER	HEINRICH			/ /		
GEDLER	HEINRICH	1862	KARLSRUHE	01/01/1882 A		F3
GEERING	EMIL		KÖNIGSFELD	01/01/1866 A		F6
GEHMANN MN WEBER	CAROLINA	1848	BLANKENLOCH	01/01/1873 A		F4
GEHMANN W FAMILY	KARL FRIEDRICH	1845	BLANKENLOCH	01/01/1873 A		F4
GEHMANN W P	CHRISTIAN		BLANKENLOCH	01/01/1873 A		F4

Lastname	Firstname	Birth Year	Birthplace	Emigration De	Prof	Source
GEHMANN W P	KARL FRIEDRICH		BLANKENLOCH	01/01/1873	A	F4
GEHMANN W P	LUISE		BLANKENLOCH	01/01/1873	A	F4
GEHRES	ERHARD JULIUS	1849	DURLACH KARLSRUHE	/ /	A	F7
GEHRING	CHRISTOPH		KARLSRUHE	01/01/1839	A	F3
GEIGER	FLORIAN		MALSCH	05/19/1883	A	F2
GEIGER	GEORG	1807	MALSCH	03/23/1846	A	F2
GEIGER	JAKOB		RICHEN	01/01/1825	A	F8
GEIGER	JOHANNES	1830	MALSCH	01/01/1832	A	F2
GEIGER	JOSEPH	1771	MALSCH	07/27/1811	A	F2
GEIGER	JOSEPH LUDWIG	1872	MALSCH	06/18/1887	A	F2
GEIGER	MARGARETHE	1758	MALSCH	01/01/1790	A	F2
GEIGER	MARTIN	1857	MALSCH	01/01/1882	A	F2
GEIGER	THEOBALD	1815	MALSCH	01/01/1859	A	F2
GEIGER W PARENTS	KAHTARINA	1840	MALSCH	01/01/1848	A	F2
GEIGER MN KASTNER	WALBURGA	1803	MALSCH	05/21/1832	A	F2
GEIGER MN REICHERT	GERTRUD	1815	MALSCH	01/01/1848	A	F2
GEIGER W FAMILY	FRANZ IGNAZ	1799	MALSCH	05/21/1832	A	F2
GEIGER W FAMILY	PAUL	1811	MALSCH	01/01/1848	A	F2
GEIGER W W	FRANZ	1761	MALSCH	01/01/1790	A	F2
GEIS	MICHEL ANTON		OBERALTENBUCH	05/27/1836	A	F5
GEISENBERGER	NIKOLAUS	1863	KARLSRUHE	01/01/1882	A	F2
GEISER	KARL	1868	KARLSRUHE	01/01/1883	A	F3
GEISER	WILHELM		FORBACH	01/01/1867	A	F6
GENNHöFER	ALOIS			/ /		
GENNHöFER	ALOIS	1777	SPESSART	01/01/1835	A	F4
GENNHöFER MN KUNZ	MAGDALENA		SCHöLLBRONN	09/06/1835	A	F4
GENNHöFER MN WAGNER	MARIA ANNA		BURBACH	06/17/1829	A	F4
GENNHöFER W FAMILY	ALOIS	1791	SPESSART	06/17/1892	A	F4
GENNHöFER W FAMILY	NIKOLAUS	1789	SPESSART	09/06/1835	A	F4
GENNHöFER W P	ALOIS	1823	SPESSART	06/17/1829	A	F4
GENNHöFER W P	IGNAZ	1827	SPESSART	06/17/1829	A	F4
GENNHöFER W P	JGNAZ	1822	SPESSART	05/21/1822	A	F4
GENNHöFER W P	JOSEF	1825	SPESSART	06/17/1829	A	F4
GENNHöFER W P	KAROLINE	1820	SPESSART	06/17/1829	A	F4
GENTNER	ALOIS	1823	MALSCH	01/01/1858	A	F2
GENTNER	FRANZ	1794	MALSCH	01/01/1858	A	
GENTNER	FRANZ	1829	MALSCH	01/01/1846	A	F2
GENTNER	FRANZ	1829	MALSCH	01/01/1858	A	F2
GENTNER	JOHANN	1833	MALSCH	01/01/1858	A	F2
GENTNER MN WESTERMAN	ELISE	1800	MALSCH	01/01/1858	A	F2
GEORG	PHILIPP		UNTERSCHWARZBACH	01/01/1859	A	F6
GEORG WW 6CH	MICHAEL		WöSSINGEN	01/01/1801		F1
GERBERICH W F	HANS		ALTFELD	04/06/1751	A	F5
GERBRICH	JOHANN		ALTFELD	05/09/1837	A	F5
GERHARDT	ULRICH		BLANKENLOCH	01/01/1854	A	F4
GERNSBECK	JOHANNES		FORBACH	01/01/1860	A	F6
GERNSBED	IGNAZ		FORBACH	01/01/1869	A	F6
GERSTNER	GREGOR		VöLKERSBACH	01/01/1846	A	F4
GERSTNER	THEKLA		VöLKERSBACH	09/03/1891	A	F4
GERSTNER MN RIHM	EVA		MöRSCH	01/01/1853	A	F7

Lastname	Firstname	Birth Year	Birthplace	Emigration	De	Prof	Source
GERSTNER W F	BERNHARD		MÖRSCH	01/01/1853	A		F7
GERSTNER W P	ANTON	1849	MÖRSCH	01/01/1853	A		F7
GERSTNER W P	AUGUST	1844	MÖRSCH	01/01/1853	A		F7
GERSTNER W P	LUDWIG	1845	MÖRSCH	01/01/1853	A		F7
GERSTNER W P	MAGDALENA	1847	MÖRSCH	01/01/1853	A		F7
GERSTNER W P	XAVER	1851	MÖRSCH	01/01/1853	A		F7
GERTEIS	CHRISTOPH		KARLSRUHE	01/01/1853	A		F3
GESCHEIDER	OTTO FRIED.AUG.	1843	DURLACH KARLSRUHE	/ /			F7
GESELL MN STRAF	ELISABETH	1839	KARLSRUHE	01/01/1881	A		F3
GEYERLE	RUDOLF	1875	DURLACH	01/01/1891	A		F3
GEYERLE	RUDOLF	1875	DURLACH	01/01/1891	A		F5
GIANI	MAX		KARLSRUHE	10/17/1850	A		F3
GIERICH	FRIEDRICH		BLANKENLOCH	01/01/1809	A		F4
GIERICH	JOHANN ADAM		BLANKENLOCH	01/01/1783	A		F4
GIESINGER	ELISABETH		SÖLLINGEN	01/01/1862	A		F7
GIESINGER	JAKOB FRIEDRICH		SÖLLINGEN	01/01/1867	A		F7
GIESINGER	JOSEF		SÖLLINGEN	01/01/1828	A		F7
GIESINGER	KARL		SÖLLINGEN	01/01/1868	A		F7
GIESINGER	MR.		SÖLLINGEN	/ /	A		F7
GIESINGER	WILHELM		SÖLLINGEN	01/01/1867	A		F7
GIMMEL	JAKOB	1837	DURLACH KARLSRUHE	/ /			F7
GISER	FRIEDRICH	1871	KARLSRUHE	01/01/1888	A		F3
GISSELBRECHT	CAMIL LUDW. TH.	1850	KARLSRUHE	01/01/1866	A		F3
GISSELBRECHT	KAROLINE LUISE	1841	KARLSRUHE	01/01/1866	A		F3
GLAIBER	FRIEDRICH	1836	VÖLKERSBACH	01/01/1860	A		F4
GLAIBER	JOSEF	1820	VÖLKERSBACH	05/21/1852	A		F4
GLAS	JAKOB		WÖSSINGEN	01/01/1737	A		F1
GLASER	AUGUST	1836	GRÖTZINGEN	01/01/1851	A		F3
GLASER	ERNST		GRÖTZINGEN	01/01/1851	A		F3
GLASER	ERNST		GRÖTZINGEN	01/01/1859	A		F5
GLASER	FERDINAND	1815	BURBACH	01/01/1855	A		F4
GLASER	FRANZ JOSEF	1804	BURBACH	/ /	A		F4
GLASER	JOHANNES	1811	BURBACH	/ /	A		F4
GLASER	KARL		GRÖTZINGEN	01/01/1852	A		F5
GLASER	KARL	1830	GRÖTZINGEN	01/01/1851	A		F3
GLASER	MARTIN		GRASFELD	01/01/1833	A		F6
GLASSNER	KARL	1852	KARLSRUHE	01/01/1878	A		F3
GLASSNER	KARL	1852	KARLSRUHE	01/01/1878	A		F6
GLASSTETTER	BERTOLD	1845	VÖLKERSBACH	01/01/1862	A		F4
GLASSTETTER	EMIL	1870	VÖLKERSBACH	10/28/1891	A		F4
GLASSTETTER	GEORG	1823	VÖLKERSBACH	01/01/1849	A		F4
GLASSTETTER	KAROLINE	1826	VÖLKERSBACH	01/01/1846	A		F4
GLASSTETTER	KRESZENS	1834	VÖLKERSBACH	10/01/1857	A		F4
GLASSTETTER	PIUS	1844	VÖLKERSBACH	/ /	A		F4
GLASSTETTER	ULBAN ISIDOR	1829	VÖLKERSBACH	04/09/1852	A		F4
GLASSTETTER MN WEBER	ANNA		SPESSART	05/23/1832	A		F4
GLASSTETTER W FAMILY	FRANZ KASPAR	1802	SPESSART	05/23/1832	A		F4
GLASSTETTER W P	ANSELM	1829	SPESSART	05/23/1832	A		F4
GLASSTETTER W P	ANTON	1831	SPESSART	05/23/1832	A		F4
GLASSTETTER W P	BARBARA	1828	SPESSART	05/23/1832	A		F4

Lastname	Firstname	Birth Year	Birthplace	Emigration	De	Prof	Source
GLASSTETTER W P	JOHANN	1826	SPESSART	05/23/1832	A		F4
GLASSTETTER W P	LIBERAT GEORG	1825	SPESSART	05/23/1832	A		F4
GLASSTäTTER	MARIA JOSEFA		ETTLINGEN	01/01/1857	A		F4
GLEISLE	HERMANN AUGUST	1875	MALSCH	01/01/1891	A		F2
GLEISLE W WIFE	FRANZ CARL	1808	ETTLINGEN	01/01/1853	A		F4
GLEISSLE	FRANZ		ETTLINGEN	01/01/1853	A		F4
GLEISSLE MN OBERT	FRANZISKA		ETTLINGEN	01/01/1853	A		F4
GOGEL	MAX JOHANN	1828	DURLACH KARLSRUHE	/ /			F7
GOLDSCHMIDT	ADOLF	1870	KARLSRUHE	01/01/1886	A		F3
GOLDSCHMIDT	CARL	1831	DURLACH KARLSRUHE	/ /			F7
GOLDSCHMIDT	CARL CHRISTOPH		DURLACH KARLSRUHE	01/01/1850	A		F7
GOLDSCHMIDT	DANIEL JOHANN	1838	DURLACH KARLSRUHE	/ /	A		F7
GOLDSCHMIDT	JOHANN		DURLACH KARLSRUHE	01/01/1854			F7
GOLDSCHMIDT	WILHELM ADAM AU		DURLACH KARLSRUHE	01/01/1843	A		F7
GOLL	HEINRICH	1863	SPRANTAL	01/01/1882	A		F8
GOLL	KARL	1859	KARLSRUHE	01/01/1884	A		F3
GOPPELSRöDER W FAMIL	CHRISTIAN		WöSSINGEN	01/01/1854	A		F1
GORENFLO	GUSTAV		KARLSRUHE	01/01/1853	A		F3
GORENFLO	OTTO		KARLSRUHE	01/01/1853	A		F3
GORENFLO W P	EMILIE	1881	FRIEDRICHSTAL	01/01/1887	A		F6
GORENFLO W P	INGO	1882	FRIEDRICHSTAL	01/01/1887	A		F6
GORENFLO W P	OSKAR	1879	FRIEDRICHSTAL	01/01/1887	A		F6
GORENFLO W P	RUDOLF	1875	FRIEDRICHSTAL	01/01/1887	A		F6
GORENFLO W P	XAVER	1876	FRIEDRICHSTAL	01/01/1887	A		F6
GOTH	FRIEDRICH	1843	KARLSRUHE	01/01/1869	A		F3
GOTTLOB	MOSES		DITTIGHEIM	01/01/1866	A		F6
GOTTREN	HEINRICH		KARLSRUHE	01/01/1827	A		F3
GRABENSTETTER	JAKOB		WEISSENSTEIN	01/01/1807	A		F8
GRAEFER MN KUNZ	MAGDALENA	1807	MALSCH	11/21/1853	A		F2
GRAEFER W FAMILY	THOMAS	1789	MALSCH	11/21/1853	A		F2
GRAF	ADAM	1842	DURLACH KARLSRUHE	/ /			
GRAF	EMIL	1861	KARLSRUHE	01/01/1881	A		F3
GRAF	FRIEDRICH		KARLSRUHE	01/01/1851	A		F3
GRAMLICH	KATHARINA		SCHLIERSTADT	01/01/1857	A		F8
GRASENEDER	CHARLES		KARLSRUHE	/ /	A		F3
GRASER	WILHELM	1873	KARLSRUHE	01/01/1891	A		F3
GRATZ	ANDREAS	1809	BURBACH	01/01/1856	A		F4
GRATZ	JAKOB	1836	BURBACH	08/16/1864	A		F4
GRATZ	JOHANN GEORG	1830	BURBACH	01/01/1856	A		F4
GRATZ	MARIA ANNE	1824	BURBACH	01/01/1856	A		F4
GRAU	ANSELM		STEINBACH	01/01/1848	A		F6
GRAU	HELENA		STEINBACH	01/01/1859	A		F6
GRAU	KATHARINA		STEINBACH	01/01/1869	A		F6
GRAU	REPOMUK		STEINBACH	01/01/1895	A		F6
GRAUGET	PETER	1792	ETTLINGEN	01/01/1845	A		F4
GRAULE	CHRISTIAN	1823	LANGENSTEINBACH	02/27/1847	A		F3
GRAULE	CHRISTOPH	1821	LANGENSTEINBACH	02/27/1847	A		F3
GRAULE	ELISABETH	1811	LANGENSTEINBACH	/ /	A		F3
GRAULE	GEORG MARTIN	1809	LANGENSTEINBACH	/ /	A		F3
GRAULE	MICHAEL	1808	LANGENSTEINBACH	01/01/1831	A		F3

Lastname	Firstname	Birth Year	Birthplace	Emigration	De	Prof	Source
GRAULE	VALENTIN	1830	LANGENSTEINBACH	03/28/1851	A		F3
GREI	FRIEDRICH	1864	KNIELINGEN	01/01/1882	A		F6
GREIF	JOHANN	1841	MALSCH	03/13/1846	A		F2
GREIF	VINZENZ	1831	MALSCH	03/13/1846	A		F2
GREIF MN GRAESSER	THERESIA	1807	MALSCH	01/01/1846	A		F2
GREIF W FAMILY	ANDREAS	1802	MALSCH	03/13/1846	A		F2
GREIF W PARENTS	JOHANNA	1833	MALSCH	03/13/1846	A		F2
GREIF W PARENTS	KATHARINA	1835	MALSCH	03/13/1846	A		F2
GREIF W PARENTS	MICHAEL	1838	MALSCH	03/13/1846	A		F2
GREIF W PARENTS	VALENTIN	1845	MALSCH	03/13/1846	A		F2
GREILE	JOSEF		ETTLINGEN	01/01/1862	A		F4
GREINER	JOHANNES		GLASHÜTTE	10/18/1803			F1
GREINER	KARL AUGUST		KARLSRUHE	/ /	A		F3
GRETSCHMANN	KARL HEINRICH		SPÖCK	01/01/1835	A		F4
GRETSCHMANN W FAMILY	AUGUST		SPÖCK	01/01/1797	A		F4
GREULE	ALBIN	1843	ETTLINGEN	04/11/1869	A		F4
GREULE	ANTON IGNATIUS	1863	ETTLINGEN	/ /	A		F4
GREULE	JOSEF	1783	ETTLINGEN	/ /	A		F4
GREULE	JOSEF	1814	ETTLINGEN	08/25/1862	A		F4
GREULE	MICHAEL		LANGENSTEINBACH	01/01/1843	A		F3
GRIEB	AUGUST FRIEDRIH	1843	DURLACH KARLSRUHE	/ /	A		F7
GRIEB	WILHELM	1875	DURLACH	01/01/1891	A		F3
GRIEB	WILHELM	1875	DURLACH	01/01/1891	A		F5
GRIEB	WILHELM	1875	DURLACH	01/01/1891	A		F6
GRIEBEL	JAKOB	1834	KNIELINGEN	01/01/1867	A		F6
GRIEBEL	JOHANN HEINRICH		KARLSRUHE	/ /	A		F3
GRIENEMAIER	GEORG ADAM		GRABEN	01/01/1814	A		F3
GRIESELICH	ERNST		KARLSRUHE	01/01/1858	A		F3
GRIESINGER MN		1835	KARLSRUHE	01/01/1887	A		F3
GRIESINGER W FAMILY	KARL FRIEDRICH	1839	KARLSRUHE	01/01/1887	A		F3
GRIESINGER W PARENTS	FRIEDRICH	1873	KARLSRUHE	01/01/1887	A		F3
GRIESINGER W PARENTS	HEINRICH	1874	KARLSRUHE	01/01/1887	A		F3
GRIESINGER W PARENTS	HERMANN	1876	KARLSRUHE	01/01/1887	A		F3
GRIESINGER W PARENTS	LUISE	1867	KARLSRUHE	01/01/1887	A		F3
GRIESINGER W PARENTS	SALOMEA	1865	KARLSRUHE	01/01/1887	A		F3
GRIESSE	KARL		KARLSRUHE	/ /	A		F3
GRIESSER	ADOLF		BUHL	01/01/1866	A		F6
GRIMM	IGNAZ	1822	OBERWEIER	01/01/1851	A		F1
GRIMM	MAXIMILLIAN	1850	BLANKENLOCH	01/01/1880	A		F4
GRIMM	NIKOLAUS	1863	SCHATTHAUSEN	01/01/1890	A		F2
GRIMM	WILHELM CHRIST	1841	DURLACH KARLSRUHE	/ /	A		
GRISCHELE	JOHANNES	1785	ETTLINGEN	/ /	A		F4
GRISCHELE	MARIA JOSEFA HE		ETTLINGEN	06/16/1869	A		F4
GRISCHELE MN VÖGELE	MARIA ANNA	1828	ETTLINGEN	/ /	A		F4
GRISCHELE W WIFE	FRANZ XAVER	1802	ETTLINGEN	/ /	A		F4
GROB	HERMANN	1877	HOCHSTETTEN	01/01/1878	A		F8
GROB	THEODOR	1875	HOCHSTETTEN	01/01/1878	A		F8
GROB W F	IMANUEL	1844	HOCHSTETTEN	01/01/1878	A		F8
GROB W F	LUISE	1853	HOCHSTETTEN	01/01/1878	A		F8
GROB W P	ADOLF	1873	HOCHSTETTEN	01/01/1878	A		F8

Lastname	Firstname	Birth Year	Birthplace	Emigration	De	Prof	Source
GROH	SOPHIE	1794	HOCHSTETTEN	01/01/1846	A		F5
GROMBACHER	LEO	1847	SCHÖLLBRONN	01/01/1869	A		F7
GROOS	MAGDL.		KARLSRUHE	/ /	A		F3
GROPP	BERNHARD	1834	RINKLINGEN	01/01/1856	A		F8
GROPP	GEORG MICHAEL	1826	RINKLINGEN	05/24/1847	A		F4
GROPP	HEINRIH EDUARD	1846	RINKLINGEN	01/01/1879	A		F4
GROPP	JOHANN GEORG		RINKLINGEN	/ /	A		F4
GROPP	KONRAD	1823	RINKLINGEN	04/13/1846	A		F7
GROPP	MARGARETHE		RINKLINGEN	02/16/1866	A		F7
GROPP	MARTIN	1828	RINKLINGEN	05/24/1847	A		F7
GROPP	REGINE	1850	RINKLINGEN	/ /	A		F7
GROPP	WILHELMINE LUIE	1858	RINKLINGEN	09/03/1879	A		F7
GROPP MN ZICKWOLF	CHRISTINA	1808	RINKLINGEN	01/01/1856	A		F7
GROSS	AUGUST		BÜHL	01/01/1878	A		F5
GROSS	CHRIST. FRIEDRI	1829	DURLACH KARLSRUHE	/ /			F7
GROSS	JOHANN		STUHLINGEN	01/01/1866	A		F6
GROSS W F	LEOPOLD		WOLSENWEIER	01/01/1866	A		F6
GROSS W FAMILY	JAKOB		KARLSRUHE	01/01/1858	A		F3
GROSSMANN	PETER CHRISTOPH		DURLACH KARLSRUHE	01/01/1849	A		F7
GRUBER	EMIL	1872	SPöCK	01/01/1888	A		F4
GRUBER	ERNESTINE		SPöCK	01/01/1866	A		F4
GRUBER	ERNST FRIEDRICH	1871	SPöCK	01/01/1888	A		F4
GRUBER	ERNST FRIEDRICH	1871	SPöCK	01/01/1883	A		F8
GRUBER	HEINRICH		SPöCK	01/01/1868	A		F4
GRUBER	JAKOB		SPöCK	01/01/1866	A		F4
GRUBER	LEOPOLD	1880	SPöCK	01/01/1892	A		F4
GRUBER	MAX	1876	SPöCK	01/01/1892	A		F4
GRUBER	MAX	1877	SPöCK	01/01/1892	A		F4
GRÜNER	FRITZ		KARLSRUHE	/ /	A		F3
GRÜNINGER W CH.	KARL ALBERT	1824	KARLSRUHE	01/01/1876	A		F3
GRÜNINGER W FATH	HERMANN	1859	KARLSRUHE	01/01/1876	A		F3
GRÜNINGER W FATH.	ERICH BERNHARD	1867	KARLSRUHE	01/01/1876	A		F3
GRÜNINGER W FATH.	OTTO	1858	KARLSRUHE	01/01/1876	A		F3
GRÜNWALD	KAROLINA		EINBACH BUCHEN	01/01/1859	A		F6
GRäFINGER	JOHANN	1839	MALSCH	01/01/1879	A		F2
GRäFINGER	PAUL	1861	MALSCH	01/01/1879	A		F2
GRäFINGER	VALENTIN	1826	MALSCH	01/01/1856	A		F2
GRäFINGER	VERONIKA	1867	MALSCH	01/01/1879	A		F2
GRäSER	KATHARINA	1844	MALSCH	10/21/1864	A		F2
GRäSER	KONRAD	1823	MALSCH	01/01/1868	A		F2
GRäSSER	FLORIAN	1853	MALSCH	01/01/1869	A		FE
GRäSSER	FRANZ KARL	1858	MALSCH	01/01/1873	A		F2
GRäSSER	KARL LUDWIG	1869	MALSCH	01/01/1880	A		F2
GRäSSER	VALENTIN	1815	MALSCH	01/01/1837	A		F2
GRäSSER	WILHELM	1850	MALSCH	01/01/1869	A		F2
GRäSSER W FAMILY	JOHANN MELCHIOR	1764	MALSCH	01/01/1880	A		F2
GRäSSER MN WESTERMAN	REGINE	1841	MALSCH	01/01/1880	A		F2
GRäSSER W PARENTS	ALBERT	1880	MALSCH	01/01/1880	A		F2
GRäSSER W PARENTS	HERMANN	1871	MALSCH	01/01/1880			
GRäSSER W PARENTS	JOSEF WILHELM	1875	MALSCH	01/01/1880	A		F2

Lastname	Firstname	Birth Year	Birthplace	Emigration	De	Prof	Source
GRäSSER W PARENTS	THEODOR MICHAEL		MALSCH	01/01/1880	A		F2
GRäULE	CHRISTOPH	1821	LANGENSTEINBACH	01/01/1847	A		F3
GRÜNWALD	CAROLINA		EINBACH	01/01/1859	A		F6
GUGEL	CHRIST. WILH		DURLACH KARLSRUHE	01/01/1855			F7
GUHL	MARIE	1885	RINKLINGEN	/ /	A		F7
GULDE	GEORG		KARLSRUHE	/ /	A		F3
GUSHURST	ADOLF	1865	ETTLINGEN	01/01/1882	A		F4
GUSHURST	BERNHARD		ETTLINGEN	01/01/1870	A		F4
GÜNTHER	FRITZ		KARLSRUHE	/ /	A		F3
GÜNTHER MN SÜSS	BARBARA	1816	LINKENHEIM	01/01/1876	A		F8
GÜNTHER W F	JOHANN	1813	LINKENHEIM	01/01/1876	A		F8
GÜNTHER W P	FRIEDERIKE	1856	LINKENHEIM	01/01/1876	A		F8
GÜNTHER W P	LUISE	1858	LINKENHEIM	01/01/1876	A		F8
GöHLER	LUDWIG		KARLSRUHE	01/01/1789	A		F3
GöRGER	KAROLINE		KARLSRUHE	01/01/1852	A		F3
GöTZ	JOHANN		DURLACH KARLSRUHE	01/01/1836			F7
GöTZ	JOSEPH		FORBACH	01/01/1869	A		F6
GöTZ	KATHARINA		GRÖTZINGEN	01/01/1853	A		F5
GöTZ	KATHARINA	1826	GRÖTZINGEN	01/01/1846	A		F3
GöTZ	LEOPOLD WILHEL	1840	DURLACH KARLSRUHE	/ /			F7
GöTZ	LUDWIG		FORBACH	01/01/1860	A		F6#
GöTZ MN HEIDT	ANNA MARIA	1800	GRÖTZINGEN	01/01/1837	A		F3
GöTZ W FAMILY	KARL	1809	GRÖTZINGEN	01/01/1837	A		F3
GöTZ W PARENTS	CHRISTINE	1836	GRÖTZINGEN	01/01/1837	A		F3
GöTZ W PARENTS	KARL	1830	GRÖTZINGEN	01/01/1837	A		F3
GöTZ W PARENTS	KATHARINA	1832	GRÖTZINGEN	01/01/1837	A		F3
GöBLIS	FRIDOLIN		SINGEN	01/01/1747	A		F6
GöTZ	BERNHARD		FORBACH	01/01/1854	A		F6
GöTZ	JOHANN GEORG		FORBACH	01/01/1854	A		F6
GÜNTER	RUDOLF	1842	SCHÖLLBRONN	/ /	A		F7
GÜNTHER	FRANZ JOSEF	1842	SCHÖLLBRONN	01/01/1866	A		F7
GÜNTHER W F	KATHARINA	1834	SCHÖLLBRONN	01/01/1869	A		F7
GÜNTHER W P	ALOISIA	1860	SCHÖLLBRONN	01/01/1869	A		F7
GÜNTHER W P	GOTTLIEB	1867	SCHÖLLBRONN	01/01/1869	A		F7
GÜNTHER W P	STEPHAN	1868	SCHÖLLBRONN	01/01/1869	A		F7
GÜNTHER W P	VIKTORIA	1864	SCHÖLLBRONN	01/01/1869	A		F7

Lastname	Firstname	Birth Year	Birthplace	Emigration	De	Prof	Source
HAAB	JOHANN JAKOB	1852	DURLACH KARLSRUHE	/ /	A		F7
HAAF	JOSEF KARL		KARLSRUHE	/ /	A		F3
HAAG	CHRISTOPH FRIED	1808	GRABEN	01/01/1866	A		F3
HAAG	JAKOB ROBERT	1875	KARLSRUHE	01/01/1891	A		F3
HAAG	KAROLINE	1848	GRABEN	01/01/1868	A		F3
HAAS	AUGUST	1844	MÜHLBURG	01/01/1867	A		F8
HAAS	JOHANN		FORBACH	01/01/1866	A		F6
HAAS	JOHANNES LEOPOD		FORBACH	01/01/1857	A		F6
HAAS	JOSEF KARL	1873	KARLSRUHE	01/01/1892	A		F3
HAAS	LUDWIG		FORBACH	01/01/1854	A		F6
HAAS	LUDWIG JULIUS	1868	NECKARGEMUND	01/01/1884	A		F1
HAAS	MARIA ANNA		FORBACH	01/01/1859	A		F6
HAAS	MAX		FORBACH	01/01/1868	A		F6
HAAS	VALENTIN		PÜLFRINGEN	01/01/1853	A		F6
HABEL	CHRISTINE		GRÖTZINGEN	/ /	A		F3
HABICH	HERMANN		KAPPELWINDECK	01/01/1885	A		F5
HABITZREUTHER	FLORIAN		KARLSRUHE	01/01/1861	A		F3
HACK	JOSEF		ETTLINGEN	/ /	A		F4
HAFENMAIER	JAKOB	1835	GRÖTZINGEN	01/01/1860	A		F3
HAFENMEYER	JOSEF		GRÖTZINGEN	/ /	A		F3
HAFFLER	JAKOB FRIEDRICH		GRABEN	01/01/1830	A		F3
HAFFNER W MOTH	FRANZ JOSF	1867	KARLSRUHE	01/01/1880	A		F3
HAFFNER W MOTH	FRIEDRICH	1870	KARLSRUHE	01/01/1882	A		F3
HAFFNER W MOTH	OTTO EDMUND	1863	KARLSRUHE	01/01/1880	A		F3
HAFFNER W MOTH	ROSA KATHARINA	1866	KARLSRUHE	01/01/1880	A		F3
HAFFNER W MOTH.	LINDA	1872	KARLSRUHE	01/01/1882	A		F3
HAFFNER WID W CH.	ROSA	1851	KARLSRUHE	01/01/1880	A		F3
HAFFNER WID. W CH.	ELISABETH	1845	KARLSRUHE	01/01/1872	A		F3
HAFLER	MARTIN		GRABEN	01/01/1872	A		F3
HAFNER	LUDWIG		GRÖTZINGEN	01/01/1846	A		F3
HAFNER	WILHEMINE		KAELSRUHE	/ /	A		F3
HAGER	JOHANN	1807	SPESSART	01/01/1881	A		F6
HAGMANN	JOSEF		BAUERBACH	01/01/1866	A		F8
HAHN	THEODOR	1875	KARLSRUHE	01/01/1891	A		F3
HAILER	FRANZ	1820	ETTLINGEN	04/13/1852	A		F4
HAILER	FRANZISKA		ETTLINGEN	01/01/1860	A		F4
HAILER	JOHANNA		WÖSSINGEN	01/01/1858	A		F1
HAILER	LEOPOLD	1838	ETTLINGEN	01/01/1854	A		F3
HAILER	LUISE		WÖSSINGEN	01/01/1858	A		F1
HAILER	MAGDALENA	1854	ETTLINGEN	09/28/1870	A		F3
HAILER MN KLUMP	MARIA	1831	ETTLINGEN	01/01/1872	A		F4
HAILER W WIFE	JOSEF		ETTLINGEN	01/17/1872	A		F4
HAINOLD MN KNODEL	SYBILLE	1786	LANGENSTEINBACH	01/01/1828	A		F3
HAINOLD W FAMILY	ADAM	1790	LANGENSTEINBACH	01/01/1828	A		F3
HAINOLD W PARENTS	CHRISTOPH	1817	LANGENSTEINBACH	01/01/1854	A		F3
HAINOLD W PARENTS	MARGARETHA	1820	LANGENSTEINBACH	01/01/1828	A		F3
HAINOLD W PARENTS	UDA	1822	LANGENSTEINBACH	01/01/1822	A		F3
HAIRER	GOTTFRIED		BLANKENLOCH	01/01/1834	A		F4
HAISCH	ERNESTINE		BLANKENLOCH	01/01/1834	A		F4
HAISCH	ERNESTINE		BLANKENLOCH	01/01/1848	A		F4

Lastname	Firstname	Birth Year	Birthplace	Emigration	De	Prof	Source
HAISCH	JOHANN	1862	BLANKENLOCH	01/01/1880	A		F4
HAISCH W FAMILY	CHRISTIAN		BLANKENLOCH	01/01/1832	A		F4
HALD	JOHANNES		LIPBURG	01/01/1859	A		F6
HAMBRECHT	PHILIPP		KARLSRUHE	/ /	A		F3
HAMMER	AUGUST	1867	KARLSRUHE	01/01/1884	A		F3
HAMMER	GEORG	1838	KARLSRUHE	01/01/1854	A		F3
HAMMER	KARL	1865	KARLSRUHE	01/01/1884	A		F3
HAMMER	LUDWWIG		KARLSRUHE	/ /	A		F3
HAMPRECHT	ALBERT		KARLSRUHE	01/01/1851	A		F3
HANG MN	MAGDALENA		ETTLINGEN	/ /	A		F4
HANG W FAMILY	ADAM		ETTLINGEN	/ /	A		F4
HANG W PARENTS .	ANTON		ETTLINGEN	/ /	A		F4
HANG W PARENTS	JOHANN		ETTLINGEN	/ /	A		F4
HANG W PARENTS	JOSEF		ETTLINGEN	/ /	A		F4
HANG W PARENTS	KATHARINA		ETTLINGEN	/ /	A		F4
HARMANN	WILHELM ANDREAS		KARLSRUHE	01/01/1860	A		F3
HARTER	JOHANN		KNIEBIS	01/01/1869	A		F6
HARTFELDER	DOROTHEA		WöSSINGEN	01/01/1832	A		F1
HARTFELDER	JOHANN ADAM		WöSSINGEN	01/01/1854	A		F1
HARTFELDER W 9 CH	CONRAD		WöSSINGEN	01/01/1782			F1
HARTFELDER WW 5CH	PHILIPP		WöSSINGEN	02/22/1803	A		F1
HARTMANN	FRIEDRICH	1865	SPöCK	01/01/1881	A		F4
HARTMANN	HEINRICH		SPöCK	01/01/1866	A		F3
HARTMANN	HEINRICH	1838	SPöCK	01/01/1868	A		F4
HARTMANN	JAKOB	1841	LANGENSTEINBACH	01/01/1864	A		F3
HARTMANN	JAKOB FRIEDRICH	1828	SPöCK	01/01/1868	A		F8
HARTMANN	KARL		SPöCK	01/01/1851	A		F4
HARTMANN	LUDWIG THEODOR	1837	SPöCK	01/01/1867	A		F8
HARTMANN	MAGDALENA	1857	LANGENSTEINBACH	/ /	A		F3
HARTMANN	MAX		SPöCK	01/01/1861	A		F4
HARTMANN	PETER		SPöCK	01/01/1847	A		F4
HARTMANN	ROSINE		SPöCK	01/01/1866	A		F4
HARTMANN MN GRETSCHA	SOPHIE	1841	SPöCK	01/01/1867	A		F4
HARTMANN MN HOFHEINZ	WILHELMINE	1830	SPöCK	01/01/1868	A		F4
HARTMANN MN KLEINSCR	ELISABETH		SPöCK	01/01/1866	A		F4
HARTMANN W F	JAKOB FRIEDRICH	1828	SPöCK	01/01/1868	A		F4
HARTMANN W F	KONRAD		SPöCK	01/01/1835	A		F4
HARTMANN W F	LEOPOLD		SPöCK	01/01/1867	A		F4
HARTMANN W F	LUDWIG THEODOR	1837	SPöCK	01/01/1867	A		F4
HARTMANN W P	AUGUST	1862	SPöCK	01/01/1868	A		F4
HARTMANN W P	ERNESTINE	1855	SPöCK	01/01/1868	A		F4
HARTMANN W P	JAKOB	1858	SPöCK	01/01/1868	A		F4
HARTMANN W P	KARL	1856	SPöCK	01/01/1868	A		F4
HARTMANN W P	KARL WILHELM	1865	SPöCK	01/01/1867	A		F4
HARTMANN W P	LUDWIG	1862	SPöCK	01/01/1868	A		F4
HARTMANN W P	MARIA		SPöCK	01/01/1867	A		F4
HARTMANN W P	MAX	1866	SPöCK	01/01/1868	A		F4
HARTWEG	MAX		KARLSRUHE	01/01/1853	A		F3
HASENMAYER	JOSEF		GRöTZINGEN	01/01/1852	A		F5
HASSEL	ZäZILIA		HEIDELBERG	01/01/1859	A		F6

Lastname	Firstname	Birth Year	Birthplace	Emigration	De	Prof	Source
HASSLER	JAKOB FRIEDRICH		GRABEN	01/01/1830	A		F5
HASSLER	KONRAD		GRABEN	01/01/1819	A		F3
HASSLER	MARTIN		GRABEN	01/01/1872	A		F5
HAUCH	ANDREAS		HUNDHEIM	01/01/1859	A		F6
HAUCK	FERDINAND	1805	SCHÖLLBRONN	01/01/1830	A		F7
HAUCK	GOTLIEB	1839	KNIELINGEN	01/01/1868	A		F6
HAUCK	PHILIPP		DURLACH KARLSRUHE	01/01/1852			F7
HAUCK MN KNOLL	FRANZISKA		SCHÖLLBRONN	/ /	A		F7
HAUCK W F	IGNAZ	1799	SCHÖLLBRONN	/ /	A		F7
HAUCK W F	IGNAZ	1842	SCHÖLLBRONN	/ /	A		F7
HAUCK W F	JOHANN	1840	SCHÖLLBRONN	/ /	A		F7
HAUCK W P	ANTON	1831	SCHÖLLBRONN	/ /	A		F7
HAUCK W P	KATHARINA	1845	SCHÖLLBRONN	/ /	A		F7
HAUCK W P	LEO	1838	SCHÖLLBRONN	/ /	A		F7
HAUCK W P	MARIA ANNA	1835	SCHÖLLBRONN	/ /	A		F7
HAUD	LUDWIG	1869	KARLSRUHE	01/01/1885	A		F3
HAUER	CHRISTOPH		BLANKENLOCH	01/01/1865	A		F4
HAUER	ERNST	1838	DURLACH KARLSRUHE	/ /			F7
HAUER	FRIEDRICH		BLANKENLOCH	01/01/1891	A		F4
HAUER	MARTIN UWE		BLANKENLOCH	01/01/1846	A		F4
HAUER	WILHELM LUDWIG	1861	BLANKENLOCH	01/01/1879	A		F4
HAUERT	FRIEDRICH ALFRE	1878	KARLSRUHE	01/01/1895	A		F3
HAUFFER	CHRISTIAN FRDR.	1877	KARLSRUHE	01/01/1893	A		F3
HAUG	FRIEDRICH	1862	KARLSRUHE	01/01/1892	A		F3
HAUG	JAKOB		MOSBACH	01/01/1859	A		F6
HAUG MN KUNZ	MARGHARETHA		SCHÖLLBRONN	01/01/1830	A		F7
HAUG W F	IGNAZ	1819	SCHÖLLBRONN	01/01/1819	A		F7
HAUG W F	JOHANN	1795	SCHÖLLBRONN	01/01/1830	A		F7
HAUG W F	JOHANN	1823	SCHÖLLBRONN	01/01/1830	A		F7
HAUG W F	JOSEF	1821	SCHÖLLBRONN	01/01/1830	A		F7
HAUG W F	MARIA ANNA	1826	SCHÖLLBRONN	01/01/1830	A		F7
HAUK	PAUL	1826	DURLACH KARLSRUHE	/ /			F7
HAUN	FRIEDRICH		DURLACH KARLSRUHE	01/01/1833			F7
HAUPT	AUGUST	1871	KARLSRUHE	01/01/1888	A		F3
HAUPT	FRIEDRICH	1869	KARLSRUHE	01/01/1887	A		F3
HAUPT	KARL LUDWIG	1876	KARLSRUHE	01/01/1894	A		F3
HAUPT	WILHELM	1867	KARLSRUHE	/ /			
HAUPT	WILHELM	1867	KARLSRUHE	01/01/1884	A		F3
HAUSER	DOROTHE	1841	ETTLINGEN	05/29/1865	A		F4
HAUSER	JOSEF	1768	MALSCH	01/01/1787	A		F2
HAUSER	KARL FRIEDRICH	1876	JÖHLINGEN	01/01/1892	A		F8
HAUSER	MATHIAS	1765	MALSCH	01/01/1787	A		F2
HAUSER	THEODOR	1875	LINKENHEIM	01/01/1881	A		F8
HAUSER	VICTORIA	1831	ETTLINGEN	/ /	A		F4
HAUSER	WALTER	1862	KARLSRUHE	01/01/1887	A		FE
HAUSER	WILHELM ANTON	1872	JÖHLINGEN	01/01/1888	A		F8
HAUSER W FAMILY	JOHANNES JAKOB	1832	BLANKENLOCH	01/01/1879	A		F4
HAUSER W P	AUGUST	1864	BLANKENLOCH	01/01/1879	A		F4
HAUSER W P	KAROLINA	1870	BLANKENLOCH	01/01/1879	A		F4
HAUSER W P	LUDWIG	1866	BLANKENLOCH	01/01/1879	A		F4

Lastname	Firstname	Birth Year	Birthplace	Emigration	De	Prof	Source
HAUSER W P	MAX	1862	BLANKENLOCH	01/01/1879	A		F4
HAUSSER	EDUARD	1837	ETTLINGEN	07/04/1854	A		F4
HAUSSER	W.M.G.	1864	KARLSRUHE	01/01/1880	A		F3
HECHT	CARL FRIEDRICH	1831	HOCHSTETTEN	01/01/1867	A		F8
HECK	FRIEDRICH		KARLSRUHE	01/01/1849	A		F3
HECK	JULIUS		BIETIGHEIM	01/01/1859	A		F6
HECK	WILHELM		KARLSRUHE	/ /	A		F3
HED	WILHELM	1871	KARLSRUHE	01/01/1890	A		F3
HEGER	CHRISTIAN		LANGENSTEINBACH	01/01/1862	A		F3
HEGER	CHRISTOPH	1819	LANGENSTEINBACH	/ /	A		F3
HEGER	GOTTLIEB	1856	LANGENSTEINBACH	01/01/1885	A		F3
HEGER	KARL	1802	LANGENSTEINBACH	01/01/1842	A		F3
HEGER	KARL	1862	LANGENSTEINBACH	/ /	A		F3
HEGER	KARL FRIEDRICH	1826	LANGENSTEINBACH	/ /	A		F3
HEGER	KATHARINA	1829	LANGENSTEINBACH	/ /	A		F3
HEGER	MAGDALENA	1817	LANGENSTEINBACH	/ /	A		F3
HEGER	MARGARETHA	1823	LANGENSTEINBACH	/ /	A		F3
HEGER	PHILIPP	1834	LANGENSTEINBACH	/ /	A		F3
HEGER	PHILIPP	1860	LANGENSTEINBACH	/ /	A		F3
HEGER MN BAUCHERT	SUSANNE		LANGENSTEINBACH	07/27/1847	A		F3
HEGER W FAMILY	KARL		LANGENSTEINBACH	07/27/1847	A		F3
HEGER W PARENTS	JOHANNES	1848	LANGENSTEINBACH	07/27/1847	A		F3
HEGER W PARENTS	MARGARETHA	1845	LANGENSTEINBACH	07/27/1847	A		F3
HEGER W PARENTS	PHILIPP CHRISTO	1841	LANGENSTEINBACH	07/27/1847	A		F3
HEIBY-HEIDEGGER	LYDIA		KARLSRUHE	/ /	A		F3
HEIDT	DOROTHEA		GRÖTZINGEN	01/01/1858	A		F5
HEIDT	DOROTHEA	1827	GRÖTZINGEN	01/01/1846	A		F3
HEIDT	ELISABETH	1829	GRÖTZINGEN	01/01/1846	A		F3
HEIDT	ERNST		GRÖTZINGEN	01/01/1846	A		F3
HEIDT	ERNST CHRISTOPH		GRÖTZINGEN	01/01/1865	A		F3
HEIDT	GEORG		GRÖTZINGEN	01/01/1817	A		F5
HEIDT	JAKOB		GRÖTZINGEN	01/01/1853	A		F3
HEIDT	JAKOB FRIEDRICH		DURLACH KARLSRUHE	01/01/1845	A		F7
HEIDT	JAKOB FRIEDRICH		GRÖTZINGEN	01/01/1865	A		F5
HEIDT	JOHANN		GRÖTZINGEN	01/01/1853	A		F3
HEIDT	JOHANN CHRISTIA	1830	GRÖTZINGEN	01/01/1851	A		F3
HEIDT	JOHANN GEORG	1806	SÖLLINGEN	01/01/1853	A		F7
HEIDT	JOHANN JAKOB		GRÖTZINGEN	01/01/1835	A		F3
HEIDT	JOHANN JAKOB		GRÖTZINGEN	01/01/1844	A		F5
HEIDT	JOSEF		SÖLLINGEN	01/01/1806	A		F7
HEIDT	MAGDALENA		GRÖTZINGEN	01/01/1853	A		F5
HEIDT MN WENZ	MARGARETHE	1851	SÖLLINGEN	01/01/1887	A		1
HEIDT W FAMILY	WILHELM	1850	SÖLLINGEN	01/01/1887	A		F3
HEIDT W P	WILHELM	1850	SÖLLINGEN	01/01/1887	A		F7
HEIDT W PARENTS	CHRISTOPH	1873	SÖLLINGEN	01/01/1887	A		F3
HEIDT W PARENTS	ERNST	1878	SÖLLINGEN	01/01/1887	A		F3
HEIDT W PARENTS	FRIEDA	1881	SÖLLINGEN	01/01/1887	A		F3
HEIDT W PARENTS	KARL	1885	SÖLLINGEN	01/01/1887	A		F3
HEIDT W PARENTS	PAULINE	1877	SÖLLINGEN	01/01/1887	A		F3
HEIDT W PARENTS	ROBERT	1883	SÖLLINGEN	01/01/1887	A		F3

Lastname	Firstname	Birth Year	Birthplace	Emigration	De	Prof	Source
HEIDUCK	ELISABETH		SÖLLINGEN	01/01/1855	A		F7
HEIDUCK	JOHANN GEORG		SÖLLINGEN	01/01/1846	A		F7
HEIDUD	ELISABETH		SÖLLINGEN	/ /	A		F7
HEIL	CARL AUGUST		LIEDOLSHEIM	01/01/1892	A		F9
HEIL	FERDINAND	1863	MÖRSCH	02/26/1881	A		F7
HEIL	GEORG		MÖRSCH	01/01/1853	A		F7
HEIL	JAKOB		MÖRSCH	01/01/1854	A		F7
HEIL	KATHARINA	1836	MÖRSCH	01/01/1854	A		F7
HEIL	LUISE	1839	MÖRSCH	01/01/1854	A		F7
HEIL	WILHELM	1851	MÖRSCH	02/20/1872	A		F7
HEIL MN BAUCH	SOPHIE		LIEDOLSHEIM	01/01/1879	A		F9
HEIL W F	AUGUST FRIEDRIH	1831	LIEDOLSHEIM	01/01/1879	A		F9
HEIL W HUSBAND	SOPHIE		LIEDOLSHEIM	01/01/1866	A		F9
HEIL W M	EMILIE		LIEDOLSHEIM	01/01/1881	A		F9
HEIL W M	GUSTAV		LIEDOLSHEIM	01/01/1881	A		
HEIL W M	JOH.CHR.		LIEDOLSHEIM	01/01/1881	A		F9
HEIL W M	KARL	1873	LIEDOLSHEIM	01/01/1881	A		F9
HEIL W P	EMILIE	1875	LIEDOLSHEIM	01/01/1879	A		F9
HEIL W P	FRIEDRICH	1859	LIEDOLSHEIM	01/01/1879	A		F9
HEIL W P	GUSTAV	1866	LIEDOLSHEIM	01/01/1879	A		F9
HEIL W P	LUDWIG	1852	LIEDOLSHEIM	01/01/1879	A		F9
HEIL W W	JOHANN		LIEDOLSHEIM	01/01/1866	A		F9
HEIL WIDOW	W CH		LIEDOLSHEIM	01/01/1881	A		F9
HEILER	BERNHARD		WÖSSINGEN	01/01/1737	A		F1
HEILER	CONRAD		WÖSSINGEN	01/01/1787	A		F1
HEILER	OTTO	1867	ETTLINGEN	01/01/1872	A		F4
HEILL	MICHEL		GRABEN	01/01/1736	A		F3
HEILL W F	MICHEL		GRABEN	01/01/1736	A		F5
HEILMANN	ANDREAS		GRABEN	01/01/1847	A		F3
HEILMANN	AUGUST FRIEDRIC		GRABEN	01/01/1781	A		F3
HEILMANN	CHRISTOPH		GRABEN	01/01/1855	A		F3
HEILMANN	CHRISTOPH		GRABEN	01/01/1856	A		F5
HEILMANN	JAKOB FRIEDRICH	1832	GRABEN	01/01/1881	A		F3
HEILMANN	JOHANN		GRABEN	01/01/1861	A		F5
HEILMANN	KARL		GRABEN	01/01/1880	A		F3
HEILMANN	LEOPOLD		GRABEN	/ /			
HEILMANN	WILHELM		GRABEN	01/01/1855	A		F3
HEILMANN MN SCHOLL	KATHARINA	1811	GRABEN	01/01/1861	A		F3
HEILMANN MN SCHOLL	KATHARINA	1831	GRABEN	01/01/1881	A		F8
HEILMANN MN WENZ	ELISABETH		GRABEN	01/01/1861	A		F3
HEILMANN W F	ANDREAS		GRABEN	01/01/1847	A		F5
HEILMANN W F	AUGUST	1862	GRABEN	01/01/1881	A		F8
HEILMANN W F	JOHANN	1821	GRABEN	01/01/1881	A		F8
HEILMANN W F	KARL	1866	GRABEN	01/01/1881	A		F8
HEILMANN W F	KAROLINE	1862	GRABEN	01/01/1881	A		F8
HEILMANN W FAMILY	JOHANN		GRABEN	01/01/1861	A		F3
HEILMANN W P	ADAM	1870	GRABEN	01/01/1881	A		F8
HEILMANN W P	CHRISTINE	1876	GRABEN	01/01/1881	A		F8
HEILMANN W P	ERNESTINE	1862	GRABEN	01/01/1881	A		F8
HEILMANN W P	KATHARINA	1865	GRABEN	01/01/1881	A		F8

Lastname	Firstname	Birth Year	Birthplace	Emigration	De	Prof	Source
HEILMANN W P	MARIA	1872	GRABEN	01/01/1881	A		F8
HEILMANN W P	WILHELMINA	1869	GRABEN	01/01/1881	A		F8
HEILMANN W PARENTS	ADAM		GRABEN	01/01/1861	A		F3
HEILMANN W PARENTS	CHRISTINE		GRABEN	01/01/1861	A		F3
HEILMANN W PARENTS	ERNESTINE		GRABEN	01/01/1861	A		F3
HEILMANN W PARENTS	KATHARINA		GRABEN	01/01/1861	A		F3
HEILMANN W PARENTS	WILHELMINE ERNT		GRABEN	01/01/1861	A		F3
HEILMANN W WIFE	LEOPOLD		GRABEN	01/01/1861	A		F3
HEILMANN WIDOWER WCH	JAKOB FRIEDRICH	1833	GRABEN	01/01/1881	A		F8
HEILMANN-WENZEL	KATHARINA		GRABEN	/ /	A		F5
HEIM	CHRISTIAN		GRÖTZINGEN	01/01/1848	A		F5
HEIM	ELISABETH	1830	GRÖTZINGEN	01/01/1851	A		F3
HEIM	MAGDALENA		GRÖTZINGEN	01/01/1846	A		F3
HEIM	REINHARD		GRÖTZINGEN	01/01/1846	A		F3
HEIM	SALOMEA	1824	GRÖTZINGEN	01/01/1851	A		F3
HEIM	ZACHARIAS	1826	GRÖTZINGEN	01/01/1851	A		F3
HEIM MN DOPF	MARGARETHA	1792	GRÖTZINGEN	01/01/1848	A		F3
HEIM W WIFE	CHRISTIAN	1791	GRÖTZINGEN	01/01/1848	A		F3
HEIMERDINGER W WIFE	MAX EMANUEL		KARLSRUHE	01/01/1866	A		F3
HEINE	JOSEF	1875	DURLACH	01/01/1892	A		F3
HEINE	JOSEF ALFRED	1875	DURLACH	01/01/1892	A		F6
HEINLE	AUGUST		GRABEN	01/01/1866	A		F3
HEINLE	AUGUST	1846	SPÖCK	01/01/1867	A		F8
HEINOLD	JAKOB	1817	LANGENSTEINBACH	/ /	A		F3
HEINOLD	LUDWIG		LANGENSTEINBACH	04/18/1854	A		F3
HEINOLD	MAGDALENA	1830	LANGENSTEINBACH	01/01/1851	A		F3
HEINRICH	CYRIAK	1829	MALSCH	01/01/1856	A		F2
HEINRICH	FRANZ JOSEF	1773	MALSCH	01/01/1795	A		F2
HEINRICH	FRANZ JOSEF	1836	MALSCH	01/01/1861	A		F2
HEINRICH	JOSEF	1867	MALSCH	10/09/1891	A		F2
HEINRICH	VERONIKA	1835	MALSCH	07/22/1854	A		F2
HEINZ	JOHANN ALBERT	1865	GRÖTZINGEN	01/01/1881	A		F3
HEINZ	MICHEL		SPÖCK	01/01/1847	A		F4
HEINZ MN HOFHEINZ	MARIA EVA	1835	SPÖCK	01/01/1867	A		F8
HEINZ W F	LUDWIG	1832	SPÖCK	01/01/1867	A		F8
HEINZ W P	KARL FRIEDRICH	1860	SPÖCK	01/01/1867	A		F8
HEINZ W P	LUDWIG	1864	SPÖCK	01/01/1867	A		F8
HEINZELMANN	JOSEF	1868	KARLSRUHE	01/01/1884	A		F3
HEIOLMANN W WIFE	LEOPOLD		GRABEN	01/01/1861	A		F5
HEISCH	CHRISTIAN		BLANKENLOCH	01/01/1832	A		F4
HEISS	AUGUST	1875	DAISBACH	01/01/1891	A		F7
HEISSLER	KARL JOHANN	1862	ETTLINGEN	02/10/1883	A		F4
HEITZ MN KÜHN	KATHARINA		MÖRSCH	06/06/1832	A		F7
HEITZ W F	LORENZ		MÖRSCH	06/06/1832	A		F7
HELLES	MICHAEL		WÖSSINGEN	01/01/1832	A		F1
HELLMUTH	MARIA		DITTIGHEIM	01/01/1866	A		F6
HELM	FRIEDRICH KARL		KARLSRUHE	/ /	A		F3
HELMBULE MN LANG	EVA MAGARETHA	1809	KARLSRUHE	01/01/1836	A		F3
HELMLE	MARIE		KARLSRUHE	/ /	A		F3
HEMBERLE W FAMILY	ADAM		BLANKENLOCH	01/01/1835	A		F4

Lastname	Firstname	Birth Year	Birthplace	Emigration	De	Prof	Source
HEMBERLE W FAMILY	GOTFRIED		BLANKENLOCH	01/01/1835	A		F4
HEMBULE	LUDWIG	1807	KARLSRUHE	01/01/1853	A		F3
HENNHOFER	JAKOB	1842	VÖLKERSBACH	01/01/1872	A		F4
HENNING	MATHäUS WILHELM		MICHELRIETH	05/20/1752	A		F5
HENNINGER	JAKOB	1831	GRÖTZINGEN	01/01/1853	A		F3
HENNINGER	JAKOB FRIEDRICH		GRÖTZINGEN	01/01/1853	A		F5
HENRIKUS	JOHANN		MONCHZELL	01/01/1859	A		F6
HEOR	AUGUST FELIX	1860	KARLSRUHE	01/01/1880	A		F3
HERBST	ADOLF	1849	HOCHSTETTEN	01/01/1867	A		F8
HERBST	ERNST KONRAD		HÖLLSTEIN	01/01/1859	A		F6
HERBST	KARL FRIEDRICH		HÖLLSTEIN	01/01/1859	A		F6
HERBST	KATHARINA		LIEDOLSHEIM	01/01/1880	A		F9
HERBST W F	DANIEL		LIEDOLSHEIM	09/10/1880	A		F9
HERBST W P	ALBERT		LIEDOLSHEIM	01/01/1880	A		F9
HERBST W P	AUGUST		LIEDOLSHEIM	01/01/1880	A		F9
HERBST W P	EMILIE		LIEDOLSHEIM	01/01/1880	A		F9
HERBST W P	KAROLINE		LIEDOLSHEIM	01/01/1880	A		F9
HERBST W P	LYDIA		LIEDOLSHEIM	01/01/1880	A		F9
HERBST W P	OTTO		LIEDOLSHEIM	01/01/1880	A		F9
HERBSTER	ANNA		GRABEN	/ /	A		F5
HERBSTER	FRIEDRICH		GRABEN	01/01/1804	A		F3
HERBSTER	LUDWIG	1862	GRABEN	01/01/1878	A		F3
HERBSTER MN	CHRISTINA	1857	GRABEN	01/01/1893	A		F3
HERBSTER W F	CHRISTINA	1867	GRABEN	01/01/1893	A		F8
HERBSTER W FAMILY	REINHARD	1854	GRABEN	01/01/1893	A		F3
HERBSTER W P	ELISABETH		GRABEN	01/01/1893	A		F8
HERBSTER W P	KARL	1891	GRABEN	01/01/1893	A		F8
HERBSTER W P	LINA	1889	GRABEN	01/01/1893	A		F8
HERBSTER W P	WILHELM FRIEDRH		GRABEN	01/01/1893	A		F8
HERBSTER W PARENTS	ALBERT		GRABEN	01/01/1893	A		F3
HERBSTER W PARENTS	ELISA	1887	GRABEN	01/01/1893	A		F3
HERBSTER W PARENTS	KARL	1891	GRABEN	01/01/1893	A		F3
HERBSTER W PARENTS	LINA	1889	GRABEN	01/01/1893	A		F3
HERBSTER W PARENTS	WILHELM FRIEDRH		GRABEN	01/01/1893	A		F3
HERM	JULIANE	1841	BURBACH	01/01/1856	A		F4
HERM	KAROLINA	1848	BURBACH	01/01/1856	A		F4
HERM	LEO	1840	BURBACH	01/01/1856	A		F4
HERM	MARIA THERESE G	1835	BURBACH	01/01/1856	A		F4
HERM	XAVER	1833	BURBACH	01/01/1856	A		F4
HERMANN	EDUARD	1859	KARLSRUHE	01/01/1887	A		F3
HERMANN	FRIEDRICH			01/01/1860	A		F6
HERMANN	GREGOR	1820	SÖLLINGEN	01/01/1865	A		F7
HERMANN	GUSTAV	1857	KARLSRUHE	01/01/1883	A		F3
HERMANN	JAKOB	1858	LINKENHEIM	01/01/1883	A		F8
HERMINGEN	THEODOR	1863	MÜHLBERG	01/01/1881	A		F6
HEROLD MN BRAUCH	CHRISTINE	1838	MÜHLBERG	01/01/1883	A		F6
HEROLD W F	JAKOB	1838	MÜHLBERG	01/01/1883	A		F6
HEROLD W P	JAKOB	1865	MÜHLBERG	01/01/1883	A		F6
HEROLD W P	KARL	1876	MÜHLBERG	01/01/1883	A		F6
HERR	GABRIEL	1832	MÖRSCH	01/01/1855	A		F7

Lastname	Firstname	Birth Year	Birthplace	Emigration	De	Prof	Source
HERR	JOSEF		MÖRSCH	01/01/1861	A		F7
HERRINGER	BARBARA	1796	BURBACH	01/01/1856	A		F4
HERRINGER	FRANZ	1807	BURBACH	01/01/1856	A		F4
HERRINGER	MARIA ANNA	1799	BURBACH	01/01/1856	A		F4
HERSCH	BERNHARD		KARLSRUHE	01/01/1857	A		F3
HERTL	CHRISTOPH		KARLSRUHE	01/01/1805	A		F3
HERTL	PHILLPP		KARLSRUHE	01/01/1805	A		F3
HERTWECK	ALBINA	1817	MALSCH	01/01/1843	A		F2
HERTWECK	FRANZISKA	1839	MALSCH	04/10/1854	A		F2
HERTWECK W PARENTS	REGINA	1830	MALSCH	04/10/1854	A		F2
HERTWECK MN HIPPLER	SUSANNE	1806	MALSCH	04/10/1854	A		F2
HERTWECK MN HORNUNG	KAROLINE	1838	MALSCH	05/17/1881	A		F2
HERTWECK MN KUNZ	VIKTORIA	1799	MALSCH	05/29/1846	A		F2
HERTWECK W FAMILY	ANDREAS	1820	MALSCH	05/29/1846	A		F2
HERTWECK W FAMILY	ANTON	1871	MALSCH	05/17/1881	A		F2
HERTWECK W FAMILY	CYRIAK	1804	MALSCH	04/10/1854	A		F2
HERTWECK W FAMILY	GEORG	1787	MALSCH	05/29/1846	A		F2
HERTWECK W FAMILY	JOSEF	1834	MALSCH	05/17/1881	A		F2
HERTWECK W PARENTS	ANDREAS	1825	MALSCH	04/10/1854	A		
HERTWECK W PARENTS	CAROLINE	1847	MALSCH	04/10/1854	A		F2
HERTWECK W PARENTS	FRANZ ANTON	1844	MALSCH	04/10/1854	A		F2
HERTWECK W PARENTS	FRANZ KARL	1835	MALSCH	05/29/1846	A		F2
HERTWECK W PARENTS	GENOVEFA	1837	MALSCH	04/10/1854	A		F2
HERTWECK W PARENTS	HELENA	1875	MALSCH	05/17/1881	A		F2
HERTWECK W PARENTS	JOSEF	1831	MALSCH	05/29/1846	A		F2
HERTWECK W PARENTS	JOSEF MICHAEL	1832	MALSCH	04/10/1854	A		F2
HERTWECK W PARENTS	JOSEPH	1878	MALSCH	05/17/1881	A		F2
HERTWECK W PARENTS	KARL	1834	MALSCH	04/10/1854	A		F2
HERTWECK W PARENTS	KATHARINA	1831	MALSCH	05/29/1846	A		F2
HERTWECK W PARENTS	KATHARINA	1867	MALSCH	05/17/1881	A		F2
HERTWECK W PARENTS	MARIA ANNA	1833	MALSCH	05/29/1846	A		F2
HERTWECK W PARENTS	STEPHAN	1873	MALSCH	05/17/1881	A		F2
HERTWECK W PARENTS	THEODOR	1838	MALSCH	05/29/1846	A		F2
HERTWECK W PARENTS	VINZENZ	1864	MALSCH	05/17/1881	A		F2
HERZ	HEINRICH	1866	KARLSRUHE	01/01/1882	A		F3
HERZOG	MICHAEL	1763	MALSCH	01/01/1787	A		F2
HESS	LEOPLD		KARLSRUHE	01/01/1850	A		F3
HESS MN PFAFFENROTH	LEOPOLDINE	1845	ETTLINGEN	01/01/1881	A		F4
HESS W FAMILY	PHILIPP	1837	ETTLINGEN	01/01/1881	A		F4
HESS W PARENTS	ANNA	1872	ETTLINGEN	01/01/1881	A		F4
HESS W PARENTS	PHILIPP	1878	ETTLINGEN	01/01/1881	A		F4
HESS W PARENTS	SOPHIE	1879	ETTLINGEN	01/01/1881	A		F4
HESS W PARENTS	THERESE	1871	ETTLINGEN	01/01/1881	A		F4
HESSELSCHWERDT	JAKOB FRIEDRICH	1865	LINKENHEIM	01/01/1883	A		F8
HETTEL W 7 PERSON	MICHAEL		FEUDENHEIM	01/01/1737			F1
HETTINGER	BERNHARD		BöDIGHEIM	01/01/1859	A		F6
HETTLINGER	AUGUST	1866	KARLSRUHE	01/01/1884	A		F3
HEUBERGER	JOSEF		SASBACH	01/01/1821	A		F8
HEUFER	FRIEDRICH		GRABEN	01/01/1872	A		F5
HEUFER	FRIEDRICH		GRABEN	01/01/1889	A		F5

Lastname	Firstname	Birth Year	Birthplace	Emigration	De	Prof	Source
HEUFER	WILHELM		GRABEN	/ /	A		F3
HEUFER-BECKER	PHILIPPINE		GRABEN	01/01/1872	A		F5
HEUSER	FRIEDRICH		GRABEN	01/01/1809	A		F3
HEUSER	FRIEDRICH		GRABEN	01/01/1872	A		F3
HEUSER	WILHELM	1849	GRABEN	01/01/1872	A		F8
HEUSER-BECKER	PHILIPPINE		GRABEN	01/01/1872	A		F3
HEUSS	KARL	1864	KNIELINGEN	01/01/1883	A		F6
HEYDUCK	JAKOB FRIEDRICH		SÖLLINGEN	/ /	A		F7
HEYDUCK	JAKOB FRIEDRICH		SÖLLINGEN	01/01/1856	A		F7
HEYDUCK	JOHANN GEORG	1846	SÖLLINGEN	01/01/1865	A		F7
HEYDUCK	PHILIPPINE		SÖLLINGEN	01/01/1862	A		F7
HEYDUD	PHILIPPINE		SÖLLINGEN	/ /	A		F7
HIEFE	HEINRICH	1868	KARLSRUHE	01/01/1884	A		F6
HILDEBRAND	FRANZISKA	1794	BURBACH	/ /	A		F4
HILDEBRAND MN FITTER	FRANZISKA	1847	MÖRSCH	03/09/1889	A		F7
HILDEBRAND W F	KARL	1842	MÖRSCH	03/09/1889	A		F7
HILDEBRAND W P	CHRISTINE	1872	MÖRSCH	03/09/1889	A		F7
HILDEBRAND W P	JOSEF	1884	MÖRSCH	03/09/1889	A		F7
HILDEBRAND W P	LINUS	1877	MÖRSCH	03/09/1889	A		F7
HILDEBRAND W P	PAULINE	1867	MÖRSCH	03/09/1889	A		F7
HILDEBRAND W P	SIMON	1875	MÖRSCH	03/09/1889	A		F7
HILDEBRAND W P	THEOBALD	1880	MÖRSCH	03/09/1889	A		F7
HILDEBRAND W P	WILHELM	1887	MÖRSCH	03/09/1889	A		F7
HILL	FRANZ		KARLSRUHE	/ /	A		F3
HILLER	MICHAEL		WÖSSINGEN	01/01/1832	A		F1
HILLES W SON	MICHAEL		WÖSSINGEN	/ /	A		F1
HILS	LUDWIG		SPÖCK	01/01/1865	A		F4
HILZ	PHIL.JAKOB	1835	DURLACH KARLSRUHE	/ /	A		F7
HIMMELSBACH	HERMANN	1880	KARLSRUHE	01/01/1897	A		F3
HIRT MN HÖFLE W CHIL	ROSA		ÜBERAUCHERN	01/01/1866	A		F6
HIRT W F	JOSEF		MÖRSCH	03/11/1858	A		F7
HIRTH	JAKOB	1822	MALSCH	03/01/1855	A		F2
HIRTH	JOHANN	1820	MALSCH	03/01/1855	A		F2
HIRTH	JOHANN	1864	MALSCH	01/01/1879	A		F2
HIRTH	JOSEF		MÖRSCH	01/01/1855	A		F7
HIRTH	KARL JOHANN	1826	MALSCH	01/01/1860	A		F2
HIRTH W F	JOSEF		MÖRSCH	01/01/1855	A		F7
HISCHERRICH	EMIL	1861	KARLSRUHE	01/01/1878	A		F3
HITSCHERICH	AMALIE	1834	MALSCH	01/01/1854	A		F2
HITSCHERICH	FLORIAN	1834	MALSCH	01/01/1854	A		F2
HITSCHERICH	FRANZ	1824	MALSCH	01/01/1854	A		F2
HITSCHERICH	FRANZ THEODOR	1831	MALSCH	07/13/1851	A		F2
HITSCHERICH	FRIEDLOLIN	1831	MALSCH	07/31/1857	A		F2
HITSCHERICH	JOHANN	1838	MALSCH	01/01/1854	A		F2
HITSCHERICH	WILHELM	1825	MALSCH	01/01/1851	A		F2
HOCHSTETTER	CARL	1833	DURLACH KARLSRUHE	/ /			F7
HOCHWARD	FRIEDRICH	1870	KARLSRUHE	01/01/1886	A		F3
HOER	EUGEN XAVER	1865	KARLSRUHE	01/01/1881	A		F3
HOFER	CHRISTIAN LUDWI	1864	DURLACH KARLSRUHE	/ /	A		F7
HOFER	HANS		GRABEN	01/01/1750	A		F3

Lastname	Firstname	Birth Year	Birthplace	Emigration	De	Prof	Source
HOFER W F	HANS		GRABEN	01/01/1750	A		F5
HOFFART	BERNHARD		OBERWEIER	01/01/1859	A		F6
HOFFARTH	JOSEF	1863	MALSCH	04/01/1880	A		F2
HOFFARTH	LUDWIG	1826	ETTLINGEN	04/18/1860	A		F4
HOFFARTH MN HOFFMANN	APOLLONIA	1815	MALSCH	11/12/1857	A		F2
HOFFARTH W FAMILY	WILHELM	1812	MALSCH	11/12/1857	A		F2
HOFFARTH W PARENTS	JOHANNES	1851	MALSCH	11/12/1857	A		F2
HOFFARTH W PARENTS	KATHARINA	1854	MALSCH	12/11/1857	A		
HOFFMANN	BENEDIGT		FORBACH	01/01/1860	A		F6
HOFFMANN	CARL LUDWIG		DURLACH KARLSRUHE	01/01/1867			F7
HOFFMANN	EDUARD	1851	KARLSRUHE	01/01/1878	A		F3
HOFFMANN	FRIEDRICH	1870	KARLSRUHE	01/01/1887	A		F3
HOFFMANN	GERTRUD		TAUBERBISCHOFSHEIM	01/01/1866	A		F6
HOFFMANN	MARTIN	1823	MALSCH	01/01/1845	A		F2
HOFHEINZ	AUGUST		SPöCK	01/01/1862	A		F4
HOFHEINZ	CHRISTIAN		SPöCK	01/01/1835	A		F4
HOFHEINZ	CHRISTIAN		SPöCK	01/01/1866	A		F4
HOFHEINZ	CHRISTIAN FERDD	1854	SPöCK	01/01/1881	A		F4
HOFHEINZ	DAVID		SPöCK	01/01/1854	A		F4
HOFHEINZ	E.FR.	1861	KARLSRUHE	01/01/1881	A		F3
HOFHEINZ	FERDINAND		SPöCK	01/01/1864	A		F4
HOFHEINZ	FRIEDERIKE		SPöCK	01/01/1846	A		F4
HOFHEINZ	KARL		SPöCK	01/01/1864	A		F4
HOFHEINZ	MAX FRIEDRICH	1854	SPöCK	01/01/1873	A		F4
HOFHEINZ	MAX FRIEDRICH	1854	SPöCK	01/01/1875	A		F8
HOFHEINZ	WILHELM FRIEDRI	1872	BLANKENLOCH	01/01/1890	A		F4
HOFHEINZ MN BETZNER	WILHELMINE	1813	SPöCK	01/01/1866	A		F4
HOFHEINZ W FAMILY	JOHANN		BLANKENLOCH	01/01/1862	A		F4
HOFHEINZ W FAMILY	LUDWIG	1803	SPöCK	01/01/1866	A		F4
HOFHEINZ W FAMILY	MICHEL		SPöCK	01/01/1847	A		F4
HOFHEINZ W P	AUGUST FRIEDRIH	1852	SPöCK	01/01/1866	A		F4
HOFHEINZ W P	ERNESTINE	1842	SPöCK	01/01/1866	A		F4
HOFHEINZ W P	KARL LUDWIG	1839	SPöCK	01/01/1866	A		F4
HOFHEINZ W P	KATHARINA	1847	SPöCK	01/01/1866	A		F4
HOFMANN	AUGUST	1866	KARLSRUHE	01/01/1883	A		F3
HOFMANN	CäCILIE	1848	MALSCH	10/06/1851	A		F2
HOFMANN	GEORG		BLANKENLOCH	01/01/1845	A		F4
HOFMANN	JOHANN JAKOB		SPöCK	01/01/1847	A		F4
HOFMANN	KATHARINA		GRABEN	01/01/1751	A		F3
HOFMANN	LUDWIG WILHELM	1873	KARLSRUHE	01/01/1890	A		F3
HOFMANN	MICHAEL		BLANKENLOCH	01/01/1846	A		F4
HOFMANN	MICHEL		SPöCK	01/01/1854	A		F4
HOFMANN	WILHELM	1864	KARLSRUHE	01/01/1881	A		F3
HOFMANN W PARENTS	KARL	1851	MALSCH	06/10/1851	A		F2
HOFMANN MN KNAM	SOPHIE	1818	MALSCH	10/06/1851	A		F2
HOFMANN MN KNAMM	SOPHIE		MALSCH	08/18/1846	A		F2
HOFMANN W FAMILY	JOHANN	1816	MALSCH	10/06/1851	A		F2
HOFMANN W PARENTS	ENGELBERTA	1844	MALSCH	10/06/1851	A		F2
HOFMANN W PARENTS	JOHANN		MALSCH	01/01/1846	A		F2
HOFMANN W PARENTS	LUITGART	1839	MALSCH	10/06/1851	A		F2

Lastname	Firstname	Birth Year	Birthplace	Emigration	De	Prof	Source
HOFMANN W PARENTS	VALENTIN	1846	MALSCH	08/18/1846	A		F2
HOFSASS	GEORG ADAM	1796	ETTLINGEN	01/01/1842	A		F4
HOG	JOHANN	1860	KARLSRUHE	01/01/1882	A		F3
HOH	JOHANN		HASSELBERG	04/28/1837	A		F5
HOH W F	HANS ADAM		HASSELBERG	05/08/1752	A		F5
HOHN	FRIEDRICH	1864	RINKLINGEN	01/01/1882	A		F7
HOHN	JAKOB FRIEDRICH	1863	RINKLINGEN	01/01/1882	A		F7
HOLLEMEYER	FR.	1864	KARLSRUHE	01/01/1881	A		F3
HOLZ	ERNST	1851	KARLSRUHE	01/01/1868	A		F3
HOLZ	FRIEDRICH		GRABEN	01/01/1790	A		F5
HOLZ	WILHELM		GRABEN	01/01/1802	A		F3
HOLZER	JOSEF		GRAFENHAUSEN	01/01/1859	A		F6
HOLZLEIBER	CLEMENS	1832	VÖLKERSBACH	01/01/1855	A		F4
HORBOLD	JOHANN		MÖNCHZELL	01/01/1866	A		F6
HORN	CHRISTOPH		EICHSEL	05/19/1752	A		F2
HORN	ERNST			/ /			
HORN	MARGARETHE		HECKFELD	01/01/1866	A		F6
HORN	PHILIPP		EICHSEL	05/19/1752	A		F2
HORN	SEBASTIAN		EICHSEL	04/26/1753	A		F2
HORN	STEPHAN		EICHSEL	05/04/1752			
HORN W FAMILY	STEPHAN		EICHSEL	01/01/1752	A		F2
HORNBERGER	MORIZ	1857	KARLSRUHE	01/01/1877	A		F3
HORNUNG	BERTOLD	1849	MALSCH	07/14/1867	A		F2
HORNUNG	FRANZ KARL	1855	MALSCH	08/21/1869	A		F2
HORNUNG	JOHANN		MALSCH	01/01/1866	A		F2
HORNUNG	WILHELMINE	1851	MALSCH	11/22/1866	A		F2
HORST	JAKOB RUDOLPH	1834	DURLACH KARLSRUHE	/ /			F7
HOTTEL WW 4CH	ANTON		OBERWEIER	01/01/1804			F1
HUBAND	KARL	1866	KARLSRUHE	01/01/1882	A		F3
HUBER	ANTON		MÖRSCH	04/11/1847	A		F7
HUBER	BARBARA		HILSBACH	01/01/1859	A		F6
HUBER	CLEMENS		WILMENDING	01/01/1852	A		F2
HUBER	GUSTAV FRIEDRIH		DURLACH KARLSRUHE	/ /			F7
HUBER	HANSJÖRG		BLANKENLOCH	01/01/1737	A		F4
HUBER	JAKOB		GRÖTZINGEN	01/01/1846	A		F3
HUBER	KASIMIR	1846	MÖRSCH	10/24/1867	A		F7
HUBER	LUISE MAGDALENA	1828	GRÖTZINGEN	01/01/1851	A		F3
HUBER	MAGDALENA		GRABEN	01/01/1854	A		F3
HUBER MN BRÄUTIGAM	ODILIE		MÖRSCH	05/07/1832	A		F7
HUBER MN FITTERER	ROSALIE		MÖRSCH	01/01/1832	A		F7
HUBER MN HARTWED	AGETHE		MÖRSCH	07/19/1853	A		F7
HUBER MN MÜLLER	FRANZISKA		MÖRSCH	11/06/1832	A		F7
HUBER W F	BENEDIKT		MÖRSCH	11/06/1832	A		F7
HUBER W F	CRISPEN		MÖRSCH	05/07/1832	A		F7
HUBER W F	DANIEL		MÖRSCH	07/19/1853	A		F7
HUBER W F	JAKOB		MÖRSCH	01/01/1832	A		F7
HUBER W F	JAKOB FRIEDRICH		GRABEN	01/01/1849	A		F5
HUBER W FAMILY	JAKOB FRIEDRICH		GRABEN	01/01/1849	A		F3
HUBER W P	JAKOB	1847	MÖRSCH	07/19/1853	A		F7
HUBER W P	PAUL	1840	MÖRSCH	07/19/1853	A		F7

Lastname	Firstname	Birth Year	Birthplace	Emigration	De	Prof	Source
HUBER W P	PIUS	1850	MÖRSCH	07/19/1853	A		F7
HUCK	GUSTAV	1837	MALSCH	01/01/1851	A		F2
HUCK	JOACHIM	1799	MALSCH	03/22/1858	A		F2
HUCK	KARL	1835	MALSCH	03/22/1858	A		F2
HUCK	PETER	1829	MALSCH	01/01/1854	A		F2
HUCK W PARENTS	MARIA EVA	1833	MALSCH	01/01/1851	A		F2
HUCK MN ABEN	GERTRUD		BURBACH	01/01/1858	A		F2
HUCK MN LAIBLE	BALBINE	1802	MALSCH	01/01/1851	A		F2
HUCK W APRENTS	JOSEF	1840	MALSCH	03/22/1858	A		F2
HUCK W FAMILY	KASPAR	1808	MALSCH	01/01/1851	A		F2
HUCK W PARENT	KAROLINE	1831	MALSCH	03/22/1858	A		
HUCK W PARENTS	AMALIE KATH.	1851	MALSCH	01/01/1851	A		F2
HUCK W PARENTS	FRANZISKA	1842	MALSCH	03/22/1858	A		F2
HUCK W PARENTS	GEORG	1827	MALSCH	03/22/1858	A		F2
HUCK W PARENTS	JOHANNES	1833	MALSCH	03/22/1858	A		F2
HUCK W PARENTS	KARL	1840	MALSCH	01/01/1851	A		F2
HUCK W PARENTS	SOPHIE	1849	MALSCH	01/01/1851	A		F2
HUCK W PARENTS	THEODOR	1853	MALSCH	03/22/1858	A		F2
HUCK W PARENTS	VERONIKA	1837	MALSCH	03/22/1858	A		F2
HUCKER	LEOPOLD	1876	KARLSRUHE	01/01/1892	A		F3
HUCKER	MARIA ANNA		MÖRSCH	01/01/1847	A		F7
HUCKER	MARIANN		MÖRSCH	01/25/1847	A		F7
HUF	CHRISTINA	1826	VÖLKERSBACH	01/01/1844	A		F4
HUF WW 5 CH	JOHANNES		WÖSSINGEN	01/01/1801			F1
HUG	WILHELM	1865	KARLSRUHE	01/01/1881	A		F3
HUGEL	FRIEDRICH		LAUDA	01/01/1866	A		F6
HUMMEL	AUGUST HEINRICH	1868	LIEDOLSHEIM	01/01/1886	A		F9
HUMMEL	JAKOB CHRISTIAN		DURLACH KARLSRUHE	01/01/1833			F7
HUMMEL	JOHANN FRIEDRIH		DURLACH KARLSRUHE	01/01/1836	A		F7
HUPF	KONSTANTIN		GRABEN	01/01/1882	A		F3
HUPF	KONSTANTIN		GRABEN	01/01/1882	A		F6
HUPF	LUDWIG		KARLSRUHE	01/01/1861	A		F3
HUPF	MICHAEL		GRABEN	01/01/1804	A		F3
HUPF	VALENTIN		KARLSRUHE	01/01/1181	A		F3
HURST	ADOLF	1840	DURLACH KARLSRUHE	/ /	A		F7
HURST	ADOLF	1890	DURLACH	/ /	A		F3
HUST	JAKOB		WÖSSINGEN	01/01/1796	A		F1
HUST	JOHANN ADAM		WÖSSINGEN	01/01/1832	A		F1
HUST	JOHANN JAKOB		WÖSSINGEN	01/01/1844	A	WEAV	F1
HUST W 2CH	ANDREAS		WÖSSINGEN	01/01/1832	A		F1
HUST W FATHER	CATHARINA		WÖSSINGEN	01/01/1832	A		F1
HUST W FATHER	JAKOB		WÖSSINGEN	01/01/1832	A		F1
HÜBLEIN	JOHANNES		EICHSEL	06/10/1833	A		F2
HÜLLER	LUISE	1869	KARLSRUHE	01/01/1886	A		F3
HÜTTNER	BERTHA	1883	GRABEN	01/01/1892	A		F8
HÜTTNER	HEINRICH		GRABEN	01/01/1879	A		F3
HÜTTNER	OTTO	1847	GRABEN	01/01/1892	A		F8
HÜTTNER	OTTO FRIEDRICH	1874	GRABEN	01/01/1892	A		F3
HÜTTNER	WILHELM	1872	GRABEN	01/01/1887	A		F3
HÜTTNER	WILHELM	1873	GRABEN	01/01/1887	A		F8

Lastname	Firstname	Birth Year	Birthplace	Emigration	De	Prof	Source
HÜTTNER MN BECKER	MAGDALENA	1840	GRABEN	01/01/1892	A		F8
HÜTTNER W F	JAKOB		GRABEN	01/01/1854	A		F5
HÜTTNER W FAMILY	OTTO	1848	GRABEN	01/01/1893	A		F3
HÜTTNER W P	HERMANN	1877	GRABEN	01/01/1892	A		F8
HÜTTNER W P	MARIE	1881	GRABEN	01/01/1892	A		F8
HÜTTNER W PARENTS	BERTHA	1884	GRABEN	01/01/1893	A		F3
HÜTTNER W PARENTS	HERMANN	1878	GRABEN	01/01/1893	A		F3
HÜTTNER W PARENTS	MARIE	1882	GRABEN	01/01/1893	A		F3
HÜTTNER W WIFE	JAKOB		GRABEN	01/01/1854	A		F3
HäFELE WW	KARL FRIEDRICH		WöSSINGEN	01/01/1828	A		F1
HäFNER	KONRAD		DIENSTADT	01/01/1866	A		F6
HäGER	CARL FRIEDRICH	1809	LANGENSTEINBACH	01/01/1847	A		F3
HäGER	GOTTFRIED	1816	LANGENSTEINBACH	01/01/1844	A		F3
HäGER	JAKOB	1783	LANGENSTEINBACH	01/01/1801	A		F3
HäGER MN SCHAUDEL	MAGDALENA	1817	LANGENSTEINBACH	01/01/1847	A		F3
HäGER W PARENTS	KARL FRIEDRICH	1839	LANGENSTEINBACH	01/01/1847	A		F3
HäGER W PARENTS	MARTIN	1846	LANGENSTEINBACH	01/01/1847	A		F3
HäGER W PARENTS	MICHAEL	1844	LANGENSTEINBACH	01/01/1847	A		F3
HäGER W PARENTS	PHILIPP	1843	LANGENSTEINBACH	01/01/1847	A		F3
HäGER W PARENTS	SUSANNE	1841	LANGENSTEINBACH	01/01/1847	A		F3
HäHN	AUGUST	1866	KARLSRUHE	01/01/1882	A		F3
HäMMER	FRIEDRICH		KARLSRUHE	01/01/1282	A		F3
HäMMERLE	JAKOB	1834	RINKLINGEN	01/01/1854	A		F7
HäMMERLE	MARTIN	1826	RINKLINGEN	01/01/1854	A		F7
HäMMERLE	MARTIN	1826	RINKLINGEN	10/24/1854	A		F7
HäUFER	CHRISTIAN		KARLSRUHE	01/01/1854	A		F3
HäUFER	JOHANN	1802	ETTLINGEN	04/09/1832	A		F4
HäUFER	LUISE		KARLSRUHE	01/01/1854	A		F3
HäUFER W WIFE	WILHELM		KARLSRUHE	01/01/1854	A		F3
HöFLE	GEORG JAKOB	1820	DIEDELSHEIM	01/01/1854	A		F7
HöFLE WW	HEIRNICH		WöSSINGEN	01/01/1845	A		F1
HöFLIN	WILHELM	1869	KARLSRUHE	01/01/1886	A		F3
HöGER	ELISABETH	1835	LANGENSTEINBACH	02/03/1854	A		F3
HöGER	GOTTFRIED	1816	LANGENSTEINBACH	01/01/1854	A		F3
HöGER	MAGDALENA	1832	LANGENSTEINBACH	01/01/1854	A		F3
HöGER	MARGARETHA	1839	LANGENSTEINBACH	01/01/1854	A		F3
HöGER MN NAGEL	ANNA	1778	LANGENSTEINBACH	/ /	A		F3
HöGER W WIFE	FRIEDRICH	1781	LANGENSTEINBACH	/ /	A		F3
HöLLMANN	FRANZ		RASTATT	01/01/1866	A		F6
HöRNER	JOHANN JöRG		EICHSEL	04/15/1785	A		F2
HöRNER WIDOW	FR.	1813	LIEDOLSHEIM	01/01/1881	A		F9
HöRRLE	KARL		KARLSRUHE	/ /	A		F3
HöFLE	GEORG JAKOB	1820	DIEDELSHEIM	01/01/1854	A		F7
HöRTH	MARIA	1877	ALTSCHWEIER	01/01/1895	A		F5

Lastname	Firstname	Birth Year	Birthplace	Emigration	De Prof	Source
ICHE	FRANZ JOSEF		SÖLLINGEN	01/01/1785	A	F4
IHLY MN DAUM	MARIA ANNA		MALSCH	01/01/1870	A	F2
IHLY MN TIEFENTHALER	JULIANE	1815	MALSCH	08/22/1846	A	F2
IHLY W FAMILY	FRANZ KARL	1833	MALSCH	01/01/1870	A	F2
IHLY W FAMILY	PETER	1811	MALSCH	08/22/1846	A	F2
IHLY W PARENTS	ELISABETH	1838	MALSCH	08/22/1846	A	F2
IHLY W PARENTS	ENGELBERTA	1841	MALSCH	08/22/1846	A	F2
IHLY W PARENTS	JOSEF	1856	MALSCH	01/01/1870	A	F2
IHLY W PARENTS	JOSEFA	1845	MALSCH	08/22/1846	A	F2
IHLY W PARENTS	KONRAD	1860	MALSCH	01/01/1870	A	F2
IHLY W PARENTS	SYMPHOROSE		MALSCH	08/22/1846	A	F2
IMBERG	FRANZ	1866	KARLSRUHE	01/01/1886	A	F3
IMMEL	JOHANN JAKOB		HOCHSTETTEN	01/01/1790	A	F5
ITTE	ANDR. CHRIST.FR		DURLACH KARLSRUHE	01/01/1846		F7
ITTE	JACOB HEINRICH		DURLACH KARLSRUHE	01/01/1847		F7

Lastname	Firstname	Birth Year	Birthplace	Emigration	De	Prof	Source
JAFFLER	ENGELHARD		STEIN	01/01/1825	A		F8
JAHRAUS MN KERTH	BARBARA		LINKENHEIM	01/01/1869	A		F8
JAHRAUS W W	CARL FRIEDRICH	1833	LINKENHEIM	01/01/1869	A		F8
JAKOB	C.P		GRABEN	/ /	A		F5
JAMMER MN GAMER	WILHELMINE	1868	GRABEN	01/01/1888	A		F3
JAMMER W FAMILY	KARL FRIEDRICH	1862	GRABEN	01/01/1888	A		F3
JAMMER W PARENTS	KARL FRIEDRICH	1887	GRABEN	01/01/1888	A		F3
JAMMERTHAL	CHRISTIAN	1851	HOCHSTETTEN	01/01/1869	A		F8
JAMMERTHAL	FRIEDRICH	1866	HOCHSTETTEN	01/01/1869	A		F8
JAMMERTHAL MN DüRR	FREDERIKE	1829	HOCHSTETTEN	01/01/1869	A		F8
JAMMERTHAL W F	KARL FRIEDRICH	1823	HOCHSTETTEN	01/01/1869	A		F8
JAMMERTHAL W P	AUGUST	1857	HOCHSTETTEN	01/01/1869	A		F8
JAMMERTHAL W P	KARL	1868	HOCHSTETTEN	01/01/1869	A		F8
JAMMERTHAL W P	LUISE	1863	HOCHSTETTEN	01/01/1869	A		F8
JENNE	RUDOLF	1827	DURLACH KARLSRUHE	/ /			F7
JERGER	JOHANN	1839	MALSCH	04/18/1864	A		F2
JOHAL	BIRSCH		RUFT	01/01/1865	A		F6
JOHANN	MICHAEL		WöSSINGEN	01/01/1782			F1
JOOS	FERDINAND	1849	BAUERBACH	01/01/1872	A		F8
JORDAN	ALBERT	1857	MÜHLBERG	01/01/1881	A		F6
JORDAN MN WELLER	KATHARINA		GRÖTZINGEN	01/01/1846	A		F3
JORDAN W FAMILY	CHRISTOPH	1810	GRÖTZINGEN	01/01/1846	A		F3
JORDAN W PARENTS	ANDREAS	1843	GRÖTZINGEN	01/01/1846	A		F3
JORDAN W PARENTS	KATHARINA	1845	GRÖTZINGEN	01/01/1846	A		F3
JORDAN W PARENTS	PHILIPP	1844	GRÖTZINGEN	01/01/1846	A		F3
JOST	ISAIAS	1866	BADEN	07/06/1880	A		F2
JOST	LEOPOLD		BRÖTZINGEN	01/01/1737	A		F2
JOURDAN	STEPHAN	1798	ETTLINGEN	01/01/1840	A		F4
JÜNGLING	FRANZ	1854	MALSCH	11/14/1883	A		F2
JÜNGLING	FRANZ KARL	1875	MALSCH	08/31/1889	A		F2
JäGLE	KARL	1853	DURLACH KARLSRUHE	/ /	A		F7
JäGLE MN		1850	DURLACH	01/01/1891	A		F3
JäGLE W FAMILY	JOSEF	1856	DURLACH	01/01/1891	A		F3
JäGLE W PARENTS	FRIEDRICH	1887	DURLACH	01/01/1891	A		F3
JäGLE W PARENTS	HEINRICH	1880	DURLACH	01/01/1891	A		F3
JäGLE W PARENTS	JOSEF	1889	DURLACH	01/01/1891	A		F3
JäGLE W PARENTS	KARL	1884	DURLACH	01/01/1891	A		F3
JÄCKLE	FRANZ JOSEF	1854	BÜHL	01/01/1871	A		F5
JÄGLE	JOSEF	1846	DURLACH	01/01/1891	A		F5
JöGEL	JOHANN		MALSCH	12/31/1896	A		F2
JöGEL MN KUNZENBACHR	FLORA		MALSCH	12/31/1896	A		F2
JöGEL W PARENTS	JOSEF	1884	MALSCH	12/31/1896	A		F2
JöGEL W PARENTS	KARL	1878	MALSCH	12/31/1896	A		F2
JöGEL W PARENTS	MARIA ANNA	1881	MALSCH	12/31/1896	A		F2
JöRGER	ANTON	1798	MALSCH	01/01/1845	A		F2
JöRGER	ELISABETH	1821	MALSCH	/ /			F2
JöRGER	KARL	1865	MALSCH	01/01/1887	A		F2
JöRGER	THEODOR	1865	MALSCH	01/01/1887	A		F2
JöRGER	THERESE	1823	MALSCH	01/01/1846	A		F2
JÖRGER MN GAGEL	LUDONIFA		BALG	01/01/1865	A		F8

Lastname	Firstname	Birth Year	Birthplace	Emigration	De	Prof	Source
JÖRGER W F	KARL		BALG	01/01/1865	A		F8

Lastname	Firstname	Birth Year	Birthplace	Emigration	De	Prof	Source
KAFFLEY	CHRISTIAN		DAXLANDEN	01/01/1835	A		F4
KAISER	GEORG		DISTELHAUSEN	01/01/1859	A		F6
KAISER	JOHANN FRIEDRIC		DURLACH KARLSRUHE	01/01/1826	A		F7
KAMMERE	CHRISTOPH		GRABEN	01/01/1861	A		F5
KAMMERER	AUGUST FRIEDRIC		KARLSRUHE	/ /	A		F3
KAMMERER	CARL HEINRICH		GRABEN	01/01/1868	A		F5
KAMMERER	CHRISTOPH		GRABEN	01/01/1840	A		F3
KAMMERER	GEORG		BLANKENLOCH	01/01/1847	A		F4
KAMMERER	HERMANN	1860	GRABEN	01/01/1879	A		F3
KAMMERER	HERMANN	1860	GRABEN	01/01/1879	A		F8
KAMMERER	JAKOB FRIEDRICH		GRÜNSWETTERSBACH	01/01/1849	A		F6
KAMMERER	KARL		SPÖCK	01/01/1865	A		F4
KAMMERER	KARL HEINRICH		GRABEN	01/01/1868	A		F3
KAMMERER	KATHARINA		GRABEN	01/01/1872	A		F3
KAMMERER	KATHARINA		GRABEN	01/01/1879	A		F5
KAMMERER	LUDWIG		GRABEN	01/01/1880	A		F3
KAMMERER	LUDWIG	1866	GRABEN	01/01/1880	A		F8
KAMMERER	LUISE		GRABEN	01/01/1872	A		F3
KAMMERER	PHILIPP		GRABEN	01/01/1878	A		F3
KAMMERER	PHILIPP		GRABEN	01/01/1878	A		F5
KAMMERER	SOPHIE	1859	LIEDOLSHEIM	01/01/1881	A		F9
KAMMERER	WILHELM		GRABEN	01/01/1833	A		F5
KAMMERER	WILHELM	1867	GRABEN	01/01/1883	A		F8
KAMMERER	WILHELM FRIEDRH		GRABEN	01/01/1883	A		F3
KAMMERER	WILHELMINE		GRABEN	01/01/1833	A		F3
KAMMERER NEES	WILHELM		GRABEN	01/01/1876	A		F5
KAMMERER W F	HEINRICH		GRABEN	01/01/1865	A		F5
KAMMERER W F	WILHELM		GRABEN	01/01/1847	A		F5
KAMMERER W FAMILY	HEINRICH		GRABEN	01/01/1865	A		F3
KAMMERER W FAMILY	WILHELM		GRABEN	01/01/1847	A		F3
KAMMERER- VEES	WILHELM		GRABEN	01/01/1876	A		F3
KAMMERER-BURGER	MAGDALENE		GRABEN	01/01/1881	A		F3
KAPFERER	EMIL	1870	KARLSRUHE	01/01/1891	A		F3
KAPPLER	JOSEF	1762	ETTLINGEN	/ /	A		F4
KAPPLER	LUDWIG		KARLSRUHE	01/01/1852	A		F3
KARCHER	CHRISTIAN JAKOB		DURLACH KARLSRUHE	01/01/1871	A		
KARCHER	FRIEDRICH	1799	KARLSRUHE	01/01/1874	A		F3
KARCHER	GUSTAV	1876	SPIELBERG	01/01/1897	A		F4
KARCHER MN KAUFMANN	CHRISTINE	1805	KARLSRUHE	01/01/1874	A		F3
KARCHER WW 2 SONS	JOSEF		OBERWEIER	01/01/1804			F1
KARLE	JAKOB		GRÖTZINGEN	/ /	A		F3
KARLE W FAMILY	LUDWIG		ETTLINGEN	/ /	A		F4
KARRER	GEORG MICHAEL		ZUSSENBACH	01/01/1859	A		F6
KASSEL	KATHARINA	1809	MALSCH	03/21/1858	A		F2
KASSEL W FAMILY	LEOPOLD	1803	MALSCH	03/21/1858	A		F2
KASSEL W P	KAROLINE	1854	MALSCH	03/21/1858	A		F2
KASSEL W PARENTS	GEORG	1844	MALSCH	01/01/1858	A		F2
KASSEL W PARENTS	KARL	1850	MALSCH	03/21/1858	A		F2
KASSEL W PARENTS	LUDWIG	1843	MALSCH	03/21/1858	A		F2
KASSEL W PARENTS	SOFIE MARGAREF	1840	MALSCH	01/01/1858	A		F2

Lastname	Firstname	Birth Year	Birthplace	Emigration	De	Prof	Source
KAST	CASPAR	1829	ETTLINGEN	04/23/1850	A		F4
KAST	JAKOB FRIEDRICH	1836	RINKLINGEN	01/01/1863	A		F7
KAST	LORENZ MARTIN	1850	RINKLINGEN	01/01/1869	A		F7
KAST	RUDOLF		ETTLINGEN	06/01/1873	A		F4
KASTLE	JAKOB KARL		KARLSRUHE	01/01/1853	A		F3
KASTNER	ADAM	1859	MÖRSCH	01/27/1888	A		F7
KASTNER	ALOIS W PARENS	1829	MALSCH	01/01/1857	A		F2
KASTNER	ANTON	1873	MÖRSCH	01/01/1887	A		F4
KASTNER	CHRESZENS	1829	MALSCH	/ /	A		F2
KASTNER	CHRISTIAN	1873	MÜHLBURG	01/01/1891	A		F8
KASTNER	GREGOR	1850	MALSCH	/ /	A		F2
KASTNER	JAKOB		WÖSSINGEN	01/01/1742			F1
KASTNER	JOHANN ADAM	1810	MÖRSCH	05/05/1832	A		F7
KASTNER	JOHANNES	1861	MALSCH	05/04/1880	A		F2
KASTNER	JOSEF	1864	MÖRSCH	04/23/1882	A		F7
KASTNER	JOSEFINE	1836	MALSCH	01/01/1857	A		F2
KASTNER	MARIA ANNA	1820	MALSCH	/ /	A		F2
KASTNER	MATHIAS	1835	MALSCH	/ /	A		F2
KASTNER	SEBALD		MÖRSCH	07/28/1832	A		F7
KASTNER	THOMAS	1821	MALSCH	/ /	A		F2
KASTNER	WILHELM	1825	OBERWEIER ALSACE	/ /	A		F2
KASTNER W PARENTS	ERNA	1842	MALSCH	03/06/1846	A		F2
KASTNER WIDOWER	PAUL	1795	MALSCH	01/17/1845	A		F2
KASTNER MN GRäSSER	WALBURGA	1803	MALSCH	01/01/1848	A		F2
KASTNER MN KELLER	GAGGENAU		MALSCH	03/06/1846	A		F2
KASTNER MN MECHLER	MAGDALENA	1803	OBERWEIER ALSACE	01/01/1857	A		F2
KASTNER MN SCHERER	ANNA		MÖRSCH	01/01/1889	A		F4
KASTNER MN SCHERER	ANNA		MÖRSCH	03/14/1889	A		F3
KASTNER MN SCHERER	ANNA		MÖRSCH	03/14/1899	A		F7
KASTNER MN WERNER	MARIA ANNA	1833	MALSCH	02/19/1857	A		F2
KASTNER W CHILDS	JAGNAZ		RASTATT	01/01/1866	A		F6
KASTNER W F	ANTON	1846	MÖRSCH	03/14/1899	A		F7
KASTNER W F	XAVER	1829	MÖRSCH	01/01/1881	A		F7
KASTNER W FAMILY	ANDREAS	1825	MALSCH	02/19/1857	A		F2
KASTNER W FAMILY	ANTON	1846	MÖRSCH	01/01/1889	A		F4
KASTNER W FAMILY	CYRIAK	1803	MALSCH	01/01/1857	A		F2
KASTNER W FAMILY	FRANZ KARL	1819	MALSCH	03/06/1846	A		
KASTNER W FAMILY	JOHANN	1801	MALSCH	01/01/1848	A		F2
KASTNER W P	ALOIS	1872	MÖRSCH	01/01/1881	A		F7
KASTNER W P	ANNA THERESE	1887	MÖRSCH	01/01/1889	A		F4
KASTNER W P	ANNA THERESE	1887	MÖRSCH	03/14/1899	A		F7
KASTNER W P	CAROLINE	1880	MÖRSCH	01/01/1889	A		F4
KASTNER W P	GENOFEVA	1871	MÖRSCH	03/14/1899	A		F7
KASTNER W P	GENOSEFFA	1871	MÖRSCH	01/01/1889	A		F4
KASTNER W P	JOHANN	1865	MÖRSCH	01/01/1881	A		F7
KASTNER W P	KAROLINE	1880	MÖRSCH	03/14/1899	A		F7
KASTNER W P	KATHARINA	1878	MÖRSCH	01/01/1889	A		F4
KASTNER W P	KATHARINA	1878	MÖRSCH	03/14/1899	A		F7
KASTNER W P	MAGDALENA	1875	MÖRSCH	01/01/1889	A		F4
KASTNER W P	MAGDALENA	1875	MÖRSCH	03/14/1899	A		F7

Lastname	Firstname	Birth Year	Birthplace	Emigration	De	Prof	Source
KASTNER W P	SERAPHINE	1880	MÖRSCH	01/01/1889	A		F4
KASTNER W P	SERAPHINE	1880	MÖRSCH	03/14/1899	A		F7
KASTNER W P	SILVESTER	1866	MÖRSCH	01/01/1881	A		F7
KASTNER W P	THOMAS	1868	MÖRSCH	01/01/1881	A		F7
KASTNER W PARENTS	ADAM	1840	MALSCH	03/06/1846	A		F2
KASTNER W PARENTS	ADOLF	1834	MALSCH	01/01/1857	A		F2
KASTNER W PARENTS	ANNA THERESE	1887	MÖRSCH	03/14/1889	A		F3
KASTNER W PARENTS	GENOFEVA	1871	MÖRSCH	03/14/1889	A		F3
KASTNER W PARENTS	JOSEF GEORG	1841	MALSCH	01/01/1857	A		F2
KASTNER W PARENTS	KAROLINE	1880	MÖRSCH	03/14/1889	A		F3
KASTNER W PARENTS	KATHARINA	1878	MÖRSCH	03/14/1889	A		F3
KASTNER W PARENTS	MAGDALENA	1875	MÖRSCH	03/14/1889	A		F3
KASTNER W PARENTS	REINHARD	1845	MALSCH	01/01/1857	A		F2
KASTNER W PARENTS	SERAPHINE	1880	MÖRSCH	02/14/1889	A		F3
KASTNER W PARENTS	WALBURGA	1829	MALSCH	01/01/1857	A		F2
KAUFMANN	ABRAHAM	1848	MALSCH	07/15/1890	A		F2
KAULE	EUGEN	1861	ETTLINGEN	11/11/1879	A		F4
KAULE	LUISE	1851	ETTLINGEN	07/31/1872	A		F4
KAUZ	HEINRICH		WÖSSINGEN	01/01/1835	A		F1
KAUZ WW	JOHANN CHRISTOH		WÖSSINGEN	01/01/1805	A		F1
KECHMER W CHILD	KATHARINA		ETTLINGEN	01/01/1872	A		F4
KECK	CHRISTIAN		FREISTETT	01/01/1859	A		F6
KEERN	JOSEF		SÖLLINGEN	/ /	A		F7
KEGEL	IGNAZ JOSEF	1821	ETTLINGEN	/ /	A		F4
KEHLHOFER	LUDWIG		KARLSRUHE	01/01/1860	A		F3
KEHLHOFER	WILHELM		KARLSRUHE	01/01/1861	A		F3
KEHLHOFER	WILHELM	1867	KARLSRUHE	01/01/1884	A		F3
KEHLHOFFER	JAKOB		KARLSRUHE	01/01/1860	A		F3
KEITEL	HEINRICH		OFTERSHEIM	01/01/1784			F1
KELLER	BARTHOLOME		BÜSINGEN	01/01/1859	A		F6
KELLER	DIONIS		MÖRSCH	01/01/1853	A		F7
KELLER	FRIEDRICH		ITTLINGEN	01/01/1825	A		F9
KELLER	FRIEDRICH AUGUST	1843	SPÖCK	01/01/1866	A		F4
KELLER MN FITTERER	ANNA		MÖRSCH	08/08/1853	A		F7
KELLER MN MÜLLER	PHILIPPINE		MÖRSCH	01/01/1853	A		F7
KELLER W F	DIONIS		MÖRSCH	01/01/1853	A		F7
KELLER W F	KARL		MÖRSCH	08/08/1853	A		F7
KELLER W P	FRANZISKA	1835	MÖRSCH	08/08/1853	A		F7
KELLER W P	LUDWINA	1849	MÖRSCH	08/08/1853	A		F7
KELLER W P	MAGDALENA	1840	MÖRSCH	08/08/1853	A		F7
KELLER W P	MONIKA	1846	MÖRSCH	08/08/1853	A		F7
KELLER W P	REGINA	1842	MÖRSCH	08/08/1853	A		F7
KELLER W P	WILHELM	1845	MÖRSCH	08/08/1853	A		F7
KELLER WW	PETER		WÖSSINGEN	01/01/1828	A		F1
KEMM	KARL LUDWIG		GRABEN	01/01/1868	A		F3
KEMM	WILHELM		GRABEN	01/01/1851	A		F3
KEMM MN GRÜNEWALD	ELISABETH		GRABEN	01/01/1847	A		F3
KEMM MN GRÜNEWALD	ELISABETH		GRABEN	01/01/1852	A		F5
KEMM W F	CHRISTOPH		GRABEN	01/01/1852	A		F5
KEMM W FAMILY	CHRISTOPH		GRABEN	01/01/1847	A		F3

Lastname	Firstname	Birth Year	Birthplace	Emigration	De	Prof	Source
KEMPTER	EMIL	1886	KARLSRUHE	/ /	A		F3
KEPPLER	CHRISTIAN		GRÖTZINGEN	01/01/1852	A		F5
KEPPLER	CHRISTINA		GRÖTZINGEN	/ /	A		F3
KERLE	MATHÄUS		ÖTIGHEIM	01/01/1795	A		F6
KERN	JAKOB		GRÖTZINGEN	01/01/1817	A		F5
KERN	JOHANN PHILIPP		WAIBSTADT	01/01/1859	A		F6
KERN	JOSEF		SÖLLINGEN	01/01/1867	A		F7
KERN	KARL		GRÖTZINGEN	01/01/1853	A		F5
KERN	LUISE		GRÖTZINGEN	/ /	A		F3
KERN	LUISE		GRÖTZINGEN	01/01/1852	A		F5
KERN	NIKOLAUS		KREUZWERTHEIM	05/23/1840	A		F5
KERNBERGER	ADAM		BRUCHSAL	01/01/1866	A		F6
KIBI	KORNELIA	1820	MALSCH	01/01/1856	A		F2
KIEFER	AUGUST		KARLSRUHE	/ /	A		F3
KIEFER	CHRISTIAN		KARLSRUHE	01/01/1844	A		F3
KIEFER	DOROTHEA		WÖSSINGEN	01/01/1829	A		F1
KIEFER	FRIEDRICH	1853	KARLSRUHE	01/01/1874	A		F3
KIEFER	GEORG JAKOB	1847	BLANKENLOCH	01/01/1869	A		F4
KIEFER	GUSTAV HEINRICH	1875	KARLSRUHE	01/01/1890	A		F3
KIEFER	JAKOB	1864	RÜPPUR	01/01/1881	A		F8
KIEFER	KARL FRIEDRICHE	1858	KARLSRUHE	01/01/1858	A		F3
KIEFER	WILHELM	1864	RÜPPUR	01/01/1882	A		F8
KIEFER MN MÜLLER	KAROLINE	1819	ETTLINGEN	01/01/1847	A		F4
KIEFER W FAMILY	JOHANN JAKOB	1812	ETTLINGEN	01/01/1847	A		F4
KIEFER W PARENTS	HEINRICH	1846	ETTLINGEN	01/01/1847	A		F4
KIENLE	HERMAN	1869	KARLSRUHE	01/01/1886	A		F3
KIES	CHRISTINE	1801	LANGENSTEINBACH	03/29/1832	A		F3
KIES	JAKOB		LANGENSTEINBACH	03/29/1832	A		F3
KIES	MARGARETHA	1815	LANGENSTEINBACH	01/01/1832	A		F3
KIESECKER W F	JOHANNES		KREDENBACH	01/01/1761	A		F5
KIESELE	KARL FRIEDRICH		KARLSRUHE	01/01/1852	A		F3
KIESSLING WW	FELIX		WÖSSINGEN	01/01/1803			F1
KIFFEL	RUDOLF		ETTLINGEN	01/01/1882	A		F4
KILIAN	HERR		SÖLLINGEN	/ /	A		F7
KILIAN	KARL		KORB/BUCHEN	12/04/1887	A		F1
KILLI	ISIDOR		VORDRACH	01/01/1859	A		F6
KIMPFER	JAKOB		DURLACH	01/01/1854	A		F6
KINDER MN	MAGDALENA	1858	GRASFELD	01/01/1883	A		F6
KINDER W F	JOHANN LUDWIG	1856	GRASFELD	01/01/1885	A		F6
KINDER W P	KAROLINE	1882	GRASFELD	01/01/1883	A		F6
KING	LUDWIG EDUARD	1855	KARLSRUHE	01/01/1872	A		F3
KINSCH	MICHAEL			/ /			
KINSCH WW	MICHAEL		WÖSSINGEN	01/01/1828	A		F1
KINZINGER	GEORG		IMPFINGEN	01/01/1866	A		F6
KIRCHBAUER	MICHAEL FRIEDRH	1853	LANGENSTEINBACH	/ /	A		F3
KIRCHBAUER MN MALTAR	MARIA KATHARINA	1800	LANGENSTEINBACH	03/24/1828	A		F3
KIRCHBAUER MN MÜLLER	KATHARINA	1848	LANGENSTEINBACH	/ /	A		F3
KIRCHBAUER W FAMILY	GEORG MARTIN	1791	LANGENSTEINBACH	03/24/1828	A		F3
KIRCHBAUER W FAMILY	JAKOB	1848	LANGENSTEINBACH	/ /	A		F3
KIRCHBAUER W PAREN	KARL	1871	SÖLLINGEN	01/01/1881	A		F7

Lastname	Firstname	Birth Year	Birthplace	Emigration	De	Prof	Source
KIRCHBAUER W PAREN	KAROLINE	1868	SÖLLINGEN	01/01/1881	A		F7
KIRCHBAUER W PAREN	MARGARETHA	1867	SÖLLINGEN	01/01/1881	A		F7
KIRCHBAUER W PARENTS	ANTONIE	1876	LANGENSTEINBACH	/ /	A		F3
KIRCHBAUER W PARENTS	FRIEDA	1881	SÖLLINGEN	01/01/1881	A		F7
KIRCHBAUER W PARENTS	FRIEDRICH	1874	LANGENSTEINBACH	/ /	A		F3
KIRCHBAUER W PARENTS	GEORG KRAFT	1820	LANGENSTEINBACH	03/24/1828	A		F3
KIRCHBAUER W PARENTS	GEORG MARTIN	1822	LANGENSTEINBACH	03/24/1828	A		F3
KIRCHBAUER W PARENTS	JULIANE	1825	LANGENSTEINBACH	03/24/1828	A		F3
KIRCHBAUER W PARENTS	LUDWIG	1882	LANGENSTEINBACH	/ /	A		F3
KIRCHBAUER W PARENTS	LUISE	1874	SÖLLINGEN	01/01/1881	A		F7
KIRCHBAUER W PARENTS	MAGDALENA	1818	LANGENSTEINBACH	03/24/1828	A		F3
KIRCHBAUER W PARENTS	PHILIPP WILHELM	1879	LANGENSTEINBACH	/ /	A		F3
KIRCHBAUER W PARENTS	REGINA	1872	LANGENSTEINBACH	/ /	A		F3
KIRCHENBAUER	ERNST LEOPOLD		SÖLLINGEN	01/01/1882	A		F7
KIRCHENBAUER	LUISE	1865	SÖLLINGEN	01/01/1881	A		F3
KIRCHENBAUER	MAX	1877	SPÖCK	01/01/1892	A		F4
KIRCHENBAUER	MICHAEL FRIEDRI	1853	LANGENSTEINBACH	/ /	A		F3
KIRCHENBAUER MN MÜLL	KATHARINA	1895	LANGENSTEINBACH	/ /	A		F3
KIRCHENBAUER MN WALT	MARIA KATHARINA	1800	LANGENSTEINBACH	03/24/1828	A		F3
KIRCHENBAUER MN WEIS	KATHARINA BARBA	1840	SÖLLINGEN	01/01/1881	A		F7
KIRCHENBAUER MN WEIS	KATHARINA BARBA	1846	SÖLLINGEN	01/01/1881	A		F3
KIRCHENBAUER W FAMIL	GEORG MARTIN	1791	LANGENSTEINBACH	03/24/1828	A		F3
KIRCHENBAUER W FAMIL	JAKOB	1848	LANGENSTEINBACH	/ /	A		F3
KIRCHENBAUER W FAMIY	KARL FRIEDRICH	1840	SÖLLINGEN	01/01/1881	A		F7
KIRCHENBAUER W P	GEORG KRAFT	1820	LANGENSTEINBACH	03/24/1828	A		F3
KIRCHENBAUER W PAREN	ANTONIE	1876	LANGENSTEINBACH	/ /	A		F3
KIRCHENBAUER W PAREN	FRIEDA	1879	SÖLLINGEN	01/01/1881	A		F3
KIRCHENBAUER W PAREN	FRIEDRICH	1874	LANGENSTEINBACH	/ /	A		F3
KIRCHENBAUER W PAREN	GEORG MARTIN	1822	LANGENSTEINBACH	03/24/1828	A		F3
KIRCHENBAUER W PAREN	JAKOB FRIEDRICH	1877	SÖLLINGEN	01/01/1881	A		F3
KIRCHENBAUER W PAREN	JULIANE	1825	LANGENSTEINBACH	03/24/1828	A		F3
KIRCHENBAUER W PAREN	KARL	1871	SÖLLINGEN	01/01/1887	A		F3
KIRCHENBAUER W PAREN	KAROLINE	1868	SÖLLINGEN	01/01/1881	A		F3
KIRCHENBAUER W PAREN	LUDWIG	1882	LANGENSTEINBACH	/ /	A		F3
KIRCHENBAUER W PAREN	MAGDALENA	1818	LANGENSTEINBACH	03/24/1828	A		F3
KIRCHENBAUER W PAREN	MARGARETHE	1867	SÖLLINGEN	01/01/1881	A		F3
KIRCHENBAUER W PAREN	PHILIPP WILHELM	1879	LANGENSTEINBACH	/ /	A		F3
KIRCHENBAUER W PAREN	REGINA	1872	LANGENSTEINBACH	/ /	A		F3
KIRCHGEHER	ELEONORA		BUCHEN	01/01/1859	A		F6
KIRNBERGER	KARL		MÖRSCH	01/01/1832	A		F7
KIRNBERGER	LORENZ		MÖRSCH	01/01/1847	A		F7
KISLING WW 7CH	PHILIPP		WÖSSINGEN	05/05/1803			F1
KISSLING WW CH	ADAM		WÖSSINGEN	01/01/1803			F1
KIST	VALENTIN	1805	LANGENSTEINBACH	/ /	A		F3
KIST MN HARTMANN	MARTHA	1802	LANGENSTEINBACH	01/01/1835	A		F3
KIST W FAMILY	MICHAEL	1802	LANGENSTEINBACH	01/01/1835	A		F3
KIST W PARENTS	PHILIPP JAKOB	1834	LANGENSTEINBACH	01/01/1835	A		F3
KISTNER	APPOLONIA	1846	MALSCH	11/03/1853	A		F2
KISTNER	CRESZENZ	1853	MALSCH	10/31/1854	A		F2
KISTNER	JAKOB	1812	MALSCH	04/12/1831	A		F2

Lastname	Firstname	Birth Year	Birthplace	Emigration	De	Prof	Source
KISTNER	LORENZ	1790	MALSCH	01/01/1890	A		F2
KISTNER	MARIA ANNA	1825	MALSCH	03/25/1832	A		F2
KISTNER	WILLIBALD		MALSCH	01/01/1832	A		F2
KISTNER MN HITSCHERH	HELENE	1803	MALSCH	03/25/1831	A		F2
KISTNER MN MAIER	MARIA EVA	1770	MALSCH	05/24/1832	A		F2
KISTNER MN SCHRAFT	GERTRUD	1817	MALSCH	02/18/1846	A		F2
KISTNER W CH	ELISABETH	1825	MALSCH	11/03/1853	A		F2
KISTNER W CH	HELENE	1839	MALSCH	10/31/1854	A		F2
KISTNER W CHILD	MARIA EVA		ETTLINGEN	01/01/1881	A		F4
KISTNER W FAMILY	DAMIAN	1815	MALSCH	02/28/1846	A		F2
KISTNER W FAMILY	GEORG	1760	MALSCH	01/01/1832	A		F2
KISTNER W FAMILY	WILLIBALD	1790	MALSCH	03/25/1832	A		F2
KISTNER W MOTHER	ROSA		ETTLINGEN	01/01/1881	A		F4
KISTNER W PARENTS	CäCILIE	1842	MALSCH	02/28/1846	A		F2
KISTNER W PARENTS	JOHANNES	1829	MALSCH	03/25/1832	A		F2
KISTNER W PARENTS	KAROLINE	1830	MALSCH	01/01/1832	A		F2
KISTNER W PARENTS	PETER	1846	MALSCH	02/28/1846	A		F2
KISTNER W PARENTS	VALENTIN	1838	MALSCH	02/28/1846	A		F2
KITTEL MN DOLZ	FRANZISKA	1800	MÖRSCH	09/09/1842	A		F7
KITTEL MN KNÄBEL	MARGARETHA		MÖRSCH	08/08/1853	A		F7
KITTEL MN SCHMADEL	MARIA ANNA		MÖRSCH	07/21/1853	A		F7
KITTEL W F	HIERONIMUS		MÖRSCH	09/09/1842	A		F7
KITTEL W F	JOSEF		MÖRSCH	07/21/1853	A		F7
KITTEL W F	ULRICH		MÖRSCH	08/08/1853	A		F7
KITTEL W P	ANTON	1849	MÖRSCH	08/08/1853	A		F7
KITTEL W P	JOSEF	1826	MÖRSCH	09/09/1842	A		F7
KITTEL W P	ULRICH	1823	MÖRSCH	09/09/1842	A		F7
KITTEL W P	XAVER	1852	MÖRSCH	07/21/1853	A		F7
KLAIBER	JOSEF		VöLKERSBACH	05/21/1852	A		F4
KLAIBER W F	JAKOB		DURLACH	01/01/1847	A		F6
KLEEHAMMER	JOHANN		FORBACH	01/01/1854	A		F6
KLEIBER	JOHANN KARL	1860	DURLACH KARLSRUHE	/ /	A		F7
KLEIBER	LUDWIG ANDREAS	1854	DURLACH KARLSRUHE	/ /	A		
KLEIN	AMBROS	1828	MÖRSCH	01/01/1854	A		F7
KLEIN	ANDREAS	1827	MALSCH	06/24/1846	A		F2
KLEIN	FRIEDRICH KARL	1829	MALSCH	06/24/1846	A		F2
KLEIN	FRIODOLIN	1831	MALSCH	06/24/1846	A		F2
KLEIN	JAKOB	1805	LANGENSTEINBACH	01/01/1840	A		F3
KLEIN	JOHANNES	1833	MALSCH	06/24/1846	A		F2
KLEIN	MAGDALENA	1836	MALSCH	06/24/1846	A		F2
KLEIN	OTTO		ETTLINGEN	/ /	A		F4
KLEIN MN BACHMEIER	VERONIKA	1801	MALSCH	06/24/1846	A		F2
KLEIN MN GREULE	ELISABETH		ETTLINGEN	/ /	A		F4
KLEIN MN SEITZ	BARBARA		ETTLINGEN	04/26/1852	A		F4
KLEIN W FAMILY	MICHAEL	1802	MALSCH	06/24/1846	A		F2
KLEIN W WIFE	JAKOB	1819	ETTLINGEN	/ /	A		F4
KLEIN W WIFE	JAKOB	1825	ETTLINGEN	04/26/1852	A		F4
KLEINFREUZ	HERR		SöLLINGEN	/ /	A		F7
KLEINHANS	ERNESTINE	1847	RINKLINGEN	01/01/1870	A		F7
KLEINHANS	JONAS	1815	RINKLINGEN	01/01/1840	A		F7

Lastname	Firstname	Birth Year	Birthplace	Emigration	De	Prof	Source
KLEINHANS	LEONHARD	1821	RINKLINGEN	01/01/1853	A		F7
KLEINHAUS	ERNESTINE	1847	RINKLINGEN	03/14/1870	A		F7
KLEINHAUS	JONAS	1815	RINKLINGEN	08/18/1840	A		F7
KLEINHAUS	LEONHARD	1821	RINKLINGEN	01/01/1853	A		F7
KLEM	PETER		WÖSSINGEN	01/01/1832	A	BUTC	F1
KLEMM	NEPOMUK		GURTWAIL	01/01/1854	A		F6
KLENERT	ADAM	1832	DURLACH KARLSRUHE	/ /	A		F7
KLENERT	CARL LUDWIG	1835	DURLACH KARLSRUHE	/ /			F7
KLENERT	FRIEDRICH	1837	DURLACH KARLSRUHE	/ /			F7
KLENERT	FRIEDRICH CARL	1839	DURLACH KARLSRUHE	/ /	A		F7
KLETT	CARL	1850	DURLACH KARLSRUHE	/ /	A		F7
KLETT WID.	MARGARETHA	1799	SÖLLINGEN	01/01/1854	A		F7
KLETTENHEIMER	FLORIAN	1829	ETTLINGEN	01/22/1855	A		F4
KLETTENHEIMER	WALBURGA	1822	ETTLINGEN	10/30/1856	A		F4
KLEY	ROBERT	1862	KARLSRUHE	01/01/1881	A		F3
KLINGEL	GEORG		EISINGEN	01/01/1825	A		F9
KLOSE	FRIEDRICH	1862	KARLSRUHE	01/01/1882	A		F3
KLOTZ	JAKOB	1855	RÜPPUR	01/01/1874	A		F8
KLUMPP	MAX	1869	KARLSRUHE	01/01/1886	A		F3
KNAB	GEORG MARTIN	1830	LANGENSTEINBACH	01/01/1848	A		F3
KNAB	JOHANN DANIEL	1828	LANGENSTEINBACH	01/01/1861	A		F3
KNAB	JULIANE	1832	LANGENSTEINBACH	01/01/1861	A		F3
KNAB MN DENNINGER	MAGDALENA	1795	LANGENSTEINBACH	02/24/1830	A		F3
KNAB MN UDELE	MARGARETHA		LANGENSTEINBACH	01/01/1830	A		F3
KNAB W FAMILY	JOHANN GEORG	1797	LANGENSTEINBACH	02/24/1830	A		F3
KNAB W FAMILY	SIMON	1788	LANGENSTEINBACH	01/01/1830	A		F3
KNAB W PARENTS	GEORG	1821	LANGENSTEINBACH	02/24/1830	A		F3
KNAB W PARENTS	JAKOB FRIEDRICH	1850	LANGENSTEINBACH	02/24/1830	A		F3
KNAB W PARENTS	KARL	1817	LANGENSTEINBACH	01/01/1830	A		F3
KNAB W PARENTS	KATHARINA	1820	LANGENSTEINBACH	02/24/1830	A		F3
KNAB W PARENTS	MAGDALENA	1820	LANGENSTEINBACH	02/24/1830	A		F3
KNAB W PARENTS	SIMON	1824	LANGENSTEINBACH	01/01/1830	A		F3
KNAM	FRIEDRICH SIMON	1785	MALSCH	01/01/1848	A		F2
KNAMM	FERDINAND	1818	MALSCH	01/01/1859	A		F2
KNAMM	FLORIAN	1837	MALSCH	01/01/1848	A		F2
KNAMM	FRANZ	1836	MALSCH	01/01/1848	A		F2
KNAMM	HELENE	1843	MALSCH	01/01/1848	A		F2
KNAMM	JOHANN	1821	MALSCH	01/01/1859	A		F2
KNAMM	JOHANNA	1816	MALSCH	01/01/1859	A		F2
KNAMM	KAROLINE	1841	MALSCH	01/01/1848	A		F2
KNAMM	LEOPOLD	1839	MALSCH	01/01/1859	A		F2
KNAMM	OTTILIE	1825	MALSCH	01/01/1848	A		F2
KNAMM	SOPHIE	1827	MALSCH	01/01/1859	A		F2
KNAMM MN RENZ	GERTRUDE	1805	MALSCH	01/01/1848	A		F2
KNAMM W FAMILY	PHILIPP	1799	MALSCH	01/01/1848	A		F2
KNAPPSCHNEIDER	JOAHNN ADAM	1843	DURLACH KARLSRUHE	/ /	A		F7
KNAPPSCHNEIDER	LISETTE		DURLACH	01/01/1865	A		F6
KNAUER	HANS		ALTFELD	/ /	A		F5
KNAUER	JOHANN CASPAR		KREDENBACH	01/01/1754	A		F5
KNAUER W F	ANDREAS		ALTFELD	04/17/1751	A		F5

Lastname	Firstname	Birth Year	Birthplace	Emigration	De	Prof	Source
KNECHT	CARL FRIEDRICH	1859	DURLACH KARLSRUHE	/ /	A		F7
KNECHT	GEORG FRIEDRICH		KARLSRUHE	/ /	A		FE
KNMAB W PARENTS	MMAGDALENA	1820	LANGENSTEINBACH	01/01/1830	A		F3
KNOBEL	WILHELM	1753	LANGENSTEINBACH	01/01/1780	A		F3
KNOCH	CHRISTIAN ROBER	1867	KARLSRUHE	01/01/1887	A		F3
KNOLL	FRANZ ANTON	1809	PFAFFENROTH	/ /	A		F7
KNOLL	KATHARINA	1798	PFAFFENROTH	/ /	A		F7
KNOLL	MARIA ANNA	1832	PFAFFENROTH	01/01/1853	A		F7
KNUTTEL	FRANZ		DITTIGHEIM	01/01/1866	A		F6
KNÄBEL	JOHANN	1839	MÖRSCH	11/17/1865	A		F7
KNÄBEL	JOSEF		MÖRSCH	01/01/1831	A		F7
KNÄBEL MN BURKARDT	UFRA		MÖRSCH	05/05/1832	A		F7
KNÄBEL MN RASTETTER	MARIA ANNA		MÖRSCH	08/08/1853	A		F7
KNÄBEL W F	SIMON		MÖRSCH	05/05/1832	A		F7
KNÄBEL W F	VALENTIN		MÖRSCH	08/08/1853	A		F7
KNÄBEL W P	JOSEF	1849	MÖRSCH	08/08/1853	A		F7
KNÄBEL W P	LUDWIG	1851	MÖRSCH	08/08/1853	A		F7
KNÖRR	FRIEDRICH		RAUENBERG	01/01/1866	A		F6
KNÖDEL	JOSEF		MÖRSCH	01/01/1831	A		F7
KOCH	AMAND		ORSCHWEIER	01/01/1852	A		F2
KOCH	BARBARA	1820	MALSCH	01/01/1853	A		F2
KOCH	DEBZELAUS ?	1815	MALSCH	01/01/1853	A		F2
KOCH	ERASMUS	1837	MALSCH	01/01/1848	A		F2
KOCH	FRANZ JOSEF	1848	MALSCH	01/01/1898	A		F2
KOCH	FRANZ KARL	1830	MALSCH	01/01/1853	A		F2
KOCH	JOHANN	1825	MALSCH	01/01/1853	A		F2
KOCH	JOHANN HEINRICH	1877	MALSCH	09/07/1893	A		F2
KOCH	JOHANNES	1845	MALSCH	02/04/1846	A		F2
KOCH	JOSEFINE	1833	MALSCH	01/01/1848	A		F2
KOCH	MARIANNE	1842	MALSCH	04/02/1846	A		F2
KOCH	MATHIAS	1824	MALSCH	01/01/1848	A		F2
KOCH	MECHTILDE		FORBACH	01/01/1854	A		F6
KOCH	NOTBURGA	1828	MALSCH	01/01/1848	A		F2
KOCH	SEBASTIAN	1828	MALSCH	01/01/1851	A		F2
KOCH	THEODOR	1840	MALSCH	04/02/1846	A		F2
KOCH	VALENTIN	1823	MALSCH	01/01/1853	A		F2
KOCH	WILHELM	1848	KARLSRUHE	01/01/1893	A		F3
KOCH MN KASTNER	LUITGARD		MALSCH	04/02/1846	A		
KOCH MN MAIER	WALBURGA	1793	MALSCH	01/01/1848	A		F2
KOCH W FAMILY	FRANZ WILHELM		MALSCH	01/01/1848	A		F2
KOCH W FAMILY	GEORG	1813	MALSCH	04/02/1826	A		F2
KOHLENREUTHER	WILHELM		MALSCH	01/01/1850	A		F2
KOHLMANN	JOSEF		DAXLANDEN	01/01/1872	A		F6
KOHLMANN	JOSEF	1864	KARLSRUHE	01/01/1872	A		F3
KOHNLE	ANDREAS		PFAFFENROTH	01/01/1854	A		
KOHNLE	ANDREAS		WÖSSINGEN	01/01/1842	A		F1
KOLLER	LEONHARD		HÜNGHEIM	01/01/1859	A		F6
KONANZ	JAKOB	1847	BRETTEN	01/01/1867	A		F8
KONFAD	BERNHARD	1862	KARLSRUHE	01/01/1883	A		F3
KONRAD	FRIEDRICH		KARLSRUHE	01/01/1868	A		F3

Lastname	Firstname	Birth Year	Birthplace	Emigration	De	Prof	Source
KONRAD	MATHäUS		GRABEN	01/01/1798	A		F5
KONSTANTIN	ANTON		UNTERWULSCHE	01/01/1861	A		F6
KOPPEL	KARL	1863	KARLSRUHE	10/10/1880	A		F3
KOREVAAR	IRMA		KARLSRUHE	/ /	A		F3
KORLE	JAKOB FRIEDRICH		GRöTZINGEN	01/01/1861	A		F5
KORN	GABRIEL		DURLACH KARLSRUHE	01/01/1832	A		F7
KORN	RUDOLF	1826	ETTLINGEN	01/01/1847	A		F4
KORN MN BESSEL	BARBARA		ETTLINGEN	/ /	A		F4
KORN W FAMILY	ALOIS		WALDMATH	04/07/1798	A		F1
KORN W WIFE	FRANZ	1776	ETTLINGEN	/ /	A		F4
KORNMÜLLER	HEINRICH		SPIELBERG	01/01/1889	A		F1
KORNMÜLLER	WILHELM	1858	RÜPPUR	01/01/1874	A		F8
KORNMÜLLER	WILHELM FRIEDRI	1863	RÜPPUR	01/01/1880	A		F8
KORWAN	KARL	1865	KARLSRUHE	01/01/1883	A		F3
KRAFFT	FRIEDRICH		RIEDERWEILER	01/01/1859	A		F6
KRAFT	ADELHEIDE	1838	MALSCH	01/01/1886	A		F2
KRAFT	ALBERT	1859	KARLSRUHE	01/01/1876	A		F3KRAT
KRAFT	ALOIS	1831	SPESSART	01/01/1846	A		F4
KRAFT	FERDINAND	1840	SPESSART	08/18/1862	A		F4
KRAFT	FRANZ IGNAZ		SPESSART	01/01/1845	A		F4
KRAFT	FRANZISKA	1810	ETTLINGEN	01/01/1832	A		F4
KRAFT	GEORG	1807	MALSCH	01/01/1832	A		F2
KRAFT	JOSEF	1778	ETTLINGEN	01/01/1818	A		F4
KRAFT	JOSEF	1833	SPESSART	02/09/1852	A		F4
KRAFT	JOSEF	1836	MALSCH	08/10/1846	A		F2
KRAFT	KARL		KARLSRUHE	01/01/1848	A		F3
KRAFT	KAROLINE	1834	MALSCH	08/10/1846	A		F2
KRAFT	STEPHAN	1849	MALSCH	/ /	A		F2
KRAFT	VERONIKA	1838	MALSCH	08/10/1846	A		F2
KRAFT MN GRäSSER	HELENE	1838	MALSCH	08/20/1880	A		F2
KRAFT MN WEISHAUPT	ELISABETH	1808	MALSCH	08/10/1846	A		F2
KRAFT W FAMILY	JOHANN BAPTIST	1837	MALSCH	08/20/1880	A		F2
KRAFT W FAMILY	KARL	1809	MALSCH	08/10/1846	A		F2
KRAFT W PARENTS	ANNA	1877	MALSCH	01/01/1880	A		F2
KRAFT W PARENTS	HERMANN	1872	MALSCH	08/20/1880	A		F2
KRAFT W PARENTS	JOHANNES	1879	MALSCH	08/20/1880	A		F2
KRAFT W PARENTS	KARL	1869	MALSCH	08/20/1880	A		F2
KRAFT W PARENTS	PIUS	1880	MALSCH	08/20/1880	A		F2
KRAFT W PARENTS	THEODOR	1870	MALSCH	08/20/1880	A		F2
KRAFT W PARENTS	THERESE	1867	MALSCH	08/20/1880	A		F2
KRALL	EDUARD	1858	KARLSRUHE	01/01/1866	A		F3
KRALL	LUDWIG		KARLSRUHE	/ /	A		F3
KRAMER	JAKOB		WöSSINGEN	01/01/1854	A		F1
KRAMER	MARIA VICTORIA		ETTLINGEN	01/01/1841	A		F4
KRAMMERER	WILHELM		KARLSRUHE	01/01/1833	A		F3
KRANK	HANS		HASSELBERG	05/20/1752	A		F5
KRANK W F	JOHANNES		BESTENHEID	05/12/1752	A		F5
KRASS	JAKOB FRIEDRICH	1841	GRABEN	01/01/1869	A		F8
KRASS MN METZGER	CHRISTINE	1846	GRABEN	01/01/1869	A		F8
KRASS W P	WILHELM FRIEDRH	1868	GRABEN	01/01/1869	A		F8

- 78 -

Lastname	Firstname	Birth Year	Birthplace	Emigration	De	Prof	Source
KRATTINGER	FRIEDRICH		KARLSRUHE	/ /	A		F3
KRAUS	ALBERT	1876	MÖRSCH	01/01/1892	A		F4
KRAUS	ALBERT	1876	MÖRSCH	09/12/1893	A		F7
KRAUS	ALBERT OTTO		ETTLINGEN	/ /	A		F4
KRAUS	AUGUST		KARLSRUHE	/ /	A		F3
KRAUS	CHRISTOPH		GRABEN	01/01/1799	A		F5
KRAUS	CHRISTOPH		GRABEN	01/01/1823	A		F3
KRAUS	FRIEDRICH		GRABEN	01/01/1793	A		F3
KRAUS	HERMANN		GRÖTZINGEN	01/01/1864	A		F5
KRAUS	JAKOB FRIEDRICH		GRABEN	01/01/1869	A		F3
KRAUS	JAKOB FRIEDRICH		GRABEN	01/01/1869	A		F5
KRAUS	PHILIPP	1829	GRABEN	01/01/1856	A		F3
KRAUS	PHILIPP	1852	GRABEN	01/01/1870	A		F3
KRAUS	SEBASTIAN	1818	SPESSART	01/01/1858	A		F4
KRAUS	WILHELM	1877	KARLSRUHE	01/01/1893	A		F3
KRAUS	WILHELM LUDWIG		GRABEN	01/01/1890	A		F3
KRAUS W WIFE	HEINRICH		SÖLLINGEN	/ /	A		F7
KRAUS-TREFFEISEN	PHILIPPINE		GRAMER	01/01/1874	A		F3
KRAUSS	AUGUST		KARLSRUHE	/ /	A		F3
KREIDEWEISS	ALEXANDER	1834	MÖRSCH	01/01/1888	A		F7
KREIDEWEISS	ANTONIE	1878	MÖRSCH	/ /	A		F3
KREIDEWEISS W F	ALEXANDER	1834	MÖRSCH	/ /	A		F3
KREIDEWEISS W P	J	1870	MÖRSCH	/ /	A		F3
KREIDEWEISS W P	JOSEF	1873	MÖRSCH	/ /	A		F3
KREIDEWEISS W P	KATHARINA	1875	MÖRSCH	/ /	A		F3
KREIDEWEISS WP	MARTHA	1881	MÖRSCH	/ /	A		F3
KREIS	MARIA EVA	1872	BÜCHIG	01/01/1890	A		F8
KRES	KARL FRIEDRICH	1859	KARLSRUHE	01/01/1871	A		F3
KRETZ	OSWALD	1825	ETTLINGEN	/ /	A		F4
KRETZ MN KÜHNER	MARGARETHA		ETTLINGEN	02/29/1852	A		F4
KRETZ MN REISS	MRGARETHA		ETTLINGEN	/ /	A		F4
KRETZ W CHILD	JOHANN		ETTLINGEN	01/01/1872	A		F4
KRETZ W CHILD	KAROLINE	1820	ETTLINGEN	01/01/1872	A		F4
KRETZ W FAMILY	LEONHARD	1808	ETTLINGEN	02/29/1852	A		F4
KRETZ W FATHER	KARL	1854	ETTLINGEN	01/01/1872	A		F4
KRETZ W PARENTS		1849	ETTLINGEN	02/29/1852	A		F4
KRETZ W WIFE	ALEXANDER		ETTLINGEN	/ /	A		F4
KREUTNER	LUDWIG	1833	KARLSRUHE	01/01/1852	A		F3
KRIEG	BARTEL		GAMBURG?	01/01/1859	A		F6
KRIEG	CHRISTOPH	1828	DURLACH KARLSRUHE	/ /			F7
KRIEG	FRIEDRICH PHILP		DURLACH KARLSRUHE	01/01/1835			F7
KRIEG	JOSEF		GAMBURG	01/01/1859	A		F6
KRIEG	SEBASTIAN		GAMBURG	01/01/1859	A		F6
KRIEGER	CHRISTOPH		GRÖTZINGEN	01/01/1851	A		F5
KRIEGER	FRIEDRICH		GRÖTZINGEN	01/01/1851	A		F5
KRIEGER	JOHANN		GRÖTZINGEN	/ /	A		F3
KRIEGER	PHILIPP		GRÖTZINGEN	01/01/1851	A		F5
KRIEGER	PHILIPP	1801	GRÖTZINGEN	01/01/1852	A		F3
KRIEGER	WILHELMINE		GRÖTZINGEN	01/01/1864	A		F3
KRIFF	ALBERT	1844	KARLSRUHE	01/01/1884	A		F3

Lastname	Firstname	Birth Year	Birthplace	Emigration	De	Prof	Source
KROHMER	KATHARINA	1849	ETTLINGEN	01/01/1872	A		F4
KRONENEWETT	CHRISTINE		PFAFFENROTH	01/01/1847	A		F7
KRONENWETT	CHRISTIAN	1863	LANGENSTEINBACH	01/01/1881	A		F3
KRONENWETT	CHRISTIAN	1863	LANGENSTEINBACH	03/14/1883	A		F3
KRONENWETT	CHRISTINE	1851	LANGENSTEINBACH	/ /	A		F3
KRONENWETT	CHRISTINE	1861	LANGENSTEINBACH	/ /	A		F3
KRONENWETT	ERNST	1848	LANGENSTEINBACH	04/12/1864	A		F3
KRONENWETT	FRIEDRICH	1859	LANGENSTEINBACH	/ /	A		F3
KRONENWETT	GEORG	1814	LANGENSTEINBACH	/ /	A		F3
KRONENWETT	GEORG	1824	LANGENSTEINBACH	01/01/1850	A		F3
KRONENWETT	GEORG	1840	LANGENSTEINBACH	/ /	A		F3
KRONENWETT	JAKOB	1818	LANGENSTEINBACH	01/01/1852	A		F3
KRONENWETT	JAKOB	1819	LANGENSTEINBACH	01/01/1836	A		F3
KRONENWETT	JAKOB	1854	LANGENSTEINBACH	/ /	A		F3
KRONENWETT	JAKOB FRIEDRICH	1800	LANGENSTEINBACH	09/29/1855	A		F3
KRONENWETT	KARL	1849	LANGENSTEINBACH	/ /	A		F3
KRONENWETT	KATHARINA	1860	LANGENSTEINBACH	/ /	A		F3
KRONENWETT	LORENZ		PFAFFENROTH	01/01/1849	A		F7
KRONENWETT	MAGDALENA	1844	LANGENSTEINBACH	01/01/1881	A		F3
KRONENWETT	MICHAEL	1804	LANGENSTEINBACH	03/25/1828	A		F3
KRONENWETT	PHILIPP	1848	LANGENSTEINBACH	02/01/1869	A		F3
KRONENWETT	PHILIPP JAKOB	1846	LANGENSTEINBACH	02/16/1869	A		F3
KRONENWETT	SUSANNE	1825	LANGENSTEINBACH	/ /	A		F3
KRONENWETT	WILHELM	1830	LANGENSTEINBACH	12/24/1850	A		F3
KRONENWETT MN	SUSANNE	1790	LANGENSTEINBACH	01/01/1829	A		F3
KRONENWETT MN HUNZIN	ANNA MARIA	1793	LANGENSTEINBACH	03/24/1828	A		F3
KRONENWETT MN KIRCHE	BARBARA	1802	LANGENSTEINBACH	01/01/1848	A		F3
KRONENWETT MN RAUSCH	MARGARETHA	1805	LANGENSTEINBACH	09/29/1855	A		F3
KRONENWETT MN TAUBEN	MARGARETHA	1807	LANGENSTEINBACH	/ /	A		F3
KRONENWETT MN WETTAC	ANNA MARIA	1817	LANGENSTEINBACH	02/27/1847	A		F3
KRONENWETT W FAMILY	FRIEDRICH	1793	LANGENSTEINBACH	01/01/1848	A		F3
KRONENWETT W FAMILY	JAKOB	1804	LANGENSTEINBACH	/ /	A		F3
KRONENWETT W FAMILY	MARTIN	1793	LANGENSTEINBACH	03/24/1828	A		F3
KRONENWETT W FAMILY	MATHäUS	1790	LANGENSTEINBACH	01/01/1829	A		F3
KRONENWETT W FAMILY	SIMON	1810	LANGENSTEINBACH	02/27/1847	A		F3
KRONENWETT W PARENTS	ANDREAS	1825	LANGENSTEINBACH	01/01/1829	A		F3
KRONENWETT W PARENTS	CHRISTINE	1828	LANGENSTEINBACH	01/01/1848	A		F3
KRONENWETT W PARENTS	ELISABETH	1827	LANGENSTEINBACH	03/24/1828	A		F3
KRONENWETT W PARENTS	GEORG	1840	LANGENSTEINBACH	02/27/1847	A		F3
KRONENWETT W PARENTS	JAKOB	1823	LANGENSTEINBACH	01/01/1829	A		F3
KRONENWETT W PARENTS	JAKOB	1828	LANGENSTEINBACH	/ /	A		F3
KRONENWETT W PARENTS	JAKOB	1830	LANGENSTEINBACH	01/01/1853	A		F3
KRONENWETT W PARENTS	JAKOB	1843	LANGENSTEINBACH	02/27/1847	A		F3
KRONENWETT W PARENTS	JOHANN GEORG	1826	LANGENSTEINBACH	08/29/1855	A		F3
KRONENWETT W PARENTS	JULIANE	1839	LANGENSTEINBACH	09/29/1855	A		F3
KRONENWETT W PARENTS	KARL	1834	LANGENSTEINBACH	01/01/1853	A		F3
KRONENWETT W PARENTS	KARL FRIEDRICH	1831	LANGENSTEINBACH	01/01/1848	A		F3
KRONENWETT W PARENTS	KATHARINA	1824	LANGENSTEINBACH	03/24/1828	A		F3
KRONENWETT W PARENTS	MAGDALENA	1823	LANGENSTEINBACH	/ /	A		F3
KRONENWETT W PARENTS	MAGDALENA	1843	LANGENSTEINBACH	09/29/1855	A		F3

Lastname	Firstname	Birth Year	Birthplace	Emigration	De	Prof	Source
KRONENWETT W PARENTS	MARGARETHA	1823	LANGENSTEINBACH	03/24/1828	A		F3
KRONENWETT W PARENTS	MARGARETHA	1832	LANGENSTEINBACH	01/01/1853	A		F3
KRONENWETT W PARENTS	MARGARETHA	1837	LANGENSTEINBACH	/ /	A		F3
KRONENWETT W PARENTS	MARGARETHA	1845	LANGENSTEINBACH	02/27/1847	A		F3
KRONENWETT W PARENTS	MATHäUS	1823	LANGENSTEINBACH	01/01/1829	A		F3
KRONENWETT W PARENTS	MATHäUS	1830	LANGENSTEINBACH	/ /	A		F3
KRONENWETT W PARENTS	SUSANNE	1825	LANGENSTEINBACH	01/01/1829	A		
KRONENWETT W PARENTS	WILHELM	1839	LANGENSTEINBACH	01/01/1853	A		F3
KROPP	JULIANA		LAUF	01/01/1859	A		F6
KROTZ MN GEIGER	KATHERINA	1799	MALSCH	05/24/1832	A		F2
KROTZ W FAMILY	CASPAR	1796	MALSCH	05/24/1832	A		F2
KROTZ W PARENTS	ELISABETH	1824	MALSCH	05/24/1832	A		F2
KROTZ W PARENTS	FRANZ KARL	1813	MALSCH	05/24/1832	A		F2
KROTZ W PARENTS	JOHANNES	1830	MALSCH	05/24/1832	A		F2
KROTZ W PARENTS	JOSEPHINE	1820	MALSCH	05/24/1832	A		F2
KRUMM	CHRISTOPH		GRöTZINGEN	01/01/1853	A		F5
KRUMM	KATHARINA		GRöTZINGEN	/ /	A		F3
KRUTINS	FRIEDRICH	1865	KARLSRUHE	01/01/1886	A		F3
KRäMER	ANNA MARIA	1857	MALSCH	10/12/1857	A		F2
KRäMER	CHRISTOPH WILH	1850	MALSCH	11/25/1854	A		F2
KRäMER	FRANZ	1773	MALSCH	01/01/1790	A		F2
KRäMER	KAROLINE	1827	MALSCH	11/25/1854	A		F2
KRäMER	MARIA ANNA	1854	MALSCH	11/25/1854	A		F2
KRäMER	MICHAEL	1810	MALSCH	04/30/1832	A		F2
KRäMER	OTTO	1874	MALSCH	04/14/1888	A		F2
KRäMER	ROSA	1856	MALSCH	10/12/1857	A		F2
KRäMER	VERONIKA	1854	MALSCH	10/12/1857	A		F2
KRäMER	WILHELM	1850	MALSCH	01/01/1890	A		F2
KRäMER MN HIRSERICH	MARIA ANNA		MALSCH	01/01/1800	A		F2
KRäMER MN LORENZ	FRANZISKA	1819	MALSCH	01/12/1857	A		F2
KRäMER W FAMILY	FRIEDRICH	1785	MALSCH	10/12/1857	A		F2
KRäMER W FAMILY	XAVER		MALSCH	01/01/1800	A		F2
KRäMMER	ADOLF	1853	KARLSRUHE	01/01/1873	A		F3
KUBACH	HEINRICH		LIEDOLSHEIM	01/01/1862	A		F6
KUCH	BURKHARD		KREUZWERTHEIM	/ /	A		F5
KUCH	ISIDOR		TAUBERBISCHOFSHEIM	01/01/1866	A		F6
KUEN	MAXIMILIAN	1833	ETTLINGEN	01/01/1856	A		F4
KUFTERER	KARL	1874	KARLSRUHE	/ /	A		F3
KUHN	CAROLINA	1850	BLANKENLOCH	01/01/1882	A		F8
KUHN	CAROLINA	1860	BLANKENLOCH	01/01/1882	A		F4
KUHN	JOHANNES	1823	MALSCH	01/01/1849	A		F2
KUHN	KARL JAKOB	1832	DURLACH KARLSRUHE	/ /	A		F7
KUHN	KAROLINE	1825	MALSCH	01/01/1848	A		F2
KUHN W F	ELISABETH	1851	BAUERBACH	01/01/1875	A		F8
KUHN W F	EMMA	1851	BAUERBACH	01/01/1875	A		F8
KUHN W F	HELENE	1862	BAUERBACH	01/01/1875	A		F8
KUHN WIDOWER W CH	KARL	1821	BAUERBACH	01/01/1875	A		F8
KUHNLE MN	MAGDALENA		GRöTZINGEN	01/01/1846	A		F3
KUHNLE W FAMILY	JAKOB	1815	GRöTZINGEN	01/01/1846	A		F3
KUHNLE W PARENTS	JOSEF	1833	GRöTZINGEN	01/01/1846	A		F3

Lastname	Firstname	Birth Year	Birthplace	Emigration De	Prof	Source
KUHNLE W PARENTS	KATHARINA	1839	GRÖTZINGEN	01/01/1846 A		F3
KUHNLE W PARENTS	LUISE	1842	GRÖTZINGEN	01/01/1846 A		F3
KUHNLE W PARENTS	MAGDALENA	1845	GRÖTZINGEN	01/01/1846 A		F3
KUMM	CHRISTOPH		GRÖTZINGEN	/ / A		F3
KUMM	GEORG		GRÖTZINGEN	01/01/1827 A		F5
KUMM	GOTTLIEB		GRÖTZINGEN	/ / A		F3
KUMM	IGNAZ JAKOB		GRÖTZINGEN	01/01/1832 A		F5
KUMM	JAKOB		GRÖTZINGEN	01/01/1870 A		F3
KUMM	JOHANN		GRÖTZINGEN	/ / A		F3
KUMM MN SCHWARZ	ELISABETH		GRÖTZINGEN	01/01/1832 A		F5
KUMM W W	JOHANN		GRÖTZINGEN	01/01/1861 A		F5
KUNLE OR KÜHNLE	MONIKA	1820	PFAFFENROTH	01/01/1850 A		F7
KUNLE OR KÜHNLE	WILHELM	1816	PFAFFENROTH	01/01/1850 A		F7
KUNZ	AMALIA	1821	PFAFFENROTH	01/01/1850 A		F7
KUNZ	BARBARA		PFAFFENROTH	01/01/1811 A		F7
KUNZ	BERNHARD	1823	MALSCH	01/01/1853 A		F2
KUNZ	FLORIAN	1802	SCHÖLLBRONN	01/01/1826 A		F7
KUNZ	FRANZ ANTON	1810	PFAFFENROTH	01/01/1858 A		F7
KUNZ	FRANZ JOSEF	1792	PFAFFENROTH	01/01/1850 A		F7
KUNZ	FRANZ KARL	1856	MALSCH	03/24/1872 A		F2
KUNZ	FRANZISKA ROSIA	1849	MALSCH	02/24/1872 A		F2
KUNZ	GERTRUD		MÖRSCH	01/01/1846 A		F7
KUNZ	HERMANN	1872	MALSCH	01/01/1890 A		F2
KUNZ	HIERONYMUS		ETTLINGEN	01/01/1866 A		F4
KUNZ	IGNAZ	1792	MALSCH	01/01/1848 A		F2
KUNZ	IGNAZ	1829	PFAFFENROTH	01/01/1850 A		F7
KUNZ	JOHANN		MALSCH	01/01/1833 A		F2
KUNZ	JOHANN	1782	SCHÖLLBRONN	01/01/1830 A		F7
KUNZ	JOHANNES	1800	PFAFFENROTH	01/01/1845 A		F7
KUNZ	KATHARINA	1808	SCHÖLLBRONN	01/01/1854 A		F7
KUNZ	KATHARINA	1826	MALSCH	08/26/1854 A		F2
KUNZ	KATHARINA	1830	MALSCH	01/01/1853 A		F2
KUNZ	MAGDALENA		SCHÖLLBRONN	01/01/1833 A		F7
KUNZ	MAGDALENA	1819	PFAFFENROTH	01/01/1850 A		F7
KUNZ	MARIANNE		ETTLINGEN	01/01/1824 A		F4
KUNZ	PETER	1820	MALSCH	06/09/1860 A		F2
KUNZ MN KASTNER	FRIEDA		MALSCH	01/01/1853 A		F2
KUNZ MN LAUINGER	SUSANNE	1804	SCHÖLLBRONN	01/01/1851 A		F7
KUNZ MN SCHMIED	MAGDALENA	1809	PFAFFENROTH	01/01/1845 A		F7
KUNZ MN SCHMIEDER	EUPHROSINE	1837	MALSCH	01/01/1869 A		
KUNZ MN STREIBIG	MARIA ANNA	1829	SCHÖLLBRONN	01/01/1848 A		F7
KUNZ MN WEISHAUPT	FRANZISKA	1824	SCHÖLLBRONN	01/01/1845 A		F7
KUNZ W F	IGNAZ	1818	SCHÖLLBRONN	01/01/1845 A		F7
KUNZ W F	KASIMIR	1806	SCHÖLLBRONN	01/01/1851 A		F7
KUNZ W F	KATHARINA	1817	SCHÖLLBRONN	01/01/1850 A		F7
KUNZ W F	SERAPHIN	1808	SCHÖLLBRONN	01/01/1848 A		F7
KUNZ W FAMILY	KARL	1845	MALSCH	01/01/1869 A		F2
KUNZ W M	AMALIE	1839	PFAFFENROTH	01/01/1850 A		F7
KUNZ W M	LINA	1843	PFAFFENROTH	01/01/1850 A		F7
KUNZ W P	GERTRUD	1834	SCHÖLLBRONN	01/01/1851 A		F7

Lastname	Firstname	Birth Year	Birthplace	Emigration	De	Prof	Source
KUNZ W P	IGNAZ	1841	SCHÖLLBRONN	01/01/1851	A		F7
KUNZ W P	JAKOB	1831	SCHÖLLBRONN	01/01/1851	A		F7
KUNZ W P	JOHANN	1829	SCHÖLLBRONN	01/01/1851	A		F7
KUNZ W P	JOSEF HERMANN	1837	SCHÖLLBRONN	01/01/1851	A		F7
KUNZ W P	LEO	1831	SCHÖLLBRONN	01/01/1848	A		F7
KUNZ W P	WILHELMINE	1844	SCHÖLLBRONN	01/01/1851	A		F7
KUNZENBACHER	GEORG	1821	MALSCH	01/01/1862	A		F2
KUNZENBACHER	JOHANN	1821	MALSCH	01/01/1880	A		F2
KUNZENBACHER	JOSEF	1803	MALSCH	01/01/1879	A		F2
KUNZENBACHER	PETER	1860	MALSCH	06/06/1879	A		F2
KUNZMANN	CHRISTINA		WÖSSINGEN	01/01/1860	A		F1
KUNZMANN	FRIED.CHRIST	1853	DURLACH KARLSRUHE	/ /	A		F7
KUNZMANN	KATHERINA BARBA		WÖSSINGEN	01/01/1861	A		F1
KUNZMANN	WILHELM	1868	GRÖTZINGEN	01/01/1884	A		F3
KUNZMANN MN STEIN	KATHARINA		WÖSSINGEN	01/01/1832	A		F1
KUNZMANN W FAMILY	MICHAEL		WÖSSINGEN	01/01/1832	A	SHOE	F1
KUNZMANN WW	ANDREAS		WÖSSINGEN	01/01/1845	A		F1
KUNZMANN WW	CHRISTOPH		WÖSSINGEN	01/01/1832	A		F1
KUNZNER	ANDREAS	1798	HELMSTADT	01/01/1825	A		F2
KURTZ	KARL FRIEDRICH	1831	GRÖTZINGEN	01/01/1851	A		F3
KURZ	JOHANN BAPTIST		SCHWEIGHAUSEN	01/01/1859	A		F6
KURZ	MAGDALENA		GRÖTZINGEN	01/01/1858	A		F5
KURZ	SALOMEA		GRÖTZINGEN	01/01/1860	A		F5
KUSSMAUL	BARBARA	1827	SÖLLINGEN	01/01/1845	A		F7
KUSSMAUL	CHRISTOPH		SÖLLINGEN	01/01/1877	A		F7
KUSSMAUL	CHRISTOPH	1845	SÖLLINGEN	01/01/1868	A		F7
KUSSMAUL	ELISABETH	1825	SÖLLINGEN	01/01/1845	A		F7
KUSSMAUL	HANNA		KARLSRUHE	/ /	A		F3
KUSSMAUL	HERR		SÖLLINGEN	/ /	A		F7
KUSSMAUL	JAKOB FRIEDRICH	1790	SÖLLINGEN	01/01/1849	A		F7
KUSSMAUL	JAKOB GEORG		SÖLLINGEN	/ /	AQ		F7
KUSSMAUL	JOHANNA		SÖLLINGEN	/ /	A		F7
KUSSMAUL	JOSEF		SÖLLINGEN	/ /	A		F7
KUSSMAUL	MARGARETHA	1830	SÖLLINGEN	01/01/1854	A		F7
KUSSMAUL MN MEKLE	MARGARETHA		SÖLLINGEN	01/01/1845	A		F7
KUSSMAUL MN WALTHER	ERNESTINE	1838	SÖLLINGEN	01/01/1880	A		F3
KUSSMAUL MN?			SÖLLINGEN	/ /	A		F7
KUSSMAUL W F	ALBRECHT	1792	SÖLLINGEN	01/01/1845	A		F7
KUSSMAUL W F	GEORG JAKOB		SÖLLINGEN	/ /	A		F7
KUSSMAUL W FAMILY	SAMUEL	1831	SÖLLINGEN	01/01/1883	A		F3
KUSSMAUL W P	BARBARA	1822	SÖLLINGEN	01/01/1845	A		F7
KUSSMAUL W P	EGIDIUS	1838	SÖLLINGEN	01/01/1845	A		F7
KUSSMAUL W P	ELISABETH		SÖLLINGEN	/ /	A		F7
KUSSMAUL W P	FRANZ		SÖLLINGEN	/ /	A		F7
KUSSMAUL W P	JOHANN GEORG		SÖLLINGEN	/ /	A		F7
KUSSMAUL W P	JOHANN JAKOB	1828	SÖLLINGEN	01/01/1845	A		F7
KUSSMAUL W P	KARL		SÖLLINGEN	/ /	A		F7
KUSSMAUL W P	MARGARETH	1843	SÖLLINGEN	01/01/1845	A		F7
KUSSMAUL W P	MARIA ELISABETH	1826	SÖLLINGEN	01/01/1845	A		F7
KUSSMAUL W PARENTS	ALBERT	1867	SÖLLINGEN	01/01/1880	A		F3

Lastname	Firstname	Birth Year	Birthplace	Emigration De	Prof	Source
KUSSMAUL W PARENTS	ALBERTINE	1875	SÖLLINGEN	01/01/1880 A		F3
KUSSMAUL W PARENTS	ELISE	1871	SÖLLINGEN	01/01/1880 A		F3
KUSSMAUL W PARENTS	ERNST FRIEDRICH	1861	SÖLLINGEN	01/01/1880 A		F3
KUSSMAUL W PARENTS	KARL WILHELM	1878	SÖLLINGEN	01/01/1880 A		F3
KUSSMAUL W PARENTS	RUDOLF	1866	SÖLLINGEN	01/01/1880 A		F3
KUSSMAUL W PARENTS	SOPHIE PAULINE	1879	SÖLLINGEN	01/01/1880 A		F3
KÜBEL MN GEIGER	APOLLONIA	1819	MALSCH	06/25/1846 A		F2
KÜBEL W FAMILY	WENDELIN		STUPFERICH	06/25/1846 A		F2
KÜBEL W PARENTS	PAULINE	1845	MALSCH	06/25/1846 A		F2
KÜCHLIN	KARL	1862	KARLSRUHE	01/01/1883 A		F3
KÜHN	JOHANNES	1823	MALSCH	01/01/1849 A		F2
KÜHN	JOSEF	1833	MALSCH	01/01/1851 A		F6
KÜHN	JULIUS		ÖRTIGHEIM	01/01/1869 A		F6
KÜHN	KAROLINE	1842	MALSCH	05/22/1854 A		F2
KÜHN W PARENTS	JOHANN LORENZ	1853	MALSCH	05/22/1854 A		F2
KÜHN MN JUNG	STEPHANIE	1821	MALSCH	05/22/1854 A		F2
KÜHN W FAMILY	ANTON	1811	MALSCH	05/22/1854 A		F2
KÜHN W PARENTS	GENOFEVA	1851	MALSCH	05/22/1854 A		F2
KÜHN W PARENTS	SABINE	1840	MALSCH	05/22/1854 A		1
KÜHNER	ANTON	1863	KARLSRUHE	01/01/1880 A		F3
KÜHNER	HEINRICH	1864	KARLSRUHE	01/01/1882 A		F3
KÜHNLE	ANDREAS		PFAFFENROT	01/01/1854 A		
KÜHNLE	MAX	1866	KARLSRUHE	01/01/1883 A		F3
KÜHNLE	PHIL.FRIEDRICH	1845	DURLACH KARLSRUHE	/ / A		F7
KÜHNLE MN UNGEMACHT	SOPHIE		PFAFFENROT	01/01/1854 A		F7
KÜNL	AUGUST	1855	KARLSRUHE	01/01/1881 A		F3
KÜNSTLE	NIKOLAUS		STEINACH	01/01/1859 A		F6
KÜNZLE	HEINRICH		KARLSRUHE	/ / A		F3
KÜNZLER	CONRAD		GRÖTZINGEN	01/01/1832 A		F5
KÜNZLER	JAKOB		GRÖTZINGEN	01/01/1847 A		F3
KÜNZLER	JAKOB	1790	GRÖTZINGEN	01/01/1846 A		F3
KÜNZLER	KONRAD	1797	GRÖTZINGEN	/ / A		F3
KÄFER	JAKOB		MIELANDINGEN	01/01/1859 A		F6
KÄLBER	JAKOB		EUTINGEN	01/01/1771 A		F9
KÄLBER	JOHANN FRANZ	1870	DURLACH	/ / A		F3
KÄLBER	JOHANN PHILIP		DURLACH KARLSRUHE	01/01/1882 A		F7
KÄLBER	LUDWIG HEINRICH	1861	DURLACH KARLSRUHE	/ / A		F7
KÄLBER	MICHAEL		EUTINGEN	01/01/1771 A		F9
KÄRCHER	EMIL	1862	KARLSRUHE	01/01/1881 A		F3
KÖHL	ANNA BARBARA		BAHLINGEN	01/01/1859 A		F6
KÖHLER	ADAM		GRABEN	01/01/1891 A		F3
KÖHLER	EDUARD	1825	ETTLINGEN	01/01/1853 A		F4
KÖHLER	HERMANN		GRABEN	01/01/1880 A		F3
KÖHLER	JOHANN	1827	ETTLINGEN	/ / A		F4
KÖHLER	JOSEF		ETTLINGEN	01/01/1857 A		F4
KÖHLER	KARL		GRABEN	01/01/1880 A		F3
KÖHLER	LEOPOLD		GRABEN	01/01/1879 A		F3
KÖHLER	LUDWIG	1874	ETTLINGEN	01/26/1894 A		F4
ÖLBLE	ANDREAS	1859	KARLSRUHE	01/01/1881 A		F3
ÖLBLE	AUGUSTE		GRAFENHAUSEN	01/01/1859 A		F6

Lastname	Firstname	Birth Year	Birthplace	Emigration	De	Prof	Source
KÖLBLE	JOSEF		GRAFENHAUSEN	01/01/1859	A		F6
KÖLMEL	JOHANN WENDELIN		ETTIGHEIM	01/01/1854	A		F9
KÖLMEL W.S.	ALEXANDER		RASTATT	01/01/1873	A		F6
KÖNIG	FRANZ		GERCHSHEIM	01/01/1866	A		F6
KÖNIG	KARL LUDWIG	1857	KNIELINGEN	01/01/1880	A		F6
KÖNIG	KARL WILHELM	1865	KNIELINGEN	01/01/1882	A		F6
KÖNIG W FAMILY	CHRISTIAN		FORBACH	01/01/1860	A		F6
KÖNIG W WIFE	JAKOB			/ /			
KÖNIGSSTÄTTER	WILHELM		KARLSRUHE	01/01/1864	A		F3
KÖPPELMANN	JOPHANN		KARLSRUHE	01/01/1850	A		F3
KÖRNER	NIKOLAUS	1864	KARLSRUHE	01/01/1882	A		F3
KÖSSLER	ADAM	1830	RINKLINGEN	01/01/1850	A		F7
KÖSSLER	ANDREAS	1847	RINKLINGEN	01/01/1878	A		F7
KÖSSLER	CHRISTINE	1833	RINKLINGEN	01/01/1854	A		F7
KÖSSLER	CHRISTOPH	1827	RINKLINGEN	01/01/1853	A		F7
KÖSSLER	FERD. WILHLEM	1862	RINKLINGEN	01/01/1882	A		F7
KÖSSLER	JOHANN PHILLIP	1851	RINKLINGEN	/ /	A		F7
KÖSSLER W P	KATHARINA FRIED	1878	RINKLINGEN	01/01/1878	A		F7
KÖSSLER MN HÖTZ	KATHARINA		WÜRMBERG	01/01/1878	A		F7
KÖSSLER W P	ANDREAS	1875	RINKLINGEN	01/01/1878	A		F7
KÖGELE	LUDWIG		WEINGARTEN	/ /	A		F8
KÖHLER	FERDINAND WILHE	1862	RINKLINGEN	01/01/1882	A		F7
KÖHLER	JAKOB		BLANKENLOCH	01/01/1835	A		F4
KÖHLER	MARTIN		BLANKENLOCH	01/01/1843	A		F4
KÖLBLE	AUGUSTE		GRAFENHAUSEN	01/01/1859	A		F6
KÖLBLE	JOSEF		GRAFENHAUSEN	01/01/1859	A		F6
KÖRNER	KARL FRIEDRICH		DURLACH	01/01/1866	A		F6
KÖRR	WILHELM	1861	MÜHLBERG	01/01/1881	A		F6
KÖSSLER	ADAM	1830	RINKLINGEN	01/01/1850	A		F7
KÖSSLER	CHRISTINE	1833	RINKLINGEN	01/01/1854	A		F7
KÖSSLER	CHRISTOPH	1827	RINKLINGEN	10/21/1853	A		F7
KÖSSLER MN GÖTZ	KATHARINA		WÜRMBERG	01/01/1878	A		F7
KÖSSLER W F	ANDREAS	1847	RINKLINGEN	01/01/1878	A		Γ7
KÖSSLER W P	ANDREAS FRIEDRH	1872	RINKLINGEN	01/01/1878	A		F7
KÖSSLER W P	KATHARINA FREDE	1878	RINKLINGEN	01/01/1878	A		F7
KÖTZLE	ADOLF	1871	MÜHLBURG	01/01/1887	A		F8
KÜBLER	WILLIBALD		DIERLINGEN	01/01/1858	A		F8
KÜHN	BARBARA	1828	MALSCH	01/01/1851	A		F2
KÜHN	ISIDOR		ÖRTIGHEIM	01/01/1865	A		F6
KÜHN	JOSEF	1833	MALSCH	01/01/1851	A		F6
KÜNSTLE	NIKOLAUS		STEINACH	01/01/1859	A		F6
KÜRNBERGER	LORENZ		MÖRSCH	01/25/1847	A		F7
KÜRNBERGER MN RASTER	ANNA MARIA		MÖRSCH	01/01/1832	A		F7
KÜRNBERGER W F	CARL		MÖRSCH	01/01/1832	A		F7

Lastname	Firstname	Birth Year	Birthplace	Emigration	De	Prof	Source
LABOR	THEODOR	1848	KARLSRUHE	01/01/1880	A		F3
LACHNER	RUDOLF	1864	ETTLINGEN	01/01/1884	A		F4
LACHNER	SIGMUND	1868	ETTLINGEN	01/01/1884	A		F4
LADHOLZ	BARBARA		MOLSENWEILER	01/01/1866	A		F6
LADHOLZ	ELISABETH		MOLSENWEILER	01/01/1866	A		F6
LAKNER	WILHELM KONRAD		DURLACH KARLSRUHE	01/01/1849	A		F7
LAMBSE	MAX	1848	KARLSRUHE	01/01/1869	A		F3
LANDER	FRIEDRICH EDUAD	1847	KARLSRUHE	01/01/1869	A		F3
LANG	AUGUST		SPöCK	01/01/1862	A		F4
LANG	CHRISTIAN		LEOPOLDSHAUSEN	01/01/1835	A		F6
LANG	ERNESTINE	1837	BLANKENLOCH	01/01/1868	A		F4
LANG	FRANZISKA	1873	MALSCH	01/01/1891	A		F2
LANG	GÜNTHER	1832	SCHÖLLBRONN	/ /	A		F7
LANG	JOHANN ADAM		BLANKENLOCH	01/01/1851	A		F4
LANG	KARL		SPöCK	01/01/1865	A		F4
LANG	KARL AUGUST	1868	SPöCK	01/01/1883	A		F4
LANG	LEOPOLD		GAMBURG WERTHEIM	01/01/1888	A		F7
LANG	LEOPOLD	1872	REICHENBACH	12/04/1888	A		F4
LANG	LUDWIG		SPöCK	01/01/1851	A		F4
LANG	MICHAEL		AUERBACH	01/01/1737	A		F6
LANG	OSKAR WENDELIN	1874	REICHENBACH	01/01/1890	A		F7
LANG	PETER	1880	MALSCH	01/01/1882	A		F2
LANG	STEFANIE	1874	MALSCH	01/01/1893	A		F2
LANG MN GLASSTETTER	KAROLINE	1852	VöLKERSBACH	01/01/1882	A		F2
LANG W F	BERNHARD		NEUSATZ	11/04/1857	A		F5
LANG W FAMILY	GEORG JAKOB		BLANKENLOCH	01/01/1835	A		F4
LANG W FAMILY	MAX	1841	MALSCH	01/01/1882	A		F2
LANG W PARENTS	JOHANN BAPTIST	1873	MALSCH	01/01/1882	A		F2
LANG W PARENTS	JOSEF	1878	MALSCH	01/01/1882	A		F2
LANGENBACH	JOHANN FRIEDRIC		DURLACH KARLSRUHE	01/01/1839			F7
LANGENBACH W D	MARTINA	1822	PFAFFENROTH	01/01/1844	A		F7
LANGENBACH W M	JOSEFINE	1844	PFAFFENROTH	01/01/1854	A		F7
LANGENBEIN	CARL CHRISTOPH		DURLACH KARLSRUHE	01/01/1845	A		F7
LANGENSTEIN	GEORG HEINRICH		MÜNZESHEIM	01/01/1774	A		F6
LANGGUTH	AMBROS	1846	SPESSART	12/20/1867	A		F4
LANGGUTH	BERTA	1843	SPESSART	10/16/1869	A		F4
LANGJAHR	ELISABETH BARBA		WöSSSINGEN	01/01/1853	A		F1
LANGJAHR	FRIEDERIKE		WöSSINGEN	01/01/1853	A		F1
LANGJAHR	JOHANN		WIFFINGEN	01/01/1854	A		F6
LANGJAHR	JOHANN		WöSSINGEN	01/01/1854	A	BRIC	F1
LANGJAHR W FAMILY	HEINRICH		WöSSINGEN	01/01/1854	A		F1
LANGJAHR W FAMILY	WILHELM		WöSSINGEN	01/01/1854	A		F1
LANGMANTEL	BARBARA		GERCHSHEIM	01/01/1866	A		F6
LAUB	LEOPOLD		ETTLINGEN	/ /	A		F4
LAUER	CARL HEINRICH	1824	DURLACH KARLSRUHE	/ /			F7
LAUER W FAMILY	NIKLAUS		KARLSRUHE	/ /	A		F3
LAUER W MOTHER	FRANZ	1823	MALSCH	05/27/1846	A		F2
LAUER W MOTHER	RONALD	1818	MALSCH	05/27/1846	A		F2
LAUER W MOTHER	ROSINA	1820	MALSCH	05/27/1846	A		F2
LAUER W MOTHER	THERESIA	1826	MALSCH	05/27/1846	A		F2

Lastname	Firstname	Birth Year	Birthplace	Emigration	De	Prof	Source
LAUER WIDOW MN MAYER	REGINE	1791	MALSCH	05/27/1846	A		F2
LAUINGER	ADOLF	1804	SCHÖLLBRONN	01/01/1839	A		F7
LAUINGER	ALOIS		SPESSART	07/31/1851	A		F4
LAUINGER	GEORG	1833	SPESSART	01/01/1854	A		F4
LAUINGER	GEORG	1850	SCHÖLLBRONN	01/01/1867	A		F7
LAUINGER	GREGOR	1850	SPESSART	01/01/1866	A		F4
LAUINGER	IGNAZ	1798	SCHÖLLBRONN	01/01/1878	A		F7
LAUINGER	JOHANN BAPTIST		SPESSART	03/26/1858	A		F4
LAUINGER	JOSEF		SCHÖLLBRONN	01/01/1839	A		F7
LAUINGER	JOSEPH	1817	BAUERBACH	01/01/1867	A		F8
LAUINGER	KARL FRIEDRICH	1804	SCHÖLLBRONN	01/01/1830	A		F7
LAUINGER	THERESE	1841	SCHÖLLBRONN	01/01/1869	A		F7
LAUINGER MN FÖRDERER	GERTRUD	1798	SCHÖLLBRONN	03/07/1821	A		F7
LAUINGER MN SCHÖNBER	MARIA ANNA	1808	ETTLINGEN	/ /	A		F4
LAUINGER W F	FRANZ	1791	SCHÖLLBRONN	03/07/1821	A		F7
LAUINGER W F	THOMAS	1787	SCHÖLLBRONN	01/01/1830	A		F7
LAUINGER W P	ISIDOR	1828	SCHÖLLBRONN	03/07/1821	A		F7
LAUINGER W P	KATHARINA	1823	SCHÖLLBRONN	03/07/1821	A		F7
LAUINGER W P	MARIA ANNA	1821	SCHÖLLBRONN	03/07/1821	A		F7
LAUINGER W P	THERESIA	1826	SCHÖLLBRONN	01/01/1830	A		F7
LAUINGER W WIFE	FRANZ XAVER		ETTLINGEN	/ /	A		F4
LAULE	FRANZ ANTON	1828	BURBACH	01/01/1856	A		F4
LAULE	JOSEF		REUTE	01/01/1823	A		F8
LAUTENSCHLAGER	CARL	1831	DURLACH KARLSRUHE	/ /			F7
LAY MN LUDWIG WID.	CHRISTINA		KARLSRUHE	01/01/1853	A		F3
LAYER	ROBERT		ETTLINGEN	01/01/1855	A		F4
LEBER	ERNST FRIED.ADA		DURLACH KARLSRUHE	01/01/1848	A		
LECHNER	FRANZ HUGO		ETTLINGEN	01/01/1854	A		F4
LECHNER	FRANZ JOSEF		ETTLINGEN	01/01/1861	A		F4
LECHNER	LEOPOLD	1830	ETTLINGEN	01/01/1863	A		F4
LEHMANN	ADOLF	1867	KARLSRUHE	01/01/1888	A		F3
LEHMANN	ARON		WENKHEIM	01/01/1866	A		F6
LEHMANN	AUGUST	1876	KARLSRUHE	01/01/1893	A		F3
LEHMANN	BURKHARD		BLANKENLOCH	01/01/1860	A		F4
LEHMANN	CHRISTINE		BLANKENLOCH	01/01/1862	A		F4
LEHMANN	KARL		BLANKENLOCH	01/01/1835	A		F4
LEHMANN	LEOPOLD		KARLSRUHE	01/01/1852	A		F3
LEHMANN	MARIANNE EMILIE	1822	ETTLINGEN	/ /	A		F4
LEHMANN	MARTIN		BLANKENLOCH	01/01/1838	A		F4
LEHMANN	NOA		BLANKENLOCH	01/01/1848	A		F4
LEHMANN	OTTO		THENINGEN	01/01/1859	A		F6
LEHMANN	OTTO	1874	BLANKENLOCH	01/01/1892	A		F4
LEHMANN	WILHELM	1876	BLANKENLOCH	01/01/1890	A		F4
LEHMANN	WILHELM	1876	BLANKENLOCH	01/01/1890	A		F8
LEHMANN MN HOFHEINZ	ELISABETH	1820	BLANKENLOCH	01/01/1868	A		F4
LEHMANN W FAMILY	BURKHARD	1815	BLANKENLOCH	01/01/1868	A		F4
LEHMANN W FAMILY	MARTIN		BLANKENLOCH	01/01/1835	A		F4
LEHMANN W P	AUGUST	1852	BLANKENLOCH	01/01/1868	A		F4
LEHMANN W P	EVA	1846	BLANKENLOCH	01/01/1868	A		F4
LEHMANN W P	LUDWIG	1860	BLANKENLOCH	01/01/1868	A		F4

Lastname	Firstname	Birth Year	Birthplace	Emigration	De	Prof	Source
LEHMANN W P	WILHELM	1852	BLANKENLOCH	01/01/1868	A		F4
LEHMANN WP	KATHARINA	1842	BLANKENLOCH	01/01/1868	A		F4
LEHMANN WP	MAX	1862	BLANKENLOCH	01/01/1868	A		F4
LEHNER	JAKOB	1872	KARLSRUHE	01/01/1890	A		F3
LEIBLIN	KARL JAKOB		KARLSRUHE	01/01/1807	A		F3
LEICHTLIN	KARL		KARLSRUHE	/ /	A		F3
LEICHTLIN	LUDWIG		KARLSRUHE	01/01/1833	A		F3
LEINBERGER	PETER		OFTERSHEIM	01/01/1784		FARM	F1
LEITZ	ANTON		KARLSRUHE	/ /	A		F3
LENT W P	IGNAZ	1846	SCHÖLLBRONN	01/01/1851	A		F7
LENZ	WILHELM	1847	RÜPPURR	01/01/1871	A		F8
LENZ MN SEIBERLICH	JULIANE		REICHENBACH	01/01/1851	A		F7
LENZ MN WEISHAUPT	LUISE	1822	SCHÖLLBRONN	01/01/1851	A		F7
LENZ W F	EGID	1807	SCHÖLLBRONN	01/01/1851	A		F7
LENZ W F	JOHANN	1820	SCHÖLLBRONN	01/01/1851	A		F7
LENZ W P	ALOISIA	1849	SCHÖLLBRONN	01/01/1851	A		F7
LENZ W P	ENGELBERT	1848	SCHÖLLBRONN	01/01/1851	A		F7
LENZ W P	FLORIAN	1849	SCHÖLLBRONN	01/01/1851	A		F7
LENZ W P	FRANZ XAVER	1843	SCHÖLLBRONN	01/01/1851	A		F7
LENZ W P	FRANZ XAVER	1845	SCHÖLLBRONN	01/01/1851	A		F7
LENZ W P	GOTTLIEB	1845	SCHÖLLBRONN	01/01/1851	A		F7
LENZ W P	IGNAZ	1846	SCHÖLLBRONN	01/01/1851	A		F7
LENZ W P	JOHANN	1842	SCHÖLLBRONN	01/01/1851	A		F7
LENZ W P	MARIA ANNA	1844	SCHÖLLBRONN	01/01/1851	A		F7
LENZ W P	MARIA LUISE	1848	SCHÖLLBRONN	01/01/1851	A		F7
LENZ W P	OTTILIE	1842	SCHÖLLBRONN	01/01/1851	A		F7
LENZINGER	CHRISTIAN LUDWI	1865	DURLACH KARLSRUHE	/ /	A		F7
LEON	JULIUS	1858	KARLSRUHE	01/01/1875	A		F3
LEONHARDT	GOTTFRIED		KARLSRUHE	/ /	A		F3
LEONHARDT W F	GEORG		BERGHAUSEN	01/01/1737	A		F6
LERCH	FERDINAND HEINR	1874	KARLSRUHE	01/01/1890	A		F3
LERCH	HEINRICH KARL		KARLSRUHE	/ /	A		F3
LEVIS	SIGMUND		KARLSRUHE	01/01/1867	A		F3
LICHTENFELS	GEORG		KARLSRUHE	/ /	A		F3
LICHTENFELS	IGNAZ	1872	RÜPPURR	01/01/1888	A		F8
LICHTENFELS	KARL FRIEDRICH	1862	RÜPPURR	01/01/1880	A		F8
LICHTENFELS	WILHELM		KARLSRUHE	/ /	A		F3
LIEB	GEORG JAKOB		FLEHINGEN	01/01/1854	A		F8
LIEBHAUSER	KARL	1864	BAUERBACH	01/01/1880	A		F8
LIEDE	RUDOLF AUG.	1857	DURLACH KARLSRUHE	/ /	A		F7
LIERMANN	CHRISTIAN		LAHR	01/01/1847	A		F6
LIND	ELISE		GRABEN	01/01/1753	A		F3
LIND	ELSE		GRABE	01/01/1753	A		F5
LIND	MARGARETHE		GRABEN	01/01/1783	A		F3
LIND	PETER		GRABEN	01/01/1750	A		F3
LIND W FAMILY	FRIEDRICH		GRABEN	01/01/1847	A		F3
LINDENMANN	FRIEDRICH		KARLSRUHE	01/01/1856	A		F3
LINDER	WILHELM	1861	HAGSFELD	01/01/1892	A		F6
LINDNER	LUISE KATHARINA	1874	HAGSFELD	01/01/1892	A		F6
LINDNER	WENDELIN ALOIS	1834	ETTLINGEN	/ /	A		F4

Lastname	Firstname	Birth Year	Birthplace	Emigration	De	Prof	Source
LING	IGNAZ		SCHÖLLBRONN	01/01/1830	A		F7
LINK	THEODOR		KARLSRUHE	01/01/1879	A		F3
LITZINGER	BURKARD		VÖLKERSBACH	01/01/1808	A		F4
LOHNER	LORENZ		BAUERBACH	01/01/1845	A		F8
LORENZ	ANTON	1768	SCHÖLLBRONN	01/01/1802	A		F7
LORENZ	GREGOR	1832	SCHÖLLBRONN	/ /	A		F7
LORENZ	NIKOLAUS	1773	MALSCH	01/01/1795	A		F2
LORENZ MN GRäSSER	JOHANNA	1827	MALSCH	08/27/1857	A		F2
LORENZ W FAMILY	ANTON	1827	MALSCH	08/27/1857	A		F2
LORENZ W PARENTS	ELISABETH	1852	MALSCH	08/27/1857	A		F2
LORENZ W PARENTS	KATHARINA	1857	MALSCH	08/27/1857	A		F2
LORENZ W PARENTS	VERONIKA	1855	MALSCH	08/27/1857	A		F2
LOTTHAMMER	JOHANNA		GRABEN	01/01/1848	A		F3
LOTTHAMMER	JOHANNE		GRABEN	01/01/1854	A		F5
LOTZ	FRIEDRICH		KARLSRUHE	/ /	A		F3
LUDWIG	CHRISTIAN		GRÖTZINGEN	01/01/1846	A		F3
LUDWIG	FRIEDRICH	1858	BLANKENLOCH	01/01/1880	A		F8
LUDWIG	FRIEDRICH	1868	BLANKENLOCH	01/01/1880	A		F4
LUDWIG	GEORG		AUERBACH	01/01/1859	A		F6
LUDWIG	JAKOB		WöSSINGEN	01/01/1852	A		F1
LUDWIG	KARL		BERGHAUSEN	01/01/1860	A		F8
LUDWIG	LUISE		WöSSINGEN	01/01/1854	A		F1
LUDWIG	MARTIN		AUERBACH /MOSBACH	01/01/1859	A		F6
LUMM	CHRISTIAN	1833	GRÖTZINGEN	01/01/1853	A		F3
LUMM	CHRISTOPH	1831	GRÖTZINGEN	01/01/1853	A		F3
LUMM	JAKOB		SÖLLINGEN	/ /	A		F7
LUMM	JULIANE		SÖLLINGEN	01/01/1853	A		F7
LUMMP MN DAUB	THEODORA		SCHÖLLBRONN	01/01/1849	A		F7
LUMMP W F	PIUS	1810	SCHÖLLBRONN	01/01/1849	A		F7
LUMMPP	MARGARETHA	1783	SCHÖLLBRONN	01/01/1830	A		F7
LUMMPP	MARGARETHA	1821	SCHÖLLBRONN	01/01/1854	A		F7
LUMMPP	NIKOLAUS	1790	SCHÖLLBRONN	01/01/1830	A		F7
LUMMPP MN LAUINGER	MARIA ANNA		SCHLUTTENBACH	01/01/1830	A		F7
LUMMPP W F	ANTON	1770	SCHÖLLBRONN	01/01/1830	A		F7
LUMMPP W P	JOSEF	1808	SCHÖLLBRONN	01/01/1830	A		F7
LUMMPP W P	JOSEF ANTON	1805	SCHÖLLBRONN	01/01/1830	A		F7
LUMPP	FIDELIS	1832	SCHÖLLBRONN	/ /	A		F7
LUMPP	GEORG	1769	OBERWEIER	01/01/1830	A		F1
LUMPP	JOHANN	1836	SCHÖLLBRONN	01/01/1852	A		F7
LUMPP	JOSEF	1837	SCHÖLLBRONN	01/01/1867	A		F7
LUMPP	KRESZENTIA	1826	SCHÖLLBRONN	01/01/1851	A		F7
LUMPP	MAGDALENA	1820	SCHÖLLBRONN	/ /	A		F7
LUMPP	MICHAEL	1828	SCHÖLLBRONN	01/01/1851	A		F7
LUMPP MN OCHS	MARIA ANNA		SCHÖLLBRONN	01/01/1842	A		F7
LUMPP W F	IGNAZ	1829	SCHÖLLBRONN	01/01/1842	A		F7
LUMPP W P	ALOIS	1828	SCHÖLLBRONN	01/01/1842	A		F7
LUMPP W P	MARIA EVA	1825	SCHÖLLBRONN	01/01/1842	A		F7
LUPPERER	MICHAEL		KNIELINGEN	01/01/1857	A		F6
LUTZ	ANDREAS	1837	DURLACH KARLSRUHE	/ /	A		F7
LUTZ W F	JOHANN THOMAS		KREUZWERTHEIM	04/21/1751	A		F5

Lastname	Firstname	Birth Year	Birthplace	Emigration	De	Prof	Source
LÄCHI	MINA		FREIBURG	01/01/1890	A		F8
LöFFEL	HEINRICH	1870	DURLACH KARLSRUHE	/ /	A		F7
LöHLENS	LUDWIG	1879	KARLSRUHE	01/01/1895	A		F3
LöWER	FRIEDRICH	1865	DURLACH KARLSRUHE	/ /	A		F7
LöWER	LUDWIG	1839	DURLACH KARLSRUHE	/ /			F7

Lastname	Firstname	Birth Year	Birthplace	Emigration	De	Prof	Source
MAAG	CHRISTOPH FRIEH	1808	GRABEN	01/01/1866	A		F8
MAAG	KAROLINE	1848	GRABEN	01/01/1868	A		F8
MAAG	WIFE OF LUDWIG		GRABEN	01/01/1888	A		F8
MAAG MN PFEIL	FRIEDRIKE	1836	GRABEN	01/01/1869	A		F3
MAAG W F	KARL	1831	GRABEN	01/01/1869	A		F8
MAAG W F	LUDWIG	1838	GRABEN	01/01/1888	A		F8
MAAG W FAMILY	CARL	1831	GRABEN	01/01/1869	A		F3
MAAG W P	FRIDERICKE CHRE	1860	GRABEN	01/01/1869	A		F8
MAAG W P	JAKOB FRIEDRICH	1869	GRABEN	01/01/1869	A		F8
MAAG W P	KARL	1867	GRABEN	01/01/1869	A		F8
MAAG W P	KARL	1868	GRABEN	01/01/1888	A		F8
MACK	LEOPOLD	1872	SPöCK	01/01/1888	A		F4
MADER	HUGO	1862	KARLSRUHE	01/01/1883	A		F3
MADER	HUGO	1862	KARLSRUHE	01/01/1884	A		F3
MADERT	JOSEF	1814	ETTLINGEN	01/01/1866	A		F4
MAI	ANTON	1850	SPESSART	10/15/1866	A		F4
MAI	JOSEF	1836	ETTLINGEN	08/03/1854	A		F4
MAI	JOSEF	1847	SPESSART	12/24/1866	A		F4
MAIER	BARTHOLOMÄ	1831	BURBACH	01/01/1857	A		F4
MAIER	ELISABETH		ETTLINGEN	01/01/1848	A		F4
MAIER	FRANZ ANTON	1835	BURBACH	01/01/1857	A		F4
MAIER	FRANZ KARL	1833	MALSCH	11/14/1857	A		F2
MAIER	FRIEDRICH		GRABEN	01/01/1890	A		F3
MAIER	JAKOB		GRÖTZINGEN	/ /	A		F3
MAIER	JAKOB	1863	KNIELINGEN	01/01/1882	A		F6
MAIER	JAKOBINE		NUSSLOCH	01/01/1859	A		F7
MAIER	JOHANN FERDINAN	1846	DURLACH KARLSRUHE	/ /			F7
MAIER	JOHANN JAKOB	1864	KARLSRUHE	01/01/1882	A		F3
MAIER	JOHANNES	1827	LANGENSTEINBACH	04/26/1853	A		F3
MAIER	KARL	1824	LANGENSTEINBACH	04/26/1853	A		F3
MAIER	KARL	1868	MALSCH	10/15/1890	A		F2
MAIER	KAROLINA		ETTLINGEN	/ /	A		F4
MAIER	KATHARINA	1826	LANGENSTEINBACH	/ /	A		F3
MAIER	LUDWIG	1824	ETTLINGEN	01/01/1845	A		F4
MAIER	LUISE	1814	BURBACH	01/01/1857	A		F4
MAIER	MAGDALENA	1867	KARLSRUHE	01/01/1884	A		F3
MAIER	MAGDALENA	1867	MALSCH	05/20/1884	A		F2
MAIER	MARIA EVA	1829	MALSCH	01/01/1856	A		F2
MAIER	MARTIN	1840	LANGENSTEINBACH	01/01/1861	A		F3
MAIER	PETER		SINGEN	01/01/1848	A		F6
MAIER	PETER JOSEF		KÜLSHEIM	01/01/1859	A		F6
MAIER	ROSINA		ETTLINGEN	/ /	A		F4
MAIER	SUSANNA	1828	LANGENSTEINBACH	/ /	A		F3
MAIER	THERESE	1830	MALSCH	08/26/1854	A		F2
MAIER	VIKTORIAN	1834	BURBACH	01/01/1854	A		F4
MAIER MN DENNINGER	CHRISTINA	1791	LANGENSTEINBACH	01/01/1832	A		F3
MAIER W 6 PERSONS	HEINRICH		WöSSINGEN	07/16/1782		FARM	F1
MAIER W CH WIDOWER	THOMAS	1800	MALSCH	11/14/1857	A		F2
MAIER W FAMILY	JUSTINUS	1825	MALSCH	01/01/1866	A		F2
MAIER W FAMILY	MICHAEL	1782	LANGENSTEINBACH	01/01/1832	A		F3

Lastname	Firstname	Birth Year	Birthplace	Emigration	De	Prof	Source
MAIER W FATHER	ENGELBERTA	1863	MALSCH	01/01/1866	A		F2
MAIER W FATHER	FERDINAND	1858	MALSCH	01/01/1866	A		F2
MAIER W FATHER	IDA	1853	MALSCH	01/01/1866	A		F2
MAIER W FATHER	ISIDOR	1860	MALSCH	01/01/1866	A		F2
MAIER W FATHER	THERESE	1851	MALSCH	01/01/1866	A		F2
MAIER W FATHR	KATHARINA	1855	MALSCH	01/01/1866	A		F2
MAIER W PARENTS	JAKOB	1822	LANGENSTEINBACH	01/01/1832	A		F3
MAIER W PARENTS	JOHANN GEORG	1817	LANGENSTEINBACH	01/01/1832	A		F3
MAIER W PARENTS	JULIANE	1810	LANGENSTEINBACH	01/01/1832	A		F3
MAIER W PARENTS	MAGDALENA	1812	LANGENSTEINBACH	01/01/1832	A		F3
MAIER W PARENTS	MICHAEL	1816	LANGENSTEINBACH	01/01/1832	A		F3
MAIER W PARENTS	PHILIPP	1819	LANGENSTEINBACH	01/01/1832	A		F3
MAISCH	AUGUSTIN	1825	MALSCH	01/01/1857	A		F2
MAISCH	FIDEL	1851	SCHÖLLBRONN	01/01/1868	A		F7
MAISCH	FRANZ PAUL	1843	SCHÖLLBRONN	01/01/1856	A		F7
MAISCH	GEORG		BULACH	01/01/1867	A		F8
MAISCH	IDA	1829	MALSCH	01/01/1857	A		F2
MAISCH	JOHANN	1837	SCHÖLLBRONN	/ /	A		F7
MAISCH MN KUNZ	KATHARINA	1795	SCHÖLLBRONN	01/01/1852	A		F7
MAISCH W F	JOHANN	1822	SCHÖLLBRONN	01/01/1852	A		F7
MALGUT	HADUMOT		KARLSRUHE	/ /	A		F3
MALL	CHRISTINE		SÖLLINGEN	/ /	A		F7
MALL	CHRISTOPH		SÖLLINGEN	/ /	A		F7
MALL	CHRISTOPH	1817	SÖLLINGTEN	01/01/1869	A		F7
MALL	ERNST FRIEDRICH	1873	SÖLLINGEN	01/01/1889	A		F7
MALL	FRANZ	1848	SÖLLINGEN	01/01/1868	A		F7
MALL	JOHANN CHRISTOH		SÖLLINGEN	/ /	A		
MALL	PHILIPP JAKOB	1869	SÖLLINGEN	01/01/1884	A		F7
MALL	U.		SÖLLINGEN	/ /	A		F7
MALL MN CHRISTENES	ERNA		SÖLLIONGEN	/ /	A		F7
MALL MN KIRCHENBAUER	KAROLINE	1845	SÖLLINGEN	01/01/1880	A		F3
MALL MN KIRCHENBAUER	KAROLINE	1845	SÖLLINGEN	01/01/1881	A		F7
MALL MN KIRCHENBAUER	MARGARETHE	1815	SÖLLINGEN	01/01/1869	A		F7
MALL W APRENTS	EMILIE LUISE	1875	SÖLLINGEN	01/01/1880	A		F3
MALL W F	JOHANN		SÖLLINGEN	/ /	A		F7
MALL W F	SAMUEL	1837	SÖLLINGEN	01/01/1881	A		F7
MALL W P	EMILIE LUISE	1875	SÖLLINGEN	01/01/1881	A		F7
MALL W P	GUSTAV ADOLF	1871	SÖLLINGEN	01/01/1881	A		F7
MALL W PARENTS	EMIL GUSTAV	1871	SÖLLINGEN	01/01/1881	A		F3
MALSCH	GEORG	1830	BUBACH	01/01/1867	A		F6
MANGOLD	CHRISTIAN		SPÖCK	01/01/1851	A		F4
MANGOLD	KARL		SPÖCK	01/01/1862	A		F4
MANGOLD	MAGARETHA		KARLSRUHE	01/01/1801	A		F3
MANGOLD	REINHARD		SPÖCK	01/01/1867	A		F4
MANGOLD W FAMILY	KARL FRIEDRICH		SPÖCK	01/01/1853	A		F4
MANZ	CäSARIUS		WINDEN	01/01/1808			F1
MANZ	FRIEDRICH	1832	DURLACH KARLSRUHE	/ /			F7
MANZ	GUSTAV	1870	KARLSRUHE	01/01/1886	A		F3
MANZ	MICHAEL		SÖLLINGEN	/ /	A		F7
MANZ	WILHELM		BLANKENLOCH	01/01/1849	A		F4

Lastname	Firstname	Birth Year	Birthplace	Emigration	De	Prof	Source
MARCH	MATHÄUS		BURBACH	01/01/1859	A		F8
MARER	LUDWIG	1848	KARLSRUHE	01/01/1870	A		F3
MARGARAF	GEORG	1802	ETTLINGEN	/ /	A		F4
MARGARAF MN MAIER	KATHARINA		ETTLINGEN	/ /	A		F4
MARGGRAF	LOTHAR		OBERLORBACH	01/01/1766			F1
MARGGRAF	WILHELM		ETTLINGEN	05/24/1852	A		F4
MARKARDT	JOHANN	1856	BLANKENLOCH	01/01/1865	A		F4
MARKART	JOHANN	1857	BLANKENLOCH	01/01/1866	A		F8
MARKELI	CHRISTIAN		DURLACH KARLSRUHE	01/01/1836	A		F7
MART	JOSEF		KARLSRUHE	01/01/1858	A		F3
MARTIN	JAKOB		TRENNFELD	01/01/1840	A		F5
MARTIN	JAKOB LUDWIG	1866	KARLSRUHE	01/01/1887	A		F3
MARTIN	JOHANN		KARLSRUHE	01/01/1800	A		F3
MARTIN	KATHARINA		DURLACH	01/01/1869	A		F6
MARTIN	RENIGIUS	1843	BEIERTHEIM	01/01/1867	A		F6
MARX	OTTILIE		FORBACH	01/01/1867	A		F6
MASINO	GEORG ADAM	1798	PFAFFENROTH	01/01/1863	A		F7
MASINO MN MAUCHER	WALBURGA	1807	PFAFFENROTH	01/01/1863	A		F7
MASINO W P	JOSEF	1834	PFAFFENROTH	01/01/1863	A		F7
MASSHALDER	CHRISTOPH		TRESCHLINGEN	01/01/1866	A		F6
MASSINO	MAGDALENA	1803	PFAFFENROTH	/ /	A		F7
MATHESIUS MN FRANZ	ANNA	1866	OBERHAUSEN	01/01/1888	A		F1
MATHOS	OTTO	1865	KÜHLBURG	01/01/1882	A		F6
MATTES	MAGDALENA		SINGEN	01/01/1859	A		F6
MATTLIN	GEORG JAKOB		KÖNIGSCHAFFHAUSEN	01/01/1859	A		F6
MAUCHER	WALBURGA	1813	PFAFFENROTH	01/01/1863	A		F7
MAUCHER MN ADAM	MARIA ANNA	1819	BURBACH	03/03/1867	A		F4
MAUCHER W FAMILY	JOHANN GEORG	1813	SCHIELBERG	03/03/1867	A		F4
MAUCHER W P	JOSEF	1849	BURBACH	03/03/1867	A		F4
MAUCHER W P	MARIA ANNA	1852	BURBACH	03/03/1867	A		F4
MAUCHER W P	OTTILIE	1846	BURBACH	03/03/1867	A		F4
MAUDERER	CRESZENTIA	1863	VÖLKERSBACH	01/01/1882	A		F4
MAUER	JOHANN		WIECHS	01/01/1856	A		F6
MAURER	BERTOLD	1855	MALSCH	01/01/1872	A		F2
MAURER	GEORG		BURBACH	01/01/1854	A		F6
MAURER MN KAMMERER	BARBARA	1832	RÜPPURR	01/01/1879	A		F8
MAURER W F	SEBASTIAN	1838	RÜPPURR	01/01/1879	A		F8
MAUS	ALEXANDER		TENGENDORF	01/01/1859	A		F6
MAX	LEOPOLD	1864	SPÖCK	01/01/1880	A		F8
MAY	ANTON	1848	SPESSART	12/22/1866	A		F4
MAY	ELISABETH	1850	SPESSART	12/22/1866	A		F4
MAY	GABRIEL	1846	SPESSART	01/01/1867	A		F4
MAY	KARL	1854	SPESSART	10/23/1869	A		F4
MAYER	ARNOLD JOHANN	1873	ETTLINGEN	01/01/1891	A		F4
MAYER	BERNHARD	1802	MALSCH	01/01/1841	A		F2
MAYER	FRANZ		SÖLLINGEN	/ /	A		F7
MAYER	FRANZISKA MAGDA	1817	BURBACH	01/01/1857	A		F4
MAYER	GEORG	1824	LANGENSTEINBACH	03/08/1843	A		F3
MAYER	GOTTFRIED	1836	LANGENSTEINBACH	01/01/1853	A		F3
MAYER	JOHANN		FORBACH	01/01/1854	A		F6

Lastname	Firstname	Birth Year	Birthplace	Emigration	De	Prof	Source
MAYER	JOHANN	1832	LANGENSTEINBACH	05/17/1851	A		F3
MAYER	JOHANN GEORG	1831	LANGENSTEINBACH	05/17/1851	A		F3
MAYER	JOHANNA	1834	LANGENSTEINBACH	01/01/1853	A		F3
MAYER	JOSEF		PRINZBACH	01/01/1859	A		F6
MAYER	KATHARINA	1838	LANGENSTEINBACH	01/01/1853	A		F3
MAYER	MARIA ANNA		PRINZBACH	01/01/1859	A		F6
MAYER	MICHAEL		STEINMAUERN	01/01/1859	A		F6
MAYER	ROSINA	1754	BURBACH	/ /	A		F4
MAYER	ROSINA	1839	LANGENSTEINBACH	01/01/1853	A		F3
MAYER	SUSANNE	1834	LANGENSTEINBACH	05/17/1851	A		F3
MAYER	THERESIA		PRINZBACH	01/01/1859	A		F6
MAYER	WILHELM	1832	LANGENSTEINBACH	05/17/1851	A		F3
MAYER W F	HEINRICH	1877	GRABEN	01/01/1894	A		F8
MAYER W FAMILY	FRANZISKA	1806	BURBACH	01/01/1857	A		F4
MAYER W P	BARTHOLOMA	1831	BURBACH	01/01/1857	A		F4
MAYER W P	FRANZ ANTON	1856	BURBACH	01/01/1857	A		F4
MAYER WIDOWER W S	FRIEDRICH	1857	GRABEN	01/01/1894	A		F8
MEFF	ALBRECHT		KARLSRUHE	01/01/1804	A		F3
MEHR	CHRISTIAN ADAM		DURLACH KARLSRUHE	01/01/1856			F7
MEHR	GABRIEL FRANZ		DURLACH KARLSRUHE	01/01/1848	A		F7
MEHR	JOHANN ANDREAS		DURLACH KARLSRUHE	01/01/1845			F7
MEHR	JOSEF	1868	KARLSRUHE	01/01/1883	A		F3
MEHRLE	ERNST	1875	KARLSRUHE	01/01/1893	A		F3
MEIER	AUGUST FRIEDRIH	1842	DURLACH KARLSRUHE	/ /	A		F7
MEIER	AUGUST WILHELM		DURLACH KARLSRUHE	01/01/1829			F7
MEIER	CARL	1830	DURLACH KARLSRUHE	01/01/1866	A		F7
MEIER	JOH.CHRIS.WILH.	1833	DURLACH KARLSRUHE	/ /			F7
MEIER	JOHANN CHRISTIN	1828	DURLACH KARLSRUHE	/ /	A		F7
MEIER	KARL		WÜHLBURG	01/01/1839	A		F6
MEIER	LEOPOLD	1853	DURLACH KARLSRUHE	/ /	A		F7
MEINGER	DANIEL		LIEDOLSHEIM	01/01/1880	A		F9
MEINZER	GEORG ADAM		BLANKENLOCH	01/01/1847	A		F4
MEINZER	GEORG JAKOB	1840	KNIELINGEN	01/01/1880	A		F6
MEINZER MN BECKER	KATHARINA	1834	HOCHSTETTEN	01/01/1868	A		F8
MEINZER MN HUSSER	ROSINE	1840	HOCHSTETTEN	01/01/1881	A		F8
MEINZER W F	JOHANN	1822	HOCHSTETTEN	01/01/1868	A		F8
MEINZER W F	K.LEOPOLD	1840	HOCHSTETTEN	01/01/1881	A		F8
MEINZER W HUSBAND	MARIE SALOMEA	1822	LIEDOLSHEIM	01/01/1869	A		F9
MEINZER W P	CARL ALBERT	1879	HOCHSTETTEN	01/01/1881	A		F8
MEINZER W P	EDUARD	1856	HOCHSTETTEN	01/01/1868	A		F8*
MEINZER W P	EMMA	1873	HOCHSTETTEN	01/01/1881	A		F8
MEINZER W P	FR.WILH.	1866	HOCHSTETTEN	01/01/1881	A		F8
MEINZER W P	FRIEDA	1861	HOCHSTETTEN	01/01/1868	A		F8
MEINZER W P	FRIEDERIKE	1877	HOCHSTETTEN	01/01/1881	A		F8
MEINZER W P	LEOPOLD	1856	HOCHSTETTEN	01/01/1868	A		F8
MEINZER W P	LUDWIG	1880	HOCHSTETTEN	01/01/1881	A		F8
MEINZER W P	ROBERT	1871	HOCHSTETTEN	01/01/1881	A		F8
MEINZER W P	WILHELM	1858	HOCHSTETTEN	01/01/1868	A		F8
MEINZER W W	FRIEDRICH WILHM		LIEDOLSHEIM	01/01/1869	A		F9
MEISTER	ALBERT	1837	WÜHLBURG	01/01/1861	A		F6

Lastname	Firstname	Birth Year	Birthplace	Emigration De	Prof	Source
MELCHOR MN KASTNER	KASTNER		ETTLINGEN	01/01/1850 A		F4
MELCHOR W WIFE	JOHANN	1816	ETTLINGEN	01/01/1850 A		F4
MELLINGER	EMIL	1873	KARLSRUHE	01/01/1891 A		F3
MENGESDORF	FRIEDRICH		MÖNCHZELL	01/01/1859 A		F6
MENNER	KLEMENZ		EBNET	01/01/1866 A		F6
MENZ	KARL ERHARD		SÖLLINGEN	/ / A		F3
MERFLINGER	KAROLINA	1840	BURBACH	01/01/1856 A		F4
MERFLINGER	MATHIAS	1812	BURBACH	01/01/1852 A		F4
MERFLINGER MN BAUER	KATHARINA	1814	BURBACH	01/01/1867 A		F4
MERFLINGER W FAMILY	SEBASTIAN	1809	BURBACH	01/01/1867 A		F4
MERFLINGER W P	ANTON	1838	BURBACH	01/01/1867 A		F4
MERFLINGER W P	BENEDIKT	1856	BURBACH	01/01/1867 A		F4
MERFLINGER W P	EUSEBIUS	1855	BURBACH	01/01/1856 A		F4
MERFLINGER W P	KAROLINE	1849	BURBACH	01/01/1867 A		F4
MERFLINGER W P	MARIM	1841	BURBACH	01/01/1867 A		F4
MERFLINGER W P	MATHILDE	1851	BURBACH	01/01/1867 A		F4
MERFLINGER W P	ROSALIA	1858	BURBACH	01/01/1867 A		F4
MERFLINGER W P	THEODOR	1843	BURBACH	01/01/1867 A		F4
MERKEL	FRANZ		ETTLINGEN	/ / A		F4
MERKL	PHILIPP JAKOB		SÖLLINGEN	/ / A		F7
MERKLE	ALBERT		KARLSRUHE	/ / A		F3
MERKLE	CHRISTIANE	1834	LANGENSTEINBACH	/ / A		F3
MERKLE	GEORG	1821	LANGENSTEINBACH	/ / A		F3
MERKLE	JAKOB	1826	LANGENSTEINBACH	01/01/1858 A		F3
MERKLE	JOHANN	1862	MÜHLBERG	01/01/1882 A		F6
MERKLE	KATHARINA	1828	LANGENSTEINBACH	/ / A		F3
MERKLE	MARGARETHA	1824	LANGENSTEINBACH	01/01/1854 A		F3
MERKLE	SIMON		GRABEN	01/01/1750 A		F5
MERKLER MN ARTMANN	JOSEFINE	1848	MÖRSCH	10/09/1889 A		F7
MERKLER MN DECK	ENGELBERTHA	1854	MÖRSCH	01/01/1881 A		F7
MERKLER W F	ANTON	1848	MÖRSCH	01/01/1881 A		F7
MERKLER W F	JOSEF	1843	MÖRSCH	10/09/1880 A		F7
MERKLER W P	HEINRICH	1873	MÖRSCH	09/10/1880 A		F7
MERKLER W P	KATHARINA	1878	MÖRSCH	01/01/1881 A		F7
MERKLINGER	JOHANN		ETTLINGEN	01/01/1853 A		F4
MERKLINGER	JOHANN	1820	SCHÖLLBRONN	01/01/1853 A		F7
MERKLINGER	JOHANNES	1776	SCHÖLLBRONN	01/01/1834 A		F7
MERKLINGER MN KUNZ	KATHARINA	1784	SCHÖLLBRONN	01/01/1834 A		F7
MERKLINGER W P	ALOISIA	1822	SCHÖLLBRONN	01/01/1834 A		F7
MERKLINGER W P	ELISABETH	1815	SCHÖLLBRONN	01/01/1834 A		F7
MERKLINGER W P	GEORG	1818	SCHÖLLBRONN	01/01/1834 A		F7
MERKLINGER W P	KASIMIR	1809	SCHÖLLBRONN	01/01/1834 A		F7
MERKLINGER W P	KATHARINA	1809	SCHÖLLBRONN	01/01/1834 A		F7
MERKLINGER W P	MAGDALENA	1820	SCHÖLLBRONN	01/01/1834 A		F7
MERKLINGER W P	SALOME	1807	SCHÖLLBRONN	01/01/1834 A		F7
MERT	JOHANNES JAKOB	1794	KARLSRUHE	01/01/1827 A		F3
MERZ	EMILIE KAROLINE	1863	WELSCHNEUREUTH	01/01/1883 A		F8
MERZ MN MARSCH	MARGARETHE	1844	WELSCHNEUREUTH ?	01/01/1881 A		F8
MERZ W F	HEINRICH	1843	WELSCHNEUREUTH ?	01/01/1881 A		F8
MERZ W P	HEINRICH	1876	WELSCHNEUREUTH	01/01/1881 A		F8

Lastname	Firstname	Birth Year	Birthplace	Emigration	De	Prof	Source
MERZ W P	JAKOB FRIEDRICH	1880	WELSCHNEUREUTH ?	01/01/1881	A		F8
METZ	HERMANN	1848	GRABEN	01/01/1867	A		F3
METZ	JOHANN		BLANKENLOCH	01/01/1835	A		F4
METZ	SOPHIE	1854	LIEDOLSHEIM	01/01/1881	A		F9
METZGER	CHRISTOPH		GRABEN	01/01/1848	A		F5
METZGER	FRITZ		GRABEN	01/01/1880	A		F5
METZGER	GUSTAV	1851	GRABEN	01/01/1870	A		F3
METZGER	HEINRICH		GRABEN	01/01/1810	A		F3
METZGER	HERMANN HEINRIH	1884	GRABEN	01/01/1891	A		F3
METZGER	JAKOB FRIEDRICH		GRABEN	01/01/1834	A		F8
METZGER	JAKOB FRIEDRICH		GRABEN	01/01/1863	A		F5
METZGER	JOHANN		GRABEN	01/01/1819	A		F3
METZGER	JOHANN JAKOB		GRABEN	01/01/1854	A		F5
METZGER	KARL	1872	GRABEN	01/01/1887	A		F3
METZGER	KARL	1872	GRABEN	01/01/1887	A		F8
METZGER	LUDWIG		GRABEN	01/01/1880	A		F3
METZGER	LUISE		GRABEN	01/01/1832	A		F5
METZGER	LUISE		GRABEN	01/01/1889	A		F3
METZGER	MARIA		GRABEN	01/01/1797	A		F3
METZGER	PHILIPP		GRABEN	01/01/1835	A		F5
METZGER	PHILIPPINE	1850	GRABEN	01/01/1869	A		F3
METZGER	ROBERT HEINRICH	1879	GRABEN	01/01/1895	A		F3
METZGER	WENDEL		GRABEN	01/01/1830	A		F5
METZGER	WENZ		GRABEN	/ /	A		F5
METZGER	WILHELM		GRABEN	01/01/1848	A		F5
METZGER	WILHELM	1865	MÜHLBERG	01/01/1882	A		F6
METZGER W F	JOHANN		GRABEN	01/01/1848	A		F5
METZGER MN	MARGARETHA	1861	GRABEN	01/01/1893	A		F3
METZGER MN SIEGEL	MARGARETHA	1857	GRABEN	01/01/1892	A		F3
METZGER MN STEGEL	MARGARETHE	1857	GRABEN	01/01/1892	A		F8
METZGER W F	AUGUST	1862	GRABEN	01/01/1892	A		F8
METZGER W F	JOHANN		GRABEN	01/01/1838	A		F5
METZGER W FAMILY	AUGUST	1862	GRABEN	01/01/1892	A		F3
METZGER W FAMILY	HEINRICH		WÖSSINGEN	01/01/1865	A		F1
METZGER W FAMILY	REINHARD	1849	GRABEN	01/01/1893	A		F3
METZGER W P	ANNA MARIA	1880	GRABEN	01/01/1892	A		F8
METZGER W P	AUGUST	1892	GRABEN	01/01/1892	A		F8
METZGER W PARENTS	ANNA MARIA	1880	GRABEN	01/01/1892	A		F3
METZGER W PARENTS	AUGUST	1891	GRABEN	01/01/1892	A		F3
METZGER W PARENTS	KARL FRIEDRICH	1888	GRABEN	01/01/1893	A		F3
METZGER W PARENTS	PHILIPPINE	1881	GRABEN	01/01/1893	A		F3
METZGER-HOHL	CHRISTINE		GRABEN	01/01/1880	A		F5
METZGER-MENZ	CHRISTIENE		GRABEN	/ /	A		F3
MEYER	ARNOLD JOHANN	1874	KARLSRUHE	01/01/1891	A		F3
MEYERHUBER	OSKAR ERWIN			01/01/1893	A		F3
MEZ	HERMANN	1848	GRABEN	01/01/1867	A		F8
MEZ	MAX		GRABEN	01/01/1888	A		F5
MEZGER	MICHAEL		UNTERÖWISHEIM	01/01/1834	A		F6
MICHAELUER				/ /			
MICHEL	IGNAZ		GERCHSHEIM	01/01/1866	A		F6

Lastname	Firstname	Birth Year	Birthplace	Emigration	De	Prof	Source
MILLOT	EDUARD	1864	KARLSRUHE	01/01/1881	A		F3
MILTENBURGER	FERDINAND	1869	KARLSRUHE	01/01/1885	A		F3
MINK MN	MAGDALENA	1806	KARLSRUHE	01/01/1866	A		F3
MINK W FAMILY	JOSEF		KARLSRUHE	01/01/1866	A		F3
MINK W PARENTS	ALBERT ADAM	1855	KARLSRUHE	01/01/1866	A		F3
MINK W PARENTS	AMALIE LUISE		KARLSRUHE	01/01/1866	A		F3
MINK W PARENTS	ERNESTINE LUISE	1850	KARLSRUHE	01/01/1866	A		F3
MINK W PARENTS	FRANZ KARL	1859	KARLSRUHE	01/01/1866	A		F3
MINK W PARENTS	FRIEDRICH LUDWG	1849	KARLSRUHE	01/01/1866	A		F3
MINK W PARENTS	SOPHIE AMALIE	1848	KARLSRUHE	01/01/1866	A		F3
MITZUM	JAKOB	1791	LANGENSTEINBACH	01/01/1850	A		F3
MITZUM MN	FRIDERIKE		LANGENSTEINBACH	/ /	A		F3
MITZUM W FATHER	ELISABETH	1818	LANGENSTEINBACH	01/01/1850	A		F3
MITZUM W FATHER	JAKOB	1820	LANGENSTEINBACH	01/01/1850	A		F3
MITZUM W FATHER	MAGDALENA	1815	LANGENSTEINBACH	01/01/1850	A		F3
MOE	JOHANN JOSEF		STEINBRUNN	01/01/1859	A		F6
MOGR W P	EMMA	1836	BURBACH	01/01/1867	A		F4
MOHR	ALOIS		OBERWEIER	01/01/1830	A		F2
MOHR	CAROLINA		OBERWEILER	01/01/1853	A		F1
MOHR	FRANZ ANTON	1806	BURBACH	01/01/1842	A		F4
MOHR W FAMILY	KONRAD	1848	BURBACH	01/01/1867	A		F4
MOHR W P	AUGUST	1847	BURBACH	01/01/1867	A		F4
MOHR W P	MATHILDE	1852	BURBACH	01/01/1867	A		F4
MOHR W P	THERESE	1839	BURBACH	01/01/1839	A		F4
MOPNER	MICHAEL		BRÖTZINGEN	01/01/1737	A		F2
MORALLER	ANTON LUDWIG	1869	KARLSRUHE	01/01/1886	A		F3
MORATH	JOSEF	1864	ALTSCHWEIER	01/01/1884	A		F5
MORATH	RUDOLF	1858	ALTSCHWEIER	01/01/1874	A		F5
MORATH MN STRITT	MARIA AGATHA		LÖFFINGEN	01/01/1854	A		F6
MORATH W P	JOHANN	1837	LÖFFINGEN	01/01/1854	A		F6
MORATH W P	JOSEF	1841	LÖFFINGEN	01/01/1854	A		F6
MORATH W P	KATHARINA	1836	LÖFFINGEN	01/01/1854	A		F6
MORATH W P	MAGDALENA	1839	LÖFFINGEN	01/01/1854	A		F6
MORATH W P	THERESIA	1843	LÖFFINGEN	01/01/1854	A		F6
MORLOCK	CHRISTIAN	1855	RINKLINGEN	01/01/1870	A		F7
MORLOCK	CHRISTOPH	1835	RINKLINGEN	01/01/1854	A		F7
MORLOCK	LORENZ	1837	RINKLINGEN	01/01/1854	A		F7
MORLOD	KARL CHRISTIAN		KARLSRUHE	01/01/1866	A		F3
MORSCH	MARTIN JOHANN	1795	RINKLINGEN	05/24/1847	A		F4
MORSCH W F	ANNA MARIA	1804	RINKLINGEN	01/01/1851	A		F7
MORSCH W P	ELISABETH	1851	RINKLINGEN	01/01/1851	A		F7
MORSCH W P	KATHARINA STEFA	1848	RINKLINGEN	01/01/1851	A		F7
MORSCH W P	LUDWIG LEOPOLD	1850	RINKLINGEN	01/01/1851	A		F7
MORSCH W P & W F	MARGARETHA	1828	RINKLINGEN	01/01/1851	A		F7
MUELLER	ANNA		KARLSRUHE	/ /	A		F3
MUFLE	KARL	1868	ETTLINGEN	01/01/1882	A		F4
MULSEITH	LUIS		KARLSRUHE	/ /	A		F3
MUNCH	WILHELM		FAHRENBACH	01/01/1866	A		F6
MUND	NIKOLAUS		MÖRSCH	07/12/1858	A		F7
MUSSGNUG	MISTER		SÖLLINGEN	/ /	A		F7

Lastname	Firstname	Birth Year	Birthplace	Emigration De	Prof	Source
MUTSCHLER	MATH. JOH. MICH		KARLSRUHE	01/01/1861 A		F3
MUTSCHLER	MATHIAS	1840	DURLACH KARLSRUHE	/ /		F7
MÜHLHAUPT	FIDEL		GEISSLINGEN	01/01/1859 A		F6
MÜHSLE	KARL	1868	KARLSRUHE	01/01/1882 A		F3
MÜLLER	ADAM		GRÖTZINGEN	01/01/1802 A		F5
MÜLLER	ADAM		GRÖTZINGEN	01/01/1803 A		F5
MÜLLER	ANNA KATHARINA		KREUZWERTHEIM	05/24/1752 A		F5
MÜLLER	AUGUSTIN		OFTERSHEIM	11/03/1819		F1
MÜLLER	CHRISTOPH	1866	LANGENSTEINBACH	01/01/1883 A		F3
MÜLLER	DYONIS		VÖLKERSBACH	01/01/1843 A		F4
MÜLLER	ELISABETH		MALSCH	01/01/1879 A		F2
MÜLLER	FERDINAND	1861	MALSCH	01/01/1879 A		F2
MÜLLER	FRIEDRICH	1872	SPIELBERG	01/01/1887 A		F4
MÜLLER	HEINRICH		SPÖCK	01/01/1855 A		F4
MÜLLER	JAKOB		BLANKENLOCH	01/01/1832 A		F4
MÜLLER	JAKOB		KARLSRUHE	/ / A		F3
MÜLLER	JAKOB	1832	DURLACH KARLSRUHE	/ /		F7
MÜLLER	JAKOB	1839	LANGENSTEINBACH	01/01/1854 A		F3
MÜLLER	JAKOB FRIEDRICH		GRÖTZINGEN	01/01/1833 A		F5
MÜLLER	JAKOB FRIEDRICH	1827	GRÖTZINGEN	01/01/1853 A		F3
MÜLLER	JOHANN		GRABEN	01/01/1865 A		F5
MÜLLER	JOHANN	1799	GRÖTZINGEN	01/01/1846 A		F3
MÜLLER	JOHANN	1817	MALSCH	01/01/1847 A		F2
MÜLLER	JOHANN JOSEPH	1850	BAUERBACH	01/01/1868 A		F8
MÜLLER	JOSEF		MALSCH	01/01/1847 A		F2
MÜLLER	JOSEF		MALSCH	01/01/1857 A		F2
MÜLLER	JOSEF	1820	MALSCH	01/01/1845 A		F2
MÜLLER	JULIUS	1870	LANGENSTEINBACH	/ / A		F3
MÜLLER	KARL FRIEDRICH	1825	GRÖTZINGEN	01/01/1854 A		F3
MÜLLER	KATHARINA		ISCHENHEIM	01/01/1859 A		F6
MÜLLER	KILIAN		OFTERSHEIM	01/01/1819		F1
MÜLLER	LUDWIG		GRABEN	01/01/1818 A		F5
MÜLLER	LUDWIG		GRABEN	01/01/1865 A		F3
MÜLLER	LUKAS	1862	MÖRSCH	01/01/1887 A		F4
MÜLLER	MARTIN		OBERWEIER	01/01/1787 A		F1
MÜLLER	MICHAEL		OBERWEIER	01/01/1787 A		F1
MÜLLER	MORITZ	1812	MALSCH	01/01/1847 A		F2
MÜLLER	PHILIPP	1858	ETTLINGEN	01/01/1872 A		F4
MÜLLER	PUIS	1869	MALSCH	01/01/1891 A		F2
MÜLLER	TOBIAS		VENDINGEN	01/01/1866 A		F6
MÜLLER	WILHELM		SÖLLINGEN	/ / A		F7
MÜLLER	WILHELM	1850	KARLSRUHE	01/01/1869 A		F3
MÜLLER	WILHELM LUDWIG	1876	BLANKENLOCH	01/01/1892 A		F4
MÜLLER	ZACHARIAS		GRÖTZINGEN	01/01/1856 A		F5
MÜLLER MN BECHLER	GENOVEVA	1817	WALPRECHTSWEILER	01/01/1854 A		F2
MÜLLER MN HOFHEINZ	CHRISTINE	1846	BLANKENLOCH	01/01/1880 A		F4
MÜLLER MN HOFHEINZ	CHRISTINE	1848	BLANKENLOCH	01/01/1880 A		F4
MÜLLER MN KRONENWETT	MAGDALENA	1845	LANGENSTEINBACH	03/17/1882 A		F3
MÜLLER W FAMILY	CHRISTIAN	1842	BLANKENLOCH	01/01/1880 A		F4
MÜLLER W FAMILY	CHRISTIAN LUDWG	1842	BLANKENLOCH	01/01/1880 A		F4

Lastname	Firstname	Birth Year	Birthplace	Emigration	De	Prof	Source
MÜLLER W FAMILY	KARL	1849	LANGENSTEINBACH	03/17/1882	A		F3
MÜLLER W FAMILY	LORENZ	1817	MALSCH	04/15/1854	A		F2
MÜLLER W P	CHRISTINE		BLANKENLOCH	01/01/1880	A		F4
MÜLLER W P	KARL		BLANKENLOCH	01/01/1880	A		F4
MÜLLER W P	LUDWIG	1872	BLANKENLOCH	01/01/1880	A		F4
MÜLLER W PARENTS	ALBERT	1879	LANGENSTEINBACH	03/17/1882	A		F3
MÜLLER W PARENTS	CHRISTINE	1873	BLANKENLOCH	01/01/1880	A		F4
MÜLLER W PARENTS	EMMA	1880	LANGENSTEINBACH	03/17/1882	A		F3
MÜLLER W PARENTS	FLORENTINE	1843	MALSCH	04/15/1854	A		F2
MÜLLER W PARENTS	JUSTINE	1841	MALSCH	04/15/1854	A		F2
MÜLLER W PARENTS	KARL		BLANKENLOCH	01/01/1880	A		F4
MÜLLER W PARENTS	KONR.BERN	1842	MALSCH	01/01/1854	A		F2
MÜLLER W PARENTS	LUDWIG	1872	BLANKENLOCH	01/01/1880	A		F4
MÜLLER W PARENTS	VERONIKA	1850	MALSCH	04/15/1854	A		F2
MÜLLERE	ANNA		KARLSRUHE	/ /	A		F3
MÜLLERW PARENTS	JOHANN NEPOMUK	1847	MALSCH	04/15/1854	A		F2
MÜLLLER WW CH	MICHAEL		WÖSSINGEN	01/01/1780		WEAV	F1
MÜNCH	CARL		GRABEN	01/01/1852	A		F3
MÜNCH	KARL		GRABEN	01/01/1852	A		F5
MÜNSTER	WILH. PHL. CHRT		DURLACH KARLSRUHE	01/01/1843	A		F7
MÜNZER	RUDOLF		DURLACH	/ /	A		F3
MÄRKY	EMIL		FREIBURG	01/01/1890	A		F8
MÖDEL	ALFRED		KARLSRUHE	/ /	A		F3
MÖGLICH	KARL AUGUST	1860	KARLSRUHE	01/01/1891	A		F3
MÖGLICH	OSKAR	1864	KARLSRUHE	01/01/1880	A		F3
MÖRDER	ANDREAS		VÖRSTETTEN	01/01/1859	A		F6
MÖRSCH	CHRISTIAN		KARLSRUHE	01/01/1856	A		F3
MÖSNER	KARL	1868	KARLSRUHE	01/01/1886	A		F3
MÖSSERT	FRIEDRICH	1864	KARLSRUHE	01/01/1883	A		F3
MÖSSINGER	BERNHARD		SÖLLINGEN	/ /	A		F7
MÖSSINGER	FRIEDRICH		SÖLLINGEN	/ /	A		F7
MÖSSINGER	JOHANN		KARLSRUHE	01/01/1849	A		F3
MÖSSINGER	LUDWIG		GRÖTZINGEN	/ /	A		F3
MÖSSINGER	LUDWIG		GRÖTZINGEN	01/01/1817	A		F5
MÖSSINGER	WILHELM		KARLSRUHE	01/01/1849	A		F3
MÖSSINGER MN SCHEUER	ELSABETH		SÖLLINGER	01/01/1849	A		F7
MÖSSINGER W CHILD.	KARL		KARLSRUHE	01/01/1849	A		F3
MÖSSINGER W FATH.	AUGUST		KARLSRUHE	01/01/1849	A		F3
MÖSSINGER W FATH.	KARL		KARLSRUHE	01/01/1849	A		F3
MÖSSINGER W W	CHRISTOPH		SÖLLINGEN	/ /	A		F7
MÖSSINGER W W	FRIEDRICH		SÖLLINGEN	01/01/1849	A		F7
MÖSSNER	ERWIN		KARLSRUHE	01/01/1825	A		F5
MÖSSNER MN KNOPF	ELSA	1799	BÜHL	01/01/1832	A		F1
MÜHLHAUPT	FIDEL		GEISSLINGEN	01/01/1859	A		F6
MÜLLER	ADAM		BLANKENLOCH	01/01/1783	A		F4
MÜLLER	ALOIS		MÖRSCH	01/01/1881	A		F7
MÜLLER	CARL	1851	RÜPPUR	01/01/1868	A		F8
MÜLLER	CHRISTIAN		MÖRSCH	01/01/1790	A		F7
MÜLLER	CHRISTINE	1845	RÜPPUR	01/01/1869	A		F8
MÜLLER	CHRISTOPH		BLANKENLOCH	01/01/1868	A		F4

Lastname	Firstname	Birth Year	Birthplace	Emigration	De	Prof	Source
MÜLLER	ELISABETH		BAUERBACH	01/01/1861	A		F6
MÜLLER	GEORG JAKOB		BLANKENLOCH	01/01/1770	A		F4
MÜLLER	JAKOB CHRISTIAN	1863	RÜPPUR	01/01/1880	A		F8
MÜLLER	JOHANN	1850	ETTLINGEN	09/30/1869	A		F4
MÜLLER	JOHANN GEORG	1849	ETTLINGEN	01/01/1872	A		F4
MÜLLER	JULIUS	1928	ETTLINGEN	07/06/1861	A		F4
MÜLLER	LEOPOLD MARTIN	1832	ETTLINGEN	01/01/1853	A		F4
MÜLLER	LUDWIG	1870	OCHSENBACH	01/01/1896	A		F7
MÜLLER	LUDWIG	1873	RÜPPURR	01/01/1888	A		F8
MÜLLER	LUKAS	1857	MÖRSCH	03/04/1889	A		F7
MÜLLER	LUKAS	1882	MÖRSCH	01/01/1887	A		F7
MÜLLER	MARKUS		MÖRSCH	03/22/1891	A		F7
MÜLLER	PHILIPP JAKOB		BURBACH	01/01/1837	A		F6
MÜLLER	WILHELM LUDWIG	1876	BLANKENLOCH	01/01/1892	A		F5
MÜLLER	ZACHARIAS		GRÖTZINGEN	01/01/1856	A		F5
MÜLLER MN HEMBACH	KAROLINA	1838	BLANKENLOCH	01/01/1868	A		F4
MÜLLER MN HOFHEINZ	CHRISTINE	1846	BLANKENLOCH	01/01/1880	A		F5
MÜLLER MN HUBER	MARARETHA	1834	MÖRSCH	07/11/1853	A		F7
MÜLLER MN MECHLER	THERESE	1842	MÖRSCH	08/01/1853	A		F7
MÜLLER W F	BENEDIKT		FORBACH	01/01/1854	A		F6
MÜLLER W F	CHRISTIAN LUDWG	1842	BLANKENLOCH	01/01/1880	A		F5
MÜLLER W F	JAKOB		MÖRSCH	08/01/1853	A		F7
MÜLLER W F	JOHANNES		MÖRSCH	07/11/1853	A		F7
MÜLLER W FAMILY	GOTTFRIED	1834	BLANKENLOCH	01/01/1868	A		F4
MÜLLER W P	ANTON	1870	MÖRSCH	08/01/1853	A		F7
MÜLLER W P	AUGUST	1867	BLANKENLOCH	01/01/1868	A		F4
MÜLLER W P	CHRISTINE	1873	BLANKENLOCH	01/01/1880	A		F4
MÜLLER W P	EMIL	1866	BLANKENLOCH	01/01/1868	A		F4
MÜLLER W P	FLORENTINE	1849	MÖRSCH	07/11/1853	A		F7
MÜLLER W P	HEINRICH	1872	MÖRSCH	08/01/1853	A		F7
MÜLLER W P	JULIUS	1865	BLANKENLOCH	01/01/1868	A		F4
MÜLLER W P	KARL	1855	BLANENLOCH	01/01/1868	A		F4
MÜLLER W P	KARL	1879	BLANKENLOCH	01/01/1880	A		F5
MÜLLER W P	KILIAN	1862	BLANKENLOCH	01/01/1868	A		F4
MÜLLER W P	LORENZ	1839	MÖRSCH	07/11/1853	A		F7
MÜLLER W P	LUDWIG	1872	BLANKENLOCH	01/01/1880	A		F4
MÜLLER W P	MARI EVA	1874	MÖRSCH	08/01/1853	A		F7
MÜLLER W P	ROSA	1878	MÖRSCH	08/01/1853	A		F7

Lastname	Firstname	Birth Year	Birthplace	Emigration	De	Prof	Source
NAGEL	AUGUST		BLANKENLOCH	01/01/1846	A		F4
NAGEL	BARBARA		BLANKENLOCH	01/01/1814	A		F4
NAGEL	BERNHARD		BLANKENLOCH	01/01/1783	A		F4
NAGEL	CHRISTIAN		BLANKENLOCH	01/01/1865	A		F4
NAGEL	CHRISTIAN	1836	LANGENSTEINBACH	04/02/1862	A		F3
NAGEL	CHRISTOPH		BLANKENLOCH	01/01/1847	A		F4
NAGEL	CHRISTOPH WILH		GRABEN	/ /	A		F5
NAGEL	DAVID		BLANKENLOCH	01/01/1845	A		F4
NAGEL	ELISABETH MARGA		BLANKENLOCH	01/01/1851	A		F4
NAGEL	ERNST	1868	BLANKENLOCH	01/01/1887	A		F4
NAGEL	FRIEDRICH		GRABEN	01/01/1811	A		F3
NAGEL	FRITZ	1862	BLANKENLOCH	01/01/1886	A		F4
NAGEL	JAKOB	1827	LANGENSTEINBACH	04/22/1864	A		F3
NAGEL	JAKOB FRIEDRICH	1827	LANGENSTEINBACH	03/02/1854	A		F3
NAGEL	JAKOB FRIEDRICH	1861	KNIELINGEN	01/01/1880	A		F6
NAGEL	JOHANN		BLANKENLOCH	01/01/1803	A		F4
NAGEL	JOHANN LUDWIG		BLANKENLOCH	01/01/1848	A		F4
NAGEL	JOSEF		BLANKENLOCH	01/01/1852	A		F4
NAGEL	KARL	1821	LANGENSTEINBACH	01/01/1847	A		F3
NAGEL	KARL LUDWIG	1865	BLANKENLOCH	01/01/1886	A		F4
NAGEL	KATHARINA	1829	LANGENSTEINBACH	04/22/1864	A		F3
NAGEL	KATHARINA	1839	LANGENSTEINBACH	04/02/1862	A		F3
NAGEL	KONRAD		GRABEN	01/01/1850	A		F3
NAGEL	LUDWIG		BLANKENLOCH	01/01/1814	A		F4
NAGEL	LUISE	1848	BLANKENLOCH	01/01/1880	A		F4
NAGEL	MAGDALENA	1832	LANGENSTEINBACH	02/03/1854	A		F3
NAGEL	MAX	1861	BLANKENLOCH	01/01/1879	A		F4
NAGEL	PETER		GRABEN	01/01/1792	A		F3
NAGEL	PHILIPP	1821	LANGENSTEINBACH	01/01/1847	A		F3
NAGEL	PHILIPP	1840	LANGENSTEINBACH	02/03/1854	A		F3
NAGEL	PHILIPP	1842	LANGENSTEINBACH	01/01/1866	A		F3
NAGEL	WILHELM		GRABEN	01/01/1835	A		F3
NAGEL	WILHELM	1841	BLANKENLOCH	01/01/1880	A		F5
NAGEL	WILHELM FRIEDRH	1863	SPRANTAL	01/01/1882	A		F6
NAGEL	WILHELM FRIEDRI	1869	BLANKENLOCH	01/01/1890	A		F4
NAGEL MN DAMBACHER	KATHARINA	1820	LANGENSTEINBACH	01/01/1847	A		F3
NAGEL MN GRIMM	CHRISTINE	1846	BLANKENLOCH	01/01/1880	A		F4
NAGEL MN NAGEL	LUISE		BLANKENLOCH	01/01/1891	A		F4
NAGEL MN SCHMIDT	FRIDERIKE	1824	LANGENSTEINBACH	01/01/1847	A		F3
NAGEL W F	JOHANN JAKOB	1851	BLANKENLOCH	01/01/1880	A		F5
NAGEL W F	KARL		BRUCHSAL	01/01/1866	A		F6
NAGEL W F	KARL FRIEDRICH		BLANKENLOCH	01/01/1891	A		F4
NAGEL W FAMILY	CHRISTIAN		BLANKENLOCH	01/01/1862	A		F4
NAGEL W FAMILY	JOHANN JAKOB	1851	BLANKENLOCH	01/01/1880	A		F4
NAGEL W FAMILY	JOHANN MICHAEL		BLANKENLOCH	01/01/1847	A		F4
NAGEL W FAMILY	JOHANN PHILIPP	1826	BLANKENLOCH	01/01/1880	A		F4
NAGEL W FAMILY	JOHANN ULRICH	1850	BLANKENLOCH	01/01/1880	A		F4
NAGEL W FAMILY	WILHELM	1841	BLANKENLOCH	01/01/1880	A		F4
NAGEL W P	AUGUST	1863	BLANKENLOCH	01/01/1880	A		F4
NAGEL W P	BERTHA	1876	BLANKENLOCH	01/01/1880	A		F4

Lastname	Firstname	Birth Year	Birthplace	Emigration	De	Prof	Source
NAGEL W P	CHRISRINE LISET	1863	BLANKENLOCH	01/01/1880	A		F4
NAGEL W P	EMILLE WILHELME	1872	BLANKENLOCH	01/01/1880	A		F4
NAGEL W P	ERNESTINE LUISE	1865	BLANKENLOCH	01/01/1880	A		F4
NAGEL W P	JOHANN LUDWIG	1861	BLANKENLOCH	01/01/1880	A		F4
NAGEL W P	KARL	1885	BLANKENLOCH	01/01/1891	A		F4
NAGEL W P	KARL GOTTFRIED	1872	BLANKENLOCH	01/01/1880	A		F4
NAGEL W P	KAROLINE	1867	BLANKENLOCH	01/01/1880	A		F4
NAGEL W P	KAROLINE CHRIST	1878	BLANKENLOCH	01/01/1880	A		F5
NAGEL W P	LISETTE LUISE	1871	BLANKENLOCH	01/01/1880	A		F4
NAGEL W P	LUISE	1876	BLANKENLOCH	01/01/1880	A		F4
NAGEL W P	LUISE KAROLINE	1879	BLANKENLOCH	01/01/1880	A		F4
NAGEL W P	LUISE KATHARINA	1868	BLANKENLOCH	01/01/1880	A		F4
NAGEL W P	MAX	1859	BLANKENLOCH	01/01/1880	A		F4
NAGEL W P	NINA	1881	BLANKENLOCH	01/01/1891	A		F4
NAGEL W P	WILHELM FRIEDRH	1873	BLANKENLOCH	01/01/1880	A		F4
NAGEL W PARENTS	KATHARINA	1847	LANGENSTEINBACH	01/01/1847	A		F3
NAGEL W PARENTS	MARIA CHRISTINE	1850	LANGENSTEINBACH	01/01/1847	A		F3
NAGELI	ANTON		SCHLICHT	01/01/1770			F1
NEES	JERG ANDREAS		GRABEN	01/01/1750	A		F3
NEES MN PLETSCH	CHRISTINE	1824	HOCHSTETTEN	01/01/1867	A		F8
NEES W F	GEORG MICHAEL	1821	HOCHSTETTEN	01/01/1867	A		F8
NEES W P	CHRISTINE	1864	HOCHSTETTEN	01/01/1867	A		F8
NEES W P	AUGUST	1862	HOCHSTETTEN	01/01/1867	A		F8
NEES W P	CARL	1841	HOCHSTETTEN	01/01/1867	A		F8
NEES W P	CAROLINE	1847	HOCHSTETTEN	01/01/1867	A		F8
NEES W P	JOHANN	1859	HOCHSTETTEN	01/01/1867	A		F8
NEES W P	LUDWIG	1857	HOCHSTETTEN	01/01/1867	A		F8
NEES W P	THEODOR	1848	HOCHSTETTEN	01/01/1867	A		F8
NEES W P	WILHELM	1866	HOCHSTETTEN	01/01/1867	A		F8
NEFF	CHRISTIAN		KARLSRUHE	01/01/1804	A		F3
NETZEBA	KARL	1872	DURLACH	01/01/1890	A		F3
NEU	FRIEDRICH GEORG	1862	KARLSRUHE	01/01/1887	A		F3
NEU	HERMANN JOSEF		MÖRSCH	07/21/1889	A		F7
NEU MN KÄSTEL	BARBARA		MÖRSCH	07/12/1853	A		F7
NEU MN RIHN	THERESE	1844	MÖRSCH	01/01/1880	A		F7
NEU W F	JOSEF BAPTIST	1846	MÖRSCH	01/01/1880	A		F7
NEU W F	SEBASTIAN		MÖRSCH	07/12/1853	A		F7
NEU W P	ALOIS	1850	MÖRSCH	07/12/1853	A		F7
NEU W P	ANTON	1844	MÖRSCH	07/12/1853	A		F7
NEU W P	DIONYS	1840	MÖRSCH	07/12/1853	A		F7
NEU W P	JOSEF	1846	MÖRSCH	07/12/1853	A		F7
NEU W P	JOSEF	1877	MÖRSCH	01/01/1880	A		F7
NEU W P	KAROLINE	1871	MÖRSCH	01/01/1880	A		F7
NEU W P	MARIA ANNA	1874	MÖRSCH	01/01/1880	A		F7
NEU W P	MICHAEL	1838	MÖRSCH	07/12/1853	A		F7
NEU W P	ROSA	1841	MÖRSCH	07/12/1853	A		F7
NEU WP	MAGDALENA	1879	MÖRSCH	01/01/1880	A		F7
NEUDERT MN SCHWAN	MARIA	1825	MALSCH	01/01/1848	A		F4
NEUDERT W FAMILY	PH'LLIP	1824	MALSCH	01/01/1848	A		F4
NEUDERT W P	JOHANN	1844	MALSCH	01/01/1848	A		F4

Lastname	Firstname	Birth Year	Birthplace	Emigration	De	Prof	Source
NEUMAIER	BARBARA	1787	SCHöLLBRONN	01/01/1829	A		F7
NEUMAIER	CHRISTOPH	1802	SCHöLLBRONN	01/01/1829	A		F7
NEUMAIER	HERMANN	1841	SCHöLLBRONN	01/01/1848	A		F7
NEUMAIER	JOHANN	1843	PFAFFENROTH	/ /	A		F7
NEUMAIER	JOSEF	1833	SCHöLLBRONN	/ /	A		F7
NEUMAIER	KATHARINA		HOFSTETTEN	01/01/1859	A		F6
NEUMAIER	KATHARINA		SCHöLLBRONN	01/01/1850	A		F7
NEUMAIER	PHILIPP ANTON	1785	SCHöLLBRONN	01/01/1829	A		F7
NEUMAIER	URBAN	1812	SCHöLLBRONN	01/01/1835	A		F7
NEUMAIER MN HEID	MAGDALENA		PFAFFENROTH	/ /	A		F7
NEUMAIER MN MERKLING	SOPHIE	1816	SCHöLLBRONN	01/01/1848	A		F7
NEUMAIER W F	DANIEL	1807	SCHöLLBRONN	01/01/1848	A		F7
NEUMAIER W P	JOSEF	1851	SCHöLLBRONN	01/01/1848	A		F7
NEUMAIER W P	MARGARETHA	1847	SCHöLLBRONN	01/01/1848	A		F7
NEUMAIER W P	THEODOR	1844	SCHöLLBRONN	01/01/1848	A		F7
NEUMAYER	GABRIEL	1828	SCHöLLBRONN	01/01/1852	A		F7
NEUMAYER	GEORG	1827	SCHöLLBRONN	01/01/1852	A		F7
NEUMAYER	JAKOB		MALSCH	01/01/1790	A		F2
NEUMAYER MN RABOLD	GERTRUD	1799	SCHöLLBRONN	01/01/1839	A		
NEUMAYER W F	JOSEF	1780	SCHöLLBRONN	01/01/1839	A		F7
NEUMAYER W P	GERTRUD	1824	SCHöLLBRONN	01/01/1839	A		F7
NEUMAYER W P	IGNAZ	1827	SCHöLLBRONN	01/01/1839	A		F7
NEUMAYER W P	JOHANN	1829	SCHöLLBRONN	01/01/1839	A		F7
NEUMAYER W P	KONSTANTIN	1831	SCHöLLBRONN	01/01/1839	A		F7
NEUMAYER W P	LEO	1834	SCHöLLBRONN	01/01/1839	A		F7
NEUMAYER W P	MATHIAS	1822	SCHöLLBRONN	01/01/1839	A		F7
NEUNDORFER	LEONHARD	1863	KARLSRUHE	01/01/1881	A		F3
NEZEBA	MAX	1843	DURLACH KARLSRUHE	/ /	A		F7
NIES	FERDINAND	1826	MALSCH	/ /	A		F2
NIES	KATHARINA		MALSCH	01/01/1846	A		F2
NIES	MICHAEL	1829	MALSCH	/ /	A		F2
NIES MN GRäSINGER	ELISABETH	1819	MALSCH	01/01/1846	A		F2
NIES MN KISTNER	WALBURGA		MALSCH	01/01/1832	A		F2
NIES W FAMILY	BONIFAZ	1803	MALSCH	01/01/1846	A		F2
NIES W PARENTS	CäCILIE	1836	MALSCH	06/22/1846	A		F2
NIES W PARENTS	ELISABETH	1842	MALSCH	06/22/1846	A		F2
NIES W PARENTS	FRANZ	1844	MALSCH	06/22/1846	A		F2
NIES W PARENTS	JAKOB	1838	MALSCH	06/22/1846	A		F2
NIES W PARENTS	JOHANN	1832	MALSCH	06/22/1846	A		F2
NIES WW	JOHANN	1807	MALSCH	01/01/1832	A		F2
NIKOLAUS WW CH	PHILIPP		WöSSINGEN	01/01/1858	A		F1
NOD	MATHIAS		OFTERSHEIM	01/01/1810			F1
NOE	FRANZ	1875	KARLSRUHE	01/01/1891	A		F3
NOHIS	JOHANN PHILIPP		OFTERSHEIM	01/01/1819			F1
NOLL	JAKOB		HUGSWEIER/LAHR	01/01/1866	A		F6
NONNENMACHER	KARL		SPöCK	01/01/1865	A		F4
NORNMüLLER	HEINRICH	1873	SPIELBERG	01/01/1889	A		F4
NOSSWAG	GOTTLIEB		SöLLINGEN	01/01/1865	A		F4
NOTTER	MISS		SöLLINGEN	/ /	A		F7
NUSSBAUMER	CHRISTIAN		KARLSRUHE	/ /	A		F3

Lastname	Firstname	Birth Year	Birthplace	Emigration	De	Prof	Source
NUTENRIETH	HERMANN EMIL	1856	KARLSRUHE	01/01/1876	A		F3
NUTHENRIED W F	KONRAD	1802	BRETTEN	01/01/1872	A		F8
NUTHENRIETH	WILHELM	1866	BRETTEN	01/01/1884	A		F8
NUTHENRIETH MN SPECH	THERESE	1818	BRETTEN	01/01/1872	A		F8
NUTHENRIETH W P	ELISE	1861	BRETTEN	01/01/1872	A		F8
NUTHENRIETH W P	KARL	1865	BRETTEN	01/01/1872	A		F8
NUTHENRIETH W P	WILHELM	1859	BRETTEN	01/01/1872	A		F8
NäGELE	JAKOB		GRABEN	01/01/1800	A		F5

Lastname	Firstname	Birth Year	Birthplace	Emigration	De	Prof	Source
OBERACKER	FRIEDRICH		LIEDOLSHEIM	01/01/1890	A		F9
OBERLE	BERNHARD	1832	MÖRSCH	01/01/1854	A		F7
OBERLE W F	JOHANN		MÖRSCH	02/01/1847	A		F7
OBERMÜLLER	CHRISTIAN		KARLSRUHE	/ /	A		F3
OBERST	ERWIN FRIEDRICH	1877	KARLSRUHE	01/01/1894	A		F3
OBERT	ANSELM CHRISTIA	1824	PFAFFENROTH	01/01/1851	A		F7
OBERT	ENODIA	1822	PFAFFENROTH	01/01/1853	A		F7
OBERT	MARIANNE INES	1806	PFAFFENROTH	01/01/1838	A		F7
OBERT	MATHIAS	1803	BURBACH	/ /	A		F4
OBERT	OTTILIE	1811	BURBACH	/ /	A		F4
OBERT	PETER	1803	BURBACH	01/01/1828	A		F4
OBERT W F	CHRISTIAN	1795	PFAFFENROTH	01/01/1838	A		F7
OBERT W P	MARKUS	1832	PFAFFENROTH	01/01/1838	A		F7
OBERT W P	VINZENZ	1828	PFAFFENROTH	01/01/1838	A		F7
OBREITER	ANTON	1832	PFAFFENROTH	01/01/1853	A		F7
OBREITER	FLORIAN	1838	PFAFFENROT	01/01/1857	A		F7
OBREITER	JOSEF	1803	PFAFFENROTH	01/01/1847	A		F7
OBREITER	JOSEF	1834	PFAFFENROTH	01/01/1854	A		F7
OBREITER	KRESZENRIA	1839	PFAFFENROTH	01/01/1854	A		F7
OBREITER	MARTIN	1831	PFAFFENROTH	01/01/1853	A		F7
OBREITER MN BAUER	STEPHANIE	1815	PFAFFENROTH	01/01/1847	A		F7
OBREITER MN MASINO	SCHOLASTIKA	1801	PFAFFENROTH	/ /	A		F7
OBREITER MN SäUBERLI	MAGDALENA	1833	PFAFFENROT	01/01/1882	A		F7
OBREITER W F	AMALIA	1867	PFAFFENROT	01/01/1882	A		F7
OBREITER W F	NIKOLAUS	1831	PFAFFENROT	01/01/1882	A		F7
OBREITER W P	DOMINIKUS	1874	PFAFFENROT	01/01/1882	A		F7
OBREITER W P	HUBERT	1859	PFAFFENROT	01/01/1882	A		F7
OBREITER W P	JOHANN ADAM	1869	PFAFFENROT	01/01/1882	A		F7
OBREITER W P	JOHANNES	1830	PFAFFENROT	/ /	A		F7
OBREITER W P	JOSEF	1836	PFAFFENROT	/ /	A		F7
OBREITER W P	MAGDALENA	1833	PFAFFENROT	/ /	A		F7
OCHS	ANDREAS	1862	SPESSART	01/01/1882	A		F4
OCHS	ANTON	1832	SPESSART	01/01/1858	A		F4
OCHS	ANTON	1846	SPESSART	01/14/1869	A		F4
OCHS	APPOLONIA		SPESSART	08/16/1854	A		F4
OCHS	BENEDIKT	1844	BURBACH	01/01/1868	A		F4
OCHS	BERTOLD	1859	SPESSART	03/20/1870	A		F4
OCHS	CONRAD	1811	VÖLKERSBACH	/ /	A		F4
OCHS	FRANZ ANTON NIO		SPESSART	01/01/1856	A		F4
OCHS	FRANZ MICHAEL	1820	VÖLKERSBACH	03/16/1851	A		F4
OCHS	GABRIEL	1833	SPESSART	04/18/1845	A		F4
OCHS	GEORG MICHAEL		LIEDOLSHEIM	01/01/1849	A		F8
OCHS	GERTRUD	1830	SPESSART	01/01/1845	A		F4
OCHS	IGNAZ	1798	SPESSART	01/01/1849	A		F4
OCHS	ISIDOR	1865	SPESSART	01/01/1882	A		F4
OCHS	JAKOB	1828	SPESSART	01/01/1846	A		F4
OCHS	JOHANN		SPESSART	04/18/1846	A		F4
OCHS	JOHANN	1768	SPESSART	/ /	A		F4
OCHS	JOHANN	1848	SPESSART	12/24/1866	A		F4
OCHS	JOHANN	1849	SPESSART	12/24/1866	A		F4

Lastname	Firstname	Birth Year	Birthplace	Emigration	De	Prof	Source
OCHS	JOHANN BAPTIST	1817	VÖLKERSBACH	08/16/1851	S		F4
OCHS	JOHANN GEORG	1844	BURBACH	01/01/1864	A		F4
OCHS	JOHANNES	1855	SPESSART	01/01/1882	A		F4
OCHS	JOSEF	1842	BURBACH	01/01/1856	A		F4
OCHS	KATHARINA		SPESSART	07/15/1881	A		F4
OCHS	KATHARINA	1836	SPESSART	01/01/1858	A		F4
OCHS	KONRAD	1811	SPESSART	01/01/1838	A		F4
OCHS	MAGDALENA	1806	BURBACH	/ /	A		F4
OCHS	MARIA JOSEFA	1830	SPESSART	01/01/1851	A		F4
OCHS	THEODOR	1864	SPESSART	07/05/1881	A		F4
OCHS MN ABEN	VERONIKA	1817	SPESSART	01/01/1856	A		F4
OCHS MN BENZ	ANNA MARIA		PFAFFENROTH	01/01/1839	A		F7
OCHS MN OCHS	MARIA ANNA		SPESSART	01/01/1852	A		F4
OCHS MN WIPFLER	GENOFEVA		SPESSART	06/29/1854	A		F4
OCHS W F	GREGOR		SCHÖLLBRONN	01/01/1839	A		F7
OCHS W FAMILY	ANTON		SPESSART	01/01/1852	A		F4
OCHS W FAMILY	FRANZ ANTON		SPESSART	06/29/1854	A		F4
OCHS W FAMILY	GEORG		SPESSART	01/01/1856	A		F4
OCHS W FAMILY	JOSEF	1811	SPESSART	01/01/1838	A		F4
OCHS W P	ANTONIA	1838	SPESSART	06/29/1854	A		F4
OCHS W P	AUGUSTA	1828	SPESSART	06/29/1854	A		F4
OCHS W P	BERTOLD	1838	SPESSART	01/01/1852	A		F4
OCHS W P	FRANZISKA	1821	SCHÖLLBRONN	01/01/1839	A		F7
OCHS W P	KAROLINE	1812	SCHÖLLBRONN	01/01/1839	A		F7
OCHS W P	KATHARINA	1834	SPESSART	01/01/1852	A		F4
OCHS W P	LUFADINA	1845	SPESSART	06/29/1854	A		F4
OCHS W P	MARIA	1838	SPESSART	06/29/1854	A		F4
OCHS W P	MARIA ANNA	1814	SCHÖLLBRONN	01/01/1839	A		F7
OCHS W P	PETER	1820	SCHÖLLBRONN	01/01/1839	A		F7
OCHS W P	STEPHANIE	1826	SPESSART	06/29/1854	A		F4
OEDER	GEORG HEINRICH		DURLACH KARLSRUHE	01/01/1845			F7
OEDER	GOTTLIEB	1837	DURLACH KARLSRUHE	/ /	A		F7
OEDER	JAKOB FRIEDRICH		DURLACH KARLSRUHE	01/01/1839	A		F7
OEDER	PHILIPP SAMUEL	1831	DURLACH KARLSRUHE	/ /			F7
OHMBERGER	KATHARINA BARBA		WASSER	01/01/1859	A		F6
OHNMACHT	JOHANN		DAUCHINGEN	01/01/1859	A		F6
OLBERT	HEINRICH		NECKARAU	01/01/1783			F1
OPPENHEIMER	HERMANN		GRÖTZINGEN	/ /	A		F3
ORTWEIN	ERNST		BÜHLERTAL	01/01/1880	A		F5
OTT	JOHANN NICOLAUS		HASSELBERG	05/24/1754	A		F5
OTT	LEONHARD		HASSELBERG	05/10/1754	A		F5

Lastname	Firstname	Birth Year	Birthplace	Emigration	De	Prof	Source
PALM	BERTHA		GRÖTZINGEN	/ /	A		F3
PALM	FANNY		GRÖTZINGEN	/ /	A		F3
PALM	ROSA		GRÖTZINGEN	/ /	A		F3
PALM	THEKLA		GRÖTZINGEN	/ /	A		F3
PAUL MN KEFFLER	FRANZISKA		MÖRSCH	02/21/1830	A		F7
PAUL W F	KARL		MÖRSCH	02/21/1180	A		F7
PAUL W P	CONRAD		MÖRSCH	02/21/1830	A		F7
PAUL W P	LUDWIG		MÖRSCH	02/21/1830	A		F7
PAUL W P	MARGARETHA		MÖRSCH	02/21/1830	A		F7
PAULI	ALOIS		MÖRSCH	02/21/1831	A		F7
PAULUS	ERNST		SPöCK	01/01/1862	A		F4
PAULUS	FRIEDRICH		SPöCK	01/01/1857	A		F4
PAULUS	MAX		SPöCK	01/01/1862	A		F4
PAULUS	WILHELMINE ELIS		SPöCK	01/01/1848	A		F4
PERINO	EDUARD	1876	KARLSRUHE	01/01/1891	A		F3
PERSON	SIGMUND		KARLSRUHE	01/01/1861	A		F3
PETER	ELISABETH		BÜHLERTAL	01/01/1896	A		F5
PETER	EMANUEL		ISSETZHEIM	01/01/1859	A		F6
PETER	GEORG		AUERBACH	01/01/1894	A		F6
PETER	JOHANN		KARLSRUHE	01/01/1802	A		F3
PETER	KARL		ISSETZHEIM	01/01/1859	A		F6*
PETER WW 3CH	MICHEL		WINDEN	01/01/1803			F1
PETERHAUS	WILHELM	1871	KARLSRUHE	01/01/1893	A		F3
· PFALZGRAF	FRIEDRICH	1845	DURLACH KARLSRUHE	/ /	A		F7
PFALZGRAF	HEINRICH		DURLACH	01/01/1849	A		F5
PFALZGRAF	HEINRICH	1825	DURLACH KARLSRUHE	/ /	A		F7
PFEFFER	JAKOB		AUERBACH	01/01/1737	A		F6
PFEIFFER	KARL JOHANN SEB	1856	ETTLINGEN	04/21/1874	A		F4
PFEIL	CHRISTOPH		GRABEN	01/01/1842	A		F3
PFEIL	FRIEDRICH		GRABEN	/ /	A		F5
PFEIL	GEORG		GRABEN	01/01/1870	A		F3
PFEIL	GUSTAV	1830	ETTLINGEN	05/07/1847	A		F4
PFEIL	HERMANN	1826	ETTLINGEN	05/07/1847	A		F4
PFEIL	JAKOB		GRABEN	01/01/1854	A		F3
PFEIL	JAKOB SIMON		GRABEN	01/01/1861	A		F5
PFEIL	JOSEF	1831	ETTLINGEN	05/07/1847	A		F4
PFEIL	KARL		GRABEN	/ /	A		F5
PFEIL	KARL WILHELM		GRABEN	01/01/1873	A		F3
PFEIL	KATHARINA	1828	ETTLINGEN	05/07/1847	A		F4
PFEIL	LUDWIG LEOPOLD		ETTLINGEN	05/07/1847	A		F4
PFEIL	MAGDALENA		GRABEN	01/01/1842	A		F3
PFEIL	MAGDALENA		GRABEN	01/01/1847	A		F5
PFEIL	PHILIPP		GRABEN	01/01/1833	A		F5
PFEIL	SIMON		GRABEN	01/01/1862	A		F3
PFEIL W F	CHRISTOPH		GRABEN	01/01/1847	A		F5
PFEIL MN SARBACHER	JAKOBINE		SCHIELBERG	05/07/1847	A		F4
PFEIL W FAMILY	IGNAZ	1798	ETTLINGEN	05/07/1847	A		F4
PFENNIG	KARL	1828	MALSCH	01/01/1847	A		F2
PFETSCHER	JOHANN ADAM		BLANKENLOCH	01/01/1846	A		F4
PFETSCHER	KAROLINE	1865	BLANKENLOCH	01/01/1882	A		F4

Lastname	Firstname	Birth Year	Birthplace	Emigration	De	Prof	Source
PFISTER	LEOPOLD	1855	ETTLINGEN	06/17/1873	A		F4
PFRANG	JOSEF		KARLSRUHE	/ /	A		F3
PFRIEMER	ELISABETH		KORK	01/01/1853	A		F6
PFRIEMER	JAKOB		KORK	01/01/1859	A		F6
PHEIL	PHILIPP		GRABEN	01/01/1833	A		F3
PHILIPP	ADAM HEINRICH		DAXLANDEN	01/01/1848	A		F6
PHILIPP	ANDREAS HEINRIH		DAXLANDEN	01/01/1852	A		F6
PHILIPP	CARL	1828	DURLACH KARLSRUHE	/ /			F7
PHILIPP	CHRISTIAN	1829	DURLACH KARLSRUHE	/ /			F7
PHILIPP	ELISABETH		DURLACH	01/01/1861	A		F6
PHILIPP	ERNST	1870	SPÖCK	01/01/1886	A		F8
PISTER	EUGEN	1876	KARLSRUHE	01/01/1892	A		F3
PISTER W CH WIDOW	IDA MN RENZ	1838	MALSCH	03/03/1884	A		F2
PISTER W MOTHER	EUGEN	1875	MALSCH	03/03/1884	A		F2
PISTER W MOTHER	MAX	1872	MALSCH	03/03/1884	A		F2
PISTER W MOTHER	VALENTIN	1866	MALSCH	03/03/1884	A		F2
PITSCHKE	LOUISE	1863	KARLSRUHE	01/01/1879	A		F3
PLATTEICHER	KARL		WÖSSINGEN	01/01/1803			F1
PLATTEICHER	MARTIN		SPÖCK	01/01/1737	A		F4
PLETSCH	HERMANN	1872	HOCHSTETTEN	01/01/1887	A		F8
PNERLE	JOSEF		MÖRSCH	01/01/1889	A		F7
POPP	JAKOB FRIEDRICH		DARMSPACH	11/16/1802			F1
POSTWEILER	WILHELM		DURLACH KARLSRUHE	01/01/1853	A		F7
PRAGER	SAMUEL		GRÖTZINGEN	01/01/1861	A		F5
PREISIG	JULIUS MATHIAS	1830	ETTLINGEN	02/27/1850	A		F4
PRIOR-JAKOB	ANNA		KARLSRUHE	/ /	A		F3
PRISSLER	CHRISTOPH		KARLSRUHE	09/08/1863	A		F3
PROBST	JOHANN		NIEDERN	01/01/1849	A		F6
PROGER	SAMUEL		GRÖTZINGEN	/ /	A		F3
PROTZ	OSKAR	1865	KARLSRUHE	01/01/1882	A		F3
PÖHLER	KONRAD		GRÖTZINGEN	01/01/1830	A		F5

Lastname	Firstname	Birth Year	Birthplace	Emigration De	Prof	Source
RAAB	IGNAZ		OBERWEIER	01/01/1830 A		F1
RAAB MN STRECH	HELENA	1822	ETTLINGEN	09/21/1854 A		F4
RAAB W FAMILY	FLORIAN		ETTLINGEN	09/21/1854 A		F4
RABER	AUGUST	1845	BLANKENLOCH	01/01/1870 A		F4
RABER	AUGUST	1861	BLANKENLOCH	01/01/1879 A		F4
RABER	ERNESTINE CHRIE		BLANKENLOCH	01/01/1869 A		F4
RABER	JAKOB FRIEDRICH		BLANKENLOCH	01/01/1838 A		F4
RABER	JOHANN LUDWIG		BLANKENLOCH	01/01/1848 A		F4
RABOLD	BALTHASAR	1830	VöLKERSBACH	10/24/1853 A		F4
RABOLD	CRESZENTIA	1834	VöLKERSBACH	10/15/1853 A		F4
RABOLD	DINE		SCHöLLBRONN	/ / A		F7
RABOLD	JOHANN		GRÜNWETTERSBACH	01/01/1867 A		F8
RABOLD	KASPAR	1830	VöLKERSBACH	10/24/1853 A		F4
RABOLD MN KUNZ	PETRONELLA	1848	SCHöLLBRON	01/01/1881 A		F7
RABOLD W F	LEO	1848	SCHöLLBRON	01/01/1881 A		F7
RABOLD W F	NAPOLEON	1850	SCHöLLBRON	01/01/1868 A		F7
RABOLD W P	AGNES	1879	SCHöLLBRONN	01/01/1881 A		F7
RABOLD W P	ELIGIUS	1878	SCHöLLBRONN	01/01/1881 A		F7
RABOLD W P	HELENA	1874	SCHöLLBRON	01/01/1881 A		F7
RABOLD W P	LEOPOLD	1875	SCHöLLBRONN	01/01/1881 A		F7
RABOLD WIDOWER W S	JOSEF	1822	SCHöLLBRONN	01/01/1868 A		F7
RADEMACHER	KARL	1861	KARLSRUHE	01/01/1879 A		F3
RAGUOT	...CHRISTIAN JA	1846	DURLACH KARLSRUHE	/ /		F7
RAGUOT	CARL FRIEDRICH		DURLACH KARLSRUHE	01/01/1845		F7
RAGUOT	GUSTAV FRIEDRIH	1825	DURLACH KARLSRUHE	/ /		F7
RAGUOT	WILH? FRIEDRICH	1849	DURLACH KARLSRUHE	/ /		F7
RAILE	ADAM		KARLSRUHE	/ / A		F3
RAILING	JOHANN	1808	PFAFFENROT	01/01/1846 A		F7
RAILING MN WEINGäRT	MARIA ANNA W CH	1802	PFAFFENROT	01/01/1854 A		F7
RAILING W M	FRANZ ANTON	1834	PFAFFENROT	01/01/1854 A		F7
RAILING W M	FRANZ J.	1829	PFAFFENROTH	01/01/1851 A		F7
RAILING W M	JOHANN VALENTIN	1827	PFAFFENROT	01/01/1854 A		F7
RAPP	WILHELM	1848	RÜPPUR	01/01/1866 A		F8
RASTETTER	ANNA	1854	ETTLINGEN	03/27/1875 A		F4
RASTETTER	BERTOLD	1855	MALSCH	01/01/1879 A		F2
RASTETTER	FRANZ	1853	ETTLINGEN	05/12/1878 A		F4
RASTETTER	KARL		DAXLANDEN	01/01/1873 A		F6
RASTETTER	KATHARINA		DAXLANDEN	01/01/1881 A		F6
RASTETTER	THOMAS		MÖRSCH	02/21/1831 A		F7
RASTETTER MN HEINRIH	BARBARA	1831	MALSCH	01/01/1858 A		F2
RASTETTER MN MÜLLER	ELISABETH		MALSCH	01/01/1879 A		F2
RASTETTER W PARENTS	BERTOLD	1855	MALSCH	01/01/1858 A		F2
RASTETTER W PARENTS	WILHELM	1855	MALSCH	01/01/1858 A		F2
RASTÄTTER	CHRISTIAN		MÖRSCH	01/01/1816 A		F7
RASTÄTTER MN BAUTSCH	BARBARA		ETTLINGEN	04/28/1847 A		F4
RASTÄTTER W FAMILY	LUDWIG	1785	ETTLINGEN	04/28/1847 A		F4
RASTÄTTER W P	BARBARA		ETTLINGEN	04/28/1847 A		F4
RASTÄTTER W P	KARL		ETTLINGEN	04/28/1847 A		F4
RASUCH	PHILIPP	1828	LANGENSTEINBACH	01/01/1853 A		F3
RATTINGER	AUGUST		GRABEN	01/01/1861 A		F5

Lastname	Firstname	Birth Year	Birthplace	Emigration	De	Prof	Source
RAU	ADAM FRIEDRICH	1807	LANGENSTEINBACH	/ /		A	F3
RAU	CARL	1837	DURLACH KARLSRUHE	/ /			F7
RAU	CHRISTOPH	1812	LANGENSTEINBACH	01/01/1828	AQ		F3
RAU	GEORG MARTIN	1846	LANGENSTEINBACH	01/01/1869	A		F3
RAU	GOTTLIEB		SCHÖLLBRON	/ /		A	F7
RAU	JAKOB	1844	LANGENSTEINBACH	01/01/1869	A		F3
RAU	JOHANN	1845	LANGENSTEINBACH	01/01/1884	A		F3
RAU	JULIANE	1844	LANGENSTEINBACH	05/30/1881	A		F3
RAU	KARL LUDWIG	1864	LIEDOLSHEIM	01/01/1882	A		F9
RAU	PHILIPP		LANGENSTEINBACH	04/08/1864	A		F3
RAU MN SCHMIDT	KATHARINA	1846	LANGENSTEINBACH	02/05/1869	A		F3
RAU W FAMILY	FRIEDRICH	1840	LANGENSTEINBACH	02/05/1869	A		F3
RAU W PARENTS	FRIEDRICH	1868	LANGENSTEINBACH	02/05/1869	A		F3
RAUCHER	JAKOB		DURLACH	01/01/1852	A		F6
RAUENBÜHLER	KARL		SCHÖLLBRON	01/01/1853	A		F7
RAUPP	CHRISTIAN		SPÖCK	01/01/1847	A		F4
RAUPP	ERNST		SPÖCK	01/01/1865	A		F4
RAUPP	JOHANN		SPÖCK	01/01/1847	A		F4
RAUSCH	ELISABETH	1824	LANGENSTEINBACH	01/01/1855	A		F3
RAUSCH	FRIEDRICH	1809	LANGENSTEINBACH	01/01/1853	A		F3
RAUSCH MN RIED	MAGDALENA	1817	LANGENSTEINBACH	01/01/1855	A		F3
RAUSCH W FAMILY	PHILIPP	1814	LANGENSTEINBACH	01/01/1855	A		F3
RAUSCH W PARENTS	JAKOB	1855	LANGENSTEINBACH	01/01/1855	A		F3
RAUSCH W PARENTS	JOHANN	1848	LANGENSTEINBACH	01/01/1855	A		F3
RAUSCH W PARENTS	KARL	1853	LANGENSTEINBACH	01/01/1855	A		F3
RAUSCH W PARENTS	KATHARINA	1844	LANGENSTEINBACH	01/01/1855	A		F3
RAUSCH W PARENTS	PHILIPP	1850	LANGENSTEINBACH	01/01/1855	A		F3
RAYLE	AUGUSTE	1870	GRABEN	01/01/1882	A		F3
RAYLE W FAMILY	LISA	1834	GRABEN	01/01/1882	A		F3
RAYLE W PARENTS	EMIL EUGEN	1863	GRABEN	01/01/1882	A		F3
RAYLE W PARENTS	KARL THEODOR	1866	GRABEN	01/01/1882	A		F3
RAYLING	CHRISTIAN	1834	PFAFFENROT	01/01/1863	A		F7
RAYLING	JOHANN GEORG		PFAFFENROT	01/01/1863	A		F7
REBELE	ANDREAS FRIEDRH		KARLSRUHE	01/01/1752	A		F3
RECHNER	PIUS		REISENBACH	01/01/1859	A		F6
REICHEL	KARL		KARLSRUHE	01/01/1853	A		F3
REICHENBACHER	GOTTFRIED	1831	SÖLLINGEN	01/01/1851	A		F7
REICHENBACHER W W	GEORG		SÖLLINGEN	/ /		A	F7
REICHENBACHER WW	JOHANN CHRISTOH		WÖSSINGEN	01/01/1845	A		F1
REICHENBADER	ADAM		SÖLLINGEN	01/01/1750	A		F7
REICHENBADER	MISTER		SÖLLINGEN	/ /		A	F7
REICHERT	ALOIS	1833	BURBACH	/ /		A	F4
REICHERT	BARBARA	1820	SPIELBERG	/ /		A	F4
REICHERT	BENEDIKT	1781	MALSCH	05/21/1832	A		F2
REICHERT	FRANZ	1809	MALSCH	05/21/1832	A		F2
REICHERT	FRANZ ANTON	1812	SCHÖLLBRONN	/ /		A	F7
REICHERT	FRANZ JOSEF	1831	BURBACH	/ /		A	F4
REICHERT	FRIEDERIKE	1813	PFAFFENROT	01/01/1846	A		F7
REICHERT	JOHANN		DURLACH	01/01/1836			F7
REICHERT	JOHANN	1759	PFAFFENROT	/ /		A	F7

Lastname	Firstname	Birth Year	Birthplace	Emigration De	Prof	Source
REICHERT	JOHANN	1783	KARLSRUHE	01/01/1832 A		F3
REICHERT	JOSEF	1812	MALSCH	05/21/1832 A		F2
REICHERT	KARL	1854	MALSCH	02/23/1867 A		F2
REICHERT	LUITGARD	1844	MALSCH	01/01/1882 A		1
REICHERT	MICHAEL		PFAFFENROT	01/01/1789 A		F7
REICHERT	VALENTIN	1806	MALSCH	05/21/1832 A		F2
REICHERT MN BECHLER	KATHARINA	1777	MALSCH	05/21/1832 A		F2
REICHERT MN BENZ	KATHARINA	1791	PFAFFENROT	01/01/1846 A		F7
REICHERT MN BUCKER	AMALIA	1822	PFAFFENROT	01/01/1846 A		F7
REICHERT MN BULLINGR	VIKTORIA	1808	MALSCH	01/01/1854 A		F2
REICHERT MN GRäSSER	MARIA ANNA		MALSCH	01/01/1882 A		F2
REICHERT MN HöGLI	MARTHA	1823	MALSCH	04/13/1853 A		F2
REICHERT MN RIPPLER	MAGDALENA		MALSCH	03/31/1846 A		F2
REICHERT W CH	XAVER		MALSCH	01/01/1832 A		F2
REICHERT W F	PETER	1793	PFAFFENROT	01/01/1846 A		F7
REICHERT W F AND P	THOMAS	1817	PFAFFENROT	01/01/1846 A		F7
REICHERT W FAMILY	BENEDIKT		MALSCH	01/01/1832 A		F2
REICHERT W FAMILY	FRANZ GEORG	1841	MALSCH	01/01/1854 A		F2
REICHERT W FAMILY	JOHANNES	1796	MALSCH	03/31/1846 A		F2
REICHERT W FAMILY	JOSEF BERNHARD	1847	MALSCH	01/01/1882 A		F2
REICHERT W FAMILY	PETER	1813	MALSCH	01/01/1854 A		F2
REICHERT W FAMILY	RUDOLF	1845	MALSCH	01/01/1882 A		F2
REICHERT W FAMILY	VINZENS	1816	MALSCH	04/13/1853 A		F2
REICHERT W FATHER	THERESE	1822	MALSCH	01/01/1832 A		F2
REICHERT W P	GENOFEVA	1841	PFAFFENROT	01/01/1846 A		F7
REICHERT W P	JOSEF	1815	PFAFFENROT	01/01/1846 A		F7
REICHERT W PARENTS	ALOIS	1842	MALSCH	04/13/1853 A		F2
REICHERT W PARENTS	AUGUSTE	1824	MALSCH	03/31/1846 A		F2
REICHERT W PARENTS	FELIX HANS	1849	MALSCH	01/01/1882 A		F2
REICHERT W PARENTS	FRANZ GEORG	1841	MALSCH	01/01/1882 A		F2
REICHERT W PARENTS	JEREMIAS	1819	MALSCH	01/01/1832 A		F2
REICHERT W PARENTS	JOSEF BERNHARD		MALSCH	01/01/1854 A		F2
REICHERT W PARENTS	KARL	1854	MALSCH	/ /		
REICHERT W PARENTS	KARL WILHELM	1848	MALSCH	04/13/1853 A		F2
REICHERT W PARENTS	LUITGART	1844	MALSCH	01/01/1854 A		F2
REICHERT W PARENTS	MAGD. CYRIAK	1859		/ /		
REICHERT W PARENTS	MARIA ANNA	1825	MALSCH	03/31/1846 A		F2
REICHERT W PARENTS	SOFIE	1844	MALSCH	04/13/1853 A		F2
REICHERT W PARENTS	TELEPHORUS	1849	MALSCH	01/01/1854 A		F2
REIF	GEORG ADAM		WEISSENSTEIN	01/01/1807 A		F8
REIF W D	JAKOB FRIEDRICH		SöLLINGEN	/ / A		F7
REIF W F	MARGARETHA		SöLLINGEN	/ / A		F7
REIFENBACHER	BERNHARD		BERGHAUSEN	01/01/1861 A		F6
REIHL	DINZENZIA		SINGEN	01/01/1859 A		F6
REIN	WILHELM	1865	KARLSRUHE	01/01/1882 A		F3
REINHARD	FRITZ		BÜHLERTAL	01/01/1878 A		F5
REINHARD	WILHELM		KARLSRUHE	01/01/1861 A		F3
REINHOLD	WILHELM AUGUST	1872	KARLSRUHE	01/01/1894 A		F3
REINIG MN JARDIN	ELISABETHA		SINSHEIM	01/01/1859 A		F6
REINIG W FAMILY	JOHANN		SINSHEIM	01/01/1859 A		F6

Lastname	Firstname	Birth Year	Birthplace	Emigration	De	Prof	Source
REININGER	WENDEL		GRABEN	01/01/1736	A		F3
REIS	CHRISTINA		DURLACH	01/01/1858	A		F5
REIS	JAKOB		DURLACH	01/01/1853	A		F5
REISENAUER	MICHAEL			/ /	A		F2
REISENAUER MN BECHLR	BARBARA	1810	MALSCH	03/16/1837	A		F2
REISENAUER MN MERKLR	FRANZISKA	1818	MALSCH	01/01/1871	A		F2
REISENAUER W CH	MICHAEL	1806	MALSCH	01/01/1871	A		F2
REISENAUER W FAMILY	MICHAEL	1808	MALSCH	03/16/1837	A		F2
REISENAUER W PARENTS	FRANZISKA	1836	MALSCH	03/16/1837	A		F2
REISENAUER W PARENTS	FRANZISKA	1860	MALSCH	01/01/1871	A		F2
REISENAUER W PARENTS	FRIDOLIN	1851	MALSCH	01/01/1871	A		F2
REISENAUER W PARENTS	KONRAD	1856	MALSCH	01/01/1871	A		F2
REISENAUER W PARENTS	MARIA ANNA	1834	MALSCH	03/16/1837	A		F2
REISENAUER W PARENTS	MICHAEL	1852	MALSCH	01/01/1871	A		F2
REISER	HEINRICH	1787	BURBACH	01/01/1866	A		F4
REISS	ALOIS		ETTLINGEN	11/26/1853	A		F4
REISS	FRIEDRICH XAVER		ETTLINGEN	12/13/1855	A		F4
REISS	GUSTAV	1833	ETTLINGEN	10/29/1852	A		F4
REISS	KARL	1837	ETTLINGEN	07/29/1852	A		F4
REISSER	IGNAZ		MALSCH	01/01/1790	A		F6
REISSNER	AUG. JAKOB	1814	DURLACH KARLSRUHE	/ /	A		F7
REITER	CHRISTINE		VöLKERSBACH	07/31/1865	A		F4
REITER	CRESZENTIA	1835	VöLKERSBACH	01/01/1857	A		F4
REITER	FRIEDA	1877	ETTLINGEN	01/01/1891	A		F4
REITER	JOHANN GEORG		VöLKERSBACH	07/31/1865	A		F4
REITER	KATHARINA		VöLKERSBACH	01/01/1866	A		F4
REITER	MARIA ANNA		ETTLINGEN	01/01/1854	A		F4
REITER	RUDOLF	1830	ETTLINGEN	10/06/1851	A		F4
REITH	FRANZ	1867	BüHLERTAL	01/01/1891	A		F5
REITZ	GEORG ADAM		DURLACH KARLSRUHE	01/01/1850	A		F7
REIZ	LEONHARDT		DURLACH KARLSRUHE	01/01/1853			F7
RELB	EUGEN		KARLSRUHE	/ /	A		F3
RENNER	ANTON		GAMSHURST	01/01/1859	A		F6
RENNER	BERCHTHOLD		GAMSHURST	01/01/1859	A		F6
RENNER	CHRISTIAN		GAMSHURST	01/01/1859	A		F6
RENNER	ELISABETH		GAMSHURST	01/01/1859	A		F6
RENNER	HEINRICH	1805	SPöCK	01/01/1881	A		F4
RENNER	RUDOLF		GAMSHURST	01/01/1859	A		F6
RENNER	RUSINE		GAMSHURST	01/01/1859	A		F6
RENTTI	MAX LUDWIG	1857	KARLSRUHE	01/01/1882	A		F3
RENZ	ANTON	1781	MALSCH	01/01/1799	A		F2
RENZ W PARENTS	MATHILDE KATHAR	1849	MALSCH	10/10/1850	A		F2
RENZ MN HOFFART	HENRIETTE	1811	MALSCH	01/23/1855	A		F2
RENZ MN MAISCH V OBR	HELENE		MALSCH	03/21/1852	A		F2
RENZ MN ZIMMER	ELISABETH	1821	MALSCH	10/10/1850	A		F2
RENZ W FAMILY	ANDREAS	1809	MALSCH	01/23/1855	A		F2
RENZ W FAMILY	JOHANN	1844	MALSCH	03/21/1852	A		F2
RENZ W FAMILY	JOSEF	1813	MALSCH	03/21/1852	A		F2
RENZ W FAMILY	KARL	1817	MALSCH	10/10/1850	A		F2
RENZ W FAMILY	KARL ARNOLD	1845	MALSCH	03/21/1852	A		F2

Lastname	Firstname	Birth Year	Birthplace	Emigration	De	Prof	Source
RENZ W PARENTS	FRANZ ANTON	1852	MALSCH	01/23/1855	A		F2
RENZ W PARENTS	JOHANNES PAUL	1842	MALSCH	01/23/1855	A		F2
RENZ W PARENTS	JOSEPHINE	1851	MALSCH	03/21/1852	A		F2
RENZ W PARENTS	KAROLINE CHARTS	1850	MALSCH	01/23/1855	A		F2
RENZ W PARENTS	MARIA ANNA	1845	MALSCH	01/23/1855	A		F2
RENZ W PARENTS	THEKLA	1842	MALSCH	03/21/1852	A		F2
RENZ W PARENTS	THERESIA	1846	MALSCH	03/21/1852	A		F2
REPPL	CARL		SöLLINGEN	/ /	A		F7
REPPL W SISTER	GEORG ADAM		SöLLINGEN	/ /	A		F7
REPPLE	KARL		SöLLINGEN	01/01/1855	A		F7
REPPLE W BROTHER	MARGARATHA		SöLLINGEN	/ /	A		F7
RESTETTER W FAMILY	FRANZ	1827	MALSCH	01/01/1858	A		F2
REUSCHLE	JOHANNES		BLANKENLOCH	04/09/1740	A		F4
REUSCHLER	JOHANNES		BLANKENLOCH	01/01/1750	A		F4
REUSS	FRIEDRICH		WÖSSINGEN	01/01/1845	A		F4
REUTER	CHRISTIAN FRIE.		KARLSRUHE	01/01/1860	A		F3
REUTER	JOHANN		HASSELBERG	04/19/1834	A		F5
REUTER W FAMILY	MARIA ANNA	1809	ETTLINGEN	02/14/1854	A		F4
REUTER W P	ADOLFINE	1839	ETTLINGEN	02/14/1854	A		F4
REUTER W P	KATHARINA	1831	ETTLINGEN	02/14/1854	A		F4
REUTER W P	MAGDALENA	1844	ETTLINGEN	02/14/1854	A		F4
REUTHER	DAMIAN	1836	VöLKERSBACH	07/03/1854	A		F4
RHEIN	JOHANN		DURLACH	01/01/1737	A		F5
RIBOLIN	MICHAEL		MALTERDINGEN	01/01/1807	A		F8
RICHTER	CARL CHRISTIAN	1829	DURLACH KARLSRUHE	/ /	A		F7
RICHTER	CHRIST. JAK	1830	DURLACH KARLSRUHE	/ /			F7
RIEB	JOHANN		SöLLINGEN	01/01/1737	A		F7
RIED	ANDREAS		LANGENSTEINBACH	01/01/1790	A		F3
RIED	ANNA MARIA	1853	LANGENSTEINBACH	/ /	A		F3
RIED	CHRISTOPH	1829	LANGENSTEINBACH	01/01/1854	A		F3
RIED	ELISABETH	1811	LANGENSTEINBACH	08/02/1854	A		F3
RIED	FRIEDRICH	1825	LANGENSTEINBACH	/ /	A		F3
RIED	JOHANN KRAFT	1816	LANGENSTEINBACH	/ /	A		F3
RIED	MAGDALENA	1810	LANGENSTEINBACH	/ /	A		F3
RIED	MICHAEL	1831	LANGENSTEINBACH	01/01/1854	A		F3
RIED	MICHAEL	1833	LANGENSTEINBACH	01/01/1850	A		F3
RIED	MICHAEL	1843	LANGENSTEINBACH	/ /	A		F3
RIED	PHILIPP	1829	LANGENSTEINBACH	01/01/1850	A		F3
RIED MN DENNINGER	KATHARINA MAGD.	1798	LANGENSTEINBACH	01/01/1850	A		F3
RIED MN KRONEWETT	CHRISTINE	1855	LANGENSTEINBACH	/ /	A		F3
RIED MN NAGEL	MARIA KATHARINA	1812	LANGENSTEINBACH	01/01/1847	A		F3
RIED MN SCHöPPLER	MAGDALENA	1820	LANGENSTEINBACH	01/01/1854	A		F3
RIED W FAMILY	GEORG	1812	LANGENSTEINBACH	01/01/1847	A		F3
RIED W FAMILY	GOTTFRIED HEINR	1853	LANGENSTEINBACH	/ /	A		F3
RIED W FAMILY	MATHäUS	1797	LANGENSTEINBACH	01/01/1850	A		F3
RIED W PARENTS	ANNA MARIA	1830	LANGENSTEINBACH	01/01/1850	A		F3
RIED W PARENTS	CHRISTINE	1879	LANGENSTEINBACH	/ /	A		F3
RIED W PARENTS	CHRISTOPH	1846	LANGENSTEINBACH	01/01/1854	A		F3
RIED W PARENTS	ELISABETH	1835	LANGENSTEINBACH	01/01/1850	A		F3
RIED W PARENTS	ELISABETH	1848	LANGENSTEINBACH	01/01/1854	A		F3

Lastname	Firstname	Birth Year	Birthplace	Emigration	De	Prof	Source
RIED W PARENTS	GEORG	1844	LANGENSTEINBACH	01/01/1847	A		F3
RIED W PARENTS	JAKOB	1838	LANGENSTEINBACH	01/01/1850	A		F3
RIED W PARENTS	JULIANE	1843	LANGENSTEINBACH	01/01/1850	A		F3
RIED W PARENTS	KARL	1827	LANGENSTEINBACH	01/01/1850	A		F3
RIED W PARENTS	KATHARINA	1821	LANGENSTEINBACH	01/01/1850	A		F3
RIED W PARENTS	LUISE	1880	LANGENSTEINBACH	/ /	A		F3
RIED W PARENTS	MAGDALENA	1817	LANGENSTEINBACH	01/01/1850	A		F3
RIED W PARENTS	MAGDALENA	1850	LANGENSTEINBACH	01/01/1854	A		F3
RIED W PARENTS	MARGARETHA	1834	LANGENSTEINBACH	01/01/1850	A		F3
RIED W PARENTS	MARGARETHA	1838	LANGENSTEINBACH	01/01/1847	A		F3
RIED W PARENTS	MARIA KATHARINA	1836	LANGENSTEINBACH	01/01/1847	A		F3
RIEF	STEFAN		DURLACH	01/01/1891	A		F3
RIEGER	FELIX	1818	MALSCH	01/01/1847	A		F2
RIEGER	KATHARINA	1836	MALSCH	01/01/1854	A		F2
RIEGER	PHILIPP	1823	MALSCH	01/01/1854	A		F2
RIEGER W FAMILY	AUGUSTIN	1787	MALSCH	01/01/1830	A		F2
RIEGER MN FINK	LUISE	1854	DÜRMERSHEIM	01/01/1882	A		F2
RIEGER MN GEIGER	FRANZISKA	1834	MALSCH	01/01/1857	A		F2
RIEGER MN KRäMER	THERESE	1789	MALSCH	01/01/1830	A		F2
RIEGER W FAMILY	ERHARDT	1828	MALSCH	01/01/1857	A		F2
RIEGER W FAMILY	WILHELM	1848	MALSCH	01/01/1882	A		F2
RIEGER W PARENTS	AUGUSTINE	1877	MALSCH	01/01/1882	A		F2
RIEGER W PARENTS	FERDINAND	1822	MALSCH	01/01/1830	A		F2
RIEGER W PARENTS	FRANZ	1875	MALSCH	01/01/1882	A		F2
RIEGER W PARENTS	FRANZ JOSEF	1856	MALSCH	01/01/1857	A		F2
RIEGER W PARENTS	JULIANE	1854	MALSCH	01/01/1857	A		F2
RIEGER W PARENTS	KARL	1827	MALSCH	01/01/1830	A		F2
RIEGER W PARENTS	KAROLINE	1828	MALSCH	01/01/1830	A		F2
RIEGER W PARENTS	LORENTZ	1824	MALSCH	01/01/1830	A		F2
RIEGER W PARENTS	VALENTIN	1820	MALSCH	01/01/1830	A		F2
RIEGER W PARENTS	WALBURGA	1822	MALSCH	01/01/1830	A		F2
RIEHLE	CHRIFOSTOMUS		UNTERENTERSBACH	01/01/1859	A		F6
RIEHM	JOHANN		MÖRSCH	01/01/1832	A		F7
RIES	MARTIN		ALTFELD	01/01/1755	A		F5
RIESE	MAGDALENA	1840	RÜPPUR	01/01/1872	A		F8
RIFFEL	BERNHARD KARL	1878	KARLSRUHE	01/01/1895	A		F3
RIFFEL	JOSEF	1836	DURLACH KARLSRUHE	/ /			F7
RIFFEL MN GRESS	ANNA MARIA	1856	PENNSYLVANIA	06/26/1888	A		F4
RIFFEL W FAMILY	RUDOLF	1857	ETTLINGEN	06/26/1888	A		F4
RIFFEL W P	JULIUS RUDOLF	1885	PENNSILVANIA	06/26/1888	A		F4
RIFFEL W P	LINA MARGARETHA	1888	ETTLINGEN	06/26/1888	A		F4
RIFFEL W P	LUISE ADELHEID	1884	MACHAMMELSBURG	06/26/1888	A		F4
RIFFLER	FRIEDRICH		KARLSRUHE	01/01/1891	A		F3
RIGOBRI	JULIUS		ETTLINGEN	08/04/1864	A		F4
RIHM	JOHANNES		MÖRSCH	06/08/1832	A		F7
RIHM	KATHARINA		MÖRSCH	06/22/1858	A		F7
RIHM	XAVER		MÖRSCH	08/08/1853	A		F7
RIHM MN FITTERER	MARIA		MÖRSCH	08/08/1853	A		F7
RIHM MN MUND	KATHARINA		MÖRSCH	07/25/1853	A		F7
RIHM W F	ALOIS		MÖRSCH	07/25/1853	A		F7

Lastname	Firstname	Birth Year	Birthplace	Emigration	De	Prof	Source
RIHM W F	XAVER		MÖRSCH	08/08/1853	A		F7
RIHM W P	ANTON	1842	MÖRSCH	07/25/1853	A		F7
RIHM W P	ANTON	1843	MÖRSCH	08/08/1853	A		F7
RIHM W P	JOHANNES	1840	MÖRSCH	07/25/1853	A		FF7
RIHM W P	JOHANNES	1852	MÖRSCH	07/25/1853	A		F7
RIHM W P	JOSEF	1838	MÖRSCH	08/08/1853	A		F7
RIHM W P	KATHARINA	1837	MÖRSCH	07/25/1853	A		F7
RIHM W P	KATHARINA	1848	MÖRSCH	08/08/1853	A		F7
RIHM W P	LUDWIG	1845	MÖRSCH	07/25/1853	A		F7
RIHM W P	MARIA	1849	MÖRSCH	07/25/1853	A		F7
RIHM W P	ROSALINDE	1848	MÖRSCH	07/25/1853	A		F7
RIHM W P	SOPHIA	1841	MÖRSCH	08/08/1853	A		F7
RITTER	JOHANN HEIN WIL		DURLACH KARLSRUHE	01/01/1845	A		F7
RITTER	LUDWIG		DURLACH KARLSRUHE	01/01/1834			
RITTERSHOFER	FRANZ JAKOB	1855	DURLACH KARLSRUHE	/ /	A		F7
RITTERSHOFER	JAKOB FRIEDRICH	1852	DURLACH KARLSRUHE	/ /	A		F7
RITTERSHOFER	WILHELM FRIEDRH		DURLACH	01/01/1829	A		F6
RITTINGER	JAKOB		OFTERSHEIM	01/01/1819			F1
RITZHAUPT	KONRAD	1848	KARLSRUHE	01/01/1866	A		F3
ROBER	KARL	1864	KARLSRUHE	01/01/1882	A		F3
RODERI WIDOW	BARBARA		WEINGARTEN	01/01/1892	A		F5
ROHR	ALOIS	1777	OBERWEIER	/ /	A		F1
ROHR	CAROLINA		OBERWEIER	01/01/1853	A		F1
ROHR	GEORG		WINDEN	01/01/1804			F1
ROHRER	GEORG		KARLSRUHE	01/01/1878	A		F3
ROLL	ANTON	1836	ETTLINGEN	01/30/1854	A		F4
ROLL	CARL	1818	ETTLINGEN	01/26/1854	A		F4
ROLL	SIMON		ETTLINGEN	01/01/1854	A		F4
ROLLE	ANTON	1864	KARLSRUHE	01/01/1883	A		F3
ROLLE MN BÖHLER	FLORENTINE	1832	KARLSRUHE	01/01/1882	A		F3
ROLLE W FAMILY	ANTON	1833	KARLSRUHE	01/01/1882	A		F3
ROLLE W PARENTS	FERDINAND	1863	KARLSRUHE	01/01/1882	A		F3
ROLLE W PARNETS	EMIL	1871	KARLRSRUHE	01/01/1882	A		F3
ROLLER	CHRISTIAN		SPPÖCK	01/01/1864	A		F4
ROLLER	CHRISTOPH		SPÖCK	01/01/1852	A		F4
ROLLER MN HOFHEINZ	LUISE	1862	SPÖCK	01/01/1883	A		F4
ROLLER W FAMILY	ERNSTINE	1830	SPÖCK	01/01/1880	A		F4
ROLLER W FAMILY	KARL	1863	SPÖCK	01/01/1883	A		F4
ROLLER W P	BERTHA	1880	SPÖCK	01/01/1883	A		F4
ROLLER W P	CAROLINE	1868	SPÖCK	01/01/1880	A		F4
ROLLER W P	FRIEDA	1864	SPÖCK	01/01/1880	A		F4
ROLLER W P	LUIS	1882	SPÖCK	01/01/1883	A		F4
ROLLER W P	LUISE	1859	SPÖCK	01/01/1880	A		F4
ROLLER W P	SOPHIE	1861	SPÖCK	01/01/1880	A		F4
ROLSHAUFER	FRIEDERIKE	1826	KARLSRUHE	01/01/1870	A		F3
ROMBACH	KARL		SÖLLINGEN	/ /			F7
ROMBACH	STANISLAUS		SÖLLINGEN	/ /	A		F7
ROMBACH	VINZENS		REUTE	01/01/1825	A		F8
ROMBACH W FAMILY	KARL		KARLSRUHE	/ /	A		F3
ROOS	CASPAR		HASSELBERG	05/20/1752	A		F6

Lastname	Firstname	Birth Year	Birthplace	Emigration	De	Prof	Source
ROOS	JOSEF	1809	MALSCH	05/23/1853	A		F2
ROOS	THERESE	1813	MALSCH	06/18/1852	A		F2
ROSENBUSCH	SALEMON		EISSIGHEIM	01/01/1866	A		F6
ROSENFELD	JOHANNES		PETERZELL	01/01/1866	A		F6
ROSENSTOCK	ELIAS		HOCHHAUSEN	01/01/1866	A		F6
ROSSWAG MN KLETT	KATHARINA	1811	SÖLLINGEN	01/01/1840	A		F7
ROSSWAG W F	JOHANN GEORG	1810	SÖLLINGEN	01/01/1840	A		F7
ROSSWAG W P	KATHARINA	1839	SÖLLINGEN	01/01/1840	A		F7
ROSSWAG W P	LUISE MARGARETH	1841	AMERIKA	01/01/1840	A		F4
ROSSWAG W P	MAGDALENA	1840	ETTLINGEN	01/01/1840	A		F4
ROSSWAG W P	MAGDALENA	1840	SÖLLINGEN	01/01/1840	A		F7
ROSSWAG W W	BERNHARD		SÖLLINGEN	/ /	A		F7
ROSTOCK	FERDINAND		GRABEN	01/01/1830	A		F5
ROTH	ADOLF	1875	LIEDOLSHEIM	01/01/1892	A		F9
ROTH	ALBERT FRIEDRIH	1875	LIEDOLSHEIM	01/01/1892	A		F6
ROTH	AUGUST	1872	LIEDOLSHEIM	01/01/1890	A		F9
ROTH	AUGUST LUDWIG	1868	LIEDOLSHEIM	01/01/1886	A		F6
ROTH	CARL CHRISTOPH	1857	LIEDOLSHEIM	01/01/1881	A		F6
ROTH	CHRISTOPH		GRABEN	01/01/1824	A		F3
ROTH	EMIL	1873	LIEDOLSHEIM	01/01/1891	A		F6
ROTH	EMILIE	1864	LIEDOLSHEIM	01/01/1880	A		F6
ROTH	FRIEDRICH		GRABEN	01/01/1872	A		F3
ROTH	FRIEDRICH	1865	LIEDOLSHEIM	01/01/1886	A		F9
ROTH	FRIEDRICH GEORG	1871	LIEDOLSHEIM	01/01/1890	A		F9
ROTH	FRITZ		GRABEN	01/01/1880	A		F5
ROTH	HEINRICH		GRABEN	01/01/1878	A		F5
ROTH	HEINRICH GUSTAV	1860	RÜPPUR	01/01/1879	A		F8
ROTH	JAKOB PHILIPP	1878	GRABEN	01/01/1893	A		F3
ROTH	JOHANN LUDWIG		LIEDOLSHEIM	01/01/1871	A		F9
ROTH	KARL FRIEDRICH		LIEDOLSHEIM	01/01/1890	A		F9
ROTH	LUDWIG		GRABEN	01/01/1881	A		F3
ROTH	PHILLIP JAKOB	1862	KARLSRUHE	01/01/1884	A		F3
ROTH	REINHARD	1850	GRABEN	01/01/1869	A		F3
ROTH	WENDEL		GRABEN	01/01/1835	A		F3
ROTH	WILHELM		GRABEN	01/01/1869	A		F3
ROTH	WILHELMINE	1832	LIEDOLSHEIM	01/01/1891	A		F9
ROTH MN	CHRISTINE	1843	GRABEN	01/01/1878	A		F3
ROTH W F	CHRISTIAN	1830	LIEDOLSHEIM	01/01/1866	A		F6
ROTH W FAMILY	HEINRICH	1858	GRABEN	01/01/1878	A		F3
ROTH W P	CHRIISTIAN	1860	LIEDOLSHEIM	01/01/1866	A		F6
ROTH W P	FRIEDRICH	1854	LIEDOLSHEIM	01/01/1866	A		F6
ROTH W P	IGNATZ	1865	LIEDOLSHEIM	01/01/1866	A		F6
ROTH W P	LUISE	1856	LIEDOLSHEIM	01/01/1866	A		F6
ROTH W P	MARGARETE	1865	LIEDOLSHEIM	01/01/1866	A		F6
ROTH W PARENTS	ANNA MARG.	1870	GRABEN	01/01/1878	A		F3
ROTH W PARENTS	ELSE	1875	GRABEN	01/01/1878	A		F3
ROTH W PARENTS	HEINRICH	1877	GRABEN	01/01/1878	A		F3
ROTH W PARENTS	KATHARINA	1872	GRABEN	01/01/1878	A		F3
ROTH W PARENTS	LUDWIG HEINRICH	1868	GRABEN	01/01/1878	A		F3
ROTH-KÖHLER	MARIE		GRABEN	/ /	A		F5

Lastname	Firstname	Birth Year	Birthplace	Emigration	De	Prof	Source
ROTHWEILER	JAKOB		BERG	01/01/1737			
ROTHWEILER W F	JAKOB		BERG	01/01/1737	A		F6
ROTTNER MN WALTER	BARBARA	1840	MÖRSCH	08/06/1868	A		F7
ROTTNER W F	EDUARD	1840	MÖRSCH	08/06/1868	A		F7
RUBEL	FRANZ KARL	1844	MALSCH	01/01/1869	A		F2
RUBEL MN GEIGER	APOLLONIA		MALSCH	01/01/1854	A		F2
RUBEL MN WEISHAUPT	MARIA	1817	MALSCH	02/07/1854	A		F2
RUBEL W FAMILY	JOSEF	1808	MALSCH	02/07/1854	A		F2
RUBEL W FAMILY	WENDELIN		MALSCH	01/01/1854	A		F2
RUBEL W PARENTS	ELISABETH	1841	MALSCH	02/07/1854	A		F2
RUBEL W PARENTS	FLORIAN	1844	MALSCH	02/07/1854	A		F2
RUBEL W PARENTS	JAKOB	1836	MALSCH	02/07/1854	A		F2
RUBEL W PARENTS	JOSEF	1837	MALSCH	02/07/1854	A		F2
RUBEL W PARENTS	KARL	1839	MALSCH	02/07/1854	A		F2
RUBEL W PARENTS	LUISE	1848	MALSCH	02/07/1854	A		F2
RUBEL W PARENTS	PAULINE	1845	MALSCH	01/01/1854	A		F2
RUDENBROD	ARTHUR	1866	ETTLINGEN	01/01/1882	A		F4
RUDENBROD	BENEDIGT		FORBACH	01/01/1864	A		F6
RUDENBROD	JOHANN		FORBACH	01/01/1860	A		F6
RUDENBROD	KAROLIN E		FORBACH	01/01/1860	A		F6
RUDENBROD	WILHELM	1862	ETTLINGEN	07/03/1883	A		F4
RUDENBROD W FAMILY	GUSTAV		FORBACH	01/01/1854	A		F6
RUDOLF	ANDREAS		ALTFELD	/ /	A		F5
RUDOLPH W F	PHILIPP		SINSHEIM	01/01/1859	A		F6
RUEBER	ALBERT			/ /			
RUF	AUGUST		GRABEN	01/01/1853	A		F3
RUF	CHRISTIAN		GRÖTZINGEN	01/01/1881	A		F3
RUF	FRIEDRICH		GRÖTZINGEN	01/01/1849	A		F3
RUF	JAKOB		GRABEN	01/01/1853	A		F3
RUF	KARL		GRABEN	01/01/1864	A		F3
RUF	KARL	1878	KARLSRUHE	01/01/1895	A		F3
RUF	MARTIN		GRABEN	01/01/1854	A		F3
RUF	MARTINA		KAPPEL	01/01/1859	A		F6
RUF W CHILD.	KARL	1823	KARLSRUHE	01/01/1852	A		F3
RUF W F	KARL		BÜHL	01/01/1866	A		F6
RUMMEL	FRANZ		ETTLINGEN	06/08/1849	A		F4
RUMMEL	FRANZ	1798	ETTLINGEN	/ /	A		F4
RUPERT	EMIL	1868	KARLSRUHE	01/01/1882	A		F3
RUPP	JAKOB	1864	LANGENSTEINBACH	/ /	A		F3
RUPP	JOHANN JAKOB	1838	SÖLLINGEN	01/01/1866	A		F7
RUPP	JOSEF		SÖLLINGEN	01/01/1865	A		F7
RUPP	KARL	1828	LANGENSTEINBACH	04/06/1864	A		F3
RUPP	KATHARINA	1837	LANGENSTEINBACH	04/06/1864	A		F3
RUPP	MAGDALENA	1834	LANGENSTEINBACH	04/06/1864	A		F3
RUPP	MARGARETHA	1830	LANGENSTEINBACH	04/06/1864	A		F3
RUPP	MARIA KATHARINA	1818	LANGENSTEINBACH	02/03/1854	A		F3
RUPP	MATHäUS	1826	LANGENSTEINBACH	01/01/1847	A		F3
RUPP	MICHAEL	1827	LANGENSTEINBACH	04/06/1864	A		F3
RUPP	WILHELM	1812	LANGENSTEINBACH	06/19/1841	A		F3
RUPP MN NAGEL	KATHARINA	1839	LANGENSTEINBACH	02/27/1868	A		F3

Lastname	Firstname	Birth Year	Birthplace	Emigration	De	Prof	Source
RUPP MN SCHWARZ	LUISE	1804	LANGENSTEINBACH	02/03/1853	A		F3
RUPP MN SPIEGEL	MARGARETHA	1839	LANGENSTEINBACH	/ /	A		F3
RUPP W FAMILY	JAKOB	1802	LANGENSTEINBACH	01/01/1853	A		F3
RUPP W FAMILY	JOHANN KARFT	1838	LANGENSTEINBACH	03/06/1868	A		F3
RUPP W PARENTS	JAKOB	1838	LANGENSTEINBACH	02/03/1854	A		F3
RUPP W PARENTS	JAKOB	1860	LANGENSTEINBACH	/ /	A		F3
RUPP W PARENTS	JULIANE	1841	LANGENSTEINBACH	02/03/1854	A		F3
RUPP W PARENTS	KARL	1843	LANGENSTEINBACH	02/03/1854	A		F3
RUPP W PARENTS	KATHARINA	1834	LANGENSTEINBACH	02/03/1854	A		F3
RUPP W PARENTS	LUISE	1829	LANGENSTEINBACH	02/03/1854	A		F3
RUPP W PARENTS	SOPHIA	1832	LANGENSTEINBACH	02/03/1854	A		F3
RUPP W WIFE	KRAFT	1838	LANGENSTEINBACH	02/27/1868	A		F3
RUPPERT	PHILIPP MARTIN	1862	DIEDELSHEIM	01/01/1880	A		F6
RUPRECHT	FRANZ	1871	KARLSRUHE	01/01/1892	A		F3
RUTHARD	HEINRICH	1821	GRABEN	01/01/1847	A		F3
RUTHARD	KARL		GRABEN	01/01/1869	A		F3
RUTTINGER	ADAM		GERCHSHEIM	01/01/1866	A		F6
RüBER	KARL WILHELM		KARLSRUHE	01/01/1857	A		F3
RüHLE	CHRISTIAN	1864	LANGENSTEINBACH	07/13/1883	A		F3
RüHLE	GOTTLIEB	1824	LANGENSTEINBACH	01/01/1850	A		F3
RüHLE	GOTTLIEB	1842	LANGENSTEINBACH	04/22/1864	A		F3
RüHLE	JAKOB		LANGENSTEINBACH	07/17/1863	A		F3
RüHLE	JOHANN GOTTLIEB	1824	LANGENSTEINBACH	01/01/1850	A		F3
RüHLE	KARL	1834	LANGENSTEINBACH	01/01/1852	A		F3
RüHLE	VALENTIN	1839	LANGENSTEINBACH	01/01/1852	A		F3
RüHLE	WILHELM	1832	LANGENSTEINBACH	04/14/1854	A		F3
RüHLE MN BAUCHERT	ROSINA	1834	LANGENSTEINBACH	03/08/1864	A		F3
RüHLE MN BEDER	KATHARINA	1837	LANGENSTEINBACH	01/01/1868	A		F3
RüHLE MN KRONENWETT	KATHARINA	1816	LANGENSTEINBACH	01/01/1847	A		F3
RüHLE MN KRONENWETT	SUSANNA	1825	LANGENSTEINBACH	09/29/1855	A		F3
RüHLE MN MART	KATHARINA	1805	LANGENSTEINBACH	01/01/1846	A		F3
RüHLE MN NAGEL	MARGARETHA BARB	1817	LANGENSTEINBACH	03/29/1864	A		F3
RüHLE MN RUPP	MAGDALENA	1830	LANGENSTEINBACH	02/18/1868	A		F3
RüHLE W FAILY	GEORG	1780	LANGENSTEINBACH	01/01/1847	A		F3
RüHLE W FAMILY	FRIEDRICH	1833	LANGENSTEINBACH	01/01/1868	A		F3
RüHLE W FAMILY	GEORG	1800	LANGENSTEINBACH	01/01/1846	A		F3
RüHLE W FAMILY	GEORG	1823	LANGENSTEINBACH	02/18/1868	A		F3
RüHLE W FAMILY	JAKOB	1810	LANGENSTEINBACH	01/01/1847	A		F3
RüHLE W FAMILY	MARTIN	1819	LANGENSTEINBACH	03/29/1864	A		F3
RüHLE W FAMILY	PHILIPP JAKOB	1828	LANGENSTEINBACH	03/08/1864	A		F3
RüHLE W FAMILY	VALENTIN	1818	LANGENSTEINBACH	09/29/1855	A		F3
RüHLE W FATHER	GOTTLIEB	1840	LANGENSTEINBACH	01/01/1847	A		F3
RüHLE W FATHER	KATHARINA	1815	LANGENSTEINBACH	01/01/1847	A		F3
RüHLE W FATHER	SUSANNA	1820	LANGENSTEINBACH	01/01/1847	A		F3
RüHLE W PARENTS	CHRISTOPH	1843	LANGENSTEINBACH	09/29/1855	A		F3
RüHLE W PARENTS	ELISABETH	1857	LANGENSTEINBACH	03/08/1864	A		F3
RüHLE W PARENTS	FRIEDRICH	1859	LANGENSTEINBACH	01/01/1873	A		F3
RüHLE W PARENTS	GEORG	1831	LANGENSTEINBACH	01/01/1846	A		F3
RüHLE W PARENTS	GEORG	1847	LANGENSTEINBACH	02/18/1868	A		F3
RüHLE W PARENTS	GEORG	1850	LANGENSTEINBACH	02/18/1868	A		F3

Lastname	Firstname	Birth Year	Birthplace	Emigration De	Prof	Source
RÜHLE W PARENTS	JAKOB	1844	LANGENSTEINBACH	03/29/1864 A		F3
RÜHLE W PARENTS	JAKOB	1857	LANGENSTEINBACH	02/18/1868 A		F3
RÜHLE W PARENTS	JAKOB	1861	LANGENSTEINBACH	03/18/1884 A		F3
RÜHLE W PARENTS	JULIAN	1847	LANGENSTEINBACH	03/29/1864 A		F3
RÜHLE W PARENTS	KARL	1857	LANGENSTEINBACH	01/01/1873 A		F3
RÜHLE W PARENTS	MAGDALENA	1838	LANGENSTEINBACH	01/01/1847 A		F3
RÜHLE W PARENTS	MARGARETHE	1849	LANGENSTEINBACH	03/29/1864 A		F3
RÜHLE W PARENTS	MARTIN	1836	LANGENSTEINBACH	01/01/1846 A		F3
RÜHLE W PARENTS	MICHAEL	1865	LANGENSTEINBACH	/ / A		F3
RÜHLE W PARENTS	PHILIPP	1860	LANGENSTEINBACH	03/08/1864 A		F3
RÜHLE W PARENTS	SUSANNE	1833	LANGENSTEINBACH	01/01/1846 A		F3
RÜHLE W PARENTS	VALENTIN	1842	LANGENSTEINBACH	01/01/1847 A		F3
RäPPLE	KATHARINA		SÖLLINGEN	/ / A		F7
RäUCHLE	EMIL		SÖLLINGEN	01/01/1861 A		F3
RöCH	SOPHIA		LAHR	01/01/1850 A		F6
RöLLER	LUDWIG	1865	SPÖCK	01/01/1881 A		F4
RöS	HEINRICH	1860	KARLSRUHE	01/01/1883 A		F3
RöSCH	CHRISTOPH	1814	GRABEN	01/01/1862 A		F3
RöSCH	ELISABETH	1806	GRABEN	01/01/1892 A		F3
RöSCH	HERMANN	1874	GRABEN	01/01/1891 A		F3
RöSCH	JAKOB FRIEDRICH		GRABEN	01/01/1879 A		F3
RöSCH	KATHARINA	1816	GRABEN	01/01/1862 A		F5
RöSCH	KATHARINA	1861	GRABEN	01/01/1862 A		F3
RöSCH	LUDWIG	1878	GRABEN	01/01/1895 A		F3
RöSCH	MARGARETHA	1809	GRABEN	01/01/1862 A		F3
RöSCH	PHILIPP	1804	GRABEN	01/01/1862 A		F3
RöSCH	WILHELM		GRABEN	01/01/1875 A		F3
RöSSLER	KARL FRIEDRICH		SPÖCK	01/01/1847 A		F4
RöSSLER W FAMILY	WILHELM		SPÖCK	01/01/1847 A		F4
RöSSNER	FRIEDRICH		DURLACH KARLSRUHE	01/01/1849		F7
RöLLER	ERNSTINE	1856	SPÖCK	01/01/1880 A		F8
RöLLER	KARL	1854	SPÖCK	01/01/1883 A		F8
RöLLER	LUDWIG	1865	SPÖCK	01/01/1881 A		F8
RöSNER	MARTIN		ISPRINGEN	01/01/1796 A		F7

Lastname	Firstname	Birth Year	Birthplace	Emigration	De	Prof	Source
SAAM W FAMILY	JOHANN		GRÖTZINGEN	01/01/1737	A		F3
SAHRBACHER	FLORENTINE		BURBACH	/ /	A		F4
SAHRBACHER	HERMANN	1849	BURBACH	01/01/1854	A		F4
SAHRBACHER	HERMINE	1841	BURBACH	01/01/1854	A		F4
SAHRBACHER	KARL	1843	BURBACH	01/01/1854	A		F4
SAHRBACHER	MARIA JOFEFA	1823	BURBACH	01/01/1856	A		F4
SAHRBACHER	THERESIA	1830	BURBACH	01/01/1856	A		F4
SALZER	FRIEDERICH	1834	LANGENSTEINBACH	01/01/1854	A		F3
SALZER	OTTO	1830	LANGENSTEINBACH	08/30/1854	A		F3
SANDBAAS	FRANZ ANTON		WÖSSINGEN	01/01/1769			F1
SANTER	ZACHARIAS		WÖSSINGEN	01/01/1853	A		F4
SARBACHER	MARTIN	1819	MALSCH	/ /	A		F2
SATTLER	JOHANN		MÖRSCH	01/01/1847	A		F7
SATTLER	JOHANN		MÖRSCH	09/23/1886	A		F7
SATTLER	JOHANNES		MÖRSCH	01/25/1847	A		F7
SATTLER	JOSEF		MÖRSCH	07/01/1891	A		F7
SATTLER MN BECKER	CAROLINE		OBERWEIER	01/01/1853	A		F1
SATTLER MN SCHNEIDER	GERTRUD		MÖRSCH	11/06/1851	A		F7
SATTLER W F	JOHANN		MÖRSCH	11/06/1851	A		F7
SATTLER W F	JOSEF	1849	MÖRSCH	11/06/1851	A		F7
SATTLER W P	MAGDALENA	1840	MÖRSCH	11/06/1851	A		F7
SATTLER WW	JOSEPH		OBERWEIER	01/01/1853	A		F1
SAUBERLICH MN GEIZ	CHRISTINE		ETTLINGEN	01/01/1847	A		F4
SAUBERLICH W FAMILY	IGNAZ UWE	1801	ETTLINGEN	01/01/1847	A		F4
SAUBERLICH W P	KATHARINA	1829	ETTLINGEN	01/01/1847	A		F4
SAUER W F	HANS ADAM		KREDENBACH	04/16/1762	A		F5
SAUERBECK	ANDREAS		DINGLINGEN	04/25/1804			F1
SAUTER	ZACHARIAS		WÖSSINGEN	01/01/1858	A		F1
SAWING	OTTO		DAXLANDEN	01/01/1893	A		F6
SAY	HELENA		DISTELHAUSEN	01/01/1866	A		F6
SCHAAF	ADOLF EMIL LUDG		KARLSRUHE	01/01/1857	A		F3
SCHAAF	JAKOB		FEUDENHEIM	01/01/1808			F1
SCHAAR W P	JOSEF	1835	PFAFFENROT	01/01/1842			F7
SCHAAR MN SCHNEIDER	KATHARINA		PFAFFENROT	01/01/1842	A		F7
SCHAAR MN SCHNEIDER	KATHARINA	1811	PFAFFENROT	01/01/1847			F7
SCHAAR W F	FRANZ		PFAFFENROT	01/01/1842			F7
SCHAAR W F	FRANZ	1804	PFAFFENROT	01/01/1847	A		F7
SCHAAR W P	BARBARA	1832	PFAFFENROT	01/01/1842			F7
SCHAAR W P	MAGDALENA	1829	PFAFFENROT	01/01/1842			F7
SCHAAR W P	MAGDALENA	1833	PFAFFENROT	01/01/1847	A		F7
SCHABER	JAKOB	1864	GRÖTZINGEN	01/01/1893	A		F3
SCHABER MN FRIEDERLE	EVA	1849	ETTLINGEN	09/06/1879	A		F4
SCHABER W FAMILY	ROBERT	1847	ETTLINGEN	09/06/1879	A		F4
SCHABER W P	ROBERT	1872	ETTLINGEN	09/06/1879	A		F4
SCHABINGER	AUGUST	1850	SPRANTAL	01/01/1882	A		F6
SCHABINGER	JOSEPHINE	1864	SPRANTAL	01/01/1882	A		F6
SCHABINGER W F	CHRISTOPH	1822	SPRANTAL	01/01/1882	A		F6
SCHABINGER WP	KARL	1862	SPRANTAL	01/01/1882	A		F6
SCHAEFER W F	JOHANN ADAM		KREDENBACH	05/19/1752	A		F5
SCHALLER	JOHANN		NÖGGENSCHWIEL	01/01/1817	A		F6

Lastname	Firstname	Birth Year	Birthplace	Emigration	De	Prof	Source
SCHARFENBERGER	HERMANN	1868	KARLSRUHE	01/01/1880	A		F3
SCHAUER	ANDREAS		FÖRCH/RASTATT	04/04/1804			F1
SCHAUFFER	HANSJÖRG		BLANKENLOCH	04/09/1750	A		F4
SCHAUFLER	ALBERT	1874	KARLSRUHE	01/01/1892	A		F3
SCHEEDER	AUGUST MICHAEL		KARLSRUHE	01/01/1866	A		F3
SCHEERERS(WITWE)W F	GEORG		KÖNDRINGEN	01/01/1866	A		F6
SCHEID	KARL FRIEDRICH		KARLSRUHE	01/01/1852	A		F3
SCHEIFLE	ERNST		KARLSRUHE	/ /	A		F3
SCHELL	CÄCILIE	1861	KARLSRUHE	01/01/1881	A		F3
SCHELL	EDMUND		HÖPFINGEN	01/01/1866	A		F6
SCHELL	ERNST FERDINAND	1876	KARLSRUHE	01/01/1893	A		F3
SCHEMSER	LUDWIG KARL	1876	KNIELINGEN	01/01/1894	A		F6
SCHENF	HEINRICH		KARLSRUHE	01/01/1804	A		F3
SCHENKEL	FRIEDRICH	1826	DURLACH KARLSRUHE	01/01/1852	A		F7
SCHENKEL	JAKOB HEINRICH		DURLACH KARLSRUHE	01/01/1846	A		F7
SCHERER	AUGUST		KARLSRUHE	01/01/1852	A		F3
SCHERER	JOHANN	1869	WALLDORF	/ /	A		F2
SCHERER	MARIANNE		MÖRSCH	01/01/1880	A		F7
SCHERER MN KUHL	MARGARETHA	1838	MÖRSCH	01/01/1881	A		F7
SCHERER W F	FRANZ		MÖRSCH	07/28/1832	A		F7
SCHERER W F	JOHANN GEORG		MÖRSCH	01/01/1881	A		F7
SCHERER W P	ANTON	1868	MÖRSCH	01/01/1881	A		F7
SCHERER W P	BENJAMIN	1864	MÖRSCH	01/01/1881	A		F7
SCHERER W P	VITAL	1863	MÖRSCH	01/01/1881	A		F7
SCHERER W P	WILHELM	1869	MÖRSCH	01/01/1881	A		F7
SCHEURER	CHRISTIAN		WÖSSINGEN	01/01/1832	A		F1
SCHEURER	FRANZ JAKOB		SÖLLINGEN	01/01/1861	A		F7
SCHEURER	GEORG JAKOB		WÖSSINGEN	01/01/1845	A		F4
SCHEURER WW	GEORG		WÖSSINGEN	01/01/1845	A		F1
SCHILLING	GEORG		REICHERTSHAUSEN	01/01/1866	A		F6
SCHILLING	KARL	1874	MÖRSCH	07/30/1890	A		F3
SCHILLING	KARL	1874	MÖRSCH	07/30/1890	A		F4
SCHILLINGER	FRANZ ANTON	1817	BURBACH	01/01/1856	A		F4
SCHILLINGER W FAMILY	FRANZ		FORBACH	01/01/1854	A		F6
SCHIMPF	GOTTFRIED		DITTIGHEIM	01/01/1866	A		F6
SCHINDEL	ERNST		KARLSRUHE	/ /	A		F3
SCHINDEL	ERNST	1872	DURLACH	01/01/1891	A		F3
SCHINDEL	FRIEDRICH KARL	1880	DURLACH/K`HE	01/01/1898	A		F3
SCHINDLER	KARL	1854	MALSCH	01/01/1881	A		F2
SCHINDLER	KARL	1862	ETTLINGEN	01/19/1884	A		F4
SCHINDLER	MARKUS		FAUTENBACH	01/01/1870	A		F5
SCHIRMEIER	VINZENS		HOFSTETTEN	01/01/1859	A		F6
SCHLATTER	LUDWIG	1865	MÜHLBURG	01/01/1884	A		F6
SCHLECHLIN	KARL FRIEDRICH	1867	KARLSRUHE	01/01/1885	A		F3
SCHLEE	GOTTHARD		WÖSSINGEN	01/01/1760	A		F1
SCHLEE	KARL	1826	ETTLINGEN	02/15/1847	A		F4
SCHLEHR	ANDREAS	1843	RINKLINGEN	06/29/1860	A		F4
SCHLEICH	JAKOB		WALLDORF	01/01/1866	A		F6
SCHLEMMER	MAX EMIL	1866	KARLSRUHE	01/01/1886	A		F3
SCHLENZ	GEORG		WILLSTETT	01/01/1859	A		F6

Lastname	Firstname	Birth Year	Birthplace	Emigration	De	Prof	Source
SCHLESSMANN W F	NICOLAUS		BESTENHEID	02/18/1773	A		F5
SCHLEYER	ROSA	1860	WÖSSINGEN	01/01/1885	A		F4
SCHLINDWEIN	AMANN	1863	KARLSRUHE	01/01/1882	A		F3
SCHLINDWEIN	JOHANNES ALOIS	1873	ETTLINGEN	01/01/1890	A		F4
SCHLINDWEIN	JOSEF ALOIS	1873	ETTLINGEN	08/04/1890	A		F4
SCHLOTTERBED	WILHELM	1849	KARLSRUHE	01/01/1870	A		F3
SCHLOTTERER	BENEDIKT		SCHÖLLBRONN	01/01/1850	A		F7
SCHLOTTERER	EGIDIUS	1840	SCHÖLLBRONN	/ /	A		F7
SCHLOTTERER MN HAUCK	THEKLA	1799	SCHÖLLBRONN	01/01/1854	A		F7
SCHLOTTERER MN STREI	MARIA URSULA	1802	SCHÖLLBRONN	01/01/1836	A		F7
SCHLOTTERER W F	BENEDIKT	1789	SCHÖLLBRONN	01/01/1854	A		F7
SCHLOTTERER W P	CRESCENTIA	1831	SCHÖLLBRONN	01/01/1854	A		F7
SCHLOTTERER W P	JOHANN ADAM	1824	SCHÖLLBRONN	01/01/1824	A		F7
SCHLOTTERER W P	JOSEF	1834	SCHÖLLBRONN	01/01/1854	A		F7
SCHLOTTERER W P	MARGARETHA	1829	SCHÖLLBRONN	01/01/1854	A		F7
SCHLOTTERER W P	THERESE	1836	SCHÖLLBRONN	01/01/1854	A		F7
SCHLOTTERER W W	EDUARD	1812	SCHÖLLBRONN	01/01/1836	A		F7
SCHMID W WIFE	ADOLF	1844	KARLSRUHE	01/01/1881	A		F3
SCHMIDT		1865	KARLSRUHE	01/01/1890	A		F6
SCHMIDT	ADAM		BLANKENLOCH	01/01/1862	A		F4
SCHMIDT	ALBERT	1855	ETTLINGEN	09/30/1873	A		F4
SCHMIDT	AUGUST		SÖLLINGEN	01/01/1861	A		F7
SCHMIDT	AUGUST KARL	1852	WÖSSINGEN	01/01/1871	A		F4
SCHMIDT	CHRISTOPH		GRÖTZINGEN	01/01/1861	A		F3
SCHMIDT	CHRISTOPH		GRÖTZINGEN	01/01/1830	A		F5
SCHMIDT	CHRISTOPH		SÖLLINGEN	01/01/1865	A		F7
SCHMIDT	GEORG	1866	KARLSRUHE	01/01/1884	A		F3
SCHMIDT	GUSTAV	1874	WÖSSINGEN	01/01/1890	A		F4
SCHMIDT	HERMANN	1836	ETTLINGEN	08/16/1858	A		F4
SCHMIDT	JAKOB		HAGENBACH	01/01/1859	A		F6
SCHMIDT	JAKOB	1845	LANGENSTEINBACH	/ /	A		F3
SCHMIDT	JAKOB	1847	LANGENSTEINBACH	05/15/1870	A		F3
SCHMIDT	JOHANN FRIEDRIH	1830	LANGENSTEINBACH	03/24/1860	A		F3
SCHMIDT	JOHANN KRAFT	1845	LANGENSTEINBACH	05/15/1870	A		F3
SCHMIDT	KAROLINA	1896	LANGENSTEINBACH	/ /	A		F3
SCHMIDT	KATHARINA	1847	LANGENSTEINBACH	01/01/1882	A		F3
SCHMIDT	LEOPOLD	1807	ETTLINGEN	01/28/1843	A		F4
SCHMIDT	LUDWIG		LANGENSTEINBACH	/ /	A		F3
SCHMIDT	MAGDALENA	1889	LANGENSTEINBACH	/ /	A		F3
SCHMIDT	MARTIN		BLANKENLOCH	01/01/1847	A		F4
SCHMIDT	PHILIPP JAKOB	1862	LANGENSTEINBACH	/ /	A		F3
SCHMIDT	WILHELM	1832	LANGENSTEINBACH	01/01/1854	A		F3
SCHMIDT	WILHELM	1850	LANGENSTEINBACH	05/15/1870	A		F3
SCHMIDT MN HÖRNER	SOPHIE		KARLSRUHE	01/01/1881	A		F3
SCHMIDT MN SCHÄFER	KAROLINE		BLANKENLOCH	01/01/1845	A		F4
SCHMIDT W FAMILY	LUDWIG		BLANKENLOCH	01/01/1845	A		F4
SCHMIEDER	AUGUST	1825	KARLSRUHE	01/01/1865	A		F3
SCHMIEDT	HEINRICH		WÖSSINGEN	01/01/1832	A		F1
SCHMIEDT	HEINRICH		WÖSSINGEN	01/01/1832	A		F4
SCHMIT	JONATHE		MOSBACH	01/01/1850	A		F6

Lastname	Firstname	Birth Year	Birthplace	Emigration	De	Prof	Source
SCHMITT	CHRISTIAN		LANGENSTEINBACH	01/01/1837	A		F3
SCHMITT	CHRISTIAN		WELSCHNEUREUTH	01/01/1857	A		F8
SCHMITT	EDUARD	1845	BAUERBACH	01/01/1869	A		F8
SCHMITT	JAKOB	1863	KARLSRUHE	01/01/1882	A		F3
SCHMITT	JOSEF	1874	MALSCH	01/01/1888	A		F2
SCHMITT	KARL		RÜSTENBACH/MOSB.	01/01/1833			F1
SCHMITT	KARL		TAUBERBISCHOFSHEIM	01/01/1859	A		F6
SCHMITT W CH	ANNA MARIA		PFAFFENROT	01/01/1847	A		F7
SCHMITT W M	HEINRICH	1825	PFAFFENROT	01/01/1847	A		F7
SCHMITT W M	IGNATIUS	1826	PFAFFENROT	01/01/1847	A		F7
SCHMITT W M	JOSEF		PFAFFENROT	01/01/1847	A		F7
SCHMäHLICH	JOHANN		FEUDENHEIM	01/01/1832			F1
SCHNECK	PETRONELLA		TAUBERBISCHOFSHEIM	01/01/1866	A		F6
SCHNEIDER	ALBERT	1834	PFAFFENROT	01/01/1854	A		F7
SCHNEIDER	BALTASAR	1823	BURBACH	01/01/1856	A		F4
SCHNEIDER	CHRISTOPH		WöSSINGEN	01/01/1854	A		F1
SCHNEIDER	CHRISTOPH		WöSSINGEN	01/01/1828	A		F4
SCHNEIDER	CHRISTOPH		WöSSINGEN	01/01/1854	A		F4
SCHNEIDER	DANIEL		WöSSINGEN	01/01/1853	A		F1
SCHNEIDER	ERHARD MARKUS	1830	PFAFFENROT	01/01/1851	A		F7
SCHNEIDER	FRANZ ANTON		MÖRSCH	01/01/1832	A		F7
SCHNEIDER	FRANZ ANTON	1836	PFAFFENROT	01/01/1854	A		F7
SCHNEIDER	FRIEDRICH		KARLSRUHE	01/01/1853	A		F3
SCHNEIDER	GEORG	1826	SPESSART	01/01/1852	A		F4
SCHNEIDER	HERMANN		GRABEN	/ /	A		F5
SCHNEIDER	IGNAZ	1777	VöLKERSBACH	/ /	A		F4
SCHNEIDER	JAKOB	1846	WöSSINGEN	01/01/1863	A		F4
SCHNEIDER	JOHANN		WöSSINGEN	01/01/1832	A		F4
SCHNEIDER	JOHANN	1816	WöSSINGEN	01/01/1832	A		F1
SCHNEIDER	JOHANNES	1823	DURLACH KARLSRUHE	/ /	A		F7
SCHNEIDER	JOSEF		MÖRSCH	01/01/1832	A		F7
SCHNEIDER	LEOPOLD	1835	PFAFFENROT	01/01/1854	A		F7
SCHNEIDER	LUISE		WöSSINGEN	01/01/1846	A		F1
SCHNEIDER	MAGDALENA	1807	PFAFFENROT	/ /	A		F7
SCHNEIDER	MAGDALENA	1826	BURBACH	01/01/1856	A		F4
SCHNEIDER	MARIA JOSEFA	1832	BURBACH	01/01/1856	A		F4
SCHNEIDER	MELCHIOR	1815	BURBACH	01/01/1856	A		F4
SCHNEIDER	RUDOLF		WöSSINGEN	01/01/1856	A		F1
SCHNEIDER W F	GEORG FRIEDRICH	1813	HOCHSTETTEN	01/01/1880	A		F8
SCHNEIDER W F	GEORG MICHAEL			/ /			
SCHNEIDER W P	MARTIN	1853	SPÖCK	01/01/1880	A		F8
SCHNEIDER W P	ROSINE	1857	SPÖCK	01/01/1880	A		F8
SCHNEIDER W W	CHRISTOPH		WöSSINGEN	01/01/1828	A	TAYL	F1
SCHNEPF	FELICIAN	1829	SPESSART	09/21/1854	A		F4
SCHNEPF	IGNAZ	1805	ETTLINGEN	01/01/1852	A		F4
SCHNEPF	IGNAZ	1822	SPESSART	09/21/1851	A		F4
SCHNETZER MN DAIGER	KATHARINA		ETTLINGEN	01/01/1849	A		F4
SCHNETZER W FAMILY	JOHANN	1801	ETTLINGEN	01/01/1849	A		F4
SCHNOCK W W	JOHANN			/ /			
SCHNäBELE	GUSTAV		KARLSRUHE	01/01/1860	A		F3

Lastname	Firstname	Birth Year	Birthplace	Emigration	De	Prof	Source
SCHNöRR	PHILLIPP	1861	KARLSRUHE	01/01/1883	A		F3
SCHOLL	ADOLF		KARLSRUHE	01/01/1852	A		F3
SCHOLL	AUGUST WILHELM		GRABEN	01/01/1892	A		F3
SCHOLL	CHRISTOPH		GRABEN	01/01/1804	A		F3
SCHOLL	ELISE		GRABEN	01/01/1737	A		F3
SCHOLL	ELISE		GRABEN	01/01/1737	A		F5
SCHOLL	FRIEDRICH		GRABEN	01/01/1831	A		F5
SCHOLL	FRIEDRICH		GRABEN	01/01/1878	A		F3
SCHOLL	FRIEDRICH		GRABEN	01/01/1881	A		F3
SCHOLL	JULIUS		KARLSRUHE	01/01/1852	A		F3
SCHOLL	KARL		GRABEN	01/01/1882	A		F3
SCHOLL	MARTIN		GRABEN	/ /	A		F5
SCHOLL	PHILIPP		GRABEN	01/01/1804	A		F5
SCHOLL	PHILIPP		GRABEN	01/01/1848	A		F3
SCHOLL	PHILIPP		GRABEN	01/01/1861	A		F3
SCHOLL	PHILIPP		GRABEN	01/01/1861	A		F5
SCHOLL	SIMON		GRABEN	/ /	A		F5
SCHOLL	WENDEL		GRABEN	01/01/1804	A		F3
SCHOLL	WILHELM		GRABEN	01/01/1881	A		F3
SCHOLL-KRüGER	JOHANNA		GRABEN	01/01/1891	A		F3
SCHOLLER	JAKOB		KARLSRUHE	01/01/1853	A		F3
SCHORB	WILHELM		BLANKENLOCH	01/01/1850	A		F4
SCHORB W FAMILY	MICHAEL		BLANKENLOCH	01/01/1836	A		F4
SCHOTT	JULIUS	1867	KARLSRUHE	01/01/1882	A		F3
SCHOTT	KARL	1874	KARLSRUHE	01/01/1890	A		F3
SCHOTTMüLLER	ANDREAS	1823	PFAFFENROT	01/01/1852	A		F7
SCHOTTMüLLER	ANTON	1827	PFAFFENROT	01/01/1852	A		F7
SCHOTTMüLLER	FLORENZ	1824	PFAFFENROT	01/01/1852	A		F7
SCHOTTMüLLER	FRANZ JOSEF	1832	PFAFFENROT	01/01/1852	A		F7
SCHOTTMüLLER	FRANZ XAVER	1833	PFAFFENROT	/ /	A		F7
SCHOTTMüLLER	JOSEF	1828	BURBACH	01/01/1856	A		F4
SCHOTTMüLLER	JOSEF	1828	PFAFFENROT	/ /	A		F7
SCHOTTMüLLER	KATHARINA	1189	BURBACH	01/01/1856	A		F4
SCHOTTMüLLER	KATHARINA	1829	PFAFFENROT	/ /	A		F7
SCHOTTMüLLER	MARIA ANNA	1819	PFAFFENROT	/ /			F7
SCHOTTMüLLER	MARIA THERESIA	1831	BURBACH	01/01/1856	A		F4
SCHOTTMüLLER	OTTILIE	1837	PFAFFENROT	01/01/1852	A		F7
SCHOTTMüLLER	SEBASTIAN	1799	PFAFFENROT	/ /			F7
SCHOTTMüLLER	SEVERIN	1835	PFAFFENROT	01/01/1852	A		F7
SCHOTTMüLLER	XAVER	1833	BURBACH	01/01/1856	A		F4
SCHRANTH	FRIEDRICH WILHM	1865	KARLSRUHE	01/01/1884	A		F3
SCHREIBER	AUGUST	1859	KNIELINGEN	01/01/1882	A		F6
SCHREIBER	CHISTIAN		WöSSINGEN	01/01/1846	A		F4
SCHREIBER	CHRISTINA		WöSSINGEN	01/01/1855	A		F1
SCHREIBER	CHRISTINE		WöSSINGEN	01/01/1856	A		F4
SCHREIBER	FRIEDRICH		WöSSINGEN	01/01/1860	A		F1
SCHREIBER	HEINRICH	1833	WöSSINGEN	01/01/1882	A		F4
SCHREIBER	HERMANN	1878	GRABEN	01/01/1892	A		F3
SCHREIBER	KATHARINA	1850	WöSSINGEN	01/01/1868	A		F4
SCHREIBER W W	CHRISTIAN		WöSSINGEN	01/01/1846	A		F1

Lastname	Firstname	Birth Year	Birthplace	Emigration	De	Prof	Source
SCHRIDEL	LUDWIG HENRICH		KARLSRUHE	01/01/1857	A		F3
SCHRIMM W F	CHRISTOPH		BERGHAUSEN	01/01/1843	A		F6
SCHROTH	ANTON	1804	PFAFFENROT	01/01/1863	A		F7
SCHROTH	FRANZ	1829	PFAFFENROT	01/01/1847	A		F7
SCHROTH	HIERONIMUS	1848	SCHÖLLBRONN	/ /	A		F7
SCHROTH	JOHANN		SCHÖLLBRONN	01/01/1848	A		F7
SCHROTH	JOSEF	1822	PFAFFENROT	01/01/1850	A		F7
SCHROTH	MARTIN		JÖHLINGEN	01/01/1858	A		F8
SCHROTH	MATHIAS	1792	PFAFFENROT	01/01/1859	A		F7
SCHROTH	SUSANNE		JÖHLINGEN	01/01/1862	A		F8
SCHROTH	SUSANNE		JÖHLINGEN	01/01/1867	A		F8
SCHROTH MN FLUTTERER	FRANZISKA		PFAFFENROT	01/01/1858	A		F7
SCHROTH MN HOFMANN	KAROLINE		ETTLINGEN	01/01/1854	A		F4
SCHROTH W F	ANTON		PFAFFENROT	/ /	A		F7
SCHROTH W FAMILY	ANTON		ETTLINGEN	01/01/1854	A		FE
SCHROTH W P		1854	ETTLINGEN	01/01/1854	A		F4
SCHROTH W P	FLORIAN	1833	PFAFFENROT	01/01/1858	A		F7
SCHROTH W P	JAKOBINE	1835	PFAFFENROT	01/01/1858	A		F7
SCHROTH W P	JOSEF	1832	PFAFFENROT	01/01/1858	A		F7
SCHROTH W P	MARIANNE	1836	PFAFFENROT	01/01/1858	A		F7
SCHROTT	FRIEDRICH CHRIP		DURLACH KARLSRUHE	01/01/1846			F7
SCHUCH	BERNHARDT		BLANKENLOCH	01/01/1834	A		F4
SCHUHMACHER	ADAM	1830	WÖSSINGEN	01/01/1850	A	CARP	F1
SCHUHMACHER	CHRISTOPH		WÖSSINGEN	01/01/1842	A		F4
SCHUHMACHER	FRIEDRICH	1866	GRÖTZINGEN	01/01/1882	A		F3
SCHUHMACHER	HEIRICH		WÖSSINGEN	01/01/1848	A		F5
SCHUHMACHER	PHILIPP		WÖSSINGEN	01/01/1850	A		F1
SCHUHMACHER W FAMILY	ADAM		WÖSSINGEN	01/01/1832	A		F1
SCHUHMACHER W FAMILY	HEINRICH		WÖSSINGEN	01/01/1832	A	FARM	F1
SCHUHMACHER WW	CHRISTOPH		WÖSSINGEN	01/01/1842	A		F1
SCHUHMAIER	HEINRICH		WÖSSINGEN	01/01/1848	A		F1
SCHULER MN METZ	KAROLINE FRIEDE	1866	LIEDOLSHEIM	01/01/1890	A		F9
SCHULER W F	CHRISTOPH FRIED	1862	LIEDOLSHEIM	01/01/1890	A		F9
SCHULER W P	FRIEDRICH		LIEDOLSHEIM	01/01/1890	A		F9
SCHULER W P	LUDWIG FRIEDRIH	1890	LIEDOLSHEIM	01/01/1890	A		F9
SCHULZ	ADOLF	1845	KARLSRUHE	01/01/1868	A		F3
SCHULZ	DANIEL	1855	KARLSRUHE	01/01/1892	A		F3
SCHUMACHER	VALENTIN		MÖNCHZELL	01/01/1859	A		F6
SCHUSTER	AUGUST	1839	BAUERBACH	01/01/1873	A		F8
SCHWAB	JOSEF	1823	LANGENSTEINBACH	01/01/1854	A		F3
SCHWALL	JOHANN		DÜRLANDEN	01/01/1818	A		F6
SCHWAN MN JGLI	CRESCENTIA	1837	MALSCH	11/19/1866	A		F2
SCHWAN W FAMILY	BENEDIKT	1833	MALSCH	11/19/1866	A		F2
SCHWAN W PARENTS	MONIKA	1861	MALSCH	11/19/1866	A		F2
SCHWAN W PARENTS	ROSA	1866	MALSCH	11/19/1866	A		F2
SCHWANDER	CHRISTIAN FRIED		DURLACH KARLSRUHE	01/01/1886	A		F7
SCHWANDER	KARL	1828	DURLACH KARLSRUHE	/ /	A		F7
SCHWANHUT	WILHELM	1877	KARLSRUHE	01/01/1893	A		F3
SCHWARZ	LEOPOLD	1830	ETTLINGEN	05/14/1850	A		F4
SCHWARZ W PARENTS	JULIE	1870	KARLSRUHE	01/01/1870	A		F3

Lastname	Firstname	Birth Year	Birthplace	Emigration	De	Prof	Source
SCHWARZ MN BUSTER	LISSETTE	1844	KARLSRUHE	01/01/1870	A		F3
SCHWARZ W FAMILY	WILHELM FRIEDRH	1846	KARLSRUHE	01/01/1870	A		F3
SCHWARZ W PARENTS	ADOLF	1869	KARLSRUHE	01/01/1870	A		F3
SCHWARZWäLDER	JOSEF		LANGENSCHILTACH	01/01/1859	A		F6
SCHWEIG	GEORG CHRISTIAN		DURLACH KARLSRUHE	01/01/1839			F7
SCHWEITZER	CHRISTIAN		UNTERKESSACH	01/01/1859	A		F6
SCHWEITZER	CHRISTINE		UNTERKESSACH	01/01/1859	A		F6
SCHWEITZER	LOTHAR	1877	KARLSRUHE	01/01/1893	A		F3
SCHWEIZER	JAKOB FRIEDRICH		KARLSRUHE	01/01/1864	A		F3
SCHWEIZER	KAROLINE		SöLLINGEN	01/01/1862	A		F7
SCHWEIZER	LOTHAR		KARLSRUHE	/ /	A		F3
SCHWEIZER	PHILIPPINE MAGD		SöLLINGEN	01/01/1865	A		F7
SCHWENDEMANN	LUDWIG		STEINACH	01/01/1850	A		F6
SCHWENDEMANN	LUDWIG		STEINACH	01/01/1859	A		F6
SCHWINDT	KARL		KARLSRUHE	01/01/1847	A		F3
SCHWäMMERLE	GOTTFRIED		WöSSINGEN	01/01/1803	A		F1
SCHWäNZ WW 3 CH	GOTTFRIED		WöSSINGEN	03/18/1803	A		F1
SCHüBEL MN KüHNER	ELISABETH	1865	SöLLINGEN	01/01/1892	A		F3
SCHüBEL W FAMILY	ANTON	1865	SöLLINGEN	01/01/1892	A		F3
SCHüBEL W PARENTS	FRANZ	1890	SöLLINGEN	01/01/1892	A		F3
SCHüBEL W PARENTS	HEINRICH	1889	SöLLINGEN	01/01/1892	A		F3
SCHüBEL W PARENTS	LUDWIG	1891	SöLLINGEN	01/01/1892	A		F3
SCHüBLY	JOHANN	1808	HELMSHEIM	01/01/1843	A		F7
SCHüDLE	CHRISTIAN FRIEH	1858	KARLSRUHE	01/01/1872	A		F3
SCHüTZ	JAKOB		KARLSRUHE	01/01/1853	A		F3
SCHüTZ	LUDWIG	1858	KARLSRUHE	01/01/1884	A		F3
SCHüTZ	PETER		DURLACH/K'HE	/ /	A		F3
SCHüTZ	PETER		WEINGARTEN	01/01/1898	A		F9
SCHüTZ W FAMILY	HEINRICH	1847	GRABEN	01/01/1888	A		F3
SCHüTZ W PARENT	HEINRICH	1876	GRABEN	01/01/1888	A		F3
SCHüTZ W PARENT	JOHANNA	1879	GRABEN	01/01/1888	A		F3
SCHüTZ W PARENT	THEODOR	1877	GRABEN	01/01/1888	A		F3
SCHäBELE	WILHELM	1860	KARLSRUHE	01/01/1877	A		F3
SCHäFER	ALEXANDER	1863	RUSSHEIM	01/01/1879	A		F9
SCHäFER	EMIL	1876	VöLKERSBACH	04/10/1892	A		F4
SCHäFER	EUGEN WILHELM	1856	KARLSRUHE	01/01/1876	A		F3
SCHäFER	FRIEDRICH WILHM	1860	KNIELINGEN	01/01/1882	A		F6
SCHäFER	LORENZ		GISSIGHEIM	01/01/1859	A		F6
SCHäFER	MAGDALENA		GISSIGHEIM	01/01/1859	A		F6
SCHäFER	MARGARETHE	1814	RINKLINGEN	02/26/1846	A		F4
SCHäFER	MICHAEL		GISSIGHEIM	01/01/1859	A		F6
SCHäFER	WILHELM	1860	KARLSRUHE	01/01/1884	A		F3
SCHäFER	WILHELM	1862	RINKLINGEN	01/01/1880	A		F4
SCHäFER W FAMILY	JOHANN PHILIPP		WöSSINGEN	01/01/1832	A		F1
SCHäFER	CAROLINA	1832	NöTTINGEN	01/01/1832	A		F6
SCHäFER	HEINRICH SEBASN	1869	RINKLINGEN	02/15/1845	A		F4
SCHäFER	PAUL		RüPPURR	01/01/1868	A		F6
SCHöNING	FRITZ EDWIN		KARLSRUHE	/ /	A		F3
SCHöPFLE	ERNST CHRISTOPH	1830	GRöTZINGEN	01/01/1851	A		F3
SCHöPFLE	JOHANN JAKOB	1801	GRöTZINGEN	01/01/1853	A		F3

- 126 -

Lastname	Firstname	Birth Year	Birthplace	Emigration	De	Prof	Source
SCHöPFLE	JOHANN MARTIN	1861	GRöTZINGEN	01/01/1881	A		F3
SCHöPFLE	JOHANNES	1790	GRöTZINGEN	01/01/1846	A		F3
SCHöPFLE MN VOLZ	BARBARA SYBILLE	1811	GRöTZINGEN	01/01/1846	A		F3
SCHöPFLE W FAMILY	HEIRICH	1806	GRöTZINGEN	01/01/1846	A		F3
SCHöPFLE W PARENTS	CHRISTIAN FRIED	1835	GRöTZINGEN	01/01/1846	A		F3
SCHöPFLE W PARENTS	HEINRICH	1840	GRöTZINGEN	01/01/1846	A		F3
SCHöPFLE W PARENTS	KAROLINE	1842	GRöTZINGEN	01/01/1846	A		F3
SCHöPFLE W PARENTS	MAGDALENA DORO	1834	GRöTZINGEN	01/01/1846	A		F3
SCHöPFLIN	MARTIN		GRöTZINGEN	01/01/1881	A		F3
SCHöPPLER	CHRISTOPH	1831	LANGENSTEINBACH	02/03/1854	A		F3
SCHöPPLER	FRIEDRICH	1830	LANGENSTEINBACH	02/03/1854	A		F3
SCHöPPLER	JOHANN	1833	LANGENSTEINBACH	08/15/1850	A		F3
SCHöPPLER	KARL MARTIN	1835	LANGENSTEINBACH	02/03/1854	A		F3
SCHöPPLER	MAGDALENA	1820	LANGENSTEINBACH	02/03/1854	A		F3
SCHöPPLER	MICHAEL	1814	LANGENSTEINBACH	01/01/1842	A		F3
SCHöFFEL	CHRISTIAN		WöSINGEN	01/01/1850	A		F4
SCHöFFER	LORENZ		SöLLINGEN	01/01/1803	A		F7
SCHöPFLE MN WALTER	ANNA		GRöTZINGEN	01/01/1855	A		F5
SCHöPFLE MN WALTER	ANNA MARIA		GRöTZINGEN	01/01/1853	A		F5
SCHöPFLE W F	JOHANN		GRöTZINGEN	01/01/1853	A		F5
SCHöPFLE W F	JOHANN JAKOB		GRöTZINGEN	01/01/1855	A		F5
SCHüBEL MN KüHNER	ELISABETH	1865	SöLLINGEN	01/01/1892	A		F7
SCHüBEL W F	ANTON	1865	SöLLINGEN	01/01/1892	A		F7
SCHüBEL W P	FRANZ	1890	SöLLINGEN	01/01/1892	A		F7
SCHüBEL W P	HEINRICH	1889	SöLLINGEN	01/01/1892	A		F7
SCHüBEL W P	LUDWIG	1891	SöLLINGEN	01/01/1892	A		F7
SEBER	HEINRICH	1768	GRABEN	01/01/1793	A		F3
SEEBER MN WERNER	MARIE CHRISTIEN	1834	GRABEN	01/01/1869	A		F3
SEEBER W F	PHILIPP MARTIN		GRABEN	01/01/1830	A		F5
SEEBER W FAMILY	AUGUST FRIEDRIC	1832	GRABEN	01/01/1869	A		F3
SEEBER W PARENTS	AUGUST FRIEDRIC	1859	GRABEN	01/01/1869	A		F3
SEEBER W PARENTS	CAROLINE FRIEDE	1863	GRABEN	01/01/1869	A		F3
SEEBER W PARENTS	CHRISTINE PHILI	1861	GRABEN	01/01/1869	A		F3
SEEBER W PARENTS	LUISE CHRISTINE	1866	GRABEN	01/01/1869	A		F3
SEEBER W PARENTS	PAULINE	1868	GRABEN	01/01/1869	A		F3
SEEFIRCHER MN BULLIR	KATHARINA		MALSCH	01/01/1891	A		F2
SEEFIRCHER W FAMILY	ANTON	1878	MALSCH	01/01/1891	A		F2
SEEFISCHER	EMMA		MALSCH	01/01/1891	A		F2
SEEFISCHER	VALENTIN	1833	MALSCH	/ /	A		F2
SEEGER	GEORG FRIEDRICH		BLANKENLOCH	01/01/1846	A		F4
SEEGER	HANS GEORG		SPöCK	01/01/1737	A		F4
SEEGER	HEINZ GEORG		SPöCK	01/01/1737	A		F4
SEEGER M FAMILY	LUDWIG		BLANKENLOCH	01/01/1862	A		F4
SEEGER W FAMILY	KARL LUDWIG		BLANKENLOCH	01/01/1862	A		F4
SEEGER W FAMILY	LUDWIG		BLANKENLOCH	01/01/1834	A		F4
SEELAND	AUGUST		SPöCK	01/01/1852	A		F4
SEELAND	CHRISTIAN		SPöCK	01/01/1852	A		F4
SEELAND	LUDWUG		KARLSRUHE	/ /	A		F3
SEEMANN	BENEDIKT		HERRENWIES	01/01/1850	A		F7
SEGER	WILHELM		BLANKENLOCH	01/01/1852	A		F4

Lastname	Firstname	Birth Year	Birthplace	Emigration	De	Prof	Source
SEIB	KARL		OBERGIMPERN	01/01/1859	A		F6
SEIDNER	JOHANN		HASSELBERG	03/06/1840	A		F5
SEIDNER	JöRG		HASSELBERG	05/20/1752	A		F5
SEIDNER W F	JOHANN MICHAEL		HASSELBERG	05/16/1754	A		F5
SEIDNER W F	PHILIPP		HASSELBERG	05/16/1754	A		F5
SEIF	GOTTLIEB	1756	LANGENSTEINBACH	03/28/1828	A		F3
SEIF MN KRONENWETT	MARGARETHA	1796	LANGENSTEINBACH	03/25/1829	A		F3
SEIF W FAMILY	JAKOB	1789	LANGENSTEINBACH	03/25/1829	A		F3
SEIF W PARENTS	GOTTLIEB	1822	LANGENSTEINBACH	03/25/1829	A		F3
SEIF W PARENTS	JAKOB	1816	LANGENSTEINBACH	03/25/1829	A		F3
SEIF W PARENTS	JOHANN MICHAEL	1819	LANGENSTEINBACH	03/25/1829	A		F3
SEIF W PARENTS	MARGARETHA	1826	LANGENSTEINBACH	03/25/1829	A		F3
SEIF W PARENTS	PHILIPP	1829	LANGENSTEINBACH	03/25/1829	A		F3
SEIFERMANN	BENEDIKT		OTTERSWEIER	01/01/1857	A		F6
SEIFERT	JOSEF	1829	ETTLINGEN	04/02/1852	A		F4
SEIFERT	JOSEF ANTON		ETTLINGEN	01/01/1850	A		F4
SEIFERT	JOSEF ANTON		ETTLINGEN	01/01/1859	A		F4
SEIFERT MN RUTHMANN	THERESE		ETTLINGEN	01/01/1845	A		F4
SEIFERT W PARENTS	LENA	1835	ETTLINGEN	01/01/1845	A		F4
SEIFERT W FAMILY	FRANZ		ETTLINGEN	01/01/1845	A		F4
SEIFERT W PARENTS	ADOLF	1839	ETTLINGEN	01/01/1845	A		F4
SEIFERT W PARENTS	FLORIAN	1841	ETTLINGEN	01/01/1845	A		F4
SEIFERT W PARENTS	FRANZISKA	1827	ETTLINGEN	01/01/1845	A		F4
SEIFERT W PARENTS	HERMANN	1833	ETTLINGEN	01/01/1845	A		F4
SEIFERT W PARENTS	JOHANNA	1844	ETTLINGEN	01/01/1845	A		F4
SEIFERT W PARENTS	KAROLINE	1843	ETTLINGEN	01/01/1845	A		F4
SEIFERT W WIFE	FRANZ	1800	ETTLINGEN	/ /	A		F4
SEILER	JOSEF		IBERG	01/01/1859	A		F6
SEILER	JOSEF	1859	KARLSRUHE	01/01/1876	A		F3
SEITH	KARL LUDWIG		LIEDOLSHEIM	01/01/1869	A		F9
SEITH W P	CHRISTOPH FRIED	1877	LIEDOLSHEIM	01/01/1890	A		F9
SEITH MN ROTH	KAROLINE	1859	LIEDOLSHEIM	01/01/1880	A		F9
SEITH MN ROTH	LUISE	1855	LIEDOLSHEIM	01/01/1890	A		F9
SEITH MN RUTTINGER	BARBARA	1840	LIEDOLSHEIM	01/01/1867	A		F9
SEITH W F	CHRISTOPH FRIED	1841	LIEDOLSHEIM	01/01/1890	A		F9
SEITH W P	FREDERICKE	1889	LIEDOLSHEIM	01/01/1890	A		F9
SEITH W P	FRIEDA	1885	LIEDOLSHEIM	01/01/1890	A		F9
SEITH W P	HERMANN AUGUST	1883	LIEDOLSHEIM	01/01/1890	A		F9
SEITH W P	KARL LUDWIG		LIEDOLSHEIM	01/01/1890	A		F9
SEITH W P	LUISE		LIEDOLSHEIM	01/01/1890	A		F9
SEITH W P	WILHELMINE	1881	LIEDOLSHEIM	01/01/1890	A		F9
SEITH W W	JOHAN DANIEL	1838	LIEDOLSHEIM	01/01/1869	A		F9
SEITH W W	KARL FRIEDRICH	1853	LIEDOLSHEIM	01/01/1880	A		F9
SEITZ	CHRISTIAN BERND	1844	LIEDOLSHEIM	01/01/1869	A		F9
SEITZ	FRIEDRICH WILHM	1871	LIEDOLSHEIM	01/01/1890	A		F9
SEITZ	GEORG		LIEDOLSHEIM	01/01/1867	A		F8
SEITZ	JOHANN ADAM		DURLACH KARLSRUHE	01/01/1865	A		F7
SEITZ	KARL LUDWIG		LIEDOLSHEIM	01/01/1893	A		F9
SEITZ	WILHELM		BLANKENLOCH	01/01/1802	A		F4
SEITZ	WILHELM	1856	LIEDOLSHEIM	01/01/1882	A		F9

Lastname	Firstname	Birth Year	Birthplace	Emigration	De	Prof	Source
SEITZ	WILHELM AUGUST	1874	BLANKENLOCH	01/01/1892	A		F4
SEITZ W F	KARL LUDWIG	1838	LIEDOLSHEIM	01/01/1879	A		F9
SEITZ MN KOCH	LINA	1845	RUSSHEIM	01/01/1881	A		F9
SEITZ MN NAGEL	ERNESTINE	1841	BLANKENLOCH	01/01/1880	A		F4
SEITZ MN ROTH	LUISE	1840	LIEDOLSHEIM	01/01/1879	A		F9
SEITZ MN ÜBERACKER	MARGARETHE		LIEDOLSHEIM	01/01/1879	A		F9
SEITZ W F	CHRISTOPH	1837	RUSSHEIM	01/01/1881	A		F9
SEITZ W F	GEORG FRIEDRICH	1839	LIEDOLSHEIM	01/01/1879	A		F9
SEITZ W FAMILY	JAKOB	1841	BLANKENLOCH	01/01/1880	A		F4
SEITZ W P	EMILIE	1872	LIEDOLSHEIM	01/01/1879	A		F9
SEITZ W P	ERNESTINE	1867	BLANKENLOCH	01/01/1880	A		F4
SEITZ W P	FRIEDERICKE	1862	LIEDOLSHEIM	01/01/1879	A		F9
SEITZ W P	HEINRICH	1864	LIEDOLSHEIM	01/01/1879	A		F9
SEITZ W P	LUISE	1879	LIEDOLSHEIM	01/01/1879	A		F9
SEITZ W P	MARTIN	1863	LIEDOLSHEIM	01/01/1879	A		F9
SEITZ W P	MINA	1866	RUSSHEIM	01/01/1881	A		F9
SEITZ W P	WILHELM	1869	BLANKENLOCH	01/01/1880	A		F4
SEITZ W P	WILHELMINE	1865	RUSSHEIM	01/01/1881	A		F9
SEIZ MN NAGEL	ERNESTINE	1841	BLANKENLOCH	01/01/1880	A		F4
SEIZ W FAMILY	JAKOB	1841	BLANKENLOCH	01/01/1880	A		F4
SEIZ W P	ERNESTINE	1867	BLANKENLOCH	01/01/1880	A		F4
SEIZ W P	KARL	1871	BLANKENLOCH	01/01/1880	A		F4
SEIZ W P	LUISE	1877	BLANKENLOCH	01/01/1880	A		F4
SEIZ W P	WILHELM	1869	BLANKENLOCH	01/01/1880	A		F4
SEMMLER	HERMANN		KARLSRUHE	/ /	A		F3
SEMMLER	HERMANN	1878	DURLACH	01/01/1893	A		F3
SERMERSHEIM	ANDREAS		RINKLINGEN	03/19/1842	A		F4
SERSTNER MN FUCHS	JOSEFA		ETTLINGEN	/ /	A		F4
SERSTNER W WIFE	ENGELBERT		ETTLINGEN	/ /	A		F4
SEUFERT	GEORG FRIEDRICH		BLANKENLOCH	01/01/1805	A		F4
SEUFERT	GEORG ULRICH	1735	BLANKENLOCH	01/01/1780	A		F4
SEUFERT	JAKOB FRIEDRICH		BLANKENLOCH	01/01/1865	A		F4
SEUFERT	JOHANN ADAM		BLANKENLOCH	01/01/1855	A		F4
SEUFFERT	KARL FRIEDRICH		KARLSRUHE	/ /	A		F3E
SEVER	HEINRICH		GRABEN	01/01/1750	A		F3
SEVERIN	KATHARINA		GRABEN	01/01/1736	A		F3
SEVERIN	MAGDALENA		GRABEN	01/01/1736	A		F3
SEYFRIED	EMANNUEL	1876	KARLSRUHE	01/01/1894	A		F3
SIEBER	KATHARINA		RINKLINGEN	01/01/1850	A		F4
SIEBER	MARGARETHE	1810	RINKLINGEN	01/01/1860	A		F4
SIEGERTH	WILHELM		WEINGARTEN	01/01/1888	A		F6
SIEGRICH	WILHELM		WEINGARTEN	06/26/1888	A		F6
SIEGRIST	CHRISTIAN		GRÖTZINGEN	01/01/1848	A		F5
SIEHS	MICHAEL		MÜHLBURG	01/01/1885	A		F6
SIGRIST	CHRISTIAN	1826	GRÖTZINGEN	01/01/1848	A		F3
SIGRIST MN BERM	KATHARINA		GRÖTZINGEN	01/01/1848	A		F3
SIGWART MN OBREITER	CäZILIA		PFAFFENROT	01/01/1857	A		F7
SIGWART W F	FLORIAN		PFAFFENROT	01/01/1857	A		F7
SILBER	RICHARD		FORBACH	01/01/1854	A		F6
SILBEREISEN	WILHELM		KARLSRUHE	01/01/1853	A		F3

Lastname	Firstname	Birth Year	Birthplace	Emigration	De	Prof	Source
SIMANN	HERMANN	1851	GRÖTZINGEN	01/01/1868	A		F3
SIMON	LUDWIG		SPÖCK	01/01/1892	A		F4
SINAUER	HEINRICH	1863	KARLSRUHE	01/01/1882	A		F3
SING	KARL LEOP. MAX	1856	KARLSRUHE	01/01/1870	A		F3
SINGER	CASPAR	1814	ETTLINGEN	01/01/1851	A		F4
SINGER	JOHANN JOAKOB		KARLSRUHE	01/01/1840	A		F3
SINGER	JOSEF	1817	WEINGARTEN	01/01/1843	A		F6
SINGRÜN	JULIA		VÖLKERBACH	01/01/1853	A		F4
SINGRÜN	JULIUS	1834	VÖLKERSBACH	04/19/1853	A		F4
SOHN	JOSEF		DIERSBURG	01/01/1859	A		F6
SOHN	PHILIPP		GRÖTZINGEN	01/01/1851	A		F3
SOLD	GOTTFRIED		DURLACH KARLSRUHE	01/01/1826			F7
SOLMS	HEINRICH		NECKARAU	03/24/1783			F1
SOMMER W F	JOHANN		KREDENBACH	08/18/1836	A		F5
SONTER W W	FRIEDRICH	1847	DIEDELSHEIM	01/01/1880	A		F6
SORNER	HERMANN	1867	KARLSRUHE	01/01/1880	A		F3
SPECK	GOTTLIEB	1849	KNIELINGEN	01/01/1867	A		F6
SPECK	LUDWIG JOHANN W	1863	RÜPPUR	01/01/1870	A		F8
SPECK	SOPHIE	1840	BETERTHEIM?	01/01/1867	A		F6
SPED	ALBERT		KARLSRUHE	/ /	A		F3
SPED	FRANZISKA		ETTLINGEN	01/01/1865	A		F4
SPED	GEORG	1812	ETTLINGEN	01/01/1854	A		F4
SPED	JOHANN GEORG		ETTLINGEN	01/01/1797	A		F4
SPED	MARTIN		ETTLINGEN	01/01/1804	A		F4
SPED	OSKAR	1859	ETTLINGEN	03/28/1870	A		F4
SPEER W CHIL.	FERDINAND	1838	KARLSRUHE	01/01/1883	A		F3
SPEER W FATH.	KATHARINA	1862	KARLSRUHE	01/01/1883	A		F3
SPEER W FATH.	WILHELM	1865	KARLSRUHE	01/01/1883	A		F3
SPEIER	XAVER		LEIBERSTUNG	01/01/1859	A		F6
SPERNÖDER	MARIA ELISABETH		SÖLLINGEN	01/01/1865	A		F7
SPIEGEL	EDMUND	1860	KARLSRUHE	01/01/1882	A		F3
SPIEGEL	PHILLIPP	1865	KARLSRUHE	01/01/1882	A		F3
SPIELER	EDUARD	1847	LIEDOLSHEIM	01/01/1892	A		F9
SPILER	FERDINAND	1877	KARLSRUHE	01/01/1891	A		F3
SPITZER	KARL	1875	KARLSRUHE	01/01/1891	A		F3
SPOHN	RICHARD	1868	KARLSRUHE	01/01/1893	A		F3
SPOHRER MN HILL	THERESE	1844	WEINGARTEN	01/01/1887	A		F5
SPOHRER W F	JOSEF	1840	WEINGARTEN	01/01/1887	A		F5
SPOHRER W P	ELISABETH	1871	WEINGARTEN	01/01/1892	A		F5
SPOHRER W P	GERTRUD	1873	WEINGARTEN	01/01/1894	A		F5
SPOHRER W P	KATHARINA	1870	WEINGARTEN	01/01/1894	A		F5
SPOHRER W P	LUISE	1880	WEINGARTEN	01/01/1894	A		F5
SPOHRER W P	MARIA THERESIA	1872	WEINGARTEN	01/01/1894	A		F5
SPRANG	BERNHARD		OBERHAUSEN	/ /	A		F1
SPRECHER	CHRISTINE		KARLSRUHE	01/01/1782	A		F5
SPRINGER	KARL	1860	ETTLINGEN	03/19/1879	A		F4
SPäTH	CHRISTIAN	1863	LANGENSTEINBACH	01/01/1882	A		F3
SPäTH WW 4CH	MATHIAS		WINDEN	01/01/1804			F1
SPäTH	ANNA	1843	ETTLINGEN	10/23/1869	A		F4
STAHL	MARIA ANNA	1846	PFAFFENROT	01/01/1869	A		F7

Lastname	Firstname	Birth Year	Birthplace	Emigration	De	Prof	Source
STAIGER	ANDREAS			/ /			
STAIGER	ANDREAS		GRÖTZINGEN	01/01/1853	A		F5
STAIGER MN KRIEGER	FR.		WÖSSINGEN	01/01/1780	A		F1
STAIGER MN KRIEGER	MAGDALENA		GRÖTZINGEN	01/01/1853	A		F3
STAIGER W FAMILY	ANDREAS		GRÖTZINGEN	01/01/1853	A		F3
STAIGER WW CH	CARL		WÖSSINGEN	01/01/1782	A		F1
STAMM	GUSTAV	1856	KARLSRUHE	01/01/1876	A		F3
STANDIN	LUDWIG	1861	NECKARAU	01/01/1889	A		F1
STARMANN	AUGUST FRIEDRIC	1868	BLANKENLOCH	01/01/1882	A		F4
STARMANN	FRIEDRICH	1864	BLANKENLOCH	01/01/1880	A		F4
STARMANN	GUSTAV FRIEDRIH	1866	BLANKENLOCH	01/01/1882	A		F4
STEBERT	WILHELM	1862	KNIELINGEN	01/01/1880	A		F6
STEFELIX	FRIEDRICH	1865	KARLSRUHE	01/01/1881	A		F3
STEFFEL	CHRISTIAN		WÖSSINGEN	01/01/1850	A		F1
STEGMÜLLER	GEORG ANTON		DURLACH KARLSRUHE	01/01/1845			F7
STEIGER	JAKOB		WÖSSINGEN	01/01/1780	A		
STEIGER	JOSEPH POPO		WÖSSINGEN	06/12/1804	A		F1
STEIGER	JULIANE		WÖSSINGEN	01/01/1854	A		F1
STEIGER W FAMILY	PHILIPP		WÖSSINGEN	01/01/1832	A		F1
STEIN	CARL ANTON	1822	ETTLINGEN	12/30/1844	A		F4
STEIN	CHRISTIAN FRIEH		WÖSSINGEN	01/01/1834	A		F1
STEIN	EMIL FRANZ	1837	ETTLINGEN	05/22/1875	A		F4
STEIN	JAKOBINE		WÖSSINGEN	01/01/1833	A		F1
STEIN	JOHANN	1830	ETTLINGEN	08/22/1850	A		F4
STEIN	LORENZ		KARLSRUHE	01/01/1803	A		F3
STEIN MN KRAUS	CÄZILIE		ETTLINGEN	01/30/1865	A		F4
STEIN W FAMILY	JOSEF	1833	ETTLINGEN	01/30/1865	A		FE
STEIN W P	WENDELIN	1863	ETTLINGEN	01/30/1865	A		F4
STEINBACH	HEINE	1879	KARLSRUHE	01/01/1893	A		F3
STEINBACH	KARL	1880	KARLSRUHE	01/01/1893	A		F3
STEINBRUNN W FAMILY	JAKOB FRIEDRICH		BLANKENLOCH	01/01/1817	A		F4
STEINBRUNNER	JAKOB FRIEDRICH		GRABEN	01/01/1825	A		F3
STEINBRUNNER W F	FRIEDRICH		GRABEN	01/01/1808	A		F5
STEINER	FRANZISKA	1833	PFAFFENROT	01/01/1854	A		F7
STEINER	GEORG ADAM	1836	PFAFFENROT	01/01/1854	A		F7
STEINER	JOSEFINE	1831	PFAFFENROT	01/01/1853	A		F7
STEINER MN GRESS	FRANZISKA		ETTLINGEN	06/16/1851	A		F4
STEINER W FAMILY	ALOIS	1800	ETTLINGEN	06/16/1851	A		F4
STEINLE	ERNST LUD.CHRI		DURLACH KARLSRUHE	01/01/1847	A		F7
STEINLE	JOHANN BURKARD		DURLACH KARLSRUHE	01/01/1838	A		F7
STEINLE	KARL THEODOR	1801	ETTLINGEN	10/17/1865	A		F4
STEINMETZ	KARL FRIEDRICH	1853	DURLACH KARLSRUHE	/ /	A		F7
STEINWACHS	MAX	1860	KARLSRUHE	01/01/1879	A		F3
STEMMER W F	MATHIAS		SÖLLINGEN	01/01/1860	A		F7
STERN	AUGUST	1865	KARLSRUHE	01/01/1880	A		F3
STEURER	ANDREAS		WÖSSINGEN	01/01/1858	A		F1
STEURER	GEORG		KORK	01/01/1859	A		F6
STEURER	GEORG ADAM		WÖSSINGEN	01/01/1854	A		F1
STEURER	MICHAEL		KORK	01/01/1859	A		F6
STIEFEL	CHRISTINE		BLANKENLOCH	01/01/1864	A		F4

Lastname	Firstname	Birth Year	Birthplace	Emigration	De	Prof	Source
STIEFEL	JAKOB		BLANKENLOCH	01/01/1852	A		F4
STIEFEL	MAIER		HOCHHAUSEN	01/01/1859	A		F6
STIEFEL MN	KAROLINE	1839	BLANKENLOCH	01/01/1866	A		F4
STIEFEL W FAMILY	KARL	1836	BLANKENLOCH	01/01/1866	A		F4
STIEFEL W P	KARL LEOPOLD	1865	BLANKENLOCH	01/01/1866	A		F4
STIEGLER	FERDINAND FRIED	1857	KARLSRUHE	01/01/1881	A		F3
STIHL	MATHIAS		KOMMINGEN	01/01/1859	A		F6
STNEZ	MARGARETHA		SEEWANGEN WALDSH.	01/01/1788			F1
STOBER	PHLIPP		SPöCK	01/01/1737	A		F4
STOBER	WILHELM		SPöCK	01/01/1849	A		F4
STOLL	LUDWIG		FORBACH	01/01/1865	A		F6
STOLZ	JAKOB KARL	1836	DURLACH KARLSRUHE	01/01/1866	A		F7
STOZ	MAGDALENA		MALTERDINGEN	01/01/1856	A		F5
STRAFBURGER	KARL		LAHR	01/01/1859	A		F6
STRANZ	HEINRICH	1836	PFAFFENROTH	01/01/1854	A		F7
STRAUB	FRIEDRICH	1874	KARLSRUHE	01/01/1892	A		F3
STRAUB	GEORG ADAM		DURLACH KARLSRUHE	01/01/1837	A		F7
STRAUB	JOSEF		ETTLINGEN	04/24/1834	A		F4
STRAUB	JOSEF	1834	ETTLINGEN	05/18/1857	A		F4
STRAUB	WENDELIN		ETTLINGEN	01/25/1865	A		F4
STRAUS	DORETH		KORB	01/01/1866	A		F6
STRAUSS	ADOLF		BARDHEIM	01/01/1866	A		F6
STRAUSS	MATHIAS		HOLZHAUSEN	01/01/1866	A		F6
STRAUSS	MORIZ		KARLSRUHE	/ /	A		F3
STRAUSS	RUDOLF JOSEF	1851	KARLSRUHE	01/01/1876	A		F3
STRAUSS	THEODOR	1863	KARLSRUHE	01/01/1883	A		F3
STREIB	GEORG	1864	KARLSRUHE	01/01/1881	A		F3
STREIBER	MICHAEL		WöSSINGEN	01/01/1803			F1
STREIBER WW CH	HEINRICH		WöSSINGEN	01/01/1802	A		F1
STREIBICH	ALOISIA	1839	SCHöLLBRONN	/ /	A		F7
STREIBICH	CASPAR	1841	SCHöLLBRONN	/ /	A		F7
STREIBICH	FRANZ JOSEF	1843	SCHöLLBRONN	/ /	A		F7
STREIBICH	MARIA ANNA	1834	SCHöLLBRONN	/ /	A		F7
STREIBICH	THERESIA	1835	SCHöLLBRONN	/ /	A		F7
STREIBIG	ANTON		SCHöLLBRONN	01/01/1858	A		F7
STREIBIG W CH	IGNAZ		SCHöLLBRONN	01/01/1852	A		F7
STREIBIG W F	ALOIS		SCHöLLBRONN	01/01/1852	A		F7
STREIBIG W F	FRANZISKA		SCHöLLBRONN	01/01/1852	A		F7
STREIBINGER	IGNAZ		SCHöLLBRONN	01/01/1853	A		F7
STREICHER	GUSTAV ADOLF		KARLSRUHE	01/01/1860	A		F5
STROBEL	MAX		KARLSRUHE	01/01/1852	A		F3
STRUBE	JAKOB		WöSSINGEN	01/01/1832	A		F1
STUDER	WILHELM FRIEDRH	1864	DIEDELSHEIM	01/01/1891	A		F6
STURM	JOHANN		WöSSINGEN	01/01/1737	A		F1
STUTZ	MAX KARL	1876	KARLSRUHE	01/01/1892	A		F3
STöRZENBACH	EDUARD	1868	KARLSRUHE	01/01/1884	A		F3
STöHRER	JOSEF		ETTLINGEN	08/12/1857	A		F4
STüRMER	WILHELM	1855	RÜPPURR	01/01/1870	A		F6
SULZER	CHR. AUG.		DURLACH KARLSRUHE	01/01/1866			F7
SUTOR	JOHANN KARL ADA	1861	KARLSRUHE	01/01/1881	A		F3

Lastname	Firstname	Birth Year	Birthplace	Emigration De	Prof	Source
SUTTER	MARTIN		BASEL	01/01/1859 A		F6
SWOBODA	JOSEF		KARLSRUHE	01/01/1782 A		F3
SÜMPFLE W PARENTS	AUGUST	1843	GRÖTZINGEN	01/01/1843 A		F3
SÜMPFLE W PARENTS	CHRISTOPH	1845	GRÖTZINGEN	01/01/1846 A		F3
SÜPFLE MN ZELLER	KATHARINA	1797	GRÖTZINGEN	01/01/1846 A		F3
SÜPFLE W FAMILY	HEINRICH	1805	GRÖTZINGEN	01/01/1846 A		F3
SÜPFLE W PARENTS	JAKOB	1841	GRÖTZINGEN	01/01/1846 A		F3
SÜSS	AUGUST		GRABEN	01/01/1857 A		F3
SÜSS	AUGUST		GRABEN	01/01/1859 A		F3
SÜSS	BALTES U CONS.		GRABEN	01/01/1737 A		F5
SÜSS	BALZER		GRABEN	01/01/1736 A		F3
SÜSS	BULTAB		GRABEN	01/01/1737 A		F3
SÜSS	ERNST		GRABEN	01/01/1881 A		F3
SÜSS	FRIEDRICH		GRABEN	01/01/1881 A		F3
SÜSS	HEINRICH		GRABEN	01/01/1881 A		F3
SÜSS	HEINRICH	1878	GRABEN	01/01/1893 A		F3
SÜSS	JAKOB KARL		SPÖCK	01/01/1854 A		F4
SÜSS	KARL		GRABEN	01/01/1879 A		F3
SÜSS	KARL		GRABEN	01/01/1880 A		F3
SÜSS	KARL		SPÖCK	01/01/1865 A		F4
SÜSS	LUDWIG		GRABEN	01/01/1868 A		F5
SÜSS	LUISE		SPÖCK	01/01/1843 A		F4
SÜSS	MAGDALENA		GRABEN	/ / A		F5
SÜSS	MARIA		SPÖCK	01/01/1847 A		F4
SÜSS	SIMON		KRAUTHEIM	01/01/1841 A		F6
SÜSS	WILHELM		GRABEN	01/01/1869 A		F3
SÜSS	WILHELM		GRABEN	01/01/1881 A		F3
SÜSS	WILHELM FRIEDRH		GRABEN	01/01/1888 A		F5
SÜSS	WILHELM JEREMIS		GRABEN	01/01/1865 A		F5
SÜSS W F	LUDWIG SIMON		GRABEN	01/01/1865 A		F5
SÜSS MN BECKER	CHRISTINE	1841	GRABEN	01/01/1888 A		F3
SÜSS MN BLAU	KATHARINA		GRABEN	01/01/1806 A		F3
SÜSS MN DOTH	KATHARINA		GRABEN	01/01/1890 A		F5
SÜSS W CHILDREN	WILHELM	1842	GRABEN	01/01/1892 A		F3
SÜSS W F	BALZER		GRABEN	01/01/1736 A		F5
SÜSS W F	KONRAD		GRABEN	01/01/1847 A		F5
SÜSS W F	SIMON		GRABEN	01/01/1868 A		F5
SÜSS W FAMILY	WILHELM FRIEDRH		SPÖCK	01/01/1847 A		F4
SÜSS W FAMILY	WILHELM FRIEDRI	1836	GRABEN	01/01/1888 A		F3
SÜSS W FATHER	KARL	1876	GRABEN	01/01/1892 A		F3
SÜSS W FATHER	KAROLINE PHILIP	1870	GRABEN	01/01/1892 A		F3
SÜSS W PARENTS	FRIEDRICH	1882	GRABEN	01/01/1888 A		F3
SÜSS W PARENTS	JOHANNA	1869	GRABEN	01/01/1888 A		F3
SÜSS W PARENTS	MAGDALENA	1874	GRABEN	01/01/1888 A		F3
SÜSS W PARENTS	PHILIPPINE	1866	GRABEN	01/01/1888 A		F3
SÜSS-DOTH	KATHARINA		GRABEN	01/01/1890 A		F3
SÜSS-WENZ	NINA		GRABEN	01/01/1880 A		F5
SäGER	ARBOGAST		DIERSBURG	01/01/1859 A		F6
SäUBERLICH	BARTHOLOMä		DURLACH KARLSRUHE	01/01/1841 A		F7
SöNLIN	ERNST JULIUS	1869	KARLSRUHE	01/01/1886 A		F3

Lastname	Firstname	Birth Year	Birthplace	Emigration	De	Prof	Source
SÜSS	LUDWIG	1872	GRABEN	01/01/1892	A		F8
SÜSS	WILHELM	1842	GRABEN	01/01/1868	A		F8

Lastname	Firstname	Birth Year	Birthplace	Emigration	De	Prof	Source
TAUBENMEIER MN KRONE	MAGDALENA	1802	LANGENSTEINBACH	02/24/1830	A		F3
TAUBENMEIER W FAMILY	JOHANN FRIEDRIC	1798	LANGENSTEINBACH	02/24/1830	A		F3
TAUBENMEIER W PARENT	ANDREAS	1829	LANGENSTEINBACH	02/24/1830	A		F3
TAUBENMEIER W PARENT	FRIEDRICH	1827	LANGENSTEINBACH	02/24/1830	A		F3
TAUBENMEIER W PARENT	MICHAEL	1824	LANGENSTEINBACH	02/24/1830	A		F3
TAUFKIRCH W PARENTS	BARBARA		KARLSRUHE	01/01/1866	A		F3
TEICHMÜLLER	HANS		KARLSRUHE	/ /	A		F3
THEILMANN W F	WILHELM		GRABEN	01/01/1834	A		F5
THIEBAUTH	PHLIPP ADAM	1811	ETTLINGEN	01/01/1850	A		F4
THOMANN	JOSEPH	1865	KARLSRUHE	01/01/1881	A		F3
THOMAS	MICHAEL	1856	KARLSRUHE	01/01/1882	A		F3
THOMAS	WILHELM	1884	KARLSRUHE	/ /	A		F3
THOMEIN	STEFAN	1862	KARLSRUHE	01/01/1886	A		F3
THORWART	GEORG		KORK	01/01/1850	A		F6
TIEFENBACHER	FRIEDRICH	1823	DURLACH KARLSRUHE	/ /	A		F7
TIEFENBACHER	LUDWIG JAKOB	1837	DURLACH KARLSRUHE	/ /	A		F7
TIGGEWS	JOSEF		KARLSRUHE	/ /	A		F3
TOMATIS MN KÜHNER	LUISE	1881	DURLACH	/ /	A		F3
TRAPP W MOTHER	FRANZ	1879	MALSCH	05/17/1881	A		F2
TRAPP MN SPäTH	JOSEFINE	1853	MALSCH	01/01/1882	A		F2
TRAPP W CH	ELISABETH	1860	MALSCH	05/17/1881	A		F2
TRAPP W FAMILY	CYRIAK	1846	MALSCH	01/01/1882	A		F2
TRAPP W PARENTS	JOSEF DANIEL	1879	MALSCH	01/01/1882	A		F2
TRAUTMANN	CRESCENZ		ETTLINGEN	05/27/1858	A		F4
TRAUTWEIN	JOHANN FRIDOLIN		SCHILTACH	01/01/1859	A		F6
TRAUTWEIN	JOHANN WILHELM	1828	KARLSRUHE	01/01/1852	A		F3
TRAUTZ	FRIEDRICH	1820	LANGENSTEINBACH	01/01/1854	A		F3
TRAUTZ MN MAIER	AUGUSTE		LANGENSTEINBACH	02/03/1854	A		F3
TRAUTZ MN RUPP	MARIA KATHARINA	1818	LANGENSTEINBACH	02/03/1854	A		F3
TRAUTZ W FAMILY	ANDREAS	1820	LANGENSTEINBACH	02/03/1854	A		F3
TRAUTZ W FAMILY	ANDREAS FRANZ		LANGENSTEINBACH	02/03/1854	A		F3
TRAUTZ W PARENTS	ANDREAS	1820	LANGENSTEINBACH	02/03/1854	A		F3
TREIBER	ADAM		MÖRSCH	01/01/1881	A		F7
TRENKLE	KARL		ELZACH	01/01/1866	A		F6
TREUER	KARL	1831	LANGENSTEINBACH	01/01/1847	A		F3
TREUER	MARGARETHA	1842	LANGENSTEINBACH	01/01/1854	A		F3
TREUER MN KRONENWETT	ANNA MARIA	1789	LANGENSTEINBACH	01/01/1849	A		F3
TREUER W FAMILY	FRIEDRICH	1774	LANGENSTEINBACH	01/01/1849	A		F3
TREUER W PARENTS	ELISABETH	1815	LANGENSTEINBACH	01/01/1849	A		F3
TREUER W PARENTS	MARTIN	1822	LANGENSTEINBACH	01/01/1849	A		F3
TREUER W PARENTS	SUSANNE	1826	LANGENSTEINBACH	01/01/1849	A		F3
TRIEB	JEREMIAS		KARLSRUHE	01/01/1861	A		F3
TRIEB	KAROLINE		KARLSRUHE	01/01/1861	A		F3
TRURTZ W PARENTS	CHRISTINE	1850	LANGENSTEINBACH	02/03/1854	A		F3
TRUTZ W PARENTS	ANDREAS	1845	LANGENSTEINBACH	02/03/1854	A		F3
TRUTZ W PARENTS	KATHARINA	1842	LANGENSTEINBACH	02/03/1854	A		F3
TRÖNDLE	FRANZ KARL		KARLSRUHE	01/01/1857	A		F3
TSCHAN	ANDREAS		SULZBACH	01/01/1867	A		F2

Lastname	Firstname	Birth Year	Birthplace	Emigration	De	Prof	Source
UBRESCH	LUISE		KARLSRUHE	01/01/1851	A		F2
UCKELE	FRIEDRICH	1840	LANGENSTEINBACH	/ /	A		F3
UCKELE	JAKOB	1838	LANGENSTEINBACH	01/01/1847	A		F3
UCKELE	KARL	1845	LANGENSTEINBACH	/ /	A		F3
UCKELE	PHILIPP	1772	LANGENSTEINBACH	01/01/1784	A		F3
UCKELE	PHILIPP	1801	LANGENSTEINBACH	/ /	A		F3
UCKELE	PHILIPP	1804	LANGENSTEINBACH	01/01/1847	A		F3
UCKELE MN	SUSANNE	1808	LANGENSTEINBACH	01/01/1847	A		F3
UDELE MN MEIER	MAGDALENA	1812	LANGENSTEINBACH	01/01/1847	A		F3
UDELE MN WETTACH	KATHARINA	1817	LANGENSTEINBACH	12/08/1847	A		F3
UDELE W FAMILY	JOHANN KRAFT	1810	LANGENSTEINBACH	12/08/1847	A		F3
UDELE W FAMILY	KARL		LANGENSTEINBACH	03/18/1829	A		F3
UDELE W FAMILY	PHILIPP	1840	LANGENSTEINBACH	01/01/1847	A		F3
UDELE W FAMILY	PHILIPP JAKOB	1810	LANGENSTEINBACH	01/01/1847	A		F3
UDELE W PARENTS	CHRISTINE	1842	LANGENSTEINBACH	01/01/1847	A		F3
UDELE W PARENTS	FRIEDRICH	1840	LANGENSTEINBACH	12/08/1847	A		F3
UDELE W PARENTS	JAKOB	1833	LANGENSTEINBACH	01/01/1847	A		F3
UDELE W PARENTS	JAKOB	1838	LANGENSTEINBACH	01/01/1847	A		F3
UDELE W PARENTS	JAKOBINE	1846	LANGENSTEINBACH	01/01/1847	A		F3
UDELE W PARENTS	MAGDALENA	1837	LANGENSTEINBACH	01/01/1847	A		F3
UDELE W PARENTS	MARGARETHE	1846	LANGENSTEINBACH	01/01/1847	A		F3
UDELE W PARENTS	MARTIN	1847	LANGENSTEINBACH	12/08/1847	A		F3
UDELE W PARENTS	PHILIPP	1838	LANGENSTEINBACH	12/08/1847	A		F3
UDELE W PARENTS	PHILIPP	1839	LANGENSTEINBACH	01/01/1847	A		F3
UDELE W PARENTS	PHILIPP	1840	LANGENSTEINBACH	01/01/1847	A		F3
UDELE W PARENTS	SUSANNE	1844	LANGENSTEINBACH	01/01/1847	A		F3
ULLRICH	FRANZ	1819	ETTLINGEN	01/01/1846	A		F4
ULMER	HANS		BOCHSTETTEN	01/01/1737	A		F6
ULRICH	JAKOB	1850	RÜPPURR	01/01/1868	A		F6
UMOLTSCH W F	CHRISTIAN	1818	BLANKENLOCH	01/01/1866	A		F8
UMOLTSCH W P	CHRISTIAN	1855	BLANKENLOCH	01/01/1866	A		F8
UMOLTSCH W P	LISELOTTE	1865	BLANKENLOCH	01/01/1866	A		F8
UMOLTSCH W P	LUDWIG	1850	BLANKENLOCH	01/01/1866	A		F8
UMOLTSCH W P	LUISE	1851	BLANKENLOCH	01/01/1866	A		F8
UNGEMACHT	BENEDIKT	1835	PFAFFENROT	01/01/1854	A		F7
UNGEMACHT	GEORG ADAM	1796	PFAFFENROT	01/01/1854	A		F7
UNGEMACHT MN LAUINGR	CRESZENZIA	1831	BUSENBACH	01/01/1854	A		F7
UNGEMACHT W M	LINA	1853	PFAFFENROT	01/01/1854	A		F7
UNGEMACHT W P	FRANZ ANTON	1843	PFAFFENROT	01/01/1854	A		F7
UNGEMACHT W P	JOSEFINE	1839	PFAFFENROT	01/01/1854	A		F7
UNGEMACHT W P	WILHELMINE	1837	PFAFFENROT	01/01/1854	A		F7
UNGEMACHT W P AND CH	MAGDALENA	1831	PFAFFENROT	01/01/1854	A		F7
UNGER	EMIL	1831	DURLACH KARLSRUHE	/ /			F7
UNGER	KARL FRIEDRICH		KARLSRUHE	01/01/1862	A		F3
UNGERER	PAUL		STRASBURG	01/01/1875			F7
UNGERER	WILHELM	1843	BERGHAUSEN	01/01/1883	A		F4
UNGERER W P	GUSTAV	1875	BERGHAUSEN	01/01/1883	A		F4
UNGERER W P	NINA	1872	BERGHAUSEN	01/01/1883	A		F4
UNGERER W P	WILHELM	1873	BERGHAUSEN	01/01/1883	A		F4
UNSER	JOHANN		ETTLINGEN	07/05/1857	A		F4

Lastname	Firstname	Birth Year	Birthplace	Emigration	De	Prof	Source
UNSER	WILHELM		ETTLINGEN	10/29/1863	A		F4
URBAN	DAVID		LEGELSHURST	01/01/1859	A		F6
URHEID	HEINRICH	1835	GRÖTZINGEN	01/01/1853	A		F3
URHEIDT	J		GRÖTZINGEN	08/18/1810	A		F3
URHEIDT	WILHELM		GRÖTZINGEN	/ /	A		F3
URHEIDT MN GÖTZ	MAGDALENA	1825	GRÖTZINGEN	01/01/1880	A		F3
URHEIDT MN HEIDT	MAGDALENA	1805	GRÖTZINGEN	01/01/1846	A		F3
URHEIDT MN ZOLLER	LUISE		GRÖTZINGEN	01/01/1883	A		F3
URHEIDT W FAMILY	FRIEDRICH	1801	GRÖTZINGEN	01/01/1846	A		F3
URHEIDT W FAMILY	GEORG FRIEDRICH	1821	GRÖTZINGEN	01/01/1880	A		F3
URHEIDT W PARENTS	AUGUST FRIEDRIH	1859	GRÖTZINGEN	01/01/1880	A		F3
URHEIDT W PARENTS	BERNHARD ULRICH	1864	GRÖTZINGEN	01/01/1880	A		F3
URHEIDT W PARENTS	CAROLINE	1835	GRÖTZINGEN	01/01/1846	A		F3
URHEIDT W PARENTS	CHRISTINE	1845	GRÖTZINGEN	01/01/1846	A		F3
URHEIDT W PARENTS	FRIEDRICH	1843	GRÖTZINGEN	01/01/1846	A		F3
URHEIDT W PARENTS	JAKOB GUSTAV	1858	GRÖTZINGEN	01/01/1880	A		F3
URHEIDT W PARENTS	JOHANN	1837	GRÖTZINGEN	01/01/1846	A		F3
URHEIDT W PARENTS	KATHARINA	1833	GRÖTZINGEN	01/01/1846	A		F3
URHEIDT W PARENTS	LUISE	1839	GRÖTZINGEN	01/01/1846	A		F3
URHEIDT W PARENTS	LUISE MAGD.	1861	GRÖTZINGEN	01/01/1880	A		F3
URHEIDT W PARENTS	MAGDALENA	1831	GRÖTZINGEN	01/01/1846	A		F3
URHEIDT W PARENTS	WILHELMINE	1841	GRÖTZINGEN	01/01/1846	A		F3
URHEIT	CONRAD		GRÖTZINGEN	/ /	A		F3
URHEIT MN CLAUS	KATHARINA	1813	GRÖTZINGEN	01/01/1846	A		F3
URHEIT W FAMILY	ZACHARIAS	1803	GRÖTZINGEN	01/01/1846			F3
URHEIT W PARENTS	DOROTHEA	1831	GRÖTZINGEN	01/01/1846	A		F3
URHEIT W PARENTS	KATHARINA	1838	GRÖTZINGEN	01/01/1846	A		F3
URHEIT W PARENTS	LUDWIG FRIEDRIC	1841	GRÖTZINGEN	01/01/1846	A		F3
URHEIT W PARENTS	PHILIPP JAKOB	1845	GRÖTZINGEN	01/01/1846	A		F3
URRHEIDT W CHILD	BARBARA	1797	GRÖTZINGEN	01/01/1851	A		F3
URRHEIDT W MOTHER	CHRISTINE	1834	GRÖTZINGEN	01/01/1851	A		F3
URZNER	LUDWIG	1856	KARLSRUHE	01/01/1883	A		F3

Lastname	Firstname	Birth Year	Birthplace	Emigration	De	Prof	Source
WEINGäRTNER	KUNIGUNDE	1813	BURBACHER	/ /	A		F4
WEINGäRTNER	LEOPOLD	1814	PFAFFENROT	/ /	A		F7
WEINGäRTNER	MARIA ANNA	1819	BURBACH	/ /	A		F4
WEINGäRTNER	PAULUS	1812	BURBACH	01/01/1852	A		F4
WEINGäRTNER	ROSALIA	1796	PFAFFENROT	/ /			F7
WEINGäRTNER	SEVERIN	1832	PFAFFENROT	01/01/1852	A		F7
WEINGäRTNER	XAVER	1805	PFAFFENROT	01/01/1839	A		F7
WEINGäRTNER MN REICT	THERESIA		PFAFFENROT	01/01/1847	A		F7
WEINGäRTNER W P	PHILIPPINE	1835	PFAFFENROT	01/01/1839	A		F7
WEINGÄRTNER	JOSEPH	1873	WÖSCHBACH	01/01/1892	A		F6
WEINIG WIDOW OF JOHA	ELISABETHA MN J		SINSHEIM	01/01/1859	A		F6
WEINLäNDER W 4 PERSN	CHRISTIAN		WÖSSINGEN	09/24/1782			F1
WEINMANN	RUDOLF	1873	KARLSRUHE	01/01/1891	A		F3
WEINMANN W PARENTS	ADOLF	1870	KARLSRUHE	01/01/1885	A		F3
WEINSCHENK	WILHELM HEINRIC	1873	KARLSRUHE	01/01/1890	A		F3
WEINSPACH	ROLAND	1880	KARLSRUHE	01/01/1896	A		F3
WEINSTEIN	FLORA	1863	MALSCH	01/01/1880	A		F2
WEINSTEIN	JAKOB	1831	ETTLINGEN	01/01/1867	A		F4
WEINSTEIN	JOSEF	1879	MALSCH	01/01/1891	A		F2
WEINSTEIN MN REICHET	ROSINE	1840	MALSCH	01/01/1891	A		F2
WEINSTEIN W FAMILY	ANTON	1840	MALSCH	01/01/1891	A		F2
WEINSTEIN W PARENTS	EMILIE	1868	MALSCH	01/01/1891	A		F2
WEINSTEIN W PARENTS	FRANZ	1885	MALSCH	01/01/1891	A		F2
WEINSTEIN W PARENTS	JOHANN	1870	MALSCH	01/01/1891	A		F2
WEINSTEIN W PARENTS	KAROLINE	1873	MALSCH	01/01/1891	A		F2
WEINSTEIN W PARENTS	LEO	1867	MALSCH	01/01/1891	A		F2
WEIS	AGATHA		NEUSATZ	01/01/1885	A		F5
WEIS	BERTA		NEUSATZ	01/01/1889	A		F5
WEIS	HERMANN		NEUSATZ	01/01/1892	A		F5
WEIS	KARL		NEUSATZ	01/01/1894	A		F5
WEIS W F	GEORG		HASSELBERG	04/09/1753	A		F5
WEISENLöHER	AUGUST	1864	KARLSRUHE	01/01/1882	A		F3
WEISHAUPT MN DAUM	EVA		VÖLKERSBACH	09/19/1850	A		F2
WEISHAUPT MN RENZ	FRANZISKA	1808	MALSCH	01/01/1851	A		F2
WEISHAUPT W CH	GERTRUD	1803	MALSCH	02/25/1846	A		F2
WEISHAUPT W FAMILY	GEORG	1805	MALSCH	01/01/1851	A		F2
WEISHAUPT W FAMILY	JOHANNES	1820	MALSCH	09/19/1850	A		F2
WEISHAUPT W MOTHER	ANTON	1838	MALSCH	01/01/1846	A		F2
WEISHAUPT W MOTHER	FRANZISKA	1831	MALSCH	02/25/1846	A		F2
WEISHAUPT W MOTHER	JOSEF	1842	MALSCH	01/01/1846	A		F2
WEISHAUPT W PARENTS	FLORA	1839	MALSCH	01/01/1851	A		F2
WEISHAUPT W PARENTS	FRIDOLIN	1843	MALSCH	01/01/1851	A		F2
WEISHAUPT W PARENTS	GEORG	1805	MALSCH	01/01/1851	A		F2
WEISHAUPT W PARENTS	JOSEF	1832	MALSCH	01/01/1851	A		F2
WEISHAUPT W PARENTS	KAROLINA	1837	MALSCH	01/01/1851	A		F2
WEISHAUPT W PARENTS	KATHARINA	1849	MALSCH	09/19/1850	A		F2
WEISHAUPT W PARENTS	MARTIN	1849	MALSCH	01/01/1851	A		F2
WEISHAUPT W PARENTS	SIMON	1844	MALSCH	01/01/1851	A		F2
WEISHAUPT W PARENTS	THERESE	1847	MALSCH	09/19/1850	A		F2
WEISHAUPT W PARENTS	VERONIKA	1835	MALSCH	01/01/1851	A		F2

Lastname	Firstname	Birth Year	Birthplace	Emigration	De	Prof	Source
WEISS	ALBRECHT		SÖLLINGEN	01/01/1845	A		F3
WEISS	APOLLONIA		SÖLLINGEN	/ /	A		F3
WEISS	BARBARA		SÖLLINGEN	01/01/1845	A		F3
WEISS	ELISABETH		SÖLLINGEN	/ /	A		F3
WEISS	ELISABETH		SÖLLLINGEN	/ /	A		F3
WEISS	HEINRICH	1858	KARLSRUHE	01/01/1875	A		F3
WEISS	JOHANN ANDREAS		KARLSRUHE	/ /	A		F3
WEISS	JOHANN KARL	1847	DURLACH KARLSRUHE	/ /			F7
WEISS	JOSEF	1831	SÖLLINGEN	01/01/1853	A		F3
WEISS	KARL		KARLSRUHE	01/01/1862	A		F3
WEISS	KARL		KARLSRUHE	01/01/1862	A		F5
WEISS	KARL FRIEDRICH	1808	KARLSRUHE	01/01/1858	A		F3
WEISS	LEONHARD		TANNENKRICH	01/01/1859	A		F6
WEISS	LUISE		SÖLLINGEN	/ /	A		F3
WEISS	OTTO	1852	KARLSRUHE	01/01/1882	A		F3
WEISS	WILHELM FRIEDRI	1839	DURLACH KARLSRUHE	/ /			F7
WEISS W F	ALBERT		SÖLLINGEN	01/01/1860	A		F7
WEISS W FAMILY	ALBRECHT		SÖLLINGEN	01/01/1860	A		F3
WEISSENBERGER	BERNHARD		WÖSCHINGEN	01/01/1859	A		F6
WEISSER	CARL AUG.	1834	DURLACH KARLSRUHE	/ /			F7
WEISSER	EMIL	1826	DURLACH KARLSRUHE	/ /			F7
WEISSER	JOSEF	1861	UNTERKIRNACH	01/01/1892	A		F5
WEISSINGER	CARL JAKOB		DURLACH KARLSRUHE	01/01/1846			F7
WEITENBACHER	WAIPURGER		STEINMAUERN	01/01/1859	A		F6
WELKER	ALOIS	1863	ETTLINGEN	01/01/1885	A		F4
WELKER	CONRAD	1850	ETTLINGEN	01/01/1882	A		F4
WELKER	EUGEN		ETTLINGEN	01/01/1872	A		F4
WELZ	XAVER		MÖRSCH	01/01/1854	A		F7
WENDLING	KARL FRIEDRICH		RHEINBISCHOFSHEIM	01/01/1859	A		F6
WENG	RUDOLF	1861	KARLSRUHE	01/01/1880	A		F6
WENGER	KONRAD		BROMBACH	01/01/1859	A		F6
WENGESDORF	HEINRICH		MÖNCHZELL	01/01/1859	A		F6
WENZ	ALBERT	1877	GRABEN	01/01/1892	A		F3
WENZ	ANDREAS		GRABEN	01/01/1890	A		F3
WENZ	AUGUST		GRABEN	01/01/1890	A		F5
WENZ	BERTA		GRABEN	/ /	A		F5
WENZ	CHRISTOPH		SÖLLINGEN	/ /	A		F3
WENZ	CHRISTOPH FRIED		GRABEN	01/01/1874	A		F3
WENZ	CONRAD		SÖLLINGEN	/ /	A		F3
WENZ	H.A		GRABEN	/ /	A		F5
WENZ	JAKOB		KARLSRUHE	/ /	A		F3
WENZ	JAKOB	1850	SÖLLINGEN	01/01/1869	A		F3
WENZ	JOHANN ADAM		WÖSSINGEN	01/01/1847	A		F1
WENZ	JOHANN FRIEDR		GRABEN	01/01/1879	A		F3
WENZ	JOHANN LUDWIG	1873	GRABEN	01/01/1888	A		F3
WENZ	JOSEF		SÖLLINGEN	01/01/1855	A		F7
WENZ	KARL LUDWIG	1862	GRABEN	01/01/1879	A		F3
WENZ	KAROLINA	1846	GRABEN	01/01/1893	A		F3
WENZ	KATHARINA		SÖLLINGEN	/ /	A		F3
WENZ	LUDWIG		GRABEN	/ /	A		F5

Lastname	Firstname	Birth Year	Birthplace	Emigration	De	Prof	Source
WENZ	MARGARETHE		GRABEN	01/01/1853	A		F5
WENZ MN MÜLLER	MAGDALENA	1836	SÖLLINGEN	01/01/1881	A		F3
WENZ MN SCHLEIFER	MARGARETHE	1847	KNIELINGEN	01/01/1876	A		F8
WENZ MN STEIGER	KAROLINE	1821	SÖLLINGEN	01/01/1880	A		F3
WENZ W F	JOHANNES	1834	SÖLLINGEN	01/01/1881	A		F7
WENZ W F	KARL FRIEDRICH	1845	KNIELINGEN	01/01/1876	A		F8
WENZ W F	MARTIN		GRABEN	01/01/1842	A		F5
WENZ W FAMILY	ADOLF	1877	SÖLLINGEN	01/01/1891	A		F3
WENZ W FAMILY	CHRISTOPH	1822	SÖLLINGEN	01/01/1880	A		F3
WENZ W FAMILY	DANIEL	1845	GRABEN	01/01/1893	A		F3
WENZ W FAMILY	JAKOB		GRABEN	01/01/1750	A		F3
WENZ W FAMILY	JAKOB	1851	SÖLLINGEN	01/01/1891	A		F3
WENZ W FAMILY	JOHANNES	1834	SÖLLINGEN	01/01/1881	A		F3
WENZ W FAMILY	PHILIP		WÖSSINGEN	01/01/1832	A		F1
WENZ W FAMILY	WILHELM	1873	SÖLLINGEN	01/01/1891	A		F3
WENZ W P	FRIEDRICH KARL		KNIELINGEN	01/01/1876	A		F8
WENZ W PARENTS	EDUARD	1856	SÖLLINGEN	01/01/1880	A		F3
WENZ W PARENTS	ELISABETH	1864	SÖLLINGEN	01/01/1881	A		F3
WENZ W PARENTS	EMILIE	1890	SÖLLINGEN	01/01/1891	A		F3
WENZ W PARENTS	ERNESTINE	1876	SÖLLINGEN	01/01/1881	A		F3
WENZ W PARENTS	HEINRICH	1877	GRABEN	01/01/1893	A		F3
WENZ W PARENTS	JAKOBINE	1860	SÖLLINGEN	01/01/1880	A		F3
WENZ W PARENTS	KARL	1891	GRABEN	01/01/1893	A		F3
WENZ W PARENTS	KAROLINE	1873	SÖLLINGEN	01/01/1881	A		F3
WENZ W PARENTS	LUDWIG	1888	GRABEN	01/01/1893	A		F3
WENZ W PARENTS	LUISE	1868	SÖLLINGEN	01/01/1891	A		F3
WENZ W PARENTS	MARIA	1867	SÖLLINGEN	01/01/1881	A		F3
WENZ W PARENTS	MINA	1881	GRABEN	01/01/1893	A		F3
WENZ W PARENTS	WILHELM	1861	SÖLLINGEN	01/01/1881	A		F3
WENZEL	CHRIST.FRIED.LU		DURLACH KARLSRUHE	01/01/1855			F7
WENZEL	FRIED.PHIL.	1853	DURLACH KARLSRUHE	/ /			F7
WERKEL	LUISE		FORBACH	01/01/1854	A		F6
WERNER	ANTON		MALSCH	/ /	A		F2
WERNER	AUGUST		GRABEN	/ /	A		F5
WERNER	ERNST		GRABEN	01/01/1861	A		F3
WERNER	ERNST		GRABEN	01/01/1861	A		F5
WERNER	FRIEDRICH	1865	KARLSRUHE	01/01/1883	A		F3
WERNER	FRIEDRICH	1868	KARLSRUHE	01/01/1884	A		F3
WERNER	IGNAZ		FORBACH	01/01/1854	A		F6
WERNER	JAKOB		GRABEN	01/01/1824	A		F5
WERNER	JAKOB		GRABEN	01/01/1881	A		F3
WERNER	JAKOB FRIEDRICH		GRABEN	01/01/1800	A		F8
WERNER	JAKOB FRIEDRICH		GRABEN	01/01/1861	A		F5
WERNER	JAKOB FRIEDRICH	1841	GRABEN	01/01/1883	A		F3
WERNER	JAKOB FRIEDRICH	1873	GRABEN	01/01/1890	A		F3
WERNER	JOHANN FRITZ		FORBACH	01/01/1854	A		F6
WERNER	JOHANN MARTIN		GRABEN	01/01/1861	A		F3
WERNER	JOHANNES	1865	KARLSRUHE	01/01/1883	A		F3
WERNER	KARL FRIEDRICH		GRABEN	01/01/1805	A		F3
WERNER	KARL MARTIN		GRABEN	/ /	A		F5

Lastname	Firstname	Birth Year	Birthplace	Emigration	De	Prof	Source
WERNER	KATHARINA	1862	GRABEN	01/01/1893	A		F3
WERNER	LUDWIG		GRABEN	01/01/1878	A		F3
WERNER	MARIE		GRABEN	01/01/1878	A		F3
WERNER	MARIE	1836	GRABEN	01/01/1856	A		F3
WERNER	MARTIN		GRABEN	01/01/1861	A		F6
WERNER	PHILIPP		GRABEN	01/01/1861	A		F3
WERNER	PHILIPP JAKOB		SÖLLINGEN	/ /	A		F3
WERNER	RICHARD		FORBACH	01/01/1864	A		F6
WERNER	WILHELM	1850	MÜHLBURG	01/01/1867	A		F8
WERNER W F	KARL FRIEDRICH		GRABEN	01/01/1865	A		F6
WERNER MN KRANTZ	FREDERIKE	1838	GRABEN	01/01/1880	A		F8
WERNER MN NEU	MARIA ANNA	1808	MALSCH	02/24/1857	A		F2
WERNER MN SCHOLL	PHILIPPINE	1830	GRABEN	01/01/1872	A		F3
WERNER MN WEISHAUPT	KATHARINA	1801	MALSCH	01/01/1855	A		F2
WERNER W CH	BEATRICE		MALSCH	02/23/1857	A		F2
WERNER W CHILDREN	PHILIPP	1832	GRABEN	01/01/1869	A		F3
WERNER W F	KARL FRIEDRICH		GRABEN	01/01/1868	A		F5
WERNER W F	MARTIN		GRABEN	01/01/1861	A		F5
WERNER W F	MARTIN	1835	GRABEN	01/01/1880	A		F8
WERNER W F	PHILIPP		FORBACH	01/01/1854	A		F6
WERNER W F	PHILIPP	1832	GRABEN	01/01/1869	A		F8
WERNER W FAMILY	ANTON	1798	MALSCH	02/24/1857	A		F2
WERNER W FAMILY	PETER	1802	MALSCH	01/01/1855	A		F2
WERNER W FAMILY	PHILIPP	1854	GRABEN	01/01/1893	A		F3
WERNER W FAMILY	VALENTIN	1824	MALSCH	02/23/1855	A		F2
WERNER W FATHER	CARL LEOPOLD	1866	GRABEN	01/01/1869	A		F3
WERNER W FATHER	HERMANN	1860	GRABEN	01/01/1869	A		F3
WERNER W FATHER	JOHANNA MAGDALE	1865	GRABEN	01/01/1869	A		F3
WERNER W FATHER	LUISE	1863	GRABEN	01/01/1869	A		F3
WERNER W MOTHER	ANTON	1841	MALSCH	02/23/1857	A		F2
WERNER W P	ALBERT	1878	GRABEN	01/01/1880	A		F8
WERNER W P	CHRISTINE	1866	GRABEN	01/01/1880	A		F8
WERNER W P	FREDERIKE	1861	GRABEN	01/01/1880	A		F8
WERNER W P	HEINRICH	1873	GRABEN	01/01/1880	A		F8
WERNER W P	HERMANN	1860	GRABEN	01/01/1869	A		F8
WERNER W P	KAROLINE	1868	GRABEN	01/01/1880	A		F8
WERNER W P	KATHARINA		GRABEN	01/01/1880	A		F8
WERNER W P	MARTIN	1862	GRABEN	01/01/1880	A		F8
WERNER W PARENTS	AMALIE	1839	MALSCH	01/01/1855	A		F2
WERNER W PARENTS	BERTA	1892	GRABEN	01/01/1893	A		F3
WERNER W PARENTS	FLORA	1841	MALSCH	01/01/1855	A		F2
WERNER W PARENTS	FRANZISKA	1832	MALSCH	02/24/1857	A		F2
WERNER W PARENTS	FRANZISKA	1833	MALSCH	01/01/1855	A		F2
WERNER W PARENTS	FRIDOLIN	1827	MALSCH	01/01/1855	A		F2
WERNER W PARENTS	ISIDOR	1837	MALSCH	01/01/1855	A		F2
WERNER W PARENTS	JOH. ADAM	1825	MALSCH	01/01/1855	A		F2
WERNER W PARENTS	JOSEF	1836	MALSCH	02/24/1857	A		F2
WERNER W PARENTS	KARL	1889	GRABEN	01/01/1893	A		F3
WERNER W PARENTS	MARIA ANNA	1833	MALSCH	02/24/1857	A		F2
WERNER W PARENTS	NIKOLAUS	1843	MALSCH	01/01/1855	A		F2

Lastname	Firstname	Birth Year	Birthplace	Emigration	De	Prof	Source
WERNER W PARENTS	PAULINE	1837	MALSCH	02/24/1857	A		F2
WERNER W PARENTS	PETER	1835	MALSCH	01/01/1855	A		F2
WERNER W PARENTS	PHILIPP	1887	GRABEN	01/01/1893	A		F3
WERNER W PARENTS	THERESE	1845	MALSCH	02/24/1857	A		F2
WERNER W WIFE	FRIEDRICH		GRABEN	01/01/1842	A		F5
WERNER W WIFE	GEORG FRIEDRICH	1814	GRABEN	01/01/1872	A		F3
WERTEL	GEORG		FORBACH	01/01/1864	A		F6
WERTEL	HEINRICH		FORBACH	01/01/1868	A		F6
WERTEL	MICHEL		FORBACH	01/01/1860	A		F6
WERTEL W F	LEONHARD		REICHERTSHAUSEN	01/01/1866	A		F6
WERTHEIMER	JAKOB	1854	BAUERBACH	01/01/1871	A		F8
WESTPHAL	ADOLF KARL	1869	KARLSRUHE	01/01/1888	A		F3
WESTPHAL	JULIUS	1868	KARLSRUHE	01/01/1888	A		F3
WETTACH	KARL	1829	LANGENSTEINBACH	01/01/1845	A		F3
WETTACH	PHILIPP	1833	LANGENSTEINBACH	02/03/1854	A		F3
WETTACH	ROBERT	1850	KARLSRUHE	01/01/1872	A		F3
WETZEBA	KARL	1872	DURLACH	01/01/1890	A		F6
WETZEL	ANTON	1822	MALSCH	01/01/1848	A		F2
WETZEL	CHRISTINE		BLANKENLOCH	01/01/1866	A		F4
WETZEL	JOHANN		BLANKENLOCH	01/01/1863	A		F4
WETZEL W F	AUGUST	1852	BLANKENLOCH	01/01/1866	A		F4
WETZEL W F	ERNESTINE	1860	BLANKENLOCH	01/01/1866	A		F4
WETZEL W F	JULIUS	1863	BLANKENLOCH	01/01/1866	A		F4
WETZEL W FAMILY	KARL		BLANKENLOCH	01/01/1866	A		F4
WETZEL W P	CHRISTINE	1857	BLANKENLOCH	01/01/1866	A		F4
WETZEL W P	FRIEDRICH	1864	BLANKENLOCH	01/01/1866	A		F4
WETZEL W P	GEORG	1854	BLANKENLOCH	01/01/1866	A		F4
WETZEL W P	KARL	1851	BLANKENLOCH	01/01/1866	A		F4
WETZEL W P	KAROLINE	1855	BLANKENLOCH	01/01/1866	A		F4
WETZEL W P	LUISE	1859	BLANKENLOCH	01/01/1866	A		F4
WEY	JOHANN		SPöCK	01/01/1854	A		F4
WICHTENBERGER	LUDWIG	1851	BAUERBACH	01/01/1872	A		F8
WICKERSHEIM	GEORG ANTON		WALTERDINGEN	01/01/1753	A		F9
WICKERT	FRIEDRICH		KARLSRUHE	/ /	A		F3
WICKERT	JAKOB		KARLSRUHE	01/01/1742	A		F3
WICT	JOHANN HEINRICH		GRABEN	07/28/1801	A		F3
WIEDERKEHR MN GUBACH	CHRISTINE		LIEDOLSHEIM	01/01/1879	A		F9
WIEDERKEHR W F	CHRISTOPH	1825	LLIEDOLSHEIM	01/01/1879	A		F9
WIEDERKEHR W P	CHRISTINE	1861	LIEDOLSHEIM	01/01/1879	A		F9
WIEGNER	CREZENTIA		STEINBACH	01/01/1853	A		F6
WIESSLER W F	NICOLAUS		BESTENHEID	05/18/1752	A		F5
WILD WW CH	JOHANNES		GLASHÜTTEN	10/18/1803			F1
WILDEMANN	JOSEPHINE	1851	MALSCH	10/10/1883	A		F2
WILDEMANN MN GRäSSIN	JOSEFA	1814	MALSCH	01/01/1855	A		F2
WILDEMANN MN KISTNER	BARBARA		MALSCH	01/01/1804	A		F2
WILDEMANN W FAMILY				/ /			
WILDEMANN W FAMILY	ANDREAS	1775	MALSCH	01/01/1804	A		F2
WILDEMANN W FAMILY	FLORIAN	1811	MALSCH	01/01/1855	A		F2
WILDEMANN W PARENTS	ANDREAS	1799	MALSCH	01/01/1804	A		F2
WILDEMANN W PARENTS	FLORA	1853	MALSCH	01/01/1855	A		F2

Lastname	Firstname	Birth Year	Birthplace	Emigration	De	Prof	Source
WILDEMANN W PARENTS	FRANZ	1838	MALSCH	01/01/1855	A		F2
WILDEMANN W PARENTS	FRANZISKA	1849	MALSCH	01/01/1855	A		F2
WILDEMANN W PARENTS	IGNAZ	1843	MALSCH	01/01/1855	A		F2
WILDEMANN W PARENTS	JOHANNES	1798	MALSCH	01/01/1804	A		F2
WILDEMANN W PARENTS	MARIA ANNA	1841	MALSCH	01/01/1855	A		F2
WILDEMANN W PARENTS	MARIA EVA	1835	MALSCH	01/01/1855	A		F2
WILDEMANN W PARENTS	WENDELIN	1797	MALSCH	01/01/1804	A		F2
WILDNIS W W	JOHANN		OBERSCHAFFHAUSEN	01/01/1825	A		F9
WILLET	LUDWIG	1873	KARLSRUHE	01/01/1894	A		F3
WILLIAM	FRITZ		KARLSRUHE	/ /	A		F3
WILLIG	ERNESTINE		UNTERKESSACH	01/01/1859	A		F6
WILLSTÄDTER	LEOPOLD	1872	GRABEN	01/01/1888	A		F8
WILMENDORF	JAKOB	1862	KARLSRUHE	01/01/1879	A		F3
WILSENELD W PARENT	CARL	1850	KARLSRUHE	01/01/1867	A		F3
WILSENFELD	ALOIS	1827	KARLSRUHE	01/01/1867	A		F3
WILSENFELD	JOHANNA	1822	KARLSRUHE	01/01/1867	A		F3
WILSENFELD W PARENTS	CHRISTIAN	1850	KARLSRUHE	01/01/1867	A		F3
WINDHOLZ	LUIS		KARLSRUHE	01/01/1857	A		F3
WINKLER	LUDWIG	1874	KARLSRUHE	01/01/1888	A		F3
WINTERGAST	MAX		KARLSRUHE	/ /	A		F3
WIPFLER	ALOIS		KARLSRUHE	/ /	A		F3
WIPFLER	ALOIS	1845	SCHÖLLBRONN	01/01/1868	A		F7
WIPFLER	AUGUST		KARLSRUHE	01/01/1858	A		F3
WIPFLER	ELISABETH	1824	VÖLKERSBACH	03/13/1852	A		F4
WIPFLER	FLORENTINE	1835	SCHÖLLBRONN	/ /	A		F7
WIPFLER	FRANZISKA	1829	SCHÖLLBRONN	/ /	A		F7
WIPFLER	JOSEF	1815	VÖLKERSBACH	04/09/1850	A		F4
WIPFLER	JOSEF BENEDIKT	1798	SCHÖLLBRONN	01/01/1830	A		F7
WIPFLER	LEOPOLD	1831	SCHÖLLBRONN	/ /	A		F7
WIPFLER	MATHäUS	1823	SCHÖLLBRONN	/ /	A		F7
WIPFLER	PAULUS	1842	SCHÖLLBRONN	01/01/1868	A		F7
WIPFLER	SEBASTIAN	1831	VÖLKERSBACH	03/13/1852	A		F4
WIPFLER	VALENTIN	1830	VÖLKERSBACH	08/31/1853	A		F4
WIRTH	CHRIST. KATHARI		GRABEN	01/01/1878	A		F5
WIRTH	CHRISTINE KATH		GRABEN	01/01/1878	A		F3
WOHLSCHLEGEL	JAKOB FRIEDRICH	1830	LANGENSTEINBACH	01/01/1850	A		F3
WOHLSCHLEGEL	JOHANNES	1844	LANGENSTEINBACH	05/05/1866	A		F3
WOHLSCHLEGEL	MAGDALENA	1853	LANGENSTEINBACH	04/15/1873	A		F3
WOHLSCHLEGEL	MARGARETHA	1848	LANGENSTEINBACH	05/05/1866	A		F3
WOHLSCHLEGEL	MICHAEL	1833	LANGENSTEINBACH	01/01/1850	A		F3
WOHLSCHLEGEL MN	CHARLOTTE		KARLSRUHE	01/01/1866	A		F3
WOHLSCHLEGEL MN DRAG	MARGARETHA		LANGENSTEINBACH	/ /	A		F3
WOHLSCHLEGEL W DAUGH	ELISABETH	1822	LANGENSTEINBACH	01/01/1850	A		F3
WOHLSCHLEGEL W FAMIL	JOSEF	1813	KARLSRUHE	01/01/1866	A		F3
WOHLSCHLEGEL W MOTHE	ELISABETH	1847	LANGENSTEINBACH	01/01/1850	A		F3
WOHLSCHLEGEL W PAREN	CARL	1851	KARLSRUHE	01/01/1866	A		F3
WOHLSCHLEGEL W PAREN	ELISE	1856	KARLSRUHE	01/01/1866	A		F3
WOHLSCHLEGEL W PAREN	ERNST	1861	KARLSRUHE	01/01/1866	A		F3
WOHLSCHLEGEL W PAREN	LUISE	1849	KARLSRUHE	01/01/1866	A		F3
WOHLSCHLEGEL W PAREN	OSKAR	1864	KARLSRUHE	01/01/1866	A		F3

Lastname	Firstname	Birth Year	Birthplace	Emigration	De	Prof	Source
WOHLSCHLEGEL W WIFE	MICHAEL	1855	LANGENSTEINBACH	06/18/1886	A		F3
WOLF	FRIEDRICH		KARLSRUHE	01/01/1836	A		F3
WOLF	GEORG	1810	WEINGARTEN	01/01/1854	A		F4
WOLF	GEORG	1856	KARLSRUHE	01/01/1879	A		F3
WOLF	HANS ADAM		MICHELRIETH	07/21/1762	A		F5
WOLF	JOSEF CHRISTIAN	1850	FLEHINGEN	01/01/1868	A		F8
WOLF	KARL	1872	KARLSRUHE	01/01/1890	A		F3
WOLF	LUDWIG	1875	KARLSRUHE	01/01/1892	A		F3
WOLF	PHILIPP		JÖHLINGEN	01/01/1842	A		F8
WOLF	PHILIPP	1848	KARLSRUHE	01/01/1880	A		F3
WOLF MN KRAUS	JOSEFINE WILHEL	1850	KARLSRUHE	01/01/1890	A		F3
WOLF W FAMILY	EMIL	1842	KARLSRUHE	01/01/1890	A		F3
WOLF W PARENTS	ELISABETH	1878	KARLSRUHE	01/01/1890	A		F3
WOLF W PARENTS	EMIL LUIS	1872	KARLSRUHE	01/01/1890	A		F3
WOLF W PARENTS	IRMA STEFANIE	1873	KARLSRUHE	01/01/1890	A		F3
WOLF W PARENTS	ROBERT EDWIN	1876	KARLSRUHE	01/01/1890	A		F3
WOLF W PARENTS	ROSA KLARA	1882	KARLSRUHE	01/01/1890	A		F3
WOLFMÜLLER	LEOPOLD	1866	KARLSRUHE	01/01/1883	A		F3
WOLZ-FIESER	LUISE		GRABEN	01/01/1890	A		F3
WUNGENAST	JOHANNES		FORBACH	01/01/1854	A		F6
WUNSCH	ALEX		FORBACH	01/01/1854	A		F6
WUNSCH	ELISABETH		FORBACH	01/01/1854	A		F6
WUNSCH	EMILIN		FORBACH	01/01/1854	A		F6
WUNSCH	FELIX		FORBACH	01/01/1854	A		F6
WUNSCH	FERDINAND		FORBACH	01/01/1854	A		F6
WUNSCH	GEORG JOSEF		KARLSRUHE	01/01/1857	A		F3
WUNSCH	JOSEPH		FORBACH	01/01/1864	A		F6
WUNSCH	KARL		FORBACH	01/01/1864	A		F6
WUNSCH	KARL		OPPENAU	01/01/1862	A		F3
WUNSCH	MAX		FORBACH	01/01/1854	A		F6
WUNSCH	RHEINHARD		FORBACH	01/01/1854	A		F6
WUNSCH	WILHELM		FORBACH	01/01/1863	A		F6
WUNSCH	XAVER		FORBACH	01/01/1861	A		F6
WUNSCH W WIFE	WILHELM		FORBACH	01/01/1867	A		F6
WUNSCH WIDOW OF	ANTON		FORBACH	01/01/1852	A		F6
WUNSE	LEO		FORBACH	01/01/1855	A		F6
WÜRTH	ROBERT	1864	KARLSRUHE	01/01/1883	A		F3
WÜRZ	GERHARD		GRABEN	01/01/1854	A		F5
WÜRZ	JULIUS	1879	KARLSRUHE	01/01/1899	A		F3
WäCHTER	EDUARD		LIEDOLSHEIM	01/01/1893	A		F9
WäGERLE	KARL		OBERGIMPERN	01/01/1850	A		F6
WöLFEL	ADOLF	1831	LANGENSTEINBACH	01/01/1851	A		F3
WöLFEL	ERNST	1832	LANGENSTEINBACH	01/01/1851	A		F3
WöLFEL	FRIEDRICH	1833	LANGENSTEINBACH	/ /	A		F3
WöLFEL	KARL FRIEDRICH	1817	LANGENSTEINBACH	01/01/1848	A		F3
WöLFEL	LUDWIG	1826	LANGENSTEINBACH	01/01/1848	A		F3
WöRNER	LUDWIG	1840	GRABEN	01/01/1868	A		F3
WöRNER	WILHELM	1863	DIEDELSHEIM	01/01/1886	A		F6
WöRZ	GUSTAV		GRABEN	01/01/1882	A		F3
WöSSNER WW 4CH	HEINRICH		WöSSINGEN	01/01/1846	A		F1

Lastname	Firstname	Birth Year	Birthplace	Emigration	De	Prof	Source
WÖHRLE MN ZIMPFER	MAGDALENA	1856	HEIMLINGEN	01/01/1872	A		F5
WÖRNER	JOSEPH		FORBACH	01/01/1854	A		F4
WÖRNER	KRESZENTIA		FORBACH	01/01/1854	A		F6
WÖRNER W F	ANTON		FORBACH	01/01/1854	A		F6
WÖRNER W F	JOHANN		FORBACH	01/01/1854	A		F6
WÖSSNER	JOHANN GEORG		GÖBRICHEN	01/01/1795	A		F6
WÜRTH	KARL FRIEDRICH	1854	RÜPPURR	01/01/1871	A		F6
WÜRTH	OTTO	1868	RÜPPURR	01/01/1884	A		F6
WÜST MN PACIUS	AUGUSTE	1827	FLEHINGEN	01/01/1884	A		F8
WÜST W F	JOHANNES	1825	FLEHINGEN	01/01/1884	A		F8
WÜST W P	JAKOB	1856	FLEHINGEN	01/01/1884	A		F8
WÜST W P	KAROLINE	1866	FLEHINGEN	01/01/1884	A		F8
WÜST W P	KATHARINA	1857	FLEHINGEN	01/01/1884	A		F8
WÜST W P	LUISE	1870	FLEHINGEN	01/01/1884	A		F8

EMIGRATION

FROM

ALSACE

Lastname	Firstname	Birth Year	Birthplace	Emigration	De	Prof	Source
ANSTETT	MICHAEL	1871	ZUTZENDORF	/ /	A		F2
ANSTETT	MICHAEL	1871	ZUTZENDORF	01/01/1888	A		F2
ANSTETT	THEOBALD	1878	ZUTZENDORF	/ /	A		F2
ANSTETT MN PETERS	MARGARETE	1868	ZUTZENDORF	01/01/1886	A		F2
ANSTETT WIDOW PETERS	CHARLOTTE	1868	ZUTZENDORF	/ /	A		F2
ARNOLD MN FOURNY	MARIE		STEINIG WENDEL	01/01/1897	A		F2
BACH	JOHANN FRIEDRIH	1834	DIEMERINGEN	01/01/1869	A		BUT
BACHMANN	GEORG		OBERMODERN	/ /	A		F2
BACHMANN	HEINRICH		OBERMODERN	/ /	A		F2
BAUER	CHRISTIAN	1835	WEISLINGEN	01/01/1841	NY		BUT
BAUER MN HOBLER	CAROLINA	1841	RATZWILLER	/ /	A		BUT
BECK	CHRISTIAN		OTTWEILER	/ /	A		F2
BIEBER	GEORG		HIRSCHLAND	01/01/1743	A		F2
BIEBER	GEORG		HIRSCHLAND	01/01/1760	A		F2
BIEBER	GEORG		HIRSCHLAND	01/01/1762	A		F2
BIEBER	JAKOB		HIRSCHLAND	01/01/1762	A		F2
BIEBER	NIKOLAUS		DURSTEL	01/01/1885	A		F2
BIEBER W 6CH	GEORG		HIRSCHLAND	01/01/1843	A		F2
BRACH	ANNA		SAARBUCKENHEIM	01/01/1886	A		F2
BRACH	FERDINAND		SAARBUCKENHEIM	01/01/1884	A		F2
BRäUNIG	JOHANN		OBERMODERN	/ /	A		F2
CONRADI W PARENTS	JOHANN ELIAS	1783	DEHLINGEN	04/25/1783	A		BUT
CONRADI MN TAMERUS	CATHARINA		DEHLINGEN	04/25/1785	A		BUT
CONRADI WW 1CH	GOTTFRIED		DEHLINGEN	04/25/1785	A		BUT
CONSTANS	HEINRICH	1829	DIEMERINGEN	/ /	A		BUT
CONSTANS	LOUISA CAROLINA	1831	DIEMERINGEN	/ /	A		BUT
CRON	JOHANN NIKOLAUS	1796	PUBERG	/ /	A		F2
CRON	NIKOLAUS		OTTWEILER	/ /	A		F2
CULLY	CATHERINA ELISE	1808	RATZWILLER	/ /	A		BUT
DROTTER	BENJAMIN		RATZWILLER	/ /	A		BUT
DROTTER	SOPHIA PHILIPPA	1828	RATZWILLER	/ /	A		BUT
DUCARN	ELISABETHA		DEHLINGEN	/ /	A		BUT
DUTT	MICHAEL	1829	OBERMODERN	/ /	A		F2
EBERHARDT	MARIA CATHARINA	1797	DIEMERINGEN	/ /	A		BUT
ECKLE	ALBERT		HARSKIRCHEN	01/01/1893	A		F2
ECKLY	EUGEN		ALSACE	01/01/1893	A		F2
ELWEIN	ANNA		ALTWEILER	01/01/1898	A		F2
ENSMINGER	CHRISTINA CATHA	1832	DIEMERINGEN	/ /	A		BUT
ENSMINGER	JOHANN CARL	1808	DIEMERINGEN	/ /	A		BUT
ENSMINGER	JOHANN CONRAD	1825	DIEMERINGEN	/ /	A		BUT
ENSMINGER	LEONIE		DIEMERINGEN	01/01/1894	A		F2
ENSMINGER	LOUISA CAROLINA		DIEMERINGEN	01/01/1838	A		BUT
ERHARD	ANNA		SAARBUCKENHEIM	01/01/1892	A		F2
ERHARD	LINA		SAARBUCKENHEIM	01/01/1889	A		F2
FARNER	JOHANN		ECKBOLSHEIM	09/09/1885	A		F2
FAUSER	SOPHIA DOROTHEA	1788	DIEMERINGEN	/ /	A		BUT
FERBER	FRIEDRICH		INGWEILER	01/01/1890	A		F2
FERBER	LUDWIG		INGWEILER	01/01/1885	A		F2
FISCHBACH	EMILIE		INGWEILER	01/01/1895	A		F2
FISCHBACH	GEORG		INGWEILER	01/01/1880	A		F2

Lastname	Firstname	Birth Year	Birthplace	Emigration	De	Prof	Source
FISCHBACH	GEORG	1880	INGWEILER	01/01/1897	A		F2
FISCHBACH	JAKOB		INGWEILER	01/01/1892	A		F2
FISCHBACH	JOHANN		INGWEILER	01/01/1881	A		F2
FISCHBACH	LINA		INGWEILER	01/01/1891	A		F2
FISCHBACH	MARGARETHA		INGWEILER	01/01/1889	A		F2
FOURNY	MARIE		STEINIG WENDEL	01/01/1897	A		F2
FRITZ	GOTTFRIED	1829	INGWEILER	/ /	A		F2
FROMM	ALFRED		PFAFFENHOFEN	01/01/1885	A		F2
FROMM	EMIL		PFAFFENHOFEN	01/01/1889	A		F2
FROMM	KARL		PFAFFENHOFEN	01/01/1883	A		F2
FROMM	LUDWIG	1880	PFAFFENHOFEN	/ /	A		F2
FUCHS	BERTHA		SAARWERDEN	01/01/1870	A		F2
FUCHS	BERTHE	1870	SAARWERDEN	/ /	A		F2
FUCHS	JULIE		SAARBUCKENHEIM	01/01/1883	A		F2
FUCHS	JULIE	1883	SAARBUCHENHEIM	/ /	A		F2
GAUP	JOHANN HEINRICH	1814	DIEMERINGEN	01/01/1836	A		BUT
GEIST	KAROLINE		DETTWEILER	01/01/1894	A		F2
GERBER	MARIA		SAARBUCKENHEIM	01/01/1864			F2
GERBER	MARIA	1864	SAARBUCKENHEIM	01/01/1890	A		F2
GERINGER	MARIE		HOLWENGEN	01/01/1872	A		F2
GERSCHHEIMER	CATHERINA BARBA	1754	WALDHAMBACH	01/01/1764	A		BUT
GERSCHHEIMER	EVA CHRISTINA	1753	WALDHAMBACH	01/01/1764	A		BUT
GERSCHHEIMER	JOHANN JACOB	1763	WALDHAMBACH	01/01/1764	A		BUT
GERSCHHEIMER	MARIA ELISABETA	1757	WALDHAMBACH	01/01/1764	A		BUT
GERSCHHEIMER MN MEDR	MARIA MAGDALENA	1729	VOLKSBERG	01/01/1764	A		BUT
GERSCHHEIMER WW CH	JOHANN PHILIPP	1728	WALDHAMBACH	01/01/1764	A		BUT
GEYER	CATHARINA	1829	RATZWILLER	/ /	A		BUT
GEYER	CHRISTIAN	1823	RATZWILLER	/ /	A		BUT
GEYER	GEORG	1827	RATZWILLER	/ /	A		BUT
GEYER	KATHARINA	1798	PUBERG	/ /	A		F2
GEYER MN SEEMANN	CATHARINA	1792	BURBACH	/ /	A		BUT
GILGER	CARL	1826	DIEMERINGEN	/ /	A		BUT
GILGER	HEINRICH	1824	DIEMERINGEN	/ /	A		BUT
GRECKMANN	PHILIPPINA		DEHLINGEN	04/25/1785	A		BUT
GREINER	ANDREAS			01/01/1749	A		BUT
GREINER	EMIL		LORENZEN	01/01/1890			F2
GUTFREUND	MARIA		SAARWERDEN	01/01/1893			F2
GöTTEL MN GRECKMANN	PHILIPPINA		DEHLINGEN	04/25/1785	A		BUT
GöTTEL/ GöTTLER PARE	CHRISTIAN WILH	1773	DEHLINGEN	04/25/1785	A		BUT
GöTTEL/GöTTLER PARE	DANIEL LUDWIG	1783	DEHLINGEN	04/25/1785	A		BUT
GöTTEL/GöTTLER PARE	JOHANN HEINRICH	1780	DEHLINGEN	04/25/1785	A		BUT
GöTTEL/GöTTLER PARE	MARIA ELISABETA	1778	DEHLINGEN	04/25/1785	A		BUT
GöTTEL/GöTTLER PARE	MARIA FRIEDERIA	1776	DEHLINGEN	04/25/1785	A		BUT
GöTTEL/GöTTLER PARE	PHILIPPINA	1775	DEHLINGEN	04/25/1785	A		BUT
GöTTEL/GöTTLER WW 6C	HEINRICH		DEHLINGEN	04/25/1785	A		BUT
HAMANN	GEORG		OBERMODERN	/ /			F2
HAMMANN	GEORG		OBERMODERN	/ /	A		F2
HEITZ	GEORG		OBERMODERN	/ /			F2
HELDT	BARBARA	1817	ROPPENHEIM	/ /	A		F2
HELDT	DANIEL	1841	ROPPENHEIM	/ /	A		F2

Lastname	Firstname	Birth Year	Birthplace	Emigration	De	Prof	Source
HELDT	FRIEDRICH	1832	ROPPENHEIM	/ /	A		F2
HELDT	GEORG	1836	ROPPENHEIM	/ /	A		F2
HELDT	KAROLINE	1828	ROPPENHEIM	/ /	A		F2
HELDT	KAROLINE	1834	ROPPENHEIM	/ /	A		F2
HELDT	MAGDALENA	1828	ROPPENHEIM	/ /	A		F2
HELDT	MAGDALENE	1821	ROPPENHEIM	/ /	A		F2
HELDT	MARTIN	1829	ROPPENHEIM	/ /	A		F2
HELDT	MICHAEL	1826	ROPPENHEIM	/ /	A		F2
HEMMERT MN KOEPPEL	CATHERINA DOROA	1781	DEHLINGEN	01/01/1828	A		BUT
HEMMERT WW	HANS NICKEL	1781	DEHLINGEN	01/01/1828	A	SHOE	BUT
HIRSCH MN KOEPPEL	MARIE ELISABETA	1821	DEHLINGEN	01/01/1867	A		BUT
HIRSCH W PARENTS	HEINRICH	1847	DEHLINGEN	01/01/1867	A		BUT
HIRSCH W PARENTS	LOUISA	1852	DEHLINGEN	01/01/1867	A		BUT
HIRSCH WW 2CH	ANDREAS	1818	DEHLINGEN	01/01/1867	A		BUT
HISSON WW CH	JOHANN GEORG	1714	WALDHAMBACH	/ /	A	WEAV	BUT
HISSONG MN MEDER	ANNA EVA	1716	WALDHAMBACH	/ /	A		BUT
HISSONG MN MEDER	ANNA MARGARETHA	1719	WALDHAMBACH	/ /	A		BUT
HISSONG W PARENTS	ANNA EVA	1747	WALDHAMBACH	/ /	A		BUT
HISSONG WW CH	JOHANN JACOB	1719	WALDHAMBACH	/ /	A		BUT
HISSONG/ HÜSSONG	JOHANN JACOB	1749	WALDHAMBACH	/ /	A		BUT
HOBLER	CATHARINA	1837	RATZWILLER	/ /	NY		BUT
HOBLER MN CULLY	CATHERINA ELISH	1808	RATZWILLER	/ /	A		BUT
HOBLER W P	CAROLINA	1841	RATZWILLER	01/01/1841	NY		BUT
HOBLER W PARENTS	PETER	1831	RATZWILLER	/ /	A		BUT
HOBLER W PARENTS	PHILIPP	1833	RATZWILLER	/ /	A		BUT
HOBLER WW CH	PETER	1807	RATZWILLER	/ /	A		BUT
HORNUNG	MARIA CATHERINA		DEHLINGEN	04/25/1785	A		BUT
HORNUNG W PARENTS	CATHARINA SOPHA	1745	DEHLINGEN	04/25/1785	A		BUT
HORNUNG W PARENTS	MARIA BARBARA	1750	DEHLINGEN	04/25/1785	A		BUT
HORNUNG W PARENTS	MARIA MARGARETA	1747	DEHLINGEN	04/25/1785	A		BUT
HORNUNG WW 3CH	HEINRICH		DEHLINGEN	04/25/1785	A		BUT
HäUSLER	GEORG		OBERMODERN	/ /			F2
IRRMANN	LUISE		SAARBUCKENHEIM	01/01/1895	A		F2
IRRMANN	MARGARETHE		SAARBUCKENHEIM	01/01/1890	A		F2
JUD	MAGDALENA		INGWEILER	01/01/1899			F2
KAMMER	FRIEDRICH		OTTWEILER	/ /	A		F2
KAMMMERER	FRIEDRICH		OTTWEILER	/ /	A		F2
KARCHER	LINA		SAARBUCKENHEIM	01/01/1889	A		F2
KERN	FRIEDRICH		DETTWEILER	01/01/1865	A		F2
KERN	FRIEDRICH	1865	DETTWEILER	/ /	A		F2
KLEIN	CATHARINA		DIEMERINGEN	01/01/1865	A		BUT
KLEIN	THEODOR		RESCINGUE	01/01/1888	A		F2
KNIPPER	CHRISTINA MARGA	1831	DIEMERINGEN	/ /	A		BUT
KNIPPER	GEORG		BIETHENHEIM	01/01/1876			F2
KOENIG	CARL NICOLAUS	1827	DIEMERINGEN	/ /	A		BUT
KOENIG	JOHANN PHILIPP	1829	DIEMERINGEN	/ /	A		BUT
KOENIG MN EBERHARDT	MARIA CATHARINA	1797	DIEMERINGEN	/ /	A		BUT
KOENIG WW 2 CH	JOHANN NICOLAUS		DIEMERINGEN	/ /	A		BUT
KOEPPEL	ANNA CHRISTINA	1795	DEHLINGEN	01/01/1828	A		BUT
KOEPPEL	CAROLINA	1846	DEHLINGEN	01/01/1863	A		BUT

Lastname	Firstname	Birth Year	Birthplace	Emigration	De	Prof	Source
KOEPPEL	CATHARINA		DIEMERINGEN	01/01/1865	A		BUT
KOEPPEL	CATHERINA DOROA	1781	DEHLINGEN	01/01/1828	A		BUT
KOEPPEL	CHRISTINA	1819	DEHLINGEN	/ /	A		BUT
KOEPPEL	MARIA ELISABETA	1821	DEHLINGEN	/ /	A		BUT
KOEPPEL W PARENTS	FRIEDRICH	1840	DEHLINGEN	01/01/1863	A		BUT
KOEPPEL W PARENTS	HEINRICH	1843	DEHLINGEN	01/01/1863	A		BUT
KOEPPEL MN RAQUET	CATHARINA	1815	OERMINGEN	01/01/1863	A		BUT
KOEPPEL W PARENTS	CATHARINA	1843	DIEMERINGEN	01/01/1865	A		BUT
KOEPPEL W PARENTS	CHRISTIAN	1845	DIEMERINGEN	01/01/1865	A		BUT
KOEPPEL W PARENTS	JACOB	1839	DEHLINGEN	01/01/1863	A		BUT
KOEPPEL WW 2 CH	CHRISTIAN		DIEMERINGEN	01/01/1865	A	BREW	BUT
KOEPPEL WW CH	JOHANN NICOLAUS	1810	DEHLINGEN	01/01/1863	A	TAYL	BUT
KREB	BARBARA		DIEMERINGEN	01/01/1752	A		BUT
KREB	JOHANN CARL	1734	DIEMERINGEN	01/01/1752	A		BUT
KREB	JOHANN MARTIN	1743	DIEMERINGEN	01/01/1752	A		BUT
KREB	JOHANNA CHRISTA	1739	DIEMERINGEN	01/01/1752	A		BUT
KREB	JOHANNES	1723	DIEMERINGEN	01/01/1752	A		BUT
KREB WIDOWER W CH	JOHANNES		DIEMERINGEN	01/01/1752	A		BUT
KREUTZER	CATHARINA MARGA	1813	DIEMERINGEN	/ /	A		BUT
KREUTZER	CHARLOTTE CATHN	1815	DIEMERINGEN	/ /	A		BUT
KREUTZER	SOPHIA CATHARIA	1811	DIEMERINGEN	/ /	A		BUT
KREUTZER MN FAUSER	SOPHIA DOROTHEA	1788	DIEMERINGEN	/ /	A		BUT
KREUTZER WW CH	PETER	1781	DEHLINGEN	/ /	A		BUT
KUCKENDUBLER	BERNHARD	1866	SCHILLERDSORF	01/01/1884	A		F2
KUCKENDUBLER	MARGARETHE		SCHILLERDORF	/ /	A		F2
KURTZ	RUDOLF		DRULINGEN	/ /			F2
KÜCKENDUBLER	BERNHARD	1866	SCHILLERSDORF	01/01/1884	A		F2
KÖPPEL	JOHANN ADAM	1822	RATZWILLER	01/01/1840	A		BUT
LEHNHARDT	JAKOB	1882	SAARWERDEN	/ /	A		F2
LETZ	CATHARINA		DIEMERINGEN	01/01/1874	A		BUT
LETZ WW	PHILIPP		INGWILLER	01/01/1873	A		BUT
LETZTER MN WURSTEISN	CATHARINA BARBA	1783	DIEMERINGEN	01/01/1828	A		BUT
LETZTER W PARENTS	CATHARINA	1803	DEHLINGEN	01/01/1828	A		BUT
LETZTER W PARENTS	CHRISTINA	1809	DEHLINGEN	01/01/1828	A		BUT
LETZTER W PARENTS	DOROTHEA	1819	DEHLINGEN	01/01/1828	A		BUT
LETZTER W PARENTS	GEORG	1821	DEHLINGEN	01/01/1828	A		BUT
LETZTER W PARENTS	MARIA CAROLINA	1825	DEHLINGEN	01/01/1828	A		BUT
LETZTER W PARENTS	SOPHIA	1814	DEHLINGEN	01/01/1828	A		BUT
LETZTER WW 6 CH	NICOLAUS	1772	BURBACH	01/01/1828	A		BUT
LISCHER MN LETZTER	CATHARINA DOROA	1803	DEHLINGEN	01/01/1828	A		BUT
LISCHER WW	PETER	1797	DEHLINGEN	01/01/1828	A		BUT
MARQUART	AMALIE		REIPERTSWEILER	/ /	A		F2
MATTER	GEORG		OTTWEILER	/ /	A		F2
MEDER	ANNA EVA	1716	WALDHAMBACH	/ /	A		BUT
MEDER	MARIA MAGDALENA	1729	VOLKSBERG	01/01/1764	A		BUT
MERCKER MN STUCKI	ELISABETH	1786	SEELHOF	/ /	A		F2
MEYER	JOHANNES	1812	OBERMODERN	/ /	A		F2
MIEGEL	CATHARINA		DIEMERINGEN	/ /	A		BUT
MUCKENDÜBLER	BERNHARD		SCHILLERSDORF	01/01/1866	A		F2
MÜGEL	CAROLINA CATHA	1829	DIEMERINGEN	/ /	A		BUT

Lastname	Firstname	Birth Year	Birthplace	Emigration	De	Prof	Source
MüGEL	CHRISTIAN	1812	DIEMERINGEN	01/01/1838	A		BUT
MüGEL	CHRISTINA LOUIA	1826	DIEMERINGEN	/ /	A		BUT
MüGEL	JOHANN PHILIPP	1824	DIEMERINGEN	/ /	A		BUT
MüGEL MN PöLCHER	SOPHIA LOUISA	1801	DIEMERINGEN	/ /	A		BUT
MüGEL WW CH	JOHANN PHILIPP	1801	DIEMERINGEN	/ /	A		BUT
MüLLER MN WEISS	ELISABETHA	1796	RATZWILLER	01/01/1817	A		BUT
MüLLER W PARENTS	JOHANN HEINRICH	1816	RATZWILLER	01/01/1817	A		BUT
MüLLER WW 1CH	ANTON	1786	WEISLINGEN	01/01/1817	A		BUT
NEHLIG	DOROTHEA		DEHLINGEN	/ /	A		BUT
PETER	GEORG	1859	SCHILLERSDORF	/ /	A		F2
PüLCHER	SOPHIA LOUISA	1801	DIEMERINGEN	/ /	A		BUT
QUIEN	DOROTHEA	1847	DEHLINGEN	01/01/1866	A		BUT
QUIEN W PARENTS	CHRISITNA	1842	DEHLINGEN	01/01/1866	A		BUT
QUIEN MN NEHLIG	FREDERICA DOROA	1808	DEHLINGEN	01/01/1866	A		BUT
QUIEN W PARENTS	FRIEDRICH	1844	DEHLINGEN	01/01/1866	A		BUT
QUIEN W PARENTS	HEINRICH	1847	DEHLINGEN	01/01/1866	A		BUT
QUIEN WW 4 CH	CHRISTIAN	1811	DEHLINGEN	01/01/1866	A	SADD	BUT
QUIRIN	SOPHIA	1796	DIEMERINGEN	01/01/1838	A		BUT
RAQUET	CATHARINA	1815	OERMINGEN	01/01/1863	A		BUT
RAUCH	GEORG		RATZWILLER	/ /	A		BUT
RAUCH MN HOBLER	CATHARINA	1837	RATZWILLER	/ /	NY		BUT
RAUSCHER MN QUIRIN	SOPHIA	1796	DIEMERINGEN	01/01/1838	A		BUT
RAUSCHER W PARENTS	CATHARINA CAROA	1826	DIEMERINGEN	01/01/1838	A		BUT
RAUSCHER W PARENTS	CATHERINA SOPHA	1823	DIEMERINGEN	01/01/1838	A		BUT
RAUSCHER W PARENTS	GEORG	1825	DIEMERINGEN	01/01/1838	A		BUT
RAUSCHER W PARENTS	JOHANN FRIEDRIH	1831	DIEMERINGEN	01/01/1838	A		BUT
RAUSCHER W PARENTS	JOHANN HEINRICH	1823	DIEMERINGEN	01/01/1838	A		BUT
RAUSCHER W PARENTS	PHILIPP CARL	1827	DIEMERINGEN	01/01/1838	A		BUT
RAUSCHER WW 6 CH	JOHANN NICOLAUS	1795	DIEMERINGEN	01/01/1838	A	FARM	BUT
REEB MN WEIDMANN	MARIE SOPHIA	1820	DEHLINGEN	01/01/1863	A		BUT
REEB W PARENTS	HEINRICH	1843	DEHLINGEN	01/01/1863	A		BUT
REEB W PARENTS	SOPHIA	1841	DEHLINGEN	01/01/1863	A		BUT
REEB WW 2 CH	HEINRICH	1817	KESKASTEL	01/01/1863	A	FARM	BUT
REICHERT	MICHAEL		OBERMODERN	/ /			F2
ROOS MN GUTFREUND	MARIA		SAARWERDEN	01/01/1893	A		F2
ROTH	LUDWIG		OTTWEILER	/ /	A		F2
RUF	CHRISTMANN	1812	OBERMODERN	/ /	A		F2
RUNTZ	JAKOB		OBERMODERN	/ /	A		F2
RUTNZ	JAKOB		OBERMODERN	/ /			F2
SC HMIDT	HEINRICH		OTTWEILER	/ /	A		F2
SCHINI	GERG	1860	BOSSELSHAUSEN	01/01/1894	A		F2
SCHINI	MICHAEL	1860	BOSSELSHAUSEN	/ /	A		F2
SCHINI	MICHAEL	1860	BOSSELSHAUSEN	01/01/1894	A		F2
SCHLOSSER	GEORG		OTTWEILER	/ /	A		F2
SCHMIDT	GEORG		OTTWEILER	/ /	A		F2
SCHMIDT	HEINRICH		OTTWEILER	/ /	A		F2
SCHMIDT MN MIEGEL	CATHARINA		DIEMERINGEN	/ /	A		BUT
SCHMIDT W PARENTS	CATHARINA CHRIS	1810	DIEMERINGEN	/ /	A		BUT
SCHMIDT W PARENTS	GEORG PETER	1813	DIEMERINGEN	/ /	A		BUT
SCHMIDT W PARENTS	JOHANN HEINRICH	1807	DIEMERINGEN	/ /	A		BUT

Lastname	Firstname	Birth Year	Birthplace	Emigration	De	Prof	Source
SCHMIDT W PARENTS	JOHANNETTA CARO	1821	DIEMERINGEN	/ /		A	BUT
SCHMIDT W PARENTS	LUDWIG	1818	DIEMERINGEN	/ /		A	BUT
SCHMIDT W PARENTS	SOPPHIA CHRISTA	1815	DIEMERINGEN	/ /		A	BUT
SCHMIDT WW 6CH	GEORG		SCHOPPERTEN	/ /		A	BUT
SCHNEPP	GEORG	1816	INGWEILER	/ /		A	F2
SCHNEPP	JAKOB	1813	INGWEILER	/ /		A	F2
SCHNEPP	MARGARETHE	1812	INGWEILER	/ /		A	F2
SCHNEPP W PARENTS	KATHARINA	1823	INGWEILER	/ /		A	F2
SCHNEPP MN MENCHHÖFR	SOPHIE	1788	INGWEILER	/ /		A	F2
SCHNEPP W FAMILY	JAKOB	1786	INGWEILER	/ /		A	F2
SCHNEPP W PARENTS	MICHAEL	1809	INGWEILER	/ /		A	F2
SCHNEPP W PARENTS	PHILIPP	1826	INGWEILER	/ /		A	F2
SCHNEPP W PARENTS	SOPHIE	1819	INGWEILER	/ /		A	F2
SCHWAB MN KOEPPEL	CHRISTINA	1819	DEHLINGEN	/ /		A	BUT
SCHWAB W HUSB 1CH	CHRISTINA	1819	DEHLINGEN	01/01/1868	A		BUT
SCHWAB W PARENTS	LUDWIG	1848	DEHLINGEN	01/01/1868	A		BUT
SCHWAB WW	LUDWIG	1823	LORENTZEN	/ /		A	BUT
SCHWAB WW 1 CH	LUDWIG	1823	LORENTZEN	01/01/1868	A		BUT
SEEMANN	CATHARINA	1792	BURBACH	/ /		A	BUT
SIEFERL	ANNA	1813	OBERMODERN	01/01/1828	A		F2
SIEGWALD	GOTTFRIED	1862	GERSTHEIM	/ /		A	F2
SIEGWALL MN WÜST	SALOME	1866	GERSTHEIM	/ /		A	F2
SIFFERTMANN	LUISE		NIEDERSCHWILLER	/ /			F2
SONTAG MN DUCARN	ELISABETHA		DEHLINGEN	/ /		A	BUT
SONTAG W PARENTS	ANNA MARIA	1805	DEHLINGEN	/ /		A	BUT
SONTAG W PARENTS	STEFAN	1808	DEHLINGEN	/ /		A	BUT
SONTAG WW 2 CH	PETER		DEHLINGEN	/ /		A	BUT
SPECHT	CATHARINA		DIEMERINGEN	01/01/1873	A		BUT
SPRECHER MN BRONNER	LOUISE		INGWEILER	/ /		A	F2
STOCK	CARL PETER	1861	BUTTEN	/ /		A	BUT
STRAUSS	JOHANN LUDWIG			01/01/1749	A		BUT
TAMERUS	CATHARINA		DEHLINGEN	04/25/1783	A		BUT
THEOBALD MN KOEPPEL	ANNA CHRISTINA	1795	DEHLINGEN	01/01/1828	A		BUT
THEOBALD WW	PETER	1793	DEHLINGEN	01/01/1828	A		BUT
TISCHBACH	GEORG	1880	INGWEILER	/ /		A	F2
TISCHBACH	JOHANN	1881	INGWEILER	/ /		A	F2
TROTTER	BENJAMIN		RATZWILLER	/ /		A	BUT
TROTTER	SOPHIA PHILIPPA	1828	RATZWILLER	/ /		A	BUT
VELTEN	MARIA MAGDALENA		RATZWILLER	/ /		A	BUT
WACK	ADOLF	1878	SAARBUCKENHEIM	/ /			F2
WAHL	FRIEDRICH	1834	ROPPENHEIM	/ /		A	F2
WEHRUNG	CAROLINE		DIEMERINGEN	01/01/1838	A		BUT
WEHRUNG	CHRISTIAN	1833	DIEMERINGEN	01/01/1838	A		BUT
WEHRUNG	GEORG	1854	WALDHAMBACH	01/01/1877	A		BUT
WEHRUNG	JOHANN HEINRICH	1852	WALDHAMBACH	01/01/1852	A		BUT
WEHRUNG WW 1CH	ADAM		DIEMERINGEN	01/01/1838	A		BUT
WEIDMANN	SOPHIA	1820	DEHLINGEN	/ /		A	BUT
WEINREB	JOSEF	1918	KARLSRUHE	08/11/1937	A		F1
WEISS	CARL	1807	RATZWILLER	/ /		A	BUT
WEISS	JOHANN PETER	1803	RATZWILLER	/ /		A	BUT

Lastname	Firstname	Birth Year	Birthplace	Emigration	De	Prof	Source
WEISS	MARGARETHA ELIH	1796	RATZWILLER	01/01/1817	A		BUT
WEISS	MARIA ELISABETA	1799	RATZWILLER	/ /	A		BUT
WEISS MN VELTEN	MARIA MAGDALENA		RATZWILLER	/ /	A		BUT
WEISS WW 3 CH	PETER	1767	RATZWILLER	/ /	A		BUT
WEISSGERBER	JAKOB		OBERMODERN	/ /	A		F2
WENDLING	JOHANN GEORG	1814	OBRMODERN	/ /	A		F2
WOHLHÜTER	MARTIN	1823	ROPPENHEIM	/ /	A		F2
WOLBER	LYDIA		SAARBUCKENHEIM	/ /			
WURSTEISEN	CATHARINA BARBA	1783	DIEMERINGEN	01/01/1828	A		BUT
ZEITER	KAROLINE		INGWEILER	01/01/1872	A		F2
ZEITLER	KAROLINE	1872	INGWEILER	/ /	A		F2

RECORDS

AVAILABLE

ON

MICROFILM

These records have been microfilmed and are
available through the Genealogical libraries
of the Church of Jesus Christ of Latter Day
Saints.

ADELSHEIM   LUTHERAN RECORDS 1607 - 1962
                   LUTHERAN RECORDS 1808 - 1870
                   JEWISH   RECORDS 1810 - 1870
                   JEWISH   RECORDS 1812 - 1912

ADERSBACH   LUTHERAN RECORDS 1652 - 1963

ALTDORF   CATHOLIC RECORDS 1740 - 1900
                   CATHOLIC RECORDS 1810 - 1850
                   CATHOLIC RECORDS 1810 - 1870
                   CATHOLIC RECORDS 1564 - 1900
                   JEWISH   RECORDS 1810 - 1870

ALTSCHWEIER   CATHOLIC RECORDS 1810 - 1870
                   CATHOLIC RECORDS 1810 - 1900

AUERBACH   LUTHERAN RECORDS 1800 - 1869
                   LUTHERAN RECORDS 1752 - 1962
                   LUTHERAN RECORDS 1576 - 1962
                   CATHOLIC RECORDS 1821 - 1867

BAHLINGEN	LUTHERAN RECORDS 1810 - 1869
BALG	CATHOLIC RECORDS 1787 - 1922
	CATHOLIC RECORDS 1810 - 1869
BLANKENLOCH	LUTHERAN RECORDS 1672 - 1961
	LUTHERAN RECORDS 1810 - 1869
	CATHOLIC RECORDS 1793 - 1869
BAUERBACH	CATHOLIC RECORDS 1585 - 1900
	CATHOLIC RECORDS 1810 - 1869
	JEWISH RECORDS 1810 - 1869
	CATHOLIC RECORDS 1810 - 1869
BERGHAUPTEN	CATHOLIC RECORDS 1736 - 1900
	CATHOLIC RECORDS 1810 - 1869
BERGHAUSEN	LUTHERAN RECORDS 1579 - 1962
	LUTHERAN RECORDS 1793 - 1869
BERGÖSCHINGEN	CATHOLIC RECORDS 1810 - 1871
BESTENHEID	LUTHERAN RECORDS 1556 - 1962
BIETIGHEIM	CATHOLIC RECORDS 1662 - 1901

BRETTEN	LUTHERAN RECORDS 1565 - 1956
	LUTHERAN RECORDS 1803 - 1869
	LUTHERAN RECORDS 1565 - 1962
	CATHOLIC RECORDS 1698 - 1900
	JEWISH RECORDS 1809 - 1810
BROMBACH	LUTHERAN RECORDS 1662 - 1962
	LUTHERAN RECORDS 1810 - 1870
	LUTHERAN RECORDS 1648 - 1964
	LUTHERAN RECORDS 1799 - 1869
BRUCHSAL	LUTHERAN RECORDS 1804 - 1963
	LUTHERAN RECORDS 1810 - 1869
	LUTHERAN RECORDS 1872 - 1918
	JEWISH RECORDS 1810 - 1869
	CATHOLIC RECORDS 1689 - 1900
	CATHOLIC RECORDS 1730 - 1904
	CATHOLIC RECORDS 1810 - 1869
	CATHOLIC RECORDS 1792 - 1823
	CATHOLIC RECORDS 1730 - 1899
	CATHOLIC RECORDS 1807 - 1869
	CATHOLIC RECORDS 1810 - 1869
	LUTHERAN RECORDS 1872 - 1918
BROTZINGEN	LUTHERAN RECORDS 1706 - 1945
BUGGINGEN	LUTHERAN RECORDS 1633 - 1962

BURBACH	CATHOLIC RECORDS 1726 - 1901
	CATHOLIC RECORDS 1810 - 1869
BUSENBACH	CATHOLIC RECORDS 1774 - 1908
	CATHOLIC RECORDS 1810 - 1869
	CATHOLIC RECORDS 1823 - 1869
BÜCHIG	CATHOLIC RECORDS 1725 - 1887
	CATHOLIC RECORDS 1810 - 1869
	LUTHERAN RECORDS 1672 - 1961
	LUTHERAN RECORDS 1810 - 1869
BÜHL	CATHOLIC RECORDS 1666 - 1900
	CATHOLIC RECORDS 1810 - 1870
	LUTHERAN RECORDS 1855 - 1962
BÜHLERTAL	CATHOLIC RECORDS 1763 - 1900
	CATHOLIC RECORDS 1810 - 1870
BÜSINGEN	LUTHERAN RECORDS 1615 - 1962
DAXLANDEN	CATHOLIC RECORDS 1802 - 1869
	CATHOLIC RECORDS 1708 - 1900
DAISBACH	LUTHERAN RECORDS 1722 - 1963
DARMSBACH	LUTHERAN RECORDS 1590 - 1962
DAUCHINGEN	CATHOLIC RECORDS 1799 - 1900

DIEDELSHEIM	LUTHERAN RECORDS 1600 - 1961
	LUTHERAN RECORDS 1803 - 1869
	CATHOLIC RECORDS 1698 - 1900
	JEWISH RECORDS 1812 - 1870
DIENSTADT	CATHOLIC RECORDS 1671 - 1900
DIERSBURG	LUTHERAN RECORDS 1682 - 1965
	CATHOLIC RECORDS 1810 - 1900
	JEWISH RECORDS 1813 - 1870
DIETENHAUSEN	LUTHERAN RECORDS 1637 - 1962
DINGLINGEN	LUTHERAN RECORDS 1630 - 1965
	LUTHERAN RECORDS 1804 - 1869
DISTELHAUSEN	LUTHERAN RECORDS 1866 - 1962
	CATHOLIC RECORDS 1670 - 1906
DITTIGHEIM	CATHOLIC RECORDS 1585 - 1902
DURLACH	LUTHERAN RECORDS 1810 - 1963
	LUTHERAN RECORDS 1690 - 1962
	LUTHERAN RECORDS 1800 - 1869
	LUTHERAN RECORDS 1685 - 1761
	LUTHERAN RECORDS 1872 - 1922
	CATHOLIC RECORDS 1810 - 1869
	CATHOLIC RECORDS 1809 - 1900

DURMERSHEIM	LUTHERAN RECORDS 1849 - 1962	
	CATHOLIC RECORDS 1660 - 1900	
DÖRLINBACH	CATHOLIC RECORDS 1646 - 1900	
	CATHOLIC RECORDS 1810 - 1870	
EBNET	CATHOLIC RECORDS 1625 - 1900	
	CATHOLIC RECORDS 1808 - 1869	
	CATHOLIC RECORDS 1645 - 1900	
	CATHOLIC RECORDS 1810 - 1870	
EICHSEL	CATHOLIC RECORDS 1735 - 1900	
EINBACH	CATHOLIC RECORDS 1810 - 1870	
	CATHOLIC RECORDS 1826 - 1909	
ELZACH	LUTHERAN RECORDS 1645 - 1963	
	CATHOLIC RECORDS 1697 - 1900	
EPFENBACH	LUTHERAN RECORDS 1642 - 1963	
	LUTHERAN RECORDS 1810 - 1869	
ETTLINGEN	LUTHERAN RECORDS 1739 - 1962	
	LUTHERAN RECORDS 1872 - 1919	
	CATHOLIC RECORDS 1689 - 1931	
	CATHOLIC RECORDS 1810 - 1869	

ETZENROT   CATHOLIC RECORDS 1823 - 1869

FAHRENBACH   LUTHERAN RECORDS 1815 - 1963
                 LUTHERAN RECORDS 1569 - 1963
                 CATHOLIC RECORDS 1810 - 1904

FAUTENBACH   CATHOLIC RECORDS 1724 - 1900
                 CATHOLIC RECORDS 1810 - 1869

FEUDENHEIM   LUTHERAN RECORDS 1632 - 1962
                 LUTHERAN RECORDS 1810 - 1870
                 CATHOLIC RECORDS 1696 - 1900
                 CATHOLIC RECORDS 1810 - 1870
                 JEWISH   RECORDS 1810 - 1870

FLEHINGEN   LUTHERAN RECORDS 1521 - 1962
                 LUTHERAN RECORDS 1808 - 1869
                 CATHOLIC RECORDS 1663 - 1900
                 JEWISH   RECORDS 1808 - 1869

FORBACH   CATHOLIC RECORDS 1810 - 1869
                 CATHOLIC RECORDS 1621 - 1909

FREIBURG   LUTHERAN RECORDS 1655 - 1929
                 MANY DIFFERENT CHURCHES
                 CATHOLIC RECORDS 1572 - 1938
                 MANY DIFFERENT CHURCH

```
FREISTETT            LUTHERAN RECORDS 1621 - 1962
                     LUTHERAN RECORDS 1810 - 1870
                     JEWISH   RECORDS 1810 - 1870

FRIEDRICHSTAL        LUTHERAN RECORDS 1703 - 1961
                     LUTHERAN RECORDS 1783 - 1869

GAMBURG              CATHOLIC RECORDS 1609 - 1921

GAMSHURST            CATHOLIC RECORDS 1663 - 1900
                     CATHOLIC RECORDS 1810 - 1869

GEISSLINGEN          CATHOLIC RECORDS 1815 - 1900

GERCHSHEIM           CATHOLIC RECORDS 1643 - 1942

GISSIGHEIM           CATHOLIC RECORDS 1612 - 1964
                     JEWISH   RECORDS 1848 - 1869

GLASHOFEN            CATHOLIC RECORDS 1800 - 1900
                     CATHOLIC RECORDS 1810 - 1870

GLASHÜTTEN SEE HASEL

GRABEN               LUTHERAN RECORDS 1645 - 1961
                     LUTHERAN RECORDS 1783 - 1869
                     JEWISH   RECORDS 1812 - 1867
```

GRAFENHAUSEN	CATHOLIC	RECORDS	1663	-	1900
	CATHOLIC	RECORDS	1810	-	1870
GRÖTZINGEN	LUTHERAN	RECORDS	1685	-	1962
	LUTHERAN	RECORDS	1793	-	1869
	JEWISH	RECORDS	1811	-	1869
GRÜNWETTERSBACH	LUTHERAN	RECORDS	1649	-	1963
	LUTHERAN	RECORDS	1800	-	1869
GURTWEIL	CATHOLIC	RECORDS	1738	-	1951
HAGSFELD	LUTHERAN	RECORDS	1594	-	1913
	LUTHERAN	RECORDS	1810	-	1869
HECKFELD	CATHOLIC	RECORDS	1727	-	1895
HEIDELBERG	LUTHERAN	RECORDS	1592	-	1808
	LUTHERAN	RECORDS	1694	-	1961
	LUTHERAN	RECORDS	1810	-	1870
	LUTHERAN	RECORDS	1649	-	1961
	LUTHERAN	RECORDS	1881	-	1946
	LUTHERAN	RECORDS	1729	-	1973
	LUTHERAN	RECORDS	1810	-	1869
	LUTHERAN	RECORDS	1866	-	1964
	LUTHERAN	RECORDS	1705	-	1963
	LUTHERAN	RECORDS	1766	-	1870

Heidelberg continued

```
                    LUTHERAN RECORDS 1569 - 1798
                    CATHOLIC RECORDS 1820 - 1863
                    CATHOLIC RECORDS 1622 - 1648
                    CATHOLIC RECORDS 1651 - 1901
                    CATHOLIC RECORDS 1810 - 1870
                    CATHOLIC RECORDS 1893 - 1907
                    CATHOLIC RECORDS 1695 - 1802
                    CATHOLIC RECORDS 1810 - 1869
                    CATHOLIC RECORDS 1810 - 1900
                    CATHOLIC RECORDS 1809 - 1870
                    LUTHERAN RECORDS 1569 - 1577
                    LUTHERAN RECORDS 1577 - 1596
                    JEWISH   RECORDS 1822 - 1870
                    JEWISH   RECORDS 1810 - 1870
                    JEWISH   RECORDS 1809 - 1810

HEIDELSHEIM         LUTHERAN RECORDS 1803 - 1869
                    CATHOLIC RECORDS 1699 - 1904
                    CATHOLIC RECORDS 1810 - 1870
                    JEWISH   RECORDS 1814 - 1870
                    JEWISH   RECORDS 1810 - 1870

HELMSHEIM           LUTHERAN RECORDS 1650 - 1962
                    LUTHERAN RECORDS 1803 - 1869
                    CATHOLIC RECORDS 1810 - 1870
                    CATHOLIC RECORDS 1699 - 1900
                    CATHOLIC RECORDS 1810 - 1869
```

HELMSTADT	LUTHERAN RECORDS 1635 - 1962
	CATHOLIC RECORDS 1705 - 1884
HERDWANGEN	LUTHERAN RECORDS 1801 - 1870
	LUTHERAN RECORDS 1810 - 1813
	CATHOLIC RECORDS 1667 - 1900
	CATHOLIC RECORDS 1800 - 1806
HERRENWIES	CATHOLIC RECORDS 1752 - 1803
	CATHOLIC RECORDS 1810 - 1870
HESSELHURST	LUTHERAN RECORDS 1765 - 1962
	LUTHERAN RECORDS 1810 - 1870
HILSBACH	LUTHERAN RECORDS 1655 - 1962
	CATHOLIC RECORDS 1699 - 1900
	JEWISH RECORDS 1801 - 1869
HOCHHAUSEN	LUTHERAN RECORDS 1602 - 1962
	JEWISH RECORDS 1812 - 1869
	CATHOLIC RECORDS 1618 - 1900
	JEWISH RECORDS 1830 - 1869
HOCHSTETTEN	LUTHERAN RECORDS 1610 - 1962
	LUTHERAN RECORDS 1810 - 1869

HOCKENHEIM	LUTHERAN RECORDS 1515 - 1962	
	LUTHERAN RECORDS 1701 - 1963	
	CATHOLIC RECORDS 1726 - 1900	
	JEWISH RECORDS 1814 - 1870	
HOLZHAUSEN	CATHOLIC RECORDS 1654 - 1900	
	CATHOLIC RECORDS 1810 - 1869	
	LUTHERAN RECORDS 1810 - 1870	
	LUTHERAN RECORDS 1581 - 1865	
HUGSWEIER	LUTHERAN RECORDS 1652 - 1962	
	LUTHERAN RECORDS 1804 - 1869	
HUNDHEIM	CATHOLIC RECORDS 1860 - 1907	
HÜNGHEIM	CATHOLIC RECORDS 1701 - 1900	
	CATHOLIC RECORDS 1810 - 1870	
	JEWISH RECORDS 1816 - 1870	
IBACH	CATHOLIC RECORDS 1843 - 1871	
	CATHOLIC RECORDS 1606 - 1900	
IFFEZHEIM	CATHOLIC RECORDS 1679 - 1900	
IMPFINGEN	CATHOLIC RECORDS 1657 - 1900	
ISPRINGEN	CATHOLIC RECORDS 1644 - 1962	

JÖHLINGEN	JEWISH RECORDS 1816 - 1869
	CATHOLIC RECORDS 1640 - 1900
	CATHOLIC RECORDS 1810 - 1869
	JEWISH RECORDS 1810 - 1869
KAPPEL	CATHOLIC RECORDS 1643 - 1900
	CATHOLIC RECORDS 1810 - 1869
	CATHOLIC RECORDS 1628 - 1900
	CATHOLIC RECORDS 1619 - 1907
	CATHOLIC RECORDS 1662 - 1934
	CATHOLIC RECORDS 1804 - 1870
KAPPELWINDECK	CATHOLIC RECORDS 1810 - 1870
	CATHOLIC RECORDS 1691 - 1900
KARLSRUHE	LUTHERAN RECORDS 1685 - 1962
	CATHOLIC RECORDS 1700 - 1960
	MANY DIFFERENT CHURCHES INCLUDIN
	DAXLANDEN AND RÜPPÜRR

KLEINEICHOLZHEIM

	LUTHERAN RECORDS 1650 - 1963
	LUTHERAN RECORDS 1810 - 1870
	JEWISH RECORDS 1747 - 1870
	JEWISH RECORDS 1810 - 1870

KNIELINGEN	LUTHERAN RECORDS 1664 - 1961
	LUTHERAN RECORDS 1783 - 1869

KOMMINGEN	CATHOLIC RECORDS 1640 - 1900
	CATHOLIC RECORDS 1810 - 1869
KORB	LUTHERAN RECORDS 1654 - 1964
	LUTHERAN RECORDS 1810 - 1870
	JEWISH RECORDS 1747 - 1870
	JEWISH RECORDS 1810 - 1870
KORK	LUTHERAN RECORDS 1580 - 1961
	LUTHERAN RECORDS 1810 - 1870
KRAUTHEIM	CATHOLIC RECORDS 1590 - 1912
	CATHOLIC RECORDS 1810 - 1870
	JEWISH RECORDS 1810 - 1870
KÜLSHEIM	CATHOLIC RECORDS 1623 - 1900
KÜRNBACH	LUTHERAN RECORDS 1555 - 1962
	LUTHERAN RECORDS 1810 - 1875
LAHR	LUTHERAN RECORDS 1680 - 1962
	LUTHERAN RECORDS 1804 - 1870
	CATHOLIC RECORDS 1849 - 1890
	JEWISH RECORDS 1858 - 1869
	LUTHERAN RECORDS 1898 - 1920

LANGENSTEINBACH

	LUTHERAN	RECORDS	1800	-	1869
	LUTHERAN	RECORDS	1752	-	1962
	LUTHERAN	RECORDS	1800	-	1864

LAUDA

| | LUTHERAN | RECORDS | 1866 | - | 1962 |
| | CATHOLIC | RECORDS | 1624 | - | 1900 |

LAUF

| | CATHOLIC | RECORDS | 1697 | - | 1900 |
| | CATHOLIC | RECORDS | 1810 | - | 1870 |

LEGELSHURST

| | LUTHERAN | RECORDS | 1616 | - | 1962 |
| | LUTHERAN | RECORDS | 1810 | - | 1870 |

LEIBERSTUG

| | CATHOLIC | RECORDS | 1810 | - | 1870 |

LEOPOLDSHAFEN

| | LUTHERAN | RECORDS | 1610 | - | 1961 |
| | LUTHERAN | RECORDS | 1810 | - | 1869 |

LEUTESHEIM

	LUTHERAN	RECORDS	1561	-	1962
	LUTHERAN	RECORDS	1561	-	1961
	LUTHERAN	RECORDS	1810	-	1870

LIEDOLSHEIM

| | LUTHERAN | RECORDS | 1578 | - | 1961 |
| | JEWISH | RECORDS | 1823 | - | 1861 |

LIENHEIM

| | CATHOLIC | RECORDS | 1700 | - | 1900 |

LINKENHEIM   LUTHERAN RECORDS 1591 - 1961

LIPBURG   LUTHERAN RECORDS 1620 - 1967

LOFFINGEN   LUTHERAN RECORDS 1873 - 1962
              CATHOLIC RECORDS 1624 - 1900
              CATHOLIC RECORDS 1810 - 1870
              CATHOLIC RECORDS 1624 - 1700

MALSCH   LUTHERAN RECORDS 1888 - 1961
              CATHOLIC RECORDS 1730 - 1900
              CATHOLIC RECORDS 1810 - 1869
              CATHOLIC RECORDS 1682 - 1900
              JEWISH   RECORDS 1811 - 1870

MALTERDINGEN   LUTHERAN RECORDS 1640 - 1962
              LUTHERAN RECORDS 1800 - 1869

MANNHEIM   LUTHERAN RECORDS 1515 - 1967
              CATHOLIC RECORDS 1600 - 1960
               INCLUDING MANY DIFFERENT CHURCHES

MERCHINGEN   LUTHERAN RECORDS 1647 - 1963
              LUTHERAN RECORDS 1810 - 1870
              JEWISH   RECORDS 1811 - 1870

MONCHZELL	LUTHERAN RECORDS 1658 - 1963
	LUTHERAN RECORDS 1810 - 1869
	CATHOLIC RECORDS 1810 - 1869
	CATHOLIC RECORDS 1858 - 1908
MOSBACH	CATHOLIC RECORDS 1811 - 1900
	CATHOLIC RECORDS 1812 - 1869
	LUTHERAN RECORDS 1565 - 1962
	CATHOLIC RECORDS 1688 - 1900
	JEWISH RECORDS 1809 - 1810
MUNDINGEN	LUTHERAN RECORDS 1618 - 1962
	LUTHERAN RECORDS 1800 - 1869
MÖRSCH	CATHOLIC RECORDS 1708 - 1900
	CATHOLIC RECORDS 1797 - 1869
MÜHLBURG	LUTHERAN RECORDS 1700 - 1962
MÜNZESHEIM	LUTHERAN RECORDS 1656 - 1977
NECKARAU	LUTHERAN RECORDS 1650 - 1962
	LUTHERAN RECORDS 1810 - 1870
	CATHOLIC RECORDS 1736 - 1903

NECKARGMÜND	LUTHERAN RECORDS 1636 - 1962	
	LUTHERAN RECORDS 1803 - 1869	
	LUTHERAN RECORDS 1810 - 1869	
	CATHOLIC RECORDS 1810 - 1869	
	CATHOLIC RECORDS 1688 - 1901	
NEIDINGEN	CATHOLIC RECORDS 1718 - 1904	
NEUSATZ	CATHOLIC RECORDS 1774 - 1900	
	CATHOLIC RECORDS 1810 - 1870	
NUSSLOCH	LUTHERAN RECORDS 1698 - 1963	
	LUTHERAN RECORDS 1810 - 1870	
	CATHOLIC RECORDS 1752 - 1900	
	CATHOLIC RECORDS 1810 - 1870	
	JEWISH RECORDS 1810 - 1870	
NÖGGENSCHWIHL	CATHOLIC RECORDS 1674 - 1900	
NÖTTINGEN	LUTHERAN RECORDS 1590 - 1962	
OBEREGGINGEN	CATHOLIC RECORDS 1765 - 1900	
OBERGIMPERN	LUTHERAN RECORDS 1593 - 1962	
	CATHOLIC RECORDS 1704 - 1904	

OBERHAUSEN	LUTHERAN RECORDS 1525 - 1962
	LUTHERAN RECORDS 1870 - 1962
	LUTHERAN RECORDS 1727 - 1901
	CATHOLIC RECORDS 1651 - 1905
	CATHOLIC RECORDS 1810 - 1869
	CATHOLIC RECORDS 1688 - 1900
OBERWEIER	CATHOLIC RECORDS 1810 - 1870
	CATHOLIC RECORDS 1692 - 1901
	CATHOLIC RECORDS 1817 - 1869
	LUTHERAN RECORDS 1598 - 1962
	CATHOLIC RECORDS 1699 - 1900
	CATHOLIC RECORDS 1810 - 1869
	CATHOLIC RECORDS 1700 - 1952
OBERWEILER	LUTHERAN RECORDS 1620 - 1967
OBRIGHEIM	LUTHERAN RECORDS 1650 - 1961
	LUTHERAN RECORDS 1650 - 1935
	CATHOLIC RECORDS 1750 - 1910
OCHSENBACH	LUTHERAN RECORDS 1672 - 1962
	LUTHERAN RECORDS 1698 - 1963
	LUTHERAN RECORDS 1804 - 1869
OFTERSHEIM	LUTHERAN RECORDS 1684 - 1963
	CATHOLIC RECORDS 1810 - 1900

OPPENAU	LUTHERAN RECORDS 1951 - 1961		
	CATHOLIC RECORDS 1628 - 1900		
ORSCHWEIER	CATHOLIC RECORDS 1810 - 1870		
	CATHOLIC RECORDS 1810 - 1873		
	JEWISH RECORDS 1819 - 1870		
OTTERSWEIER	LUTHERAN RECORDS 1855 - 1962		
	CATHOLIC RECORDS 1641 - 1900		
	CATHOLIC RECORDS 1810 - 1870		
PETERZELL	LUTHERAN RECORDS 1704 - 1961		
PFAFFENROT	CATHOLIC RECORDS 1810 - 1869		
PFORZHEIM	LUTHERAN RECORDS 1648 - 1870		
	LUTHERAN RECORDS 1706 - 1945		
	LUTHERAN RECORDS 1690 - 1698		
	LUTHERAN RECORDS 1895 - 1926		
	LUTHERAN RECORDS 1607 - 1961		
	LUTHERAN RECORDS 1718 - 1826		
	LUTHERAN RECORDS 1766 - 1827		
	CATHOLIC RECORDS 1784 - 1901		
	JEWISH RECORDS 1810 - 1869		
	JEWISH REOCRDS 1810 - 1870		

PRINZBACH	CATHOLIC RECORDS 1651 - 1900
	CATHOLIC RECORDS 1810 - 1869
PÜLFRINGEN	CATHOLIC RECORDS 1726 - 1901
RAPPENAU	LUTHERAN RECORDS 1654 - 1962
	JEWISH RECORDS 1813 - 1869
RASTATT	LUTHERAN RECORDS 1839 - 1920
	LUTHERAN RECORDS 1775 - 1963
	CATHOLIC RECORDS 1648 - 1916
	LUTHERAN RECORDS 1860 - 1920
RAUENBERG	CATHOLIC RECORDS 1800 - 1900
	CATHOLIC RECORDS 1721 - 1900
REICHENBACH	CATHOLIC RECORDS 1823 - 1869
	CATHOLIC RECORDS 1838 - 1892
	CATHOLIC RECORDS 1810 - 1869
	CATHOLIC RECORDS 1831 - 1869
	CATHOLIC RECORDS 1831 - 1900
	LUTHERAN RECORDS 1635 - 1962
	LUTHERAN RECORDS 1800 - 1869
	LUTHERAN RECORDS 1640 - 1963
	LUTHERAN RECORDS 1650 - 1964

REISENBACH   CATHOLIC RECORDS 1660 - 1903

REUTE   CATHOLIC RECORDS 1594 - 1947
                 CATHOLIC RECORDS 1810 - 1869

RHEINBISCHOFSHEIM LUTHERAN RECORDS 1581 - 1965
                 LUTHERAN RECORDS 1810 - 1870

RHEINSHEIM   CATHOLIC RECORDS 1692 - 1901

RICHEN   LUTHERAN RECORDS 1640 - 1887
                 LUTHERAN RECORDS 1654 - 1963
                 LUTHERAN RECORDS 1810 - 1870
                 CATHOLIC RECORDS 1699 - 1899
                 CATHOLIC RECORDS 1810 - 1870

RINKLINGEN   LUTHERAN RECORDS 1565 - 1962
                 LUTHERAN RECORDS 1803 - 1869
                 CATHOLIC RECORDS 1698 - 1900

RUST   JEWISH   RECORDS 1811 - 1870
                 CATHOLIC RECORDS 1652 - 1900
                 CATHOLIC RECORDS 1810 - 1870

RÜPPURR SIEHE KARLSRUHE

SACHSENHAUSEN   LUTHERAN RECORDS 1556 - 1962

SASBACH   CATHOLIC RECORDS 1697 - 1930
                CATHOLIC RECORDS 1810 - 1870
                CATHOLIC RECORDS 1657 - 1900
                CATHOLIC RECORDS 1810 - 1869

SCHATTHAUSEN   LUTHERAN RECORDS 1669 - 1940

SCHIELBERG   CATHOLIC RECORDS 1672 - 1900
                CATHOLIC RECORDS 1810 - 1869

SCHILTACH   LUTHERAN RECORDS 1558 - 1963

SCHLATT   CATHOLIC RECORDS 1606 - 1952

SCHLIERSTADT   CATHOLIC RECORDS 1668 - 1900
                CATHOLIC RECORDS 1810 - 1870

SCHLOSSAU   CATHOLIC RECORDS 1660 - 1903
                CATHOLIC RECORDS 1810 - 1872

SCHLUTTENBACH   CATHOLIC RECORDS 1692 - 1901
                CATHOLIC RECORDS 1810 - 1869

SCHÖLLBRONN	CATHOLIC RECORDS 1613 - 1890
	CATHOLIC RECORDS 1810 - 1869
	LUTHERAN RECORDS 1810 - 1870
	LUTHERAN RECORDS 1605 - 1964
	CATHOLIC RECORDS 1699 - 1906
SCHWEIGHAUSEN	CATHOLIC RECORDS 1646 - 1900
SCHWEIGHAUSEN	CATHOLIC RECORDS 1804 - 1870
SENNFELD	LUTHERAN RECORDS 1717 - 1982
	LUTHERAN RECORDS 1808 - 1869
	JEWISH RECORDS 1811 - 1869
	JEWISH RECORDS 1811 - 1870
SINGEN	LUTHERAN RECORDS 1743 - 1962
	LUTHERAN RECORDS 1620 - 1962
	LUTHERAN RECORDS 1863 - 1964
	CATHOLIC RECORDS 1645 - 1900
SINSHEIM	LUTHERAN RECORDS 1685 - 1963
	CATHOLIC RECORDS 1699 - 1900
	CATHOLIC RECORDS 1722 - 1900
	JEWISH RECORDS 1812 - 1870
SINZHEIM	CATHOLIC RECORDS 1623 - 1909
	CATHOLIC RECORDS 1809 - 1869

SPESSART	CATHOLIC RECORDS 1663 - 1900
	CATHOLIC RECORDS 1810 - 1869
SPIELBERG	LUTHERAN RECORDS 1752 - 1962
	LUTHERAN RECORDS 1810 - 1962
	CATHOLIC RECORDS 1810 - 1869
SPÖCK	LUTHERAN RECORDS 1667 - 1962
	LUTHERAN RECORDS 1783 - 1869
SPRANTAL	LUTHERAN RECORDS 1695 - 1962
	LUTHERAN RECORDS 1808 - 1869
STAFFORT	LUTHERAN RECORDS 1667 - 1962
	LUTHERAN RECORDS 1783 - 1869
STEBBACH	LUTHERAN RECORDS 1675 - 1962
	LUTHERAN RECORDS 1810 - 1870
	JEWISH RECORDS 1813 - 1869
	JEWISH RECORDS 1813 - 1870
	JEWISH RECORDS 1811 - 1870
STEIN	LUTHERAN RECORDS 1654 - 1962
	CATHOLIC RECORDS 1810 - 1900
STEINNACH	CATHOLIC RECORDS 1676 - 1902

```
STEINBACH        CATHOLIC RECORDS 1810 - 1870
                 CATHOLIC RECORDS 1810 - 1900
                 CATHOLIC RECORDS 1683 - 1907
                 CATHOLIC RECORDS 1810 - 1870

STEINMAUER       CATHOLIC RECORDS 1727 - 1901

STÜHLINGEN       LUTHERAN RECORDS 1885 - 1962
                 CATHOLIC RECORDS 1664 - 1947

STUPFERICH       CATHOLIC RECORDS 1646 - 1900
STUPFERICH       CATHOLIC RECORDS 1795 - 1869

SULZBACH         CATHOLIC RECORDS 1802 - 1900
                 CATHOLIC RECORDS 1817 - 1869
                 LUTHERAN RECORDS 1652 - 1961
                 LUTHERAN RECORDS 1683 - 1964
                 CATHOLIC RECORDS 1809 - 1901
                 CATHOLIC RECORDS 1810 - 1869
                 CATHOLIC RECORDS 1811 - 1869
                 CATHOLIC RECORDS 1811 - 1942
                 LUTHERAN RECORDS 1652 - 1963

SÖLLINGEN        LUTHERAN RECORDS 1610 - 1963
                 LUTHERAN RECORDS 1793 - 1869
                 CATHOLIC RECORDS 1717 - 1900
```

TAIRNBACH   LUTHERAN RECORDS 1688 - 1962

TANNENKIRCH   LUTHERAN RECORDS 1556 - 1962
                   LUTHERAN RECORDS 1800 - 1869

TAUBERBISCHOFSHEIM
                   LUTHERAN RECORDS 1864 - 1962
                   CATHOLIC RECORDS 1597 - 1936

TENGEN   CATHOLIC RECORDS 1640 - 1895
                   CATHOLIC RECORDS 1810 - 1869

TENINGEN   LUTHERAN RECORDS 1591 - 1962
                   LUTHERAN RECORDS 1800 - 1869

TRESCHKLINGEN   LUTHERAN RECORDS 1604 - 1962

UNTERENTERSBACH CATHOLIC RECORDS 1849 - 1900

UNTERGIMPERN   LUTHERAN RECORDS 1593 - 1962

UNTERKESSACH   LUTHERAN RECORDS 1658 - 1963
                   LUTHERAN RECORDS 1810 - 1870

UNTERKIRNACH   CATHOLIC RECORDS 1784 - 1900

UNTERSCHWARZACH LUTHERAN RECORDS 1622 - 1964
                LUTHERAN RECORDS 1803 - 1870

VOCKENROT   LUTHERAN RECORDS 1556 - 1962

VOLKERTSHAUSEN CATHOLIC RECORDS 1630 - 1900

VÖLKERSBACH   CATHOLIC RECORDS 1686 - 1900
                CATHOLIC RECORDS 1810 - 1869

VÖRSTETTEN   LUTHERAN RECORDS 1676 - 1962
                LUTHERAN RECORDS 1800 - 1869

WAIBSTADT   LUTHERAN RECORDS 1722 - 1963
                CATHOLIC RECORDS 1598 - 1900
                JEWISH   RECORDS 1809 - 1810
WALDMATT   CATHOLIC RECORDS 1810 - 1870

WALLDORF   LUTHERAN RECORDS 1698 - 1963
                LUTHERAN RECORDS 1651 - 1962
                LUTHERAN RECORDS 1698 - 1961
                KATHOLIC RECORDS 1810 - 1870
                KATHOLIC RECORDS 1697 - 1895

WASSER   LUTHERAN RECORDS 1640 - 1965

WEHR	LUTHERAN RECORDS 1888 - 1961
	CATHOLIC RECORDS 1643 - 1900
WEIL	CATHOLIC RECORDS 1810 - 1869
	LUTHERAN RECORDS 1739 - 1962
	LUTHERAN RECORDS 1799 - 1869
WEINGARTEN	LUTHERAN RECORDS 1695 - 1961
	LUTHERAN RECORDS 1791 - 1837
	CATHOLIC RECORDS 1699 - 1899
	CATHOLIC RECORDS 1795 - 1869
	JEWISH RECORDS 1810 - 1869
	JEWISH RECORDS 1821 - 1870
	CATHOLIC RECORDS 1795 - 1869
	CATHOLIC RECORDS 1787 - 1900
WEINHEIM	LUTHERAN RECORDS 1693 - 1961
	LUTHERAN RECORDS 1651 - 1800
	LUTHERAN RECORDS 1801 - 1938
	LUTHERAN RECORDS 1686 - 1821
	CATHOLIC RECORDS 1722 - 1900
	JEWISH RECORDS 1811 - 1869
WEISSENSTEIN	LUTHERAN RECORDS 1648 - 1870
	LUTHERAN RECORDS 1693 - 1930

WELSCHNEUREUTH	LUTHERAN RECORDS 1700 - 1962	
	LUTHERAN RECORDS 1803 - 1869	
WENKHEIM	LUTHERAN RECORDS 1792 - 1962	
	CATHOLIC RECORDS 1666 - 1900	
WIECHS	LUTHERAN RECORDS 1605 - 1962	
	CATHOLIC RECORDS 1839 - 1957	
	CATHOLIC RECORDS 1694 - 1900	
	CATHOLIC RECORDS 1810 - 1869	
WILFINGEN	CATHOLIC RECORDS 1814 - 1902	
WILFERDINGEN	LUTHERAN RECORDS 1620 - 1962	
WILLSTÄTT	LUTHERAN RECORDS 1592 - 1964	
	LUTHERAN RECORDS 1810 - 1870	
WOLFENWEILER	LUTHERAN RECORDS 1810 - 1870	
	LUTHERAN RECORDS 1655 - 1962	
	LUTHERAN RECORDS 1810 - 1870	
WÖSCHBACH	CATHOLIC RECORDS 1727 - 1924	
	CATHOLIC RECORDS 1810 - 1869	
WÖSSINGEN	LUTHERAN RECORDS 1691 - 1962	

ÖHNINGEN   CATHOLIC RECORDS 1611 - 1900

ÖNSBACH   CATHOLIC RECORDS 1792 - 1900
                 CATHOLIC RECORDS 1810 - 1869

RECORDS OF ALSACE AVAILABLE ON MICROFILM

ALTWEILER
NEAR FORBACH   CATHOLIC RECORDS   1723 - 1737
                      CATHOLIC RECORDS   1808 - 1882

ALTWEILER
NEAR ZABERN   LUTHERAN RECORDS   1756 - 1807
                      CIVIL   RECORDS   1792 - 1872

BIETLENHEIM   LUTHERAN RECORDS   1600 - 1793
                      CIVIL   RECORDS   1792 - 1899

BOSSELSHAUSEN   LUTHERAN RECORDS   1736 - 1792
                      CIVIL   RECORDS   1792 - 1872

BURBACH   LUTHERAN RECORDS   1698 - 1869
                      CIVIL   RECORDS   1793 - 1872

BUTTEN   LUTHERAN RECORDS   1740 - 1798
                      CIVIL   RECORDS   1792 - 1872

DEHLINGEN   LUTHERAN RECORDS   1704 - 1794
                      CIVIL   RECORDS   1792 - 1872

DETTWEILER	CATHOLIC	RECORDS	1690	-	1793
	LUTHERAN	RECORDS	1668	-	1792
	CIVIL	RECORDS	1792	-	1872
DIEMERINGEN	LUTHERN	RECORDS	1588	-	1799
	CIVIL	RECORDS	1793	-	1872
DRULINGEN	LUTHERAN	RECORDS	1685	-	1941
	CIVIL	RECORDS	1793	-	1872
DURSTEL	LUTHERAN	RECORDS	1695	.	1787
	CIVIL	RECORDS	1793	-	1872
ECKBOLSHEIM	CATHOLIC	RECORDS	1687	-	1789
	LUTHERAN	RECORDS	1609	-	1792
	CIVIL	RECORDS	1793	-	1872
GERSTHEIM	CATHOLIC	RECORDS	1682	-	1792
	LUTHERAN	RECORDS	1594	-	1792
	CIVIL	RECORDS	1793	-	1872
HARSKIRCHEN	CATHOLIC	RECORDS	1728	-	1794
	LUTHERAN	RECORDS	1698	-	1799
	CIVIL	RECORDS	1792	-	1872

HIRSCHLAND	LUTHERAN RECORDS	1698 - 1799
	CIVIL RECORDS	1792 - 1872
INGWEILER	CATHOLIC RECORDS	1689 - 1792
	LUTHERN RECORDS	1614 - 1815
	CIVIL RECORDS	1792 - 1872
KESKASTEL	CATHOLIC RECORDS	1642 - 1793
	LUTHERAN RECORDS	1698 - 1794
	CIVIL RECORDS	1792 - 1872
LORENTZEN	CATHOLIC RECORDS	1680 - 1809
	LUTHERAN RECORDS	1671 - 1794
	CIVIL RECORDS	1792 -1872
OBERMODERN	LUTHERAN RECORDS	1568 - 1843
	CIVIL RECORDS	1792 - 1872
ORMINGEN	CATHOLIC RECORDS	1649 - 1793
	LUTHERAN RECORDS	1758 - 1794
	CIVIL RECORDS	1682 - 1872
OTTWEILER	CIVIL RECORDS	1792 - 1872

PFAFFENHOFEN	CATHOLIC	RECORDS	1721	- 1792
	LUTHERAN	RECORDS	1545	- 1792
	CIVIL	RECORDS	1792	- 1872
PUBERG	LUTHERAN	RECORDS	1780	- 1792
	CIVIL	RECORDS	1792	- 1872
RATZWILLER	CIVIL	RECORDS	1792	-1872
REIPERTSWILLER	LUTHERAN	RECORDS	1736	- 1790
	CIVIL	RECORDS	1792	- 1872
ROPPENHEIM	CATHOLIC	RECORDS	1679	- 1793
	LUTHERAN	RECORDS	1688	- 1791
	CIVIL	RECORDS	1792	- 1872
SAARWERDEN	CATHOLIC	RECORDS	1738	- 1805
	CIVIL	RECORDS	1792	- 1872
SCHILLERSDORF	LUTHERAN	RECORDS	1672	- 1792
	CIVIL	RECORDS	1792	-1872
SCHOPPERTEN	CIVIL	RECORDS	1792	- 1872

WALDHAMBACH	LUTHERAN	RECORDS	1683	- 1792
	CIVIL	RECORDS	1792	- 1822
WEISLINGEN	CIVIL	RECORDS	1792	- 1872
WESTHOFEN	CATHOLIC	RECORDS	1762	1792
	LUTHERAN	RECORDS	1579	- 1793
	CIVIL	RECORDS	1792	- 1872
ZUTZENDORF	LUTHERAN	RECORDS	1633	- 1819
	CIVIL	RECORDS	1792	- 1872